THE
QUEST FOR
COMPETITIVENESS

THE
QUEST FOR
COMPETITIVENESS

Lessons from America's
Productivity and Quality Leaders

Edited by Y. K. SHETTY
and VERNON M. BUEHLER

FOREWORD BY GEORGE M. C. FISHER

Q

QUORUM BOOKS
New York • Westport, Connecticut • London

Library of Congress Cataloging-in-Publication Data

The Quest for competitiveness : lessons from America's productivity
  and quality leaders / edited by Y. K. Shetty and Vernon M. Buehler ;
  foreword by George M. C. Fisher.
        p.   cm.
    Selected lectures sponsored by Utah State University's Partners
  Program, 1979-1989.
    ISBN 0-89930-546-6 (lib. bdg. : alk. paper)
      1. Industrial productivity—United States. 2. Quality of
  products—United States. 3. Competition, International.
  I. Shetty, Y. Krishna. II. Buehler, Vernon M.
  HC110.I52Q47   1991
  338.7'4'0973—dc20   89-49433

British Library Cataloguing in Publication Data is available.

Library of Congress Catalog Card Number: 89-49433
ISBN: 0-89930-546-6

First published in 1991

Quorum Books, 88 Post Road West, Westport, CT 06881
An imprint of Greenwood Publishing Group, Inc.

Printed in the United States of America

The paper used in this book complies with the
Permanent Paper Standard issued by the National
Information Standards Organization (Z39.48-1984).

10 9 8 7 6 5 4 3 2 1

Copyright Acknowledgments

The editors and publisher gratefully acknowledge the following sources for
granting permission to use copyrighted material:

Chapter 3 is reprinted by permission of the publisher from *Productivity
Improvement* by Vernon Buehler and Krishna Shetty © 1981 AMACOM, a
division of American Management Association, New York. All rights reserved.

Chapters 7 and 10 are reprinted by permission of the publisher by eds. Y. K.
Shetty and Vernon M. Buehler, *Quality, Productivity, and Innovation.* Copyright
1987 by Elsevier Science Publishing Co., Inc.

Chapters 4, 12, 16, 17, 27, and 32 are reprinted from *Competing Through
Productivity and Quality,* edited by Y. K. Shetty and Vernon M. Buehler, 1988.
By permission of Productivity Press.

Gratefully dedicated

to H. Ross Perot

As a leading crusader for quality education in the United States and for his unstinting efforts in attempting to bring his message on "competitiveness" to hundreds of Utah State University's students and friends of its Partners Program, we dedicate this volume to H. Ross Perot, one of America's foremost entrepreneurs of the twentieth century. Regrettably, his planned lecture for January 19, 1989, at Utah State University's Sixth Annual Human Resources Seminar, was cancelled because of unforeseen circumstances. Without question, his creative genius, zest for hard work, business achievements and patriotic fervor make him the ultimate role model for aspiring young entrepreneurs on campuses and elsewhere around the globe.

Contents

Contents

x   Contents

Foreword

George M. C. Fisher

How can America enhance productivity?

In this seventh volume in their series on quality and productivity, the editors have assembled answers to this question as provided by the renowned authorities and experienced industrialists who lectured at Utah State University's student-managed Partners Program seminars during 1979-89. Although their methods differ markedly, these gurus seem to agree on certain basic points: top management needs to be permanently involved in quality; robots and automation alone are inadequate; and quality circles are of little use except as an adjunct to other methods.

The editors have provided a highly useful collection of philosophies and techniques that have proved valuable to all types of organizations in designing programs to enhance competitiveness thorugh quality and productivity. Readers will benefit from understanding these approaches as they integrate the techniques into programs tailored to fit their diverse environments.

Labor-management teamwork seems essential in all approaches for solving the quality, productivity, and competitiveness concerns in America. Worker participation or employee involvement has a controversial history in the US where the labor movement has tended to regard it as a device for busting unions. However new evidence shows that self-managing work teams can have a massive impact on productivity because of flexible work practices, worker satisfaction, reduced absenteeism, and so forth.

Furthermore, most will agree with the editors that U.S. competitiveness will benefit from increased teamwork in other areas. Walls between designers, manufacturing engineers, and other specialties are disappearing. Teams are developing innovative products to improve quality, shorten delivery times, lower inventories, and upgrade productivity. Such benefits are further magnified by the cooperative efforts of supplier-producer-dealer teams.

Closer business-government cooperation is proving helpful
in formulating public policy on trade, antitrust, consum-
erism, and other issues.   Joint university-industry
centers should expedite the commercialization of new
ideas.   A teamwork environment is the key to productivity.

At Motorola teamwork has played an essential role in
our company's being selected as one of the only three
winners of the first Baldrige National Quality Award.
Bringing a product to market invovles not only finding
out what the customer wants, but also working closely
with vendors, and designing the product so that it can be
manufactured at the highest quality and lowest cost
standards.

In compiling these timely insights, the editors have
provided a valuable resource to educators, practitioners,
policy makers, and society in general.

Preface

This volume contains lectures by the "giants" of industry, academia, and the consulting world on quality, productivity, and competitiveness. Approximately 1000 lectures sponsored by Utah State University's renowned Partners Program during 1978-89 were combed in selecting this collection of sage counsel by the likes of W. Edwards Deming, Joseph M. Juran, Lester C. Thurow, Hewlett-Packard's John Young and Florida Power and Light's Joe C. Collier.

Initiated in 1970, the Partners Program provided a forum where thousands of students as aspiring entrepreneurs and hundreds of practitioners could discuss emerging management issues that were often yet to be printed in textbooks. This unique student-managed partnership with industry evolved to satisfy both a strong student desire for meaningful interaction with the real world and a deep conviction by the GMs, IBMs, DECs and others, that they should share their changing views on competitiveness with students.

The Partners Program benefits greatly from the loyalty of over 600 business partners and the generosity of several visionaries, such as the late George S. Eccles and his successor, Spencer F. Eccles, CEO of the First Security Corporation, who sponsored many of these speakers in the renowned Eccles Distinguished Lecture Series.

As coeditors, we are convinced that America's entrepreneurial spirit and free enterprise system, in which the marketplace picks the winners, will respond to the global competitive challenge by making continuous incremental improvements in quality and productivity. Furthermore, with the emergence of the information age in which brain-based activities rather than material resources will dominate, the U.S. competitiveness should be strengthened because of America's legendary ability to create new ideas and technology.

Our confidence stems from the lessons gained from these lecturers and elsewhere concerning: (1) the spreading recognition among U.S. firms of all sizes that they must think globally; (2) the streamlining of factory processes to slash inventories, material costs, and production time; (3) the paring of management layers to force designers, engineers, production workers, and marketers to work as a team; (4) the harnessing of computer technology to make small batches of customized products at low cost; (5) the enlightened attitude of labor and management in adopting teamwork practices that empower the workforce to improve quality and productivity; (6) the growing awareness of the crucial importance of speed in commercializing new technology; (7) the institutionalization of continuous productivity improvement in all sectors; (8) the nurturing, reinforcing, and mobilizing of cohesive corporate cultures to support the demand for innovation, flexibility, and ever-improving levels of productivity and quality; (9) the gradual changing of public policy on such issues as antitrust and technology transfer, to catch up with the fast changing competitive needs of U.S. firms in the global marketplace; and (10) the increasing realization that regaining market share rests less on further dollar depreciation and more on export awareness by both small and large firms, as well as on increased spending for R & D plant/equipment, and education/training.

Despite our optimism about America's success in the race for competitive improvement, our experience as educators makes us cautious about whether the academic community will adequately meet its responsibilities to upgrade curricula in a timely manner to prepare students to be global competitors in the twenty-first century. Our reservations rest on the findings of a recent survey of the members of the American Academy of Management. The participants criticized themselves for "closed loop/ little influence on the outside world" thinking. A comprehensive study of accredited business schools conducted by the American Assembly of the Collegiate Schools of Business also found a prevalent attitude of "complacency, ossification, and irrelevancy".

We believe that educators must (1) interact with business better to understand each other's needs and actions; (2) modify curricula in statistics, participative management, total quality control, foreign languages and cultures, and general management to prepare graduates for broad-based flexible assignments; (3) conduct research on the management of culture change and quality strategies to determine the best approaches for transforming firms into total quality control, market-driven, high-performance entities; and (4) join with industry and others in partnerships for sharing emerging ideas to help restore America's competitive position in the global marketplace.

Finally, we gratefully acknowledge the assistance of hundreds of student managers of USU's Partners Program who, with minimal supervision willingly and conscientiously planned, organized, and conducted seminars on energizing management issues during this past decade. Kristen Henrie Walton, who typifies the work ethic orientation of these students, prepared these manuscripts with flawless accuracy and exceptional timeliness.

PART I

The Quest for Competitiveness

1

Productivity, Quality, and the Competitive Advantage

Y. K. Shetty and
Vernon M. Buehler

Enhancing the global competitiveness of American business has become a major issue and continues to receive much attention at the national and business level. Improving U.S. competitiveness in domestic and international markets would help to reduce inflationary pressures, raise the standard of living, create jobs, strengthen the dollar in international markets, and improve the balance of trade. For individual companies it is the most fruitful approach for improving profitability.

Many scholars and managers have expressed their views on American competitiveness. They have pinpointed reasons for the decline of U.S. competitiveness and proposed measures to correct the problem. The President's Commission on Industrial Competitiveness, in its report, *Global Competition: The New Reality*, concluded that the nation's ability to compete has declined over the past two decades; a number of indicators, including increasing trade deficits, loss of market share by American hightechnology industries, declining rates of return in vital manufacturing sectors, declining productivity growth rates and stagnant real wages, demonstrate the problem. The commission's recommendations include increased research and development, removal of antitrust barriers, more improved manufacturing, effective use of human resources, improved labor-management relations, and improved trade and investment policy.

In a 1988 report, *Picking Up the Pace: The Commercial Challenge to American Innovation*, the Council on Competitiveness, a nonpartisan group that represents 151 prestigious chief executives of business, higher education, and labor organizations, recommends that the old "research-driven" model of innovation be supplemented with a new model. America's once commanding technological lead has been eroded significantly by foreign competitors, not due to a lack of inventiveness here but because the U.S. has failed to move its discoveries from the drawing board to the marketplace fast enough. The report calls for new federal policies specifically designed to help industry commercialize technological advances quickly. For example, the report demands that technology issues be part of deliberations on broader economic policy. The government has largely ignored these issues, leading to policies that have inadvertantly hurt the nation's ability to compete internationally.

The MIT Commission on Industrial Productivity scrutinized the American economy by examining eight industries that generate nearly 30 percent of U.S. manufacturing output. Its report, *Made in America: Regaining the Productive Edge*, identifies a series of weaknesses in U.S. businesses, including outdated strategies, provincial thinking, short time horizons, technological attitudes that favor invention over production, neglect of human resources (especially education), failures of cooperation both within companies and between companies and their suppliers and government, and industries that operate against their own best intersts. To correct these weaknesses, the MIT Commission urges industry, government, and educational institutions to take the following actions:

1. Learn to live in a world economy;

2. Cultivate a new "economic citizenship" that gives individuals more responsibility;

3. Blend cooperation and individuality by "flattening" organizations;

4. Provide for the future by investing heavily in basic education and technical literacy; and

5. Focus on producing products in the most modern way.

These and other reports on U.S. competitiveness pinpoint the reasons for the loss of competitiveness and recommend ways to address the problem. One major theme running through these reports is that public policy and business initiatives should be developed together to enhance U.S. competitiveness. They also caution that although effective public policy measures are necessary to provide a healthy environment in which businesses can operate, the major responsibility for restoring America's competitiveness resides with business. The business sector has definitely gotten the message. Many business executives believe that to be fully effective, the private sector must improve the quality and cost competitiveness of its products. As Allan F. Jacobson, chairman and CEO of 3M, so aptly put it, "There are only three issues critical to business success--innovation, productivity, and total quality." John Young, CEO of Hewlett-Packard and chairman of both the President's Commission on Industrial Competitiveness and the Council on Competitiveness has said, "In today's competitive environment, ignoring the quality issue is tantamount to corporate suicide. Companies that continuously produce high-quality products have lower manufacturing costs, higher profit margins, and capture a larger and larger share of the market."

PRODUCTIVITY AND QUALITY

Productivity growth, a measure of how fast output increases relative to inputs (labor, capital, and natural resources), in the United States has been slowing since the mid-1960s and declined in the 1970s. In spite of its recent improvements, the lag in productivity growth is putting the United States behind other industrialized countries. Likewise, the ability of U.S. industry to provide quality products--defined as satisfying the levels of relevance, uniformity, and dependability required by customers--has also deteriorated seriously in recent years.

Productivity can be defined simply as a ratio of output to input. Output is the number of units produced in a given period by a worker, a plant, a firm, or a nation's economy. Inputs are the resources used to produce certain outputs. A typical product is a combination of raw materials, machinery, labor, energy, and many other factors. Inputs are combined in the manufacturing process into products or outputs. Productivity indicates how well an organization utilizes its labor, capital, and raw material resources: the fewer resources per unit of output, the more productive the process is. There is a direct link between productivity and competitive advantage. Improved productivity clearly reduces costs and enhances competitiveness and profitability.

Quality is a complex concept. In simple terms, quality is a key attribute that customers use to evaluate products or services. Attributes associated with quality however, vary among products. For an automobile, for example, quality may include performance, durability, styling, comfort, safety, finish, speed, competence of repair, and value. Airline quality may include ease of check-in, cabin cleanliness, food, flight attendants' courtesy, and other variables. Quality attributes may also vary between firms; for instance, quality standards probably differ between Lord & Taylor department stores and K-Mart discount stores, between Mercedes and Volkswagen automobiles. Since quality has so many components or dimensions, it is often difficult to define precisely, but, definitions usually consider performance features: reliability, conformance, durability, serviceability, aesthetics, and overall reputation or perceived quality. The specific definition and relative importance of these factors can vary from market to market.

Quality must be defined from the customer's perspective. Hence, a firm's products and services must be compared to the products or services offered by competitors. American business tends to examine quality largely from the perspective of management. Since, the customer defines quality, however, management must accept the customer's perspective. It is not easy to identify customer requirements, so these must be examined continuously. Companies known for product or service quality use several methods to determine desirable quality-related attributes, including customer surveys, focus groups, customer comments, constant interaction with the customer, and other methods. Once quality has been defined, a firm can test conformance and correct any problems.

Finally, quality must also include the criteria that customers use when they perceive value, a perspective that involves the concept of relative value. Relative value can be envisioned as the formula, Value=Quality/Price. Product preference is thus determined by the value of the perceived quality/price ratio of one product in relation to another competing product.

SOURCES OF COMPETITIVE ADVANTAGE

Productivity and quality are two major sources of competitive advantage. Improved productivity clearly reduces costs and enhances competitiveness and profitability. Such an advantage allows a firm to use its cost advantage to increase profit margins, lower prices, or both. Traditionally, in the United States, quality and productivity have often been considered as distinctly different issues, even though the two concepts are closely linked. Quality is concerned with both the outputs and the inputs of the production process. Since productivity is the ratio of outputs to inputs, an increase in inputs and a decline in outputs lowers productivity. A deterioration in the quality of the products or services can disrupt schedules, delay deliveries, increase rework and scrap, waste manpower, materials, and machine time, and increase warranty costs. Reworking products, inspecting parts, and losing product as scrap represent increased input and decreaed output; in other words, lower productivity.

On the one hand, poor quality products and services not only increase costs but also affects sales. For example, poor quality may result in rejection and substantially diminish the chance of selling the customer a replacement product, thus precipitating a decline in the level of output. Furthermore, the damage to the company reputation can eventually cause incalculable losses in terms of reduced sales and market share lost to competitors.

On the other hand, businesses that improve quality acquire a competitive advantage through quality-induced product differentiation or the creation of something perceived as unique throughout the industry. Product differentiation on the basis of quality creates a defensible competitive position and protects a firm against inroads of rival firms. Customers who prefer quality products are willing to pay more. Customer loyalty and the uniqueness associated with quality are difficult barriers for new competing firms to surmount. In short, productivity and quality improvement are important sources of competitive advantage.

QUALITY AND PROFITABILITY

Is a strategy to improve productivity and product quality profitable? The link between productivity and profitability is well established. Although the literature on product quality is voluminous, the linkage between quality and profitability has not been as carefully explored. U.S. firms have traditionally viewed quality and productivity as distinctly different concepts. Efforts to improve quality have therefore been perceived to increase costs and reduce both productivity and profitability. In recent years scholars such as W. Edwards Deming, Joseph M. Juran, Philip B. Crosby, and others have attempted to correct this misconception. According to Deming, quality is productivity. He contends that productivity improves and costs decrease as quality is improved. A company captures the market and becomes more profitable when it couples lower prices with higher quality. Crosby says quality is free, but disregarding quality is costly. In short, it pays to do jobs right the first time.

In their popular book, *In Search of Excellence: Lessons from America's Best-Run Companies*, Thomas J. Peters and Robert H. Waterman demonstrated that the well-managed U.S. corporations that are most profitable also emphasize product and service quality. Their research confirmed that companies such as Hewlett-Packard, IBM, Marriott, Procter and Gamble, Johnson and Johnson, Maytag, Merck, and Walt Disney provided quality products and services and also ranked in the top of their respective industries in at least four out of six financial criteria over a twenty-year period. The financial criteria included compound asset growth, compound equity growth, the average ratio of market value to book value, average return on total capital, average return on equity, and the average return of sales. The results clearly showed that America's best-run companies use product quality to enhance profit performance.

A large-scale study, conducted by the Strategic Planning Institute of Cambridge, Massachusetts, provided more quantitative data concerning the link between quality and profitability. This study, "Profit Impact of Marketing Strategies" (PIMS), involved 1,200 businesses. The quality ratings were based on executives' estimates of the proportion of sales of (a) products clearly superior in quality to those of their largest competitors, (b) those of equivalent quality, and (c) those of inferior quality. Both return on investment and net profits as a percentage of sales rose as relative quality increased. The return on investment ranged from 13 percent for the businesses that ranked themselves in the lowest one-fifth product quality category to 30 percent for those that ranked in the highest one-fifth, a statistically significant difference. Businesses selling high-quality products or services are generally more profitable than those whose products are of lower quality.

How does product quality affect profitability? Quality can increase profits by lowering costs, increasing sales, or a combination of both factors.

QUALITY REDUCES COSTS...

Quality reduces costs and thus increases productivity in several ways. Eliminating defects or errors reduces labor and/or machine hours. It also reduces inspection costs and the level of inventories for replacements. Reducing scrap and waste reduces the cost of materials. Fewer warranty claims decrease the material and labor required to repair defective products. A reduction in service costs decreases labor costs. A low-cost producer can use its cost advantage to increase profit margins and/or lower prices for improved sales.

Substantial cost savings accrue from reduced re-work, less scrap, and lower inspection, warranty, and product liability costs. IBM estimates that 30 percent of its manufacturing cost, the total cost of detection and appraisal, was the direct result of not doing it right the first time. Hewlett-Packard calculated that as much as 25 percent of its manufacturing assets were tied up in reacting to quality problems. Eliminating these costs could increase output by a similar percentage, triggering a comparable percentage increase in profitability.

Calculating the cost of poor quality is one of the best ways to convince top managers and employees that quality significantly affects productivity and profitability. The cost of poor quality is simply any expenditure, in manufacturing and service, above that incurred if the product were built right the first time. Total quality costs typically include expenditures concerning: (1)

prevention costs--steps taken to assure that tasks are always done right the first time, which include quality planning, worker training, and supplier education; (2) appraisal costs--costs associated with evaluating whether a task has in fact been done right the first time, including product inspection and testing; (3) internal failures--costs associated with correcting mistakes, including rework and scrap; and (4) external failures--costs associated with any failures experienced by the customer, including costs of warranty and product liability.

In most companies, such cost information is not readily available. Accounting information systems focus on financial data and not on data concerning the cost of poor quality. Although many companies seem to recognize the need for better quality, their financial and accounting systems do not yet reflect product quality information.

AND ENHANCES SALES

Quality also affects a firm's sales and market share. First, a reputation for higher quality decreases the elasticity of demand and provides opportunities for companies to charge higher prices and earn higher profit margins. Second, a reputation for quality also improves chances of enhancing sales and market share. PIMS data confirm that high-quality products and services increase sales and market share. Businesses that improved quality increased their market share five or six times faster than those whose products declined in quality, and three times faster than those whose quality was similar to that of their competitors. Even when increasing quality required more expensive materials and manufacturing processes, the price differentials typically exceeded the higher costs.

Quality improvement is a powerful means of building market share. Research based on PIMS data concerning the relationship ob advertising, price, product quality, and market share showed that (a) changes in the relative product quality are strongly related to changes in market share; (b) relative advertising had only a modest relationship to changes in market share; and (c) the relative changes in price were not related to changes in market share. The benefits of simply lowering prices are short-lived as competitors quickly match decreases in price. Quality improvement, on the other hand, is much more difficult for other companies to match; it requires more time, money, and creativity.

A decline in quality can suddenly lower sales, harm the competitive position of a company, and reduce customer loyalty. Failure to correct quality errors can lead to incalculable losses. A leading manufacturer of appliances estimates that one in three dissatisfied customers will complain to the company; however, each dissatisfied customer complains to at least 15 friends and acquaintances. One "Big-Three" automobile company estimated that a single dissatisfied owner of a luxury car costs the company no fewer than 100 lost sales in a single year. Recent studies conducted by Ford Motor Company show that satisfied customers tell eight other people about their car, while dissatisfied customers complain to 22 people.

Recognizing the importance of productivity and quality, many companies have taken initiatives aimed at improving productivity and quality to gain competitive advantage. Though some companies have made substantial improvements, many have not yet fully recaptured a reputation for product quality. A recent study conducted by the American Society for Quality Control (ASQC) showed that eight out of ten executives believe that product quality plays a very important role in making U.S. companies more competitive with foreign nations and that quality will be essential to their own companies' ability to compete in intensely competitive marketplaces. Major corporations throughout the United States are vigorously addressing this competitive challenge. They have launched a variety of initiatives to improve productivity and to produce better quality products and services.

Productivity and quality are widely recognized as two major sources of competitive advantage. This volume contains papers by some of the best known authorities on policy measures and practical guidelines for enhancing productivity and quality. It contains specific recommendations by world-renowned experts such C. Jackson Grayson, W. Edwards Deming, Joseph M. Juran, Thomas J. Peters, Philip B. Crosby, Rosabeth Moss Kanter, and others. It also provides the detailed experiences of a number of firms such as Hewlett-Packard, IBM, Texas Instruments, Ford, 3M, Nucor, Lincoln Electric, Xerox, and Dana who are America's productivity and quality leaders on the day-to-day policies and practices that contribute to competitive success. The contributors, representing a broad range of large American businesses, provide guidelines for developing and implementing successful productivity and quality improvement programs. The emphasis throughout is on the role of human resources and manufacturing strategy in enhancing productivity and quality. The focus is on practices that have proven effective in terms of managing people, quality, productivity, and manufacturing strategy. In summary, this volume provides well-tested policies and practices with regard to the various features of productivity and quality improvement initiatives. These ideas will provide invaluable assistance to companies in search of successful productivity and quality improvement initiatives for competitive success.

PART II

America's
Productivity and
Quality Leaders

2

Introduction

Y. K. Shetty and
Vernon M. Buehler

This section contains papers by world-renowned productivity and quality experts--educators and consultants with varied practical experiences. These papers clearly define the productivity and quality challenges that American businesses face and provide several approaches and guidelines for solving these problems. Their recommendations provide corporate managers with authoritative perspectives on changes in productivity and quality practices that can help U.S. business improve its competitiveness in world markets.

JOHN W. KENDRICK

Professor Kendrick, an international authority on productivity, defines the concept and then identifies sources of growth of labor productivity in the U.S. economy. He emphasizes that productivity is the key to profitability at the company level; in the concluding section of the paper he moves from a macro (national) emphasis to consider productivity improvement within a micro (organizational) context. Discussing the experiences of a number of companies (such as Honeywell, Northrop, and Kaiser Aluminum), Kendrick suggests certain preconditions for the success of productivity improvement programs. These include an effective organization for productivity improvement, worker involvement, productivity measurement, specific productivity goals, and an effective monitoring and communications system.

C. JACKSON GRAYSON

As chairman of the American Productivity and Quality Center in Houston, C. Jackson Grayson is well known for his efforts to improve productivity and quality in the United States. His paper, "Productivity for All Seasons: Yesterday, Today, and Tomorrow," traces the role of productivity in the rise and decline of nations and then discusses the major lessons of his findings. He says, "As the present world productivity leader, the United States would do well to keep these lessons in mind as it contemplates the twenty-first century, and those now challenging the U.S. for economic leadership."

According to Grayson, the United States is losing its productivity lead, and the overall U.S. response to the problem is not sufficient. If the United States continues to decline, it will result from a failure to maintain productivity leadership in a highly competitive global economy. The implications for this nation and for the world are enormous, since productivity provides business profits, jobs, real wages, education, health care, and defense. Ultimately productivity determines the rank of nations. That is why it is important to pay more attention to productivity; how to measure it, how to compare relative productivities across nations, how to identify the sources and obstacles to productivity growth, and how to make productivity growth the win-win strategy for humanity. Productivity is the challenge for the global economy. We need a global focus on productivity improvement for the benefit of all.

W. EDWARDS DEMING

W. Edwards Deming, a world-renowned consultant for the improvement of quality and productivity, says that management is solely responsible for declines in product quality. According to him, deadly obstacles or barriers to high quality exist, including: (1) lack of constancy of purpose to plan products and services that will have a market, keep the company in business, and provide jobs; (2) emphasis on short-term profits and short-term thinking (just the opposite of constancy of purpose to stay in business), fed by the fear of takeovers and by demands from bankers and owners for dividends; (3) personal review systems (evaluations of performance, merit ratings, annual reviews, or annual appraisals, by whatever name), for people in management, the effects of which are devastating; (4) mobility of management, leading to job hopping from one company to another; and (5) use of only visible figures for management, with little or no consideration of figures who are unknown or unknowable.

Deming believes that there must be a transformation, not just solutions to immediate problems, and that this can be brought about only by top management. Business firms must look ahead and plan for the future if they are to stay in business. In this paper he lists fourteen points of management that should lead to improved produc- tivity, quality, and the transformation of Western-style management. They highlight such concepts as quality coming first, customer focus, continuous improvement, employee involvement, and partnership with suppliers.

Deming contends that as efforts to improve quality succeed, productivity improves and costs go down. With better quality at lower prices, a company captures the market and provides ever more jobs. A further important gain is happier employees--people who are happy to have the opportunity to take part in company-wide improvement. Thus, improvements in quality have a cascading effect. Productivity goes up, and customers are happier with better quality at lower prices. Deming says that situa- tion occurs in the Western world only when the top management works actively and with devotion in transform- ing Western-style management.

THOMAS J. PETERS

Thomas J. Peters, once a management consultant with McKinsey & Company, along with Robert H. Waterman, Jr., has been investigating how the best-run U.S. companies attained and maintain that status. The results of their investigation are reported in *In Search of Excellence*. They are based on studying forty-three models of U.S. companies, including Bechtel, Boeing, Caterpillar Trac- tor, Dana, Delta Airlines, Digital Equipment, Emerson Electric, Flour, Hewlett-Packard, IBM, Johnson & Johnson, McDonald's, Procter & Gamble, and 3M. According to Peters and Waterman, these best-run companies consistent- ly exhibit certain core characteristics that constitute eight attributes of excellence:

1. A bias for action. A do-it, fix-it, or try-it mentality prevails, rather than waiting for more analysis and expert opinion.
2. Closeness to the customer. They are obsessed with being close to the customer, emphasizing quality, service, and reliability.
3. Autonomy and entrepreneurship. Managers are en- couraged to act like entrepreneurs.
4. Simple form and a lean staff. Units remain at a small, manageable size; a lean staff avoids bureau- cracy.
5. Productivity through people. The employees are the root of productivity, quality, and growth.
6. Hands-on, value-driven leadership. Excellent companies, through their leaders, talk to their workers constantly and remind them of the company

philosophy through word and deed. The key is the
value system, which becomes a culture for the
company.
7. Sticking to their knitting. They do not acquire a
business that they do not know how to run.
8. Simultaneous loose and tight controls. They maintain a balance, controlling a few variables tightly
but allowing a great deal of flexibility in the
others.

These excellent companies believe in the importance of
superior quality and productivity. They value people as
the root source of productivity and quality. Drawing
lessons from the best-run U.S. companies, Peters says
that superior performers understand their products and
customers, pay attention to details, and are involved in
constant experimentation. Whether it is computers,
potato chips, hotels, or chocolate chip cookies, a
company can have virtually any market it wants, if it
provides quality products and is "simply, plainly,
humanly courteous" to its customers. Superior quality
and customer service are the key, from Maytag in the
washing machine business, to Hewlett-Packard in the
instrumentation business, to Mars in the candy bar
business, and to Frito-Lay in the potato chip business.
The customer will pay money only if we give him or her
something worth paying for--quality product and service.
Based on the experience of the best-run firms, Peters
says that when it comes to product/service quality, we
are enamored with statistical quality and control,
quality circles, automation, CAD/CAM, robotics, and the
like. These are important techniques, but they are, at
most, the icing on the cake. The cake is people who live
quality, decade in and decade out. If the best-run
companies' simple formula for success is the magic of
constant experimentation, superior quality, superior
customer service, and customer courtesy, then the basis
of such success is people. The most important people are
not the executives, but the real people, the rank and
file. Quality is an all-hands game. In short, people
are the most important source of productivity, quality,
and profitability in a company. They are the foundation
and the cornerstone on which all else is built.

LESTER C. THUROW

Lester C. Thurow's paper, "Can America Compete in the
World Economy?" employs a three-level grid in discussing
the causes of American productivity problems. The first
grid is an industry-by-industry examination of productivity growth. The second grid deals with capital and labor
inputs. The third grid concerns adverse external shocks,
such as sudden large jumps in energy costs or the imposi-

tion of new environmental or safety rules. After analyzing productivity problems in these areas, Thurow attributes declining productivity to several factors: shifts from high-productivity industries to services and other low-productivity industries; inadequate investment in plant and equipment to match fast-growing labor forces, thus causing the capital-labor ratio to fall; energy shocks; environmentalism; sagging research and development; inept management; and other problems. He believes that no single factor killed American productivity growth; hence, no one single measure can revive it. Thurow believes that the contributions of labor, capital, management, and public policy must match those of the competitor nations if America is to be competitive. A world-class economy demands world-class inputs. Institutions and incentives must therefore be reformulated to foster the desired market results. He believes that America has the capacity to do what is necessary to compete with other countries.

JOSEPH M. JURAN

Joseph M. Juran's intriguing paper, "The Quality Trilogy" cites nine premises for charting a new direction in managing quality in a company. Serious obstacles or non-uniformities (multiple functions, multiple levels of hierarchy, and multiple product lines) must be overcome, however, to find a universal way of thinking about quality that fits all functions, levels, and product lines. Juran proposes the underlying concept of the quality trilogy, consisting of three basic quality-oriented processes: (1) quality planning as a process for preparing to meet quality goals, with an end result of meeting those goals: (2) quality control as a process for meeting quality goals during operations, with the end result of conducting operations in accordance with the quality plan; and (3) quality improvement as the process for breaking through to unprecedented levels of performance, with the end result of conducting operations at levels of quality distinctly superior to planned performance. His paper concludes with persuasive illustrations of the quality trilogy for training in management for quality and for strategic quality planning.

PHILIP B. CROSBY

In his fascinating paper, "The Pragmatic Philosophy of Phil Crosby," Crosby relates his experiences with managing quality starting in the 1950s. These include how he arrived at the concept of "Zero Defects" while managing quality for the Pershing project at the Martin Company. After preaching this philosophy and gaining experience at several firms, he wrote *Quality is Free*, in the late 1970s and set up Philip Crosby Associates for training executives on the following "Absolutes of Quality Management": (1) the definition of quality is conformance to requirements; (2) the system of causing quality is prevention; (3) the performance standard for quality is Zero Defects; and (4) the measurement of quality is the price of non-conformance. Crosby contends that quality is the result of policy: firms can decide to have or not have it. He concludes with the following profile of a quality-troubled company as spelled out in his popular 1984 book, *Quality Without Tears*: (1) they never deliver exactly what they have agreed to provide; (2) they have a "fix-it" organization; (3) they do not have a clear performance standard; (4) they have no idea what nonconformance costs; and (5) they think all of this is someone else's fault.

STEVEN C. WHEELWRIGHT

In his paper, "Building Excellence in Manufacturing," Professor Wheelwright discusses several aspects of this goal, including the concept of corporate strategy, in which manufacturing plays a key competitive role. Wheelwright then analyzes how U.S. manufacturing conforms to these precepts. U.S. manufacturing industries are often viewed as the "end of the line," second class, and not very important. Wheelwright instead contends that manufacturing is generally under-utilized as a competitive weapon. Companies often ignore the fact that excellence in manufacturing provides a strong competitive advantage because excellence is difficult to copy. Wheelwright also notes that there are many new technologies and approaches that can make manufacturing a creative and dynamic field.

Wheelwright identifies the following factors in successful manufacturing firms:

1. They have very clear business strategies and have articulated and consistently pursued functional strategies.
2. They have tremendous discipline and are sharply focused in all aspects of their business.
3. They integrate all the functions well.
4. Managers take initiative and are leaders.

According to Wheelwright, these successful manufacturing companies are not competent at everything but they are superior at the one or two aspects that are most important to their businesses.

ROSABETH MOSS KANTER

In her essay, "Managing Change in Innovative Organizations," Rosabeth Kanter, author of one of the most talked-about books, *The Change Masters*, discusses the environment that allows people to master change adequately and to develop corporate support for winning the new competitive game in the business world. This is a new game: everything is in flux; technology is changing rapidly; customers, employees, and users are more demanding and willing to shop around; and the whole structure of the industry is changing. It is very difficult to win a game like this using conventional methods, so innovation is critically important.

Kanter says that in order to win the competitive game, businesses must do a number of things. First, they should focus on a few things that they know how to do very well, to build on competence and avoid the distraction of trying to keep up with too many things. Second, they should develop the ability to move quickly to gain the benefit of "first mover" advantage. Third, they must be flexible enough to keep bending and re-directing to take advantage of new opportunities that arise in an environment of constant change, where technology provides an opportunity a minute. Behind these three actions, partnership is essential. The best strategy is to befriend all the groups in the environment on whom the company depends--customers, employees, and suppliers. Finally, we need a particular corporate environment. Stimulating innovation and entrepreneurship derive from an integrative organization, in which people pull together rather than apart, joint projects and joint developments are encouraged, communication and information knit everything together, and shared goals for a business create unanimity of purpose. The real issue in managing an innovative organization, according to Kanter, is to create more opportunity for people themselves to take charge of change.

ARMAND V. FEIGENBAUM

"Challenge to America's Industrial Leadership" by Armand V. Feigenbaum outlines several major trends. First, quality has become crucial to the industrial strength of the United States. Second, American industry has made substantial quality gains; the full job of international quality leadership however, is still a long way ahead. Third, accelerating the rate of quality improvement is the single most important competitive challenge facing the United States. After tracing the weaknesses in U.S. quality improvement initiatives, Feigenbaum outlines seven bench marks for building effective company-wide programs:

1. That quality is not a technical or departmental function but is instead a systematic process that extends throughout the company.
2. That quality must be organized to recognize that while it is everybody's job in the company, it will become nobody's job unless this company quality process is correctly structured to support both the quality work of individuals as well as quality teamwork among departments.
3. That the quality improvement emphasis must take place in marketing, in development and enginee-ring, in manufacturing, and particularly in servic-es, not merely in production for the factory workers only.
4. That quality must be perceived in this process as what the buyer wants and needs to satisfy his requirements for use, not what the company needs to satisfy its requirements for marketing and produc-tion efficiency.
5. That modern quality improvement requires the application of new technology, ranging from quality design techniques to computer-aided quality manage-ment measurement and control.
6. That widespread quality improvement is achieved only through the help and participation of all the men and women in the company.
7. That all of these changes come about when the company has established a clear, customer-oriented quality management system throughout the organiza-tion.

The power and continuity of strong total quality programs are becoming a major competitive strength for American business growth. The key to success is that the company must have a total quality improvement program that is managed for maximum effectiveness.

WICKHAM SKINNER

In his profound paper, "The Productivity Paradox Explained," Harvard Professor Wickham Skinner, recipient of the coveted McKinsey Prize for the best article in the *Harvard Business Review* and an early champion of improv-ing manufacturing strategy, says that the U.S. has made an extraordinary turnaround in productivity and quality in the 1980s but we have not yet regained our competitive ability. He cautions that the productivity and quality strategies of the 1980s will not be enough in the fierce-ly competitive market of the 1990s when more attention to speed and flexibility in product development will be needed to win customers. Skinner has three major con-cerns for the 1990s: (1) managers are focusing on short-run operations and failing to look at fundamental manufacturing structural problems of make-or-buy, capacity, equipment and process technology, and the infrastructure of operating systems; (2) the best management people are not going into production, manufacturing and operations management; and (3) the traditional functional organization creates barriers that must be replaced with teams so that we can remove a serious impediment to adapting to the global competitive environment.

MARTIN STARR

Columbia University's Martin Starr, a leading U.S. academician in management science and productivity, presents some highly stimulating views on their studies of time-based management in his paper, "How Fast Response Organizations Achieve Global Competitiveness." In fast-response organizations, managers do not wait for something to happen before taking action. They are prepared to create new situations and to visualize and respond to likely new scenarios. Faster-response business units are more successful than slower-response competitors because they cut lead time, lag time, think time, communication time, and so forth. Starr concludes that time is the dimension that business must use for leverage. His message is that the old, traditional, bureaucratic organization can no longer prosper, or even survive, in the global business environment.

SUMMARY

Just as one finds little consensus on the causes for the slowdown in U.S. productivity--inadequate capital investment and R & D, age/sex workforce composi-tion, energy costs, inflation, government regulations, etc.--so there is no agreement among these gurus on the best methods for correcting our lagging productivity. Having stated that, however, one finds agreement on certain basic points for improving quality and productivity. These authorities believe that until top management becomes permanently involved in quality, nothing will work. They see little hope for relying primarily on robots, automation, or other gadgetry. They have little use for quality circles except as an adjunct to other methods and systemic changes. Beyond that, one finds that each authority has an emphasis: Deming stresses managerial philosophy and statistical methods, Juran emphasizes setting annual goals and assigning teams to work on them; Crosby relies on inspirational messages to motivate managers; Feigenbaum aims at designing and installing total quality control so that the same statistical and engineering methods can be applied company-wide, to marketing and distribution as well as on the factory floor. As will be described in Section III, many firms have found that some mix of these approaches has proved useful in enhancing quality, productivity, and competitiveness.

3

Background and Overview of Productivity Improvement Programs

John W. Kendrick

It is true that government can do a great deal to improve the climate within which enterprise operates, but we can't wait for government to act to help facilitate productivity improvement. Productivity at the company level is the key to profitability. Our competitive system produces very real incentives for productivity improvements. We can go ahead and, as we have done for the last 200 years, continue to make those improvements and innovations at the company level to increase outputs of goods and services that people want in relation to the resources that are used in their production.

WHAT IS PRODUCTIVITY?

That brings me to my first point: What is productivity? It is the relationship of outputs of goods and services in real physical volume to inputs of the basic labor and nonhuman resources used in the production process, also measured in physical units such as hours worked, machine hours, and so forth. If output is related to all the inputs (which I think is the most desirable kind of measure), output per unit of total input is basically the productivity formula: O/I.

If you include all of the inputs, this measure will get at the net saving of cost elements or inputs per unit of output achieved over time as a result of technological change and the other factors that make it possible to increase production with a given volume of resources. Since this input is a composite measure, including human and nonhuman resources, you can look at it as a weighted

average of output in relation to weighted inputs. Output
in relation to labor-hours alone is the usual productivity measure. (We used to call it output per man-hour, but
now we have desexed the term "man-hour" and just talk
about labor-hours or hours worked, it means the same
thing.)

Then we have output in relation to capital inputs.
These are the capital goods, plants, equipment, and
inventory stocks. In this category we also include land
and natural resources, as well as other broad major
groupings of inputs: output per unit of materials,
supplies, and other purchased goods and services--includ-
ing energy. As we are able to increase output in relation to each of these, of course, we increase the efficiency of the productive process. Not only are we
concerned with saving on labor per unit of output (thereby making it possible to increase production with the
existing or growing labor force), but we are interested
in conserving on capital goods because capital is scarce.
It comes at a cost of saving and investment, just as
labor comes at a cost of work and has the alternative use
of leisure, which is desirable.

The alternative use of the investment and saving that
goes into the making of capital goods is consumption,
which is a desirable alternative. In the case of the raw
materials that go into production, the alternative is
conservation for future generations. So, by improving
productivity we're able to conserve, a buzz word these
days. In fact, I found nobody who really objects to the
idea of improving productivity; it's only rational to try
to produce a given output with fewer inputs, since these
inputs have desirable alternative uses.

As I pointed out, we measure outputs and inputs in real
terms. I won't go into technicalities, but most of the
outputs and the inputs are aggregates of the components,
which may be very diverse when you are looking at the
whole business economy. The business gross product
comprises thousands of different kinds of goods. So, in
effect, you have a weighted quantity aggregate--quanti-
ties of given periods weighted by the prices of a based
period--so that over time you are holding prices constant
and the aggregate is moving as the quantities of output
move. And similarly with inputs, you are measuring the
quantities of hours weighted by base-period wage rates or
average hourly compensation so that the labor input moves
as hours move but not as wage rates move. Because this
is a technical relationship, you want to look at the
relative quantity movements not obscured by price changes, wage changes, and so forth. This kind of a ratio
basically signifies technological improvement.

People who have studied economics should remember the
production function: With varying quantities of labor
and capital, you produce a certain quantity of output,
and you can vary combinations to get at the least-cost

combination, depending on the relative prices of the factors. What you are getting when productivity goes up is a shift of this production function in which you are now able to produce the same quantities with less of one or both of the factors, so that you have saved real cost and with given quantities of the factors you are able to produce more. Of course, this has been the source of rising standards of living in this country, which have gone up 2 or 3 percent a year on the average during this century. Also, at the national level, it is important as an anti-inflationary element, because to the extent that productivity rises, it helps offset the increases in wage rates and in other input prices. The rise in productivity strengthens our economy and our position in the world economy.

PRODUCTIVITY AT THE INDUSTRY AND COMPANY LEVELS

At the industry level, the relative changes in productivity are great. We have a spectrum of rates of change. Some industries rank very high--airlines, pipelines, electric utilities, communications, and technology-based manufacturing industries, such as electric machinery and equipment. Others (some of the older industries such as shoe making and the waterways of this country) have shown very little productivity increase. One industry for which I devised measures for the postwar period showed a drop--local transit. (That's not surprising: More and more people are using their own personal cars, and fewer are riding buses. Therefore, bus traffic has gone down and the roads are getting clogged.) Generally, this kind of spectrum is associated with relative price changes. Industries with high productivity change have low relative price changes. This stimulates sales to the extent that there is an elasticity of demand, which goes right along with what the economists say: If relative prices fall, people tend to buy more of the goods.

The relative changes in productivity have accounted for changes in the industrial structure of the economy. In general, the high-productivity industries which have been able to reduce relative price have captured more of the market. They've grown relatively, and often their employment has grown as well. In fact, I think that labor has much more to fear from the unprogressive employer who doesn't keep up technologically than from the progressive employer who is improving products and processes.

At the company level, productivity is the key to profitability. If you are competing with other companies that are paying more or less the same wage rates and the same prices for materials and energy, and that are charging more or less the same prices for their outputs, the only way your profit can be greater is by using fewer inputs per unit of outputs so that your costs per unit are less. Higher productivity is the key to company profitability. The companies with higher productivity have higher profit margins. If they increase productivity faster than their competitors do, they can enjoy an increase in profit.

If productivity goes up less rapidly, profit margins tend to decline. Therefore, our competitive system produces very real incentives for productivity improvement. Companies try to improve their technology relative to competitors either offensively in order to widen their margins or defensively with respect to competitors who have introduced better technology. They must imitate the leaders and also improve their technology in order to preserve and maintain their profit margin. So, over the centuries before we even heard of the word productivity, companies were improving productivity. They were forced to by the competitive market system.

Incidentally, even the socialist countries are thinking more of trying to use market pricing and competition as a means of spurring their managers to reduce costs through innovation. Recently, while I was lecturing in the Soviet Union, my audience kept asking me how we stimulate our plant managers to innovate. It's a real problem there because of so much red tape in getting anything done. The managers don't particularly like to change techniques and get new allocations from Gosplan. Their bonuses are based on meeting production quotas. If you experiment, you may not meet the quota in the first year or two with new methods.

THE MACRO-ECONOMIC BACKGROUND

A summary view of what has been happening to a weighted average of output and productivity in all the enterprises of the economy, and in the industries into which firms or establishments are grouped, is given in Table 3.1. The rates of change are based on estimates for the U.S. private domestic business economy, which comprises about 80 percent of GNP, prepared by the Bureau of Labor Statistics (BLS) in the U.S. Department of Labor. The table and discussion of this section have been added since the conference paper was first published in 1981 in order to bring the background material up to date.

Everyone is now well aware that, following respectable gains in real gross product and productivity during the first quarter-century after World War II, there was a marked slowdown beginning in 1973. The growth of real gross product per hour of all persons employed dropped from an average of almost 3 percent a year between 1948 and 1973 to only 0.6 percent 1973-81. Including capital as well as labor inputs, multifactor productivity even showed a small absolute decline after 1973.

Table 3.1
Output and Productivity in the US Private
Business Economy 1948-1988, by Subperiod

(Average annual percentage rates of change)

Output: real gross product	3.6	2.0	3.7	3.3
Output/hour of all persons	2.9	0.6	1.7	2.2
Multifactor productivity	2.0	-0.2	1.3	1.4

Source: Bureau of Labor Statistics,
U.S. Department of Labor

It is less well known that since 1981 there has been a significant pickup in rates of growth of output and productivity. But, as the table shows, productivity growth did not recover fully to the pre-1973 rates. The recovery that did occur was due largely to the reversal of most of the negative forces that had caused the slowdown, as reviewed briefly below. Although limited, the productivity pickup helped hold down the inflation rate after 1982, just as the slow-down had contributed to accelerating inflation during the 1973-81 period.

A major force behind the productivity slump was a decline in the rate of technological progress. Real outlays for research and development levelled out from the mid-1960s to the latter 1970s, then began to grow smartly again. Taking account of the lags between R & D and embodiment of inventions in new products and process-es, this variable helps explain both the slow-down, and the pickup after 1981.

Investments in new plants and equipment per worker did not decline much after 1973 and played a minor role in the slowdown. But the oil shocks rendered some energy intensive capacity obsolete, and contributed to the accelerating inflation. Having to cope with inflation diverted managerial attention, and clouded the longer-term outlook for investment.

Another major factor was the slowdown in growth of real gross product after 1973, and the subsequent recovery after the 1981-82 recession. This affected opportunities for economies of scale and rates of utilization of capacity. After shrinking following 1973, these volume factors again became favorable during the 1980s.

Increased government regulations was a negative factor in the 1970s since they raised costs and inputs without increasing real GNP as measured. They were less negative in the 1980s, however, as social regulations became less onerous, and some economic regulations were lifted, pro-moting competition as in the airlines.

Prior to 1973, shifts of resources, particularly out of agriculture into more remunerative uses, promoted produc-tivity. Since 1973 these shifts have not been important.

Deterioration of national resource reserves has been a mildly negative tendency, especially since 1970 when productivity in mineral industries began to decline.

Investment in human resources has continued to rise quite steadily right through the 1970s and 1980s. There are some indications, however, such as S.A.T. scores, that the average quality of education was declining up until the early 1980s when a modest reversal took place.

Changes in the age-sex mix of the labor force reduced the average age and experience of workers in the 1970s, but the changes became favorable in the 1980s as the baby-boomers entered the prime working ages.

It is difficult to measure changes in the average efficiency of all workers in the country under a given technology, as can be done by work measurement techniques in individual companies. Some people think efficiency declined after the end of the Vietnam War. But the productivity slowdown and increasing international competition with American products have led to a major expansion of cooperative efforts by labor and management over the past decade to improve productivity. They may well have contributed to the pickup since 1981, although over the long run it is technological progress that is basic to rising productivity. But it is to human resource programs that the rest of this article is devoted, for they can have dramatic short- and medium-term effects.

JOINT LABOR-MANAGEMENT PRODUCTIVITY EFFORTS

Basically, productivity improvement and cost reduction are normal functions of management. It is axiomatic that the unique function of management is innovation: doing things better; trying to figure out better ways to produce better products at a lower cost, and also to manage an enterprise or an organization efficiently with a given technology--that is, to operate at maximum efficiency relative to potential, and to increase levels of efficiency. But by systematically tapping the reservoir of knowledge, creativity, and productivity inherent in the work-force, management can enhance productivity.

The first efforts to set up labor-management committees go back to World War II when Donald Nelson, the head of the War Production Board, called for the formation of joint labor-management productivity committees throughout American industry. Before the end of the war, more than 7 million workers were under such organizations. In general, it was felt that these committees were effective in enhancing productivity with meetings in various organizational units, offices, or plants, and with workers contributing or receiving ideas and being motivated to improve productivity and to recognize its importance to the war effort. And, indeed, during World War II, productivity did rise quite dramatically.

Since then there have been other developments that have promoted labor-management efforts and company programs in nonunionized as well as unionized companies. One of these has been in the area of international competition. In 1971, the United Steelworkers of America, in its contract with the steel companies, agreed to set up productivity committees in all the plants in the industry. That clause was renewed in subsequent contracts because of the competition from Germany and Japan, where productivity was rising faster and prices were falling relative to U.S. prices.

Another cause for the formation of these committees and programs has been government regulation. First of all, in regulated industries, such as the telephone industry and electric and gas utilities, the public utility commissions often want evidence that the companies are improving efficiency before they grant rate increases to cover increased costs; they don't want just a cost-plus pass-through to the customer.

I have testified for the Bell Companies as to the success of their efforts in improving productivity. In a National Productivity Center pamphlet called "Improving Company Productivity: A Description of Selected Company Programs," one of the five or six companies included was Detroit Edison. It so happened that before it would grant rate increases, the Michigan State Public Service Commission required measurement of productivity and evidence that Detroit Edison was improving its productivity.

In 1971, we got into much more regulation, partly because of the productivity slowdown and the acceleration of inflation. In August of that year, President Nixon called for a 90-day wage-price freeze, followed by Phase II of the anti-inflation program, in which controls were instituted. Jackson Grayson, the man chosen to head that effort, later formed the American Productivity Center in Houston, because he was convinced that the best way to combat inflation was through increasing productivity--not price controls.

Under Phase II, companies had to justify their applications for price increases by showing that their cost per unit had risen. However, with regard to the labor costs per unit, they had to show how much of the wage increase could be counteracted by gains in output per hour. Most companies didn't know how to measure their productivity. Jackson Grayson substituted, at my recommendation, the industry rates of change, because this gave companies an incentive to beat the industry rate and thus be able to widen profit margins if they could.

Actually, in 1972 and 1973, under the price-control program, productivity increased quite rapidly, because there was a built-in incentive to increase productivity. Similarly, when utilities' rates are set and their wages are rising, they have an incentive to improve productivity to offset that cost increase and preserve their profit margins or at least minimize the erosion of profit margin while they are waiting for the commissions to increase their rates to help cover their increased costs.

The main ideas which have been addressed by joint labor-management committees in the industries where they operate and by the productivity improvement programs are generally those where labor has a particular input, because in the end management has to make the big decisions on how much to invest in new plant and equipment and how much to spend for R&D. But these committees can address areas where labor has a particular significance, and some of these areas include the more efficient use of materials and reducing defects.

Beech Aircraft, for example, had a zero-defects program. This meant trying to improve reworking, improve quality, improve recovery and salvage of materials--which is particularly important in a period where material prices are rising rapidly--and likewise to conserve energy which is another major cost factor today. Even such things as agreeing to reduce the temperature in the winter by two degrees or to increase the temperature in the summer by two degrees save energy.

The committees try to suggest ways to improve on maintenance and on the repair and use of equipment, to reduce machine set-up time and downtime, and to improve work design. This is particularly important, since nobody knows his job better than the worker. He often can suggest very important ways either to simplify the job and get greater productivity, or to enrich it.

If the job is too boring, you want enrichment rather than simplification. But the whole area of job design is one in which cooperative efforts can be very fruitful. Some of the simple personnel matters are important, such as absenteeism, tardiness, amount of overtime, the amount of unproductive time, and so on. It is important to increase safety, reduce accidents, improve health and morale, and prevent alcoholism and drug abuse. Although some unions don't like the industrial engineering approach, in some companies, with the cooperation of labor, it has been able to expand work measurement and productivity measurement. Labor can help in the planning of training programs, in the design of tools or of products, and in layouts and organization of work. These committees can help reduce grievances and improve communications in order to catch developing problems and nip them in the bud. One important problem in the office is to reduce paperwork. Business is always complaining about all the paperwork the government requires, and yet within companies, there is a lot of paperwork which can often be cut down, thus reducing costs.

But productivity improvement programs are not for every company. First of all, you have to have a top management that is willing to experiment, that is not autocratic (or is at least willing to involve workers at all levels to a greater extent in production problems), that believes in the importance of human resources, that is serious about trying to improve performance, and that is able to get the support of front-line supervisors and foremen. Also, if there is a union, you need the union's cooperation, particularly in those industries that have problems, like apparel, shoes, or steel, or other industries facing foreign competition.

Unions recognize that the health of companies in their industry is very important to their job security and their improvements in real wages. I think that unions basically recognize the importance of increased productivity and are willing to cooperate if there is a good enough atmosphere in the company. And if it's a nonunion company, you would of course need a good enough relationship with labor and enough mutual trust to permit a fair try at a program of this sort.

SEVEN KEY ELEMENTS OF SUCCESSFUL PRODUCTIVITY PROGRAMS

In summary, here are seven key elements of any successful productivity program. First of all, there has to be an effective organization for productivity improvement with top management support, and someone must be responsible to top management for the program. Honeywell called him or her the productivity administrator. There were also productivity coordinators in the various divisions, plants, and departments, who chaired the group meetings with workers in these various organizational units. There was a steering committee of productivity coordinators at Honeywell. There are various ways the productivity improvement program can be organized: It can be carried on through existing line management, although even there, there has to be somebody responsible. There should be training of the supervisors and foremen and of the productivity coordinators, if you have a special organization, in how to go about tapping the ideas of workers through meetings or suggestions.

Second, the program should involve workers at all levels with groups in each self-contained unit within the company, whether office or plant. The committees are basically advisory to management. This isn't participative management with labor participating in the final decisions; the committees make recommendations, but management maintains ultimate decision-making authority. As far as the joint labor-management committees are concerned, here again their work should not and does not infringe on provisions of the labor contract, but it is supplemental to the contract. And not only are workers involved, but their contribution should be recognized through awards and rewards. This is a somewhat controversial area involving how monetary incentive should be worked in. Everyone is aware of the Scanlon Plans which provide bonuses. As their measures show reduced costs per unit, or increased profit, a bonus is periodically paid to workers. In other cases, individual workers are paid bonuses for particular cost-saving suggestions. In general, it is felt that some kind of monetary incentive helps in addition to recognition. Some people argue that since a major element in wage increases is productivity improvement anyway, labor is being paid for the productivity improvement in a generalized sense. I think that in many programs, it is felt that something additional is certainly motivating to a greater extent than not having a special incentive.

Third, the productivity improvement program should be linked with measurement. This means measurement not only of company productivity in terms of output per hour or per unit of input, but of other supplemental measures that are helpful: work measurement, measurement of personnel matters, absenteeism, and so on. All of these measures help in the program in that they make it possible to set goals to monitor and evaluate results. Productivity measurement in companies got a big boost back in the late 1940s and early 1950s when the Bureau of Labor Statistics had a program of plant-level measurement and a good many companies continued these measurement efforts. Then, with price controls and price standards, many more companies have come in. But accurate measurements depend on meaningful definitions of productivity.

Fourth, there should be adequate information resources available to the program--materials relating to productivity improvement techniques and the worthwhile suggestions that are made within the company, as well as resources from outside such as the publications of the former National Productivity Center, or the American Productivity Center. Resources also include the 28 private productivity centers. (There are about two dozen states that have productivity centers and private quality-of-work centers.) Material about all these outside resources should be available in the company.

Fifth is the development of plans, goals, and objectives with respect to improving productivity through reducing waste and accidents, or through whatever objectives may be set jointly by labor and management.

Sixth is the need for effective communication, both "up" and "down." This is an effort to get an input from workers, and should be "up" even more often than down. But it is also a way of transferring technology from one department to another where it is applicable. Where one department has hit on some good scheme through the productivity committees, you can transfer these ideas throughout the company. Usually there is a productivity newsletter which also contains material of use in the various units.

And finally, there should be a periodic review, evaluation, and analysis of the program, its results and benefits, and the obstacles encountered (such as fear for job security), and so on. The question to be posed is how to keep these programs living and useful after the start-up period. The United Steelworkers program has been going since 1971. Can interest be maintained and continued at a vital and creative level? Presumably many of the good ideas come in the first year or two, but with less frequent meetings, I would think that the kind of organization that I've discussed could continue to yield good results, although perhaps at a lower level, thus making a continuing contribution to greater profitability.

4

Productivity for All Seasons: Yesterday, Today, and Tomorrow

C. Jackson Grayson

Productivity, in the long run, is the single most important factor that influences (a) the survival of businesses, (b) the economic, political, and military strength of
nations, and (c) the world's standard of living.

It provides profits, jobs, real wages, education,
health care, roads, defense, and--ultimately--produc-
tivity determines the rank of nations.

Given this critical and central role of productivity in
the well-being of all nations, it is incredible how relatively under-used productivity is in determining public
policy in governments, how often productivity is misused
or not used at all in running profit and nonprofit organizations, how many myths and misunderstandings there are
about productivity, and--compared to other economic con-
cepts--how relatively little is done to measure it, to
integrate it into economic theory, or to understand very
well why it grows and why it declines.

I want to share with you a few of my views, based on
ten years of work in the American Productivity Center,
about "Productivity: Yesterday, Today, and Tomorrow."

PRODUCTIVITY YESTERDAY: THE RISE AND DECLINE OF NATIONS

Why is productivity "yesterday" important? For the
same reasons we find history of value.

We can learn from the past--clues as to what caused
productivity to grow, to stagnate, and to decline in
nations, and attempt to arrive at some "lessons from
history" to guide us in the future.

When I first did reading in history focusing on productivity, I presumed, as do most people, that "growth"
through productivity started fairly soon after man
stopped his nomadic wanderings around 8000 B.C. and

settled down to agriculture, and that it accelerated even more around 4500 B.C. when the first "civilizations" were formed. That's not quite right.

There was almost no growth in income per person (or population) from 8000 B.C. until the 1700s--almost a 10,000 year period! There was some absolute growth in population and incomes, but spread out over thousands of years, the rate of growth was almost imperceptible.

Of course, there were wealthy civilizations--Babylon, Persia, Phoenicia, Egypt, Rome. All accumulated fabulous wealth. The income per person in Rome is estimated by some to have been about $250-300 in today's dollars, not bad considering the 1987 estimate for the PRC is about $230. But their wealth didn't come from growth as we know it today. It came primarily from taking it away from one another--thighbone bashing, war and plunder, expropriation, and "beggar-thy-neighbor" trading. It was mostly a "win-lose" world.

Growth through productivity--"win-win"--is really an invention of Western civilization, and it is only about 200 to 250 years old. Since then, only three nations have led the world in productivity growth. Can you guess who they are?

Most people immediately assume England, as the home of the Industrial Revolution, was the first leader. That is wrong. The world's first productivity leader was the Netherlands. Angus Maddison, former chief economist of the OECD, names the Dutch as the world's first real productivity leader, pacing the world for most of the 18th century--from about 1700-1785. As the world leader, they grew rich, powerful, and finally, complacent as the world leader. They shouldn't have: the British were coming.

England began to improve its productivity growth in the last quarter of the 18th century, as the first effects of the Industrial Revolution were felt. Hargreave's Spinning Jenny (1764) permitted a 16-fold productivity inncrease in spinning soft welt. Arkwright's spinning frame (1768), Watt's steam engine (1776), and other technical developments began to increase the rate of England's productivity growth. The word "productivity" first appeared in print in 1766, interestingly not in England, but in France.

England's average rate of productivity growth was a steady, though tiny, 0.5 percent per year for the last few decades of the 18th century. But that rate of growth--plus Dutch stagnation--was sufficient for the British to pass the Dutch in productivity level around 1785.

England became number one--the world's second productivity leader. It became the technological wonder and workshop of the world, as Landes put it, "...the very model of industrial excellence and achievement," and had incredible world economic power.

But the British, like the Dutch before them, became complacent, idealized themselves and their own past, and didn't look back to see if anybody was gaining. They should have. Two major competitors--America and Germany--were growing faster in productivity than the British.

It was very important to note that even though British productivity was still growing at an average rate of 1.3 percent during this period, England was losing! America's productivity was growing faster, at a rate of 2.1 percent. Though the difference in productivity growth rates was very small--only 0.8 percent, this small difference, compounded over time, was enough for the United States to pass England in productivity level in the 1890s.

The United States became number one, the productivity leader of the world, the position it still holds today.

To recap:

	Leader	Years as No. 1
1700–1785	Netherlands	85
1785–1890	England	105
1890–1988	United States	98

The rise and decline of nations is the tale of long distance runners. Relative positions change slowly, but they do change. It is, as Landes said, "a race without a finishing line."

Now, the trillion dollar question: Is there to be a fourth number one? Who? When? And what are the implications if the leadership changes hands?

No one can answer any of those questions with certainty, but from my review of the history of productivity ten "lessons" emerged that would be well to remember as we turn to productivity today:

1. Complacency is the cancer of leadership and seems to infect all leaders.
2. Leaders overlook the relative growth rates of their challengers.
3. Productivity changes are so slow that leaders fail to sense, in time, the cumulative gains made by challengers.
4. Initial size of nations is not a predictor of winners.
5. Gainers have drive, hunger, desire--the "eye of the tiger" that focuses their energies.
6. Challengers stress education very heavily.

7. Gainers copy the leaders, adapt, and improve.
8. Quality improvement and customer focus are key strategies of challengers.
9. Protection helps challengers; it hurts leaders.
10. The leader's ability to adjust diminishes over time.

As the present world productivity leader, the United States would do well to keep these lessons in mind as it contemplates the 21st century and those now challenging the U.S. for economic leadership. And there are challengers.

PRODUCTIVITY TODAY: COMPETITIVENESS

It would be hard to find anyone who does not now know that there has been a serious decline in the rate of American productivity (GNP/hour, business sector):

Year	Rate of Growth
1948–65	3.2%
1965–73	2.1
1973–77	1.1
1977–87	1.0
1987	0.9

Numerous researchers have attempted to find the causes of the slowdown. They have rounded up a number of traditional economic suspects: inadequate capital investments and R & D, age/sex work force composition, energy costs, inflation, government regulations, and more.
However, none of the suspects has been convicted, for there is still wide disagreement on the degree of influence of the various suspects, plus there are those among us who do not believe that the traditional list contains all suspects. To make matters worse, nearly every researcher, even after exhaustive econometric calculations, has been left with as much as 40 to 50 percent of the slowdown simply unexplainable. This "residual" has been appropriately called by some the "measure of ignorance." In other words, we still don't completely understand it.
While we are trying to figure out what caused our slowdown, other nations, particularly in Asia, have been growing much faster in productivity and now challenge the productivity leadership of the U.S. There are problems measuring and comparing productivity across nations,

which I will discuss later, but for the moment, let's use the most widely available yardstick: GDP (Gross Domestic Product)/employee.

GDP/Employee

1986 U.S. Dollars (Purchasing Power)		Growth Rates 1973-86
United States	$37,565	0.5%
Canada	35,670	1.2
Netherlands	32,415	0.7
France	31,667	2.2
Belgium	30,543	2.0
Germany	30,390	2.2
Norway	30,114	2.4
U.K.	26,448	1.5
Japan	25,882	2.8

Though the U.S. is still the world productivity leader, if one assumes that the trend rates of 1973-86 were to continue, then the United States would lose its leadership to a number of nations in the next few decades.

Leadership Trend

Country	Year Leadership Lost
Canada	1994
France	1996
Norway	1998
W. Germany	1999
Belgium	2000
Japan	2003

Of course, trend rates do not have to continue. But if they do, by the year 2003, the U.S. will rank seventh in productivity level (GDP/Employee) among leading industrialized nations. History shows that when a nation loses the productivity lead, in subsequent decades, it also loses the world economic and political leadership. That could occur in the early part of the 21st century.

There is, however, some encouraging news and some factors that argue against the decline possibility:

1. The United States has recently had a surge in manufacturing productivity, and the problem is solved.
2. The measures of service sector productivity are imperfect, and the slowdown may not be as extensive as believed.

3.   The challengers, having almost "caught up" will now
      slow down their faster pace and not overtake the
      U.S.
4.   The United States is now sufficiently awake to the
      problem and will adjust and retain its leadership.

I hope that the above is true. But I do not think so.
That is why I wrote a book just published in February,
coauthored with Carla O'Dell, called *American Business:
A Two-Minute Warning*, which says, among other things:

-    The United States is still losing (not "has lost")
     the productivity lead.
-    While the news about manufacturing productivity is
     encouraging, the trend in productivity growth of
     the service sector (nearly 70 percent of the GNP)
     is almost zero, and trends do not change quickly.
-    Though some of the productivity measures are
     imperfect, especially in services, we have not
     changed the measures and the trends are still
     essentially telling the right story.
-    The overall U.S. response is still not sufficient.
-    History shows that challengers do not have to slow
     down when they reach the leader's level--almost
     everyone passed England.

And--one of the lessons of history--relative differences matter. A small difference of even less than 1
percent compounds slowly, but inexorably, and topples
leaders.
    If the U.S., like England, becomes a "weary Titan"--to
borrow Joseph Chamberlain's phrase--and declines, it will
be because of a failure to maintain its productivity
leadership in a hotly competitive global economy. Should
that occur, the implications for this nation and for the
world are enormous.
    That is why it is very important for the United States
and other nations to pay more attention to productivity--
how to measure it, how to compare relative productivities
across nations, what the sources and obstacles are to
productivity growth, and how we can make productivity
growth the win-win strategy for all citizens of this
earth.
    That's the challenge of productivity tomorrow.

PRODUCTIVITY TOMORROW: THE GLOBAL ECONOMY

"Plate tectonics" is the study of the ebb and flow of
land masses--continents--and the forces that affect them.
Similarly, forces are at work producing major changes in
world economies which might be called "economic tectonics." Both are a process of destruction and creation,
changing the face of the globe.

Economic tectonics is reshaping international competition, entire industries, notions of comparative advantage, even the concept of national economies. Instead of breaking apart like the continents, the 186 economies of the world are flowing together--imploding--becoming more integrated, interrelated, and inter-dependent.

As Dorothy in *The Wizard of Oz* says, "Toto, I don't think we're in Kansas anymore." She's right. While the world has not yet become Marshall McLuhan's global village, the first outline of the competitive characteristics of this new global economy are becoming apparent:

Characteristics of the Global Economy

1. *Global Production*: Products made and services delivered everywhere by everybody.
2. *Technology*: Technology no longer the monopoly of advanced nations; copying, improving, and rapidly applying may pay off better than inventing.
3. *Comparative Advantage*: Dynamic and man-made, not static and fixed by nature. Natural resource-poor nations can become strong international competitors.
4. *Human Capital*: The greatest value added source, not physical capital or natural resources.
5. *Financial*: Incredible financial power coming from the Orient, especially Japan--the financial powerhouse of the 21st century.
6. *Flexibility*: A premium on rapid adaptation, not specialized skills.
7. *Protection*: Increased danger of world trade barriers and retaliatory trade wars.
8. *Quality*: Ever more important, especially in service/information-oriented economies.
9. *Arbitrage*: Jobs and factories moving across nations to obtain lower costs, highest productivity, and quality.
10. *Commoditization*: Declining importance of traditional commodities and quick commoditization of technical advancements.
11. *Centrally planned economies*: The entrance and integration of centrally planned economies into the world economy.
12. *Haves and Have-nots*: The wealth gap that is likely to grow between economically advanced and less developed nations.
13. *Multi-polar world*: The end of U.S. economic hegemony, and the emergence of a multi-polar economy.
14. *Pacific Basin*: The economic center of the world in the 21st century. The Asian-Pacific nations alone will create over 20 percent of the world GDP by the year 2000--the equal of the U.S. or Europe. And one of every two people on earth will live in Asia.

You know the world is changing when Coca-Cola earned more in 1987 in Japan than it did in the U.S., when Italy passed England in 1987 in GDP/capita, and when seven of the top ten banks in the world are Japanese! Given these system-wrenching changes, how can firms, industries, nations monitor and adjust to the changes?

Productivity is the one factor, more than any other, that can help to monitor, organize and channel the destructive-creative economic tectonic forces for tomorrow. I suggest productivity as the organizing theme for the global economy.

If that is to happen, we have a lot of work to do.

The main points I want to stress up front are:

1. A major effort must be made to raise the level of productivity understanding, productivity consciousness, productivity education, and usage of productivity in business, government, and non-profit organizations in all nations.
2. Better international comparative productivity data are needed. All nations need to work together to improve comparability standards.
3. The United States has the best productivity data system in the world right now. But it needs major improvement, and it should be prepared to help others who wish assistance.
4. There is not a lot of time for these changes to be made if the world is to avoid some undesirable consequences.

TO BEGIN

Time is too limited today to outline all the steps that would be required to launch such a large-scale effort, but it is important to begin. For the United States, I suggest as a first step that we set a national goal of 2.5 percent annual productivity improvement, ask the new President--whoever that may be--to announce it in the spring of 1989.

Many agencies of government, and many firms in the private sector would need to be consulted, brought into the thinking, discussing, organizing, and planning process as to how the nation could work toward this goal-- getting productivity explicitly considered in public policy formulation, improving productivity in government, improving productivity in firms and industries, and so on.

In the remainder of my time today, I would like to focus my remarks on only one, but very important, area-- productivity statistics: the way we keep score.

PRODUCTIVITY STATISTICS

The U.S. has one of the best productivity statistics gathering and dissemination programs in the world. Even so, it needs improvement.

In 1979, a panel formed by the National Academy of Science did a comprehensive review of government data on productivity, and came up with 23 recommendations. The main categories:

- Measurement of output (especially quality, health, education, regulations)
- Measurement of inputs (capital, labor, intermediate inputs, and multi-factor measures)
- Measurement of sources of change
- International comparisons of output and productivity
- Presentation and interpretation of productivity measures
- Interagency cooperation and coordination
- Interfirm comparisons

The panel's Chairman, Al Rees, pointed out that their work came uncomfortably close to reviewing the entire body of economic statistics collected by the federal government. I faced the same problem in this lecture, for if I were to look at all statistics that impact productivity, I would need to examine needs for improved statistics in savings, investment, R & D, education, trade, interest, price indexes, and many others. (This illustrates the pervasiveness of productivity as a central economic concept for nations.)

A report on the status on the panel's recommendations was prepared in 1983 for the White House Conference on Productivity. It showed much progress on many of the recommendations, and work continues.

It is not possible to comment on each recommendation, but I do want to indicate several items to which I think high priority should be given. This statement of needs neither overlooks nor is intended to disparage past accomplishments or ongoing progress. What it does mean is that we need to move forward even further and faster:

- Quality--improved measures of quality changes in products and services
- Services--improved measures for the service sector
- Industries--deeper and wider coverage of industries
- Total factor--expand to two-digit SIC code level
- SIC codes--more frequent revisions in SIC codes to reflect more rapid shifts in the economy
- Revisions--reduce magnitude of revisions
- Statistical enclave--the organization of some body inside government to work toward coordinating data collection and data exchange in government

- Users--involve users in design, analysis, and dissemination of data; not only train managers in statistics, but also train statisticians in management
- Forecasting--improve the accuracy of forecasts of productivity, for it is such a critical component of GNP growth. Every 1 percent increase in productivity adds about $32 billion to real GNP.

Though all these are important, the area where I see the greatest need for expanded work is in the <u>international</u> area.

COMPARATIVE ECONOMIC STATISTICS

The major gap in productivity statistics, in my opinion, is the international arena--sector and industry level and trend comparisons among nations. It is increasingly important for several reasons.

Developed nations. Developed nations need relative productivity data if they are to stay ahead of hardcharging challengers. No longer can they remain inwardfocused, complacent about their lead, and stick with old industries, techniques, and ideas. Firms need such data to know when their productivity is declining relative to others--how fast, in what industries, and whether they are gaining or falling behind.

The populations of the developed nations are also aging fast. The OECD projects that by 2020, the U.S. will have 16 percent of its population 65 and older; Japan 21 percent; France 20 percent; U.K. 15 percent, and Germany a whopping 22 percent. The challenge will be to keep these nations adjusting, not resisting change, and to have sufficient productivity to afford the higher pension and health costs of an older, non-working population.

Rapid change. The need for timely knowledge about relative productivity differentials has always existed-- England might not have met her economic fate had she seen such data, in time, in the late 19th century.

Today, such information is not only still needed, it is needed rapidly. Enormous advances in transportation, communication, and widespread education have collapsed time and geography and redistributed skills and technology at an incredibly fast rate. A two-year lag in productivity data could be fatal for some industries. For example, the day after the announcement of superconductivity, MITI called a meeting of business executives, scientists, and government officials to launch a scientific and commercial program to exploit the potential of superconductivity as fast as developments occur. Comparative advantage these days is about as fleeting as fame.

Centrally planned economies. All together, the centrally planned economies (CPEs) of the world constitute almost 25 percent of world GNP--not an insignificant figure. However, political differences have, in the past, largely sealed off those nations from comparable data collection and analysis.

For example, CPEs do not use the two most familiar measures of national output, namely GDP and GNP. Instead, they call aggregated national income "Net Material Product" (NMP), a term which connotes material output and those services deemed "productive."

Glasnost and perestroika are now opening a window for the CPEs to become part of the global economic community. If the world is to seize this opportunity to build a truly global economy, their data and relative productivities need to be integrated into the global economy.

DEVELOPING NATIONS (LDC's)

It is clear that the differences in GNP per person across the globe are largely explained by differences in productivity, and the LDCs are evidence of that.

The GNP of China, the most populous nation on earth, is exceeded by the GNP of four relatively tiny western European nations--U.K., France, West Germany, and Italy. Pakistan, with close to 100 million has about 15 times as many people as Switzerland, but with a GNP about one-third as large. The explanation is lower relative productivity.

And it could get worse. The LDCs continue to expand their populations at a fast clip. While the LDC population growth rates have slowed a little to about 2 percent annually, that rate is still four times faster than the industrial market countries rate of 0.5 percent. Ben Wattenberg estimates that the fraction of total world population in the western community will be only 13 percent by 2010, dropping to 5 percent by 2085. By the year 2000, the developing nations of the world will constitute 80 percent of the world's population of an estimated 6.2 million people, and how they fare will impact world growth and world peace.

The LDCs of the world need not only productivity information as a guide to development, but also assistance on how to improve productivity. For if they do not, the lower productivity of LDCs forces these nations to compete on the basis of protection, subsidies, low wages and profits, and a low standard of living--thus trapping an ever-larger part of the world in unending relative poverty.

Finally, unless developed nations' productivity growth rates stay robust, the LDCs markets will dry up, and they will be effectively frozen at their current levels of poverty, disease, and ignorance: an inhumanity and a

danger. With large populations constituting a majority
of the world, many with large debt levels and a growing
gap between the have/have-nots, the situation is a
ticking economic time bomb.

WHAT DATA DO WE HAVE NOW?

We do have some comparative productivity data now,
generated by national governments, OECD, national productivity centers, Asian Productivity Organization, IMF,
World Bank, CIA, UN, associations, consultants, newspapers and magazines, and others.

But what it all adds up to is pretty deficient, compared to what is needed. The main bases for comparisons
now are:

-   *GDP/Capita*: GDP (Gross Domestic Products) divided
    by the entire population. Levels and growth rates
    are available for most nations. It is a measure of
    national wealth, but not a good productivity
    measure, as GDP is divided by every man, woman, and
    child whether he or she works or not.
-   *GDP/Employee*: GDP divided by the employed labor
    force. A better productivity measure, but it does
    not account for the difference among nations in
    hours worked. Available in levels and trends for
    major nations, and trend data for selected indus-
    tries.
-   *GDP/Hour*: GDP divided by hours worked or paid.
    The best productivity measure, but generally not
    available internationally for comparisons, except
    for manufacturing productivity in advanced indus-
    trial nations, and even then only growth rates, not
    levels.
-   *Currency conversions*: Market exchange rates are
    available for most all nations, except for CPEs. To
    attempt to improve comparability, "purchasing power
    parity" exchange rates are used for most major
    nations.

WHY ARE DATA HARD TO OBTAIN?

There are a number of reasons why such data have not
been collected extensively to date:
-   A belief that comparative data are not needed,
    especially when the world grew more slowly and
    economies were more isolated.
-   Difficulties in obtaining data from some nations,
    where such data either do not exist or are avail-
    able only with long lags.
-   Differing definitions, methods of estimating, and
    classification systems for the various components

of productivity: base years, hours worked, capital, output, industries, etc.

- Nations not always on the same calendar year complicate the job of comparison.
- Lack of language skills to read, write, or communicate with a multitude of nations make it difficult to gather and interpret data.
- Data secrecy, controlled markets, and artificial official exchange rates in centrally planned nations.
- Low interest (thus, low priority) up until now in comparative international statistics by politicians, government officials, businessmen, and many economists.
- Lack of funds to expand statistical work.

WHAT DATA ARE NEEDED?

The following is a list of what I think should be adopted as minimum goals of improving international productivity statistics: (Data are also needed for other relevant economic statistics, such as savings, investment, R & D, etc.)

- *Two key productivity indicators*: GDP/Employee and GDP/Hour--for nations, for sectors, and for industries, both as to levels and growth rates.
- *Data standards*: A standardized system for recording or converting economic data for comparison purposes.
- *Timeliness*: Data not more than 12 months old across the world.
- *Currency conversion*: An improved and constantly updated system for converting currencies to a common denominator for comparisons ("purchasing power parities").
- *CPEs*: The conversion of centrally planned and mixed economies data into comparative terms, even if imputation and estimation are required.

None of the above will be easy or swift. But few projects could be of as much importance, not only for the United States, but for the world. Even if the measures can't be precise or as neat as we would like, at least let's develop surrogates, proxies, estimates, and label them as such.

Though it may sound heretical to a purist, I agree with a teacher of mine who once said, "If it's worth doing, it's worth doing badly."

HOW TO BEGIN?

I suggest that the U.S. take a leadership role, initiated by the Bureau of the Census.

Seek simultaneously the involvement and participation of organizations in the U.S. and all over the world. As an example, involve the U.S. Departments of Labor, Commerce, and State; OECD; national productivity centers; American Productivity Center; consulting and accounting firms; and CPEs, perhaps through the Council for Mutual Economic Assistance (COMECON). The American Productivity Center would be glad to be a part of the effort.

The Census Bureau already has a network of thousands and experience in international coordination of data through its International Statistical Programs Center (ISPC), the Foreign Demographic Analysis Division (FDAD), and the International Demographic Data Center (IDDC). There are undoubtedly other units and individuals in Census, Labor, and Commerce who could form a cadre of expertise to initiate the effort.

WHERE WILL THE FUNDS COME FROM?

This will cost money. While everyone acknowledges the importance of data for decision making, providing funds for statistics gets extremely low priority in the federal budget of the U.S., and probably the same is true in most other nations.

Such funds are grudgingly allocated, always in small increments and within traditional fields. To make it worse, budget cuts in the U.S. have impaired the overall statistical effort--statistical funding is one of the first to go. Funds for statistics do not have the sex appeal or political clout of new bridges, Social Security, and weapon systems.

Regardless, I recommend large-scale funding of an improved productivity (and other economic) statistics effort even in the face of large U.S. budget deficits. The funds are a necessity, an investment in the future of the U.S.--economically and militarily.

Economically, each 1 percent gain in productivity adds about $32 billion in real dollars to the economy annually. Militarily, history repeatedly shows that when an economy declines, military power erodes. There is a significant correlation over time between economy strength and military strength. If there is no other way to secure funds, it would be a good investment in defense to cut the U.S. defense budget to fund this program.

MILESTONES

Some short-term goals should be set for the first five-year period. But for the bulk of the effort, I would set the year 2000 as the goal for reaching all major milestones--that's only 12 years away.

PRODUCTIVITY: A UNIFYING THEME

What are the dangers if we don't do this? Stagnation, poverty, and war. History shows that when nations feel economically trapped or great powers see early stages of decline, they often resort to war. If war is avoided by the major powers, then stagnation and poverty are likely to be the lot of a growing majority of the world's population. While in the past they had to, or were willing to, tolerate these disparities, such is not likely to be the case in the future.

I have four children, aged 8 to 28. And I want them to grow up in a win-win world, for themselves and for all the people on this globe. The rising tide could lift all boats and even rescue those under water. If that is to happen my strong belief is that the single greatest contributor will be a universal rise in productivity growth all over the globe. I would rather all of us work on a productivity gap than a missile gap.

It is toward that end that I call for a global focus on productivity improvement, beginning today. Let's call it "Productivity 2000."

Parts of this lecture were adapted from the book by C. Jackson Grayson, Jr., and Carla O'Dell, *American Business: A Two-Minute Warning* (New York: Free Press, 1988).

5

Transformation of Western-Style Management

W. Edwards Deming

The decline of Western industry, which began in 1968 and 1969, a victim of competition, has reached little by little a stage that can be characterized only as a crisis. The decline is caused by Western-style management, and it will continue until the cause is corrected. In fact, the decline may be ready for a nose dive. Some companies will die a natural death, victims of Charles Darwin's inexorable law of survival of the fittest. In other companies there will be awakening and conversion of management.

What happened? U.S. industry knew nothing but expansion from 1950 to around 1968. U.S. goods had the market. Then, one by one, many companies awakened to the reality of competition from Japan.

Little by little, one by one, the manufacture of parts and materials moved out of the Western world into Japan, Korea, Taiwan, and now Brazil for reasons of quality and price. More business is carried on now between the United States and the Pacific Basin than across the Atlantic Ocean.

A sudden crisis, like Pearl Harbor, brings everybody out in full force, ready for action, even if they have no idea what to do. But a crisis that creeps in catches its victims asleep. Some awaken in a drowse; some awaken to action; others will go on sleeping.

Management in an expanding market is fairly easy. It is difficult to lose when business simply drops into the basket. But when competition presses into the market, knowledge and skill are required for survival. Excuses ran out. By 1969, the comptroller and the legal department began to take charge for survival, fighting a defensive war, backs to the wall. The comptroller does his best, using only visible figures, trying to hold the company in the black, unaware of the importance for management of figures that are unknown and unknowable. The legal department fights off creditors and predators that are on the lookout for an attractive takeover. Unfortunately, management by the comptroller and the legal department brings only further decline.

The decline is accelerated by the aims of management to boost the quarterly dividend and maximize the price of the company's stock. Quick returns, whether by acquisition, divestiture, paper profits, or creative accounting, are self-defeating. The effect in the long run erodes investment and ends up as just the opposite to what is intended.

A far better plan is to protect investment by plans and methods to improve product and service, accepting the inevitable decrease in costs that accompany improvement of quality and service, thus reversing the decline, capturing the market with better quality and lower price. As a result, the company stays in business and provides jobs and more jobs.

FORCES CAUSING THE DECLINE

For years, price tag and not total cost of use governed the purchase for materials and equipment. Work standards, quotas, exhortation, numerical goals devoid of methods to achieve them, failure to invest in knowledge, and failures of training and supervision have contributed to the decline.

Other forces are still more effective:

1. Lack of constancy of purpose to plan product and service that will have a market, keep the company in business, and provide jobs;
2. Emphasis on short-term profits: short-term thinking (just the opposite from constancy of purpose to stay in business), fed by fear of unfriendly takeover and by push from bankers and owners for dividends;
3. Personal review system or evaluation of performance, merit rating, annual review, or annual appraisal, by whatever name, for people in management, the effects of which are devastating;
4. Mobility of management: job hopping from one company to another;
5. Use of visible figures only for management, with little or no consideration of figures that are unknown or unknowable.

Two forces that are peculiar to industry in the United States are:

6. Excessive medical costs;
7. Excessive costs of warranty, fueled by lawyers who work on contingency fees*.

Anyone could add more inhibitors. One, for example, is the choking of business by laws and regulation and by legislation brought on by special interest groups, the effect of which is, too often, to nullify the work of standardizing committees of industry, government, and consumers.

Still another force is the system of detailed budgets, which leaves a division manager no leeway. In contrast, the Japanese manager is not bothered with details. He has complete freedom except for one item; he cannot transfer to other uses his expenditure for education and training.

USE OF MERIT RATING SYSTEMS

Many U.S. companies have systems by which everyone in management or in research receives from his or her superiors a rating every year. Some government agencies have a similar system. Management by objectives, on a go/no-go basis, is another name for the same evil. Management by fear would be a better name, as someone in Germany suggested. The effect if devastating.

It nourishes short-term performance, annihilates long-term planning, builds fear, demolishes teamwork, nourishes rivalry and politics.

It leaves people bitter, others despondent and dejected, some even depressed, unfit for work for weeks after receipt of a rating, unable to comprehend why they are inferior.

It is unfair, because it ascribes to the people in a group differences that may be caused by the system they work in.

The idea of merit rating is alluring. The sound of the words captivates the imagination: Pay for what you get; get what you pay for; motivate people to do their best, for their own good. The effect of the merit rating is exactly the opposite of what the words promise. Everyone propels himself forward, or tries to, for his own good, on his own life preserver. The organization is the loser.

Moreover, a merit rating is meaningless as a predictor of performance, except for someone who falls outside the limits of differences attributable to the system that the people work in.

OTHER OBSTACLES

1. Hope for quick results (instant pudding)
2. The excuse that "our problems are different"
3. Inept teaching in schools of business
4. Failure of schools of engineering to teach statistical theory
5. Statistical teaching centers fail to prepare students for the needs of industry. Students learn statistical theory for enumerative studies and then see them applied in class and in textbooks to analytical problems. They learn to calculate estimates of standard errors of the result of an experiment and in other analytic problems in which there is no such thing as a standard error. They learn tests of hypothesis, null hypothesis, and probability levels of significance. Such calculations and the underlying theory are excellent mathematical exercises, but they provide no basis for action, no basis for evaluating the risk of predicting the results of the next experiment, nor of tomorrow's product, which is the only question of interest in a study aimed at improving the performance of a process or a product.

   Statistical work in industry in the Western world, along with other techniques, will become more useful and important and broader in scope, as little by little management makes the changes that are necessary for survival. Meanwhile, people with master's degrees in statistical theory accept jobs in industry and government to work with computers. It is a vicious cycle. Statisticians who do not know what statistical work is are satisfied to work with computers. Management, likewise, has no knowwledge about statistical work in industry, and sowmehow supposes that computers are the answer. Statisticians and management thus misguide each other and keep the vicious cycle rolling.

   Statisticians and other technical people can reach maximal usefulness in industry, including service industries, only by adopting as their main purpose help to management, to make the changes that are necessary for survival.
6. The supposition by management that the workforce could turn out quality if they would only apply full force their skill and effort. The fact is that nearly everyone in Western industry--management and workforce--is impeded by barriers to pride of workmanship.
7. Reliance on quality circles, employee involvement, employee participation groups, quality of work life, anything to get rid of the problems of people. Without management's participation, these shams deteriorate and break up after a few months.

The big task ahead is to get management involved in management for quality. Applications of techniques within the system as it exists often accomplish great improvements in quality, productivity, and reduction of waste.

IMPORTANT MANAGEMENT DATA ARE NOT VISIBLE

The comptroller runs the company on visible figures. This is a sure road to decline. Why? Because the most important figures for management are not visible: They are unknown and unknowable. Do courses in finance teach students the importance of the unknown and unknowable loss

-   from a dissatisfied customer?
-   from a dissatisfied employee, one who, because of correctible faults of the system, cannot take pride in his work?
-   from the annual rating on performance, the socalled merit rating?
-   from absenteeism (purely a function of supervision)?

Do courses in finance teach students about the increase in productivity that comes from people who can take pride in their work? Do they teach students about the multiplying effect of a happy customer?

THE FOURTEEN POINTS OF MANAGEMENT

There is now a theory of management. No one can say that there is nothing about management to teach. If experience by itself would teach management how to improve, then why are we in the predicament? Everyone doing his or her best is not the answer that will halt the decline. It is necessary that everyone knows what to do and then does his or her best.

The fourteen points of management apply anywhere, to small organizations as well as to large one, to the service industry as well as to manufacturing.

1. Create constancy of purpose toward improvement of product and service, with the aim to become competitive, stay in business, and provide jobs.
2. Adopt the new philosophy. We are in a new economic age created by Japan. Transformation of Western-style management is necessary to halt the continued decline in industry.
3. Cease dependence on inspection to achieve quality. Eliminate the need for inspection on a mass basis

by building quality into the product in the first place.

4. End the practice of awarding business on the basis of price tag. Purchasing must be combined with design of product, manufacturing, and sales, to work with the chosen supplier, the aim being to minimize total cost, not merely initial cost.

5. Improve constantly and forever every activity in the company, to improve quality and productivity, and thus constantly decrease costs.

6. Institute training and education on the job, including management.

7. Institute supervision. The aim of supervision should be to help people and machines and gadgets to do a better job.

8. Drive out fear, so that everyone may work effectively for the company.

9. Break down barriers between departments. People in research, design, sales, and production must work as a team to foresee problems in production and in use that may be encountered with the product or service.

10. Eliminate slogans, exhortation, and targets for the work force asking for zero defects and new levels of productivity. Such exhortations only create adversarial relationships, as the bulk of the causes of low quality and low productivity belong to the system and thus lie beyond the power of the work force.

11. Eliminate work standards that prescribe numerical quotas for the day. Substitute aids and helpful supervision, using methods to be described.

12a. Remove the barriers that rob hourly workers of their right to pride of workmanship. The responsibility of supervisors must be changed from sheer numbers to quality.

b. Remove the barriers that rob people in management and in engineering of their right to pride of workmanship. This means, *inter alia*, abolishment of both the annual or merit rating and management by objective.

13. Institute a vigorous program of education and retraining. New skills are required for changes in techniques, materials, and services.

14. Put everybody in the company to work in teams to accomplish the transformation.

WHAT IS REQUIRED FOR CHANGE

The first step is for Western management to awaken to the need for change. Change may not be easy for everybody.

Top management will agree to carry out the new philosophy. They will explain by seminars and other means to a critical mass of people in the company why change is necessary, and that the change will involve everybody. Everyone must understand the fourteen points, the deadly diseases, and the obstacles. Top management and everyone else must feel pain and dissatisfaction with past performance and must have the courage to change. Top management must break out of line, even to the point of exile among their peers.

As everyone knows, applications of techniques within the system as it exists often accomplish spectacular results, great improvements in quality and productivity, and reduction of waste. Anyone who attends a meeting of the American Society for Quality Control comes away convinced that the great problems of the United States already solved. It is easy to be fooled. An example (not mine) is a simple change in the tracker for the seat of an automobile, with eventual reduction of failures from 42% to 2%. Another simple example saved a company $186,000 a day, calculations for which were accomplished in less than half an hour. The fact is that the management of the company must somehow save thirty times this amount to become competitive.

The sad fact is that despite the accomplishments posted, however spectacular they may be, they are insignificant in comparison with the losses caused by Western-style management. What these colossal accomplishments do is prolong by a few months the life of the patient, whose demise in one form or another is assured by Western-style management.

6

Secrets to Growth: What Makes "Best-Run" Firms Run?

Thomas J. Peters

As I was writing this chapter, I was wondering where to start to make it appropriate for such a diverse audience of readers. After a great deal of careful consideration, I decided to write about chickens. I do this for a very serious reason. Bob Waterman and I are often accused of having a particularly soft spot in our hearts for the Hewlett-Packards, the IBMs, and the other wizards of the high-technology markets. The reality is that, in many respects, our greatest excitement comes from finding astonishing examples of places where "it can't be done." Nobody represents it better than East Coast media star Frank Perdue, who also runs a chicken business. His business is Perdue Farms.

SUPERIOR PERFORMERS

Mr. Perdue will tell you that in every single year since 1930, economists have predicted, with that special precision that is reserved for their trade, that Americans have had it with chicken. There's no more room in the market. And yet, headquartered in the thriving metropolis of Salisbury, Maryland, Mr. Perdue has managed to fashion a three-quarter-billion-dollar chicken company.

When we think about chicken, we think about the word commodity in the same breath. They forgot to tell Perdue about that. On his pound of frier or roaster he garners margins that are about 800% above the industry average. They get about a quarter of a penny a pound on the average in the industry, and Frank gets two or two and a half

cents. Now we also all know, from Economics I, that if
you're peddling friers and roasters, and if you get 800%
more than the next guy, your share of the market is
likely to be zero or perhaps a little bit less. Well,
Mr. Perdue competes in some fairly competitive urban
markets: Norfolk, Richmond, Washington, Baltimore,
Philadelphia, Boston, and the New York metropolitan area.
His lowest share of the market in any of those cities is
around 60%.

Mr. Perdue says that there is no difference between a
Ferrari and a chicken wing. He says you can put unlimited quality into any product. In his simple-minded view
he just says, "If you believe in the unlimited ability
to improve quality and behave with integrity in all of
your business dealings, then the rest of that 'stuff'--
market share, growth, profitability--will take care of
itself."   It's those very simple views that we have
observed from one end of the United States to the other,
from the computer business to the chicken wing business.

UNDERSTAND YOUR PRODUCT

Let me put my framing remarks in a slightly different
context. I recently attended an august annual event in
San Diego--the meeting of the *Business Week* Corporate
Planners One Hundred. They are the top business strate-
gists from the GMs, the GEs, the Citibanks, and the Chase
Manhattans. I was the chairman for this event, and one
of my duties was to introduce people. One of my copartic-
ipants, whom I introduced, was a fellow named Ken Schoen.

Ken is an executive vice president and sector head in
the 3M Company. About two minutes before Ken was to
speak, somebody handed me his biography. In front of
this body of sedate, seven-piece-suit types, with my
microphone turned on, I burst out laughing when I scanned
his biography, because in that simple biography there was
a lot of the story of the 3M Company. Ken Schoen was
born in St. Paul, raised in St. Paul, educated in St.
Paul, and lives in St. Paul. He began as a quality-
control chemist, became a foreman, production engineer,
production manager, production superintendent, plant
manager, division manufacturing manager, general manager,
and fourteen promotions later became executive vice
president. You don't have to do much more than glance at
that little picture to be able to say to yourself, "Here
is a fellow who probably understands the product!"

Now you see, I think that kind of stuff is important,
because one of my part-time jobs is teaching at Stanford's Graduate School of Business. In 1984, for the
umpteenth consecutive year, the business school deans
voted us the number one business school in the United
States. Since there aren't many business schools overseas, that means we're the best in the world, we're

Mecca. Well, right after talking to Schoen, I had an
occasion to go through the course descriptions of the
ninety-one electives that we were teaching our second-
year MBAs at Stanford. Only three out of the ninety-one
dealt with selling or manufacturing. There's a little
difference here. According to the world of Stanford,
88/91 of what's important doesn't have anything to do
with making the product or selling the product. You
wouldn't get that view past Ken Schoen or Frank Perdue.
Now it's not all a bad news story, since the three course
that are taught are up from one for the previous year.
We're getting there!

Well, we discovered no magic. We discovered intensity,
care, concern, commitment, and passion. We write in *In
Search of Excellence* about Joe Gerard, the car salesman.
His record is as epic as Frank Perdue's. Here's a fellow
who, for ten consecutive years, sold twice as many cars
as the number two human being in the world. That's
called dominating your niche. His magic, he says, is
that he cares. He says, "The great restaurants in this
country have love and care coming out of their kitchens.
When somebody buys a car from me, they're going to feel
just like they do when they walk out of a great restaurant." He shows it. He sends people cards, tells them
Joe's alive and well and thinking about them. Now that
may not seem like a big deal to you; I didn't think it
was either at first, but then I started thinking about
it. I'm forty-one years old now and have been buying
cars for approximately twenty-five years. The *next* card
I get from a car salesman will be number one. Suddenly
these funny little things, like sending people cards,
sound like a big deal. Joes does do it to a bit of an
excess perhaps. He sends cards when the kids get to be
driving age, and he sends them to the aunts, the uncles,
the nieces, the nephews, and the in-laws. He sends cards
on Christmas, Easter, birthdays, Valentine's Day, Columbus Day, Veterans Day, Presidents Day, and Chinese New
Year. He sends 13,000 cards a month. Moreover, he says
he loves to go to baseball games, especially if they're
poorly pitched, because every time there's a hit, he
leaps up in the air and throws out 200 calling cards.
Now that's my idea of marketing!

This is really the point. I had a great year in '83,
as you might guess. Nonetheless, as a great as it was,
I can point to the highlight very easily. Right before
Christmas I went down to Burbank, California, and visited
the Lockheed-California Company--or more specifically, I
visited Kelly Johnson of the Lockheed Company. He is the
fellow who brought the term Skunk Work from L'il Abner to
U.S. industry. He is the fellow who is responsible for
half of what flies, or has flown, in the past twenty-five
or thirty years in the skies around us. He's responsible
for the F-80, F-104, C-130, U-2, SR-71, and a whole bunch
of other planes. More significantly, this turned-on

Skunk Work of Kelly Johnson's performs some miracles. A typical, but not unusual, Johnson story that I collected was the situation in which Mr. Johnson took on an ailing satellite program. It had a 12 1/2% success rate and was years behind when he got involved. It had 1,271 people inspecting a single subcontractor. In one year Mr. Johnson was able to reduce the 1,271 a bit--to 35 get the thing back on schedule, and increase the efficiency from 12 1/2% to 98%. I get so darned irritated when I wander around U.S. business listening to mangers say, "Let's go after a 4%-a-year annual white-collar productivity increase, whether we need it or not." From the world of Kelly Johnson to the world of Frank Perdue, to the world of Joe Gerard, to the world of the top Girl Scout cookie-selling troop, the superior performers outdo the rest by 500%, 600%, 700%, and 800%, not 1% or 2% at the margin. I think every manager and would-be manager should set those targets at 500% and 600%. We see that it can be done from chicken wings to complex weapon systems.

PAY ATTENTION TO TRIVIA

Well, this is a paradox. I have challenged you, on the one hand, to seek 1,000% increases in productivity, and now I'm going to turn right around, in the next breath, and say that it all comes from trivia. I consider myself America's number one trivia fanatic in the world of business. I have said to many people of late that I have boiled down my entire five years of work on this project to a single question. The question I ask is, why is it that, in a $20 billion industry, only Walt Disney Productions has figured out how to keep a park clean? It comes in part, from trivia. Disney has no "customers": they simply have "Guests." And moreover, heaven help you should you be an insider at Disney and fail to capitalize the letter "G" in Guest in any of your correspondence. Well, again, maybe that sounds like trivia, like Mr. Gerard and his cards. I thought, at least, that it was interesting. But then it came to take on greater significance for me.

Recently, a plane I was on, heading for Denver in the middle of the night, made a quick stop in Salt Lake City. Because we were a little behind schedule, we were at the gate in Salt Lake for only three or four minutes. As the Salt Lake passengers were getting ready to come aboard, the head flight attendant turned to her colleague, presumably thinking that the rest of us were out of earshot, and said, "Here come the animals." One company president said to me the other day, "There's just a heck of a lot of things you can do to animals that you can't do to guests." We see it all over the country: In the retailing business, the analog is, "Boy those stores look great until the idiots come in and mess them up." I do most of my work in Silicon Valley, with the technology companies, and the analog there is just as bad: "Boy we make a great product, if only our customers had IQs over thirty and understood how to use them." On it goes. I call the whole phenomenon by the term TDC, Thinly Disguised Contempt for the customer.

But let's look at the flip side. I would guess that over a period of two years I have spoken on 100 or 150 occasions to audiences in which I was joined by executives of various companies from around the country, including sometimes their customers, or with trade associations. Interestingly enough, and I don't consider these coincidences, two times during those occasions one of the persons I was with started his speech by saying those two wonderful words, thank you--"Thank you to our customers who are out here in the audience. We hope that we can merit your continued business." Now to me it's just a little bit odd that both of those times the two wonderful words came from an executive of the International Business Machine Company. That's the detail, the so-called trivia, that is at the heart of the distinctive edge of the Marriotts, the McDonalds, the Hewlett-Packards, and the IBMs.

CONSTANT EXPERIMENTATION

Well, I want to cover three or four points very quickly. Bob Waterman and I talk rather ceaselssly these days about champions, Skunk Works, and constant experimentation. All of those terms are messy, and they connote tough management problems. Well, the reason we have an obsession with these sloppy terms is that in harsh, cold reality, extending from the world of miracle drugs to the world of computers, virtually every invention, small or large, comes from the *wrong* person in the *wrong* division of the *wrong* company in the *wrong* industry at the *wrong* time for the *wrong* reason with a *wrong* set of end users. That's the sole reason we argue for these strange traits.

Here's a nice example of a company that experiments, and it suggests that it can be done even when a company gets big. Out in Menlo Park, California, is a wonderful company called Raychem, which is a three-quarter-billion-dollar maker of high-technology, sophisticated connectors and the like. They recently passed their twenty-fifth anniversary. At that anniversary event their chairman and founder, Paul Cook, estimated that Raychem has had about 200,000 products go through their product line. A winner at Raychem is a 100% market share, with a 95% operating margin, in a $5 million market. He collects such products as one would collect balls on a Christmas tree. This is typical of what we find in this sizable, three-quarter-billion-dollar company. One of their field service engineers, in the North Sea area, came across a

leak in an offshore oil platform, underneath the sea. In
120 hours they brought basic researchers from Menlo Park
and from Swindon, England, built a site, developed a
truly state-of-the-art new product, prototyped it, de-
bugged it, and installed it.   It's now a $20 million
product that has a lot of unintended uses. The contrast
to this came when I told this story at a seminar: a
fellow from another company that's a little bit more
bureaucratic than Raychem said to me, "Tom, you know in
our company at the end of 120 hours you'd be darned lucky
to have cut your travel orders to get out of Menlo Park,
California."

"Ready, Fire, Aim." This term was stolen from me
without attribution by a fellow named Arch McGill, when
he was the president of a large share of American Bell.
I didn't make much of it when he stole it from me and
made it his logo because, first, he's a good friend and,
second, I stole it--without attribution--from American
Express.

If experimenting is the key, then obviously the experi-
menter is essential. I could bore you with systematic in-
house studies from IBM and Procter & Gamble, from the
National Science Foundation--they all say the same thing:
Whenever anything happens anywhere, there is a persistent, determined, irrational champion involved.   Peter
Drucker's beautiful phrase, in his autobiography: "Whenever anything is being accomplished, it is being done, I
have learned, by a monomaniac with a mission." In fact,
my sad conclusion from life in general is that any company with more than four people on the payroll is a hopeless bureaucracy. The ability to get anything done, anywhere, requires that kind of persistence.   At the 3M
Company they're simply open about it, saying, "We expect
our champions to be irrational."   They say, "We like to
cut off the project team funding three or four times,
because that's the only way to peel it back to the
fanatics."

Perhaps the most beautiful word in the English language, surprisingly enough, is failure.   If we are
serious about creating entrepreneurial environments, then
we have no choice but to let our people make mistakes.
We openly pray that they persist and that they learn from
each and every one of those mistakes. Yet failure is a
beautiful word. Mary Kay Ash and Thomas Alva Edison both
uttered the same line: "I failed my way to success." I
think anybody who is honest would say the same thing.

This particular sentence comes from the president of a
computer company in Silicon Valley, and it is not his
utterance after the third martini.   It is a formal,
written part of this brief corporate philosophy.   It
says, "We tell our people to make at least ten mistakes
a day. If your not making ten mistakes a day, you're not
trying hard enough." If we want young men and women to
step out and take risks and be entrepreneurial, we must

own up to the fact that we who are managers have seedy backgrounds ourselves. The reason we succeeded was not because we're smarter, but because we fouled up more times, because we have more bruises and bumps. And yet I know manager after manager who gets promoted and then sits there, in the sterile splendor of his office, acting as if he got there because he had a career record of 100 at bats and 100 home runs. It doesn't exactly induce other people to step out and take a risk. Don Estridge, the president of IBM Entry Systems Division and the PC inventor, in fact, said almost exactly the same thing: "If you don't let people make mistakes, there is no ownership whatsoever."

CUSTOMER COURTESY

The second part of my remarks focuses on an extremely unpleasant topic in many respects, unpleasant as an American, as a consumer, as a businessman. Buck Rodgers is the IBM marketing vice president. What else would you have your marketing vice president called? Rodgers made this comment a while back: "If you get satisfactory service in this country, from your corner grocery store, local hardware store, or your friendly computer company, it's darn near a miracle." I wish I could find room to disagree with him. I do a little bit. I would omit the "darn near." Bob Waterman and I have concluded, independently, that whether it is computers, potato chips, hotels, or chocolate chip cookies, you can have virtually any market you want in the United States if you are simply, plainly, humanly courteous to your customers. You may have one or two other players up there with you, but you won't have more than one or two.

And when I say courtesy I want to make it clear that I mean plain, garden-variety, down-to-earth, mundane, common, human courtesy. Here is typical example of what I mean. This is very homely, I know. It was a Friday afternoon before Christmas, and we were having a party at our house. On the way home I stopped by a local wine and liquor store to pick up a case of wine. I picked out the wine and waited to get to the head of the line. American Express was being a little bit user-unfriendly at a peak hour, and it took about three minutes for my card to clear. When it cleared, the clerk bagged my case of wine and I turned to go out. Sitting on the counter next to the clerk was one of those thick, old-fashioned, glass-walled jars containing a bunch of little foil-wrapped mints. The clerk reached in the jar, picked out a two-cent mint, dropped it into my bag, and said, "Look, that delay was thoroughly inexcusable. I truly apologize for it and hope it doesn't happen again. You know we value your business. Come back and see us again soon. Have a nice weekend." For two *cents* he bought my loyalty

for life! It doesn't happen anymore. That's what we're
talking about.

SUPERIOR CUSTOMER SERVICE

   When talking about service I admit that I have a favorite company in this country. That company is Frito-Lay.
I love them because it just can't be done. They are
working off of the world's silliest economic proposition.
Now, I want you to roleplay with me, if you will, for
about forty-five seconds. I teach a Business Strategy
course at Stanford, and my students make presentations
about various business proposals. Well, let's assume
that's happening now, and you take my part. A fellow
walks in. "Hello, how are you? What's your name?" you
ask. He answers, "Herman Lay." You reply, "Fine. What
have you decided on as a business?" He coolly replies,
"Potato chips," You're getting excited already. You
say, "Herman, look, one of the main things we teach in
this course is segmentation of the market. What have you
chosen as your market?" He says, "I got it narrowed down,
boss." You ask, "Well, what is it. Herman?" His quick
reply is "America." You say, "Well, given this brilliant
strategic insight, this wonderful product, this narrowing
of the market, what kind of shares are you going after?"
He calmly replies, "Oh 80,90%." Your response is, "Right
Herman!" You do not ask him to leave, but you escort him
out through the door.
   But that's exactly what Frito-Lay has done. They have
sales of nearly $3 billion--potato chips and pretzels.
They are much bigger than Pepsi-Cola. They have an 80% to
90% market share in about three-quarters of the United
States. Their margins are about one and three-quarters
times the industry average, and they promise the mom-and-
pop gas station in the boondocks and the Safeway store in
downtown Oakland alike a minimum 99.5% chance of a daily
sales and service call on a seventy-nine-cent item. Make
no mistake about what I'm talking about: It's those
10,000 spotless, white Frito-Lay trucks running around
the countryside. The average salesperson has about ten
stops on his route. About eight of them are corner bars
and grills or gas stations and two of them, maximum, are
the Safeways, the Luckys, the Krogers. He spends three
hours a day selling and servicing that seventy-nine-cent
product in the Safeway store. You wonder why the other
guys have a little trouble getting shelf space! Frito-
Lay invented a market on the basis of superior service.
Other people would have written this off as a commodity
market, if they had thought of it at all.
   Arch McGill made this obvious comment--obvious but
often ignore: "The customer perceives service in his or
her own terms." As much as we know it, we don't acknowledge it. The customer doesn't care a bit what the com-

pany service policy manual says. The customer doesn't
care about the algorithms for peakload, retail floor,
work force balancing. The customer views the world in
his or her own, sweet, emotional, irrational, idiosyn-
cratic, real-time terms.

And it <u>is</u> an unfair world in which we live. I work
with Don Burr, chairman of People Express, in New Jersey.
Don and I were talking about it, and he stated the case
beautifully. Here was his comment pertaining to the
airline industry: "Coffee stains on the flip-down tray
means that we do the engine maintenance wrong." That's
exactly right. I want to seriously argue and leave with
you as a proposition that, in my opinion, the *single* most
significant, distinctive advantage of the IBM Company and
McDonald's alike is that these two institutions are the
two best wiper-uppers of coffee stains in the United
States. They will not let you catch them with a coffee
stain.

Now, there are two ways to look at this statement. You
can do what most companies do, and wring your hands,
gnash your teeth, and talk about what a horrible world we
live in. Or you can turn it around and say, "Wow, what
an incredible opportunity!" Which is, of course, what
Marriott, Frito-Lay, IBM, McDonald's, and Disney have
done. I have a friend who lives in Cupertino, California.
He's in his mid-fifties. He started skiing when he was
about six years old, which means that he has been skiing
for half a century. We were talking about this stuff,
and he says, "I'll give you an example, Tom, on the positive side. You know, I probably have skied nearly every
resort in the world. In all that time I've run into a
unique service at a resort in the California Sierras. At
the head of the lift line, before you get on the chair
lift, there's a little dispenser with a Kleenex box in
it. You can use the Kleenex to wipe your goggles while
you're going up the lift. I cannot tell you," he adds,
"how many of my 'sophisticated' friends refer to the
whole darn resort as the "Kleenex Box Resort!" And that's
right on. It explains the power of the Hewlett-Packards,
the IBMs, the McDonalds. The power is in those long-term
memories of the cumulation of a million tiny little
things done just a tiny bit better (or worse).

In our world today, whether you are a reader of *Cosmo-
politan*, *The New Republic*, or *Playboy*, we are all inun-
dated with computer ads. Heaven help us. Every one of
them seems to say the same thing: "Our electrons go
around faster than their electrons." With one exception.
Of course, the one exception (coincidentally?) comes
from old mother blue in Armonk. IBM runs an ad with a
picture of a pillow with the IBM logo embroidered on it.
The tag line reads: "What most people want from a computer company is a good night's sleep." This is pure,
unadulterated genius.

RESPECT FOR PEOPLE: THE KEY TO SUPERIOR QUALITY

When it comes to quality we're enamored in this country with statistical quality control, quality circles, automation, CAD/CAM, robotics, and the like. They are important techniques, but they are, at most, the icing on the cake. The cake is people who *live* quality--decade in and decade out. If you had your choice or businesses to go into, my guess is that your first choice wouldn't be candy bars, dog food, or rice. And yet Mars, Inc., has a $5 billion candy bar, dog food, and rice business. Returns to shareholders are conservatively estimated at several times the industry average. The magic is quality. Mr. Mars didn't like to spend time in committee meetings or with his vice presidents. (He had a clever way of avoiding the latter. He runs a $5 billion company with a corporate staff of twenty. That helps, since he doesn't have to meet with many vice presidents.) Also, until Mr. Mars reached his eighties, he liked to spend his time in the factories and corner stores of America, checking the Mars, M&Ms, and Snickers displays. It was said that when Mr. Mars would find a single miswrapped candy bar or misprinted label, his normal response was to ask the offending factory to send him a carton of the candy bars. He would then carry them into his weekly officers' operating meeting in McLean, Virginia, and throw the candy bars, one at a time, at the officers.

Forrest Mars, Herman Lay, Frank Perdue, Ray Kroc, and J. Willard Marriott each had an incredibly important advantage over most of today's managers. None of those fellows ever took a course in "operations research" at Leland Stanford University's Engineering Department. Each of those fools thought that you could make a billion dollars worth of eighteen-cent items--and they'd all work. I mean that's ridiculous! They didn't understand statistics. The only thing that proves them right is the real world.

At the end of the day at a recent seminar I gave, a fellow who was the president of an insurance company said, "Look, Tom, you're talking about balance. We've gone too far in this analytical, quantitative stuff. Now we've got to come back and balance it out with informal things and still maintain the controls." I was tired. I said, "Yes, sir, that is exactly what I mean." Then a hand rose in the back of the audience. The speaker was a sixteen-year manufacturing manager from Procter & Gamble. He said, "That's a bunch of nonsense. It is not balance. We haven't got all of these control systems in our factories. We haven't got any MRP systems. We only have some comparative information on factory-versus-factory performance. I'll tell you about quality. I remember well when I was about a four-year P and G'er and supervisor for the first time. A call came at one-thirty in the morning from the district sales manger. He said,

'George, you have a problem with a soap bar down here.'
Down here was about 200 miles away. 'George, think you
could be down here by six A.M. to look at it?' The tone
of voice suggested more than an invitation. When you
have finished your first 200-mile ride through the back
hills of Tennessee to look at one blankety-blank thirty-
four-cent bar of soap, you suddenly get the idea that the
Procter & Gamble Company is a bit serious about quality.
They do not have to subsequently send you a 300-page
manual to prove it."

It's living the quality message. I get so irate with
my friends at Hewlett-Packard, whom I love so much. They
tell us about the marvels of quality circles. Well, of
course, the circles are great at Hewlett-Packard because
Hewlett-Packard has respected the individual since the
time the company opened its doors. And they expect
everybody to contribute creatively. In that context the
quality circle is a beautiful device. Absent that commitment it's nothing.

CUSTOMERS WILL PAY FOR VALUE

Some companies are driven by the dictum of "low costs
at all costs." This can lead to serious trouble, as
we've seen during the recession. An IBM manager stated
to me a while back, "There is a vast difference between
competitive costs and low cost. You must have a competitive cost structure, but on the other hand I've never
known a company with a low-cost *attitude*, over the long
haul, that's been a winner."

The American Business Conference, which is a newly
formed lobbying group that represents America's long-
neglected, mid-sized growth companies, recently reported
the results of a study. The American Business Conference
includes companies between $25 million and $1 billion in
sales that have more than doubled in size since the early
1980s. Members include the high-tech companies, as you'd
expect, but also Dunkin' Donuts, A.T. Cross, and Lenox
China. The study reports that in forty-three of these
forty-five superbly managed mid-sized companies, the businesses discriminated them-selves from others by making
higher value-added products and services for which the
customer paid.

From Maytag in the washing machine business, to Hewlett-Packard in the instrumentation business, to Mars in
the candy bar business, to Frito-Lay in the potato chip
business, we simply find that the customer will pay money
if only we give him or her something worth paying for.
In fact, I go so far in this as to say that if I were
allowed to be czar for one day, I would do one and only
one thing: I would strike the word commodity from the
business person's language. When we start calling things

commodities we come to treat them as commodities: we take
the service and quality out of them.

I do some work with the head of a personal computer
company in Silicon Valley. We've started to use the word
commodity with reference to the home personal computer
field. In one of my chats with this fellow I wanted to
talk to him about this word commodity. We were both
trained as engineers and therefore don't know our left
feet from our right in the field of mass marketing. I
thought, "What would two dumb engineers clearly agree was
a commodity?" I noodled around a little bit and thought,
"One-ply toilet paper, where can you go from there?" So
on my way to visit him I decided to conduct five minutes
of solid and systematic market research. I stopped at a
cooperatively owned grocery store in Palo Alto, in which
I priced a four-roll package of generic, one-ply toilet
paper, that lovely stuff that disintegrates in the bag on
the way home as often as not. It was priced at seventy-
nine cents. Two blocks later I stopped at a 7-11 and
priced the Procter & Gamble Charmin entrant into the one-
ply sweepstakes. It was going for $1.99. So you add
$1.20 to one-play toilet paper by going two blocks--with
a different service delivery vehicle (7-11) and a 150-
year total commitment to quality at Procter & Gamble. It
can be done, and you don't have to be a follower of the
stock market to realize that the shareholders of Procter
& Gamble and the Southland Corporation, the owners of 7-
11, have done a tiny bit better than the owners of the
cooperatively owned grocery stores and generic toilet
paper makers.

In fact, this goes to the absurd extremes, which is
sort of where I like to push it. In most communities in
America, when you think about tacky, you think about the
neighborhood laundromat. And yet one of the most explo-
sive and fastest-growing businesses in the United States
is a midwestern chain of laundromat-wine bars! It can be
done! You can find a way to add value to that product.
This, of course, is their logo, which I love: "Enjoy our
suds while you wash your duds."

TRUST IN PEOPLE

Well, if our magic is the simple magic of constant experimentation, superior customer service, customer courtesy, superior quality, then obviously the most important
people are not the executives, but the *real* people. It's
an all-hands game.

The greatest privilege of my career--past, present, or
future--was when I had the great opportunity to be on the
Stanford Business School faculty while Rene McPherson,
the former Dana Corporation chairman, was our dean. I
once heard him describe Dana as having one of the rotten-
est product lines ever granted by God to a *Fortune* 500

company. He turned it, during the decade of the 1970s, into the number two returner on total capital among the *Fortune* 500. Battered in the recession by the industries it had supported. Dana's comeback has been nothing short of remarkable. McPherson's focus was plain and simple: Turn the company back over to the people who do the work. He was a little shy about it. He sometimes had trouble getting that message through to middle managers. So he ran nondescript little ads in major magazines. They said, for instance, "Talk back to the boss." He says he loved what happened when he ran them. The phone would ring off the hook during the following days. First-line supervisors would ask, "What in the world have you done this time? I got seven of these advertisements taped on my door, and it's only eight in the morning." He said, "My response to that was always the same: I guess you must be starting to get the message.' "It was a simple focus. It was described to perfection by this statement: "The manager's job is to keep the bureaucrats off the back of the productive people."

I'm going to ask you to imagine that you are at an old, established, tin-bending, unionized company in Toledo, Ohio. Imagine for a minute that you are in Toldeo during February in an old company. Then read this 1983 statement by a Dana executive vice president--"We have no corporate procedures at Dana. We threw the books away in the late sixties. We eliminated reports and sign-offs. We installed trust." It can be done. Interestingly enough, Don Estridge, who is the PC fellow at IBM, made almost exactly the same statement. He said, "We don't need checks and balances. We need trust."

COMMITMENT PRODUCES RESULTS

Please join me for a brief excursion in academic psychology. It will last just thirty seconds. This is an experiment Bob Waterman and I wrote up in the book in an obscure corner. It has come front and center to Bob and me because we believe that the two most significant words in the English language are ownership and commitment. Some industrial psychologists selected some adult subjects and told them they were going to engage in an industrial hygiene experiment concerning the effects of noise on productivity. The subjects were given some difficult puzzles to solve and some proofreading to do while a raucous audiotape played in the background. The tape consisted of two persons speaking Armenian, one person speaking Spanish, noise from a mimeograph machine and a typewriter, and street noise. Half the people were given a big button that they could push. If you pushed the button, the noise went away. So the experiment was simple: What is the effect of button pushing on productivity? Well, the outcome was dull. As you'd guess, the

people with the buttons solved five times more puzzles
and made one-quarter as many proofreading errors. What
was interesting, however, was that in all the times the
experiment was repeated, never once did any human being
push his or her button. The mere fact that people
thought they had a tiny degree of control over their
environment led to improvement in the performance. It is
so powerful as to be frightening.

But let's get out of the lab quickly and return to the
real world, at the Edison, New Jersey, Ford Motor Company
assembly plant. Ford is experimenting with some of the
same productivity devices in this big, old assembly
plant. They have given each person in the multi-thou-
sand-person facility a button that he or she can push.
And if anyone pushes the button, the whole line shuts
down! That is a gutsy move by the plant manager. The
results show that people will push the button. Twenty to
thirty times a day somebody shuts down the line to make
a little quality adjustment. The good news is that the
shutdown lasts only about ten seconds on the average, and
so you're talking just 200 seconds a day, and they've
been able to keep productivity even. There have been
some other interesting little indicators of success,
however. The number of defects per car during an eight-
month period fell modestly, from 17.1 to 0.8 The number
of cars requiring rework when they come off the end of
the line has been reduced by 97%. The average union
grievance back-log has fallen from the mid-200s to seven.

In this same vein, Sarah Clifton is the most important
business person in America. Her calling card reads,
"Sarah Clifton, Supreme Commander." Sarah works for the
W. L. Gore Company, headquartered in Newark, Delaware.
This quarter-billion-dollar successful company makes the
breathing synthetic Gortex fabric, among other things.
Sarah works on a production line. Bill Gore doesn't
stand on formality. He said, basically, "Sarah, what do
you want to be?" Sarah wanted to be a supreme commander.
Why the heck not? A serious question: Have you ever
heard of a supreme commander with an absenteeism problem?
As you'd expect, Bill Gore's philosophy is very simple
and to the point: "We can't run this business. We
learned over twenty-five years ago to let the business
run itself. Commitment, not authority, produces results."

This is the bad-news side of the story. I sometimes
think that out of omission, not commission, American
managers stay awake at night trying to find ever-better
ways to make their people just a teensy bit shorter when
they come to work the next morning. My colleagues and I
were called in to work with an aircraft company. They
called us in because they had a "quality problem."
That's the euphemism in the industry for "the planes
don't fly so good, so often." We focused our attention
on the life and times of the first-line manufacturing

supervisor. Twenty of us went off-site for four days to
analyze, in minute-by-minute detail, what it's like to be
a first-line manufacturing supervisor. This is typical
of what we found. He has thirty-five people working for
him and nearly $2 to $4 million of capital equipment
under his or her control. Yet he can't buy an $8.95
bucket of paint to clean up his work space without getting a vice president to approve. We tell people they're
responsible for the quality reputation of the company,
for our number one asset, our people, for our number two
asset, our capital. Yet we don't trust them to spend
$8.95 wisely. We treat people like children and then
stand back in utter dismay when they actually behave like
children in response to it. We made these guys a deal.
We said, "You can have these rules. We acknowledge the
need for them, as long as you'll do us one tiny favor.
Every time you write a rule, place at the end of it this
parenthetical statement, in red, in the policy manual:
"We're doing this because we don't trust you!" If you
can accept that, then you can keep the rule."

Now, if you're like me and you spent $50,000 on a
Stanford MBA education, you say, "We have to do this
because of fiduciary responsibilities." We learn all
sorts of words like fiduciary at Stanford and Harvard.
To that poor soul in a manufacturing shop, it's simply
that we don't trust him. He doesn't know about fiduciary.

To change direction 180°, I have this hypothesis that I
don't wish to test because, frankly, I could be wrong. My
hypothesis is that there's giant stone lintel over the
entrance to Harvard Business School. And deeply etched
into the stone is the phrase, "All ye who enter here
shall never smile again. American business is darn
serious stuff." But from Hewlett-Packard to IBM, from
Mary Kay to Tupperware, we found people who could smile.
We all know it, whether it's the turned-on sales branch,
the turned-on store, or the turned-on accounting depart-
ment--things that work are filled with the three magic
words: fun, zest, and enthusiasm.

The fastest-growing billion-dollar company in the
United States today is the Limited Stores in Columbus,
Ohio. They have a tiny staff, but on that staff is a
full-time person who is responsible only for nonmonetary
compensation. One little part of it is this lovely magazine. It has the most beautiful title I've ever seen.
It's called *Applause Applause*. Whether you need it or
not, it comes out every two weeks. With pictures and
words, it celebrates the success of a minimum 500 people
by name.

CONCLUSION

I said at the beginning that we discovered no magic: I
lied.   I've had the greatest experience that any human
being could expect by getting to know dynamic business
leaders. This included the opportunity to go to Newark,
Delaware, and meet Bill Gore, the opportunity to know
Rene McPherson, the opportunity to know Tom Beebe, who
was the Delta Air Lines chairman, and also Bill Hewlett
of Hewlett-Packard, Sam Walton of Bentonville, Arkansas,
and the Wal-Mart Company.   The one thing that those
individuals share at the end of the day, the one piece of
true magic, is that each and every one of them has a
bone-deep belief in the dignity and the worth and the
creative potential of each person in their organizations.
That's the magic. That's the foundation and the cornerstone of which it's all built.

7

Can America Compete in the World Economy?

Lester C. Thurow

Anemic productivity growth stands as America's central economic problem. If productivity cannot be reaccelerated, Americans can only look forward to a very slow rise in their standard of living regardless of how successful they are in inflation-proofing the economy, lowering unemployment, restoring a more reasonably valued dollar, eliminating budget deficits, or in dealing with any of their other economic problems. Rapid productivity growth is essential to America's future.

When disaster strikes, it is human nature to look for someone to blame as the villain. Such a reaction is easy to understand. If only we could find the villain responsible for our troubles, all we would need to do is to punish him and the disaster would disappear--or so we all sometimes like to think. Unfortunately, if the case of slow productivity were viewed as a melodrama all of the actors would wear black hats, none would wear white hats. Each American is part of the problem and each American will have to be part of the solution if there is to be a solution.

Similarly there is no magic button to be pushed--that one single thing which, if it were to be done, would cure the problem. An autopsy of American productivity growth would record "death by a thousand cuts" when it came to the line "cause of death." No one single thing killed American productivity growth, no one single thing can revive it. Death by a thousand bandages is much harder to apply than one big operation. Each of us is in favor of bandaging the 999 "cuts" caused by others and leaving the one caused by himself. Each of us envisions a

patient that could survive our one cut.   Each of us is
right.   The patient could survive any one cut, but if no
cut is bandaged because each of us defends his own cut,
the patient bleeds to death.   And in this case the
patient is our collective economic future.

DECLINE IN PRODUCTIVITY GROWTH:
THREE-LAYERED GRID ANALYSIS

   American productivity is best analyzed on a three-layer
grid.   The first grid consists of an industry-by-industry
examination of productivity growth.   The aim is to find
those particular industry-specific problems that have led
to lower productivity growth.   While statistically all of
the national decline can be traced to some particular industry, to say that productivity has fallen in some particular industry is not to say that the cause is to be
found in that industry.   If the real cause of poor productivity performance was too little capital or an un-
skilled, poorly motivated work force, these factors would
show up as lower productivity in some particular industry, but the real problems would lie elsewhere.   The job
of the productivity analyst is to separate real industry-
specific problems from those that only look as if they
are industry-specific problems.
   The second grid consists of the capital and labor inputs into the economy.   What part of the decline in productivity can be attributed to reductions in either the
quantity or quality of capital and labor going into the
economy?   Since higher real (inflation-corrected) earnings can only be generated by higher productivity, slowdowns in productivity growth must show up as slowdowns
in income growth for some factor of production.   As a
result such slowdowns in income growth can be used to
attribute productivity declines to capital and labor. If
real hourly earnings or returns to capital are down or
growing more slowly, the earnings of these factors are
down because they have become less efficient.   (Technically the economist is assuming that each factor of
production is paid its marginal product and that less
labor efficiency does not show up as less income for
capital or vice versa.)
   As is the case with an industry-by-industry analysis
all of the slowdown in productivity growth can be attributed to deteriorations in either capital or labor since
declining productivity must be matched by declining
incomes for some factor of production.   As before, however, attribution is not necessarily causation.   If the
real productivity problem was an industry-specific
problem, such as having to drill deeper (use more resources) to find fewer barrels of oil, then this industry-specific problem would show up as lower average
earnings for capital and labor in the oil drilling in-

dustry.   To diagnose the problem as a capital-labor
problem would be to misdiagnose it.   Real capital-labor
problems must be separated from phony ones.

The third grid is composed of adverse external shocks
such as sudden large jumps in energy prices, the imposi-
tion of new environmental or safety rules, or droughts
that lower farm output per unit of input.   Some adverse
shocks such as environmental regulations are controllable; others such as droughts are not.   At this point,
however, the goal is simply to determine what part of the
observed decline is caused by factors external to the
economy itself.

As a result the productivity analyst must move across
this three-layered grid searching for the ultimate causal
factors.   As is always true in economics, judgment is required to assign causation to different statistical results.   Numbers are often true but misleading or meaningless.

SPECIFIC INDUSTRY PROBLEMS: FIRST GRID EFFECT

Statistically, the national decline in productivity can
be disaggregated into slower productivity growth rates
within individual industries and to shifts in output from
high productivity industries to low productivity industries.   If within-industry productivity growth rates are
examined, there is unrelieved gloom.

In the 1977-83 period, the last period for which detailed industry data are now available, every single
industry recorded a lower growth rate than it had from
1948 to 1965.   While there were no industries with falling productivity in the first period, there were five
such industries in the latter period.   At the end of each
year these industsries were slightly less efficient than
they had been at the beginning of that year.   Other industries had to have substantial positive gains in productivity just to keep the nation from slipping below
zero.

In addition if low-productivity industries such as
agriculture are contracting in size relative to high
productivity industries, national productivity expands.
Agriculture used to be doing so; it no longer is.   Conversely if low-productivity industries such as services
are expanding relative to high-productivity industries,
national productivity contracts.   Unfortunately, in the
period from 1977 to 1983 such shifts were working against
national productivity growth.

In 1983, productivity was almost five times as high in
communications as it was in agriculture, forestry, and
fisheries.   Such differences are not surprising and do
not necessarily indicate that one industry is more efficient than another.   Technology dictates, for example,
that some industries use much more capital per worker

than others. This leads those industries to produce more
per hour of work but does not necessarily lead to higher
total efficiency (output per unit of all inputs—capital,
labor, land, and natural resources combined). If one
were trying to rank American industries based on their
efficiency, one would want to look at total factor
productivity and not labor productivity, but total factor
productivity isn't available on a detailed industry-by-
industry basis. In any case, the current goal is not a
ranking of industries based on their overall efficiency
but an understanding of why labor productivity is growing
more slowly. Shifts from industries with high labor productivity to industries with low labor productivity are
not necessarily bad, but they do have negative consequences for measures of national labor productivity.
    When such shifts and slowdowns are examined, there seem
to be five industry-specific problems:

THE SHIFT OUT OF AGRICULTURE

    From 1948 to 1965 the movement out of agriculture was
strongly enhancing national productivity growth.   Although agriculture has had an above average rate of
growth of productivity since World War II, it had, and
still has, a level of productivity well below that of
other industries. In 1948 agriculture's productivity was
just 40 percent of the national average. As a result
every worker released from agriculture and employed by
other industries represented, on average, a 60 percentage
point jump in productivity.
    From 1948 to 1965, 9.1 billion man-hours of work (or 8
percent of the total number of hours worked in the entire
private economy) left agriculture to enter industrial employment. By the early 1970s, however, this process was
nearing an end, and from 1977 to 1983 less than 0.2 billion man-hours of work were released from agriculture.
    As agriculture declined from 17 to 5 percent of all
hours worked, national productivity was being enhanced.
A very low productivity industry was shrinking and its
workers were taking jobs with much higher productivity.
But his source of national productivity growth had to
end—no industry can forever shrink—as it did after
1972.
    If agricultural employment had not been shrinking from
1948 to 1965, American productivity would only have grown
at a 3.0 percent rather than 3.3 percent per year. Thus
the shrinkage of agricultural employment explains 12
percent (0.3 percentage points) of the observed drop (2.5
percentage points) in the national productivity growth
rate between the 1948-65 and 1977-82 periods.
    Identifying a cause does not, however, automatically
lead to a solution. America cannot go back to the era
when workers were leaving agriculture in massive numbers

and contributing to national productivity growth. Agriculture no longer employs a large fraction of the labor force. America is simply faced with a new stage in its development. To get the old rate of productivity growth, new sources of productivity growth will have to be found.

A MYSTERY IN CONSTRUCTION

Where constructions's productivity was once well above the national average, it is now 39 percent below the national average and 25 percent below its own 1968 peak. While construction productivity grew in 1983 (3.9 percent), it has been falling for most of the past fifteen years.

Because the construction industry builds the plants and installs the equipment used by other industries, a fall in construction productivity is much more important than its own size (6.2 percent of total hours of work) would indicate. If a country's construction industry becomes inefficient, the costs of installing plant and equipment rise for other industries; less plant and equipment can be purchased per dollar spent. These other industries consequently buy less plant and equipment and, having invested less, suffer from slower rates of productivity growth. With inferior construction productivity, U.S. Steel and Nippon Steel, for example, could buy identical steel mills and U.S. Steel would still not be able to compete, since it would cost U.S. Steel more to set up the mill in the United States than it would cost Nippon Steel to set up the same mill in Japan. As a consequence, construction productivity has major ripple effects on the rest of the economy.

If construction productivity had continued to grow at its 1948-65 pace instead of falling at its 1977-83 pace, 13 percent of the decline in national productivity would have disappeared. The decline in construction productivity is a major mystery, however. No one knows what caused it; no one knows how to reverse it.

Various explanations for the decline in construction productivity have been advanced, but none of them is entirely convincing. Inefficient union work rules are one possibility but this suggestion has to confront the fact that unionized construction is rapidly becoming a smaller and smaller fraction of total construction. If union work rules were the problem, one would expect to see productivity grow as unions become less important in the construction business. In fact the decline in unionization and the decline in productivity have gone hand-in-hand.

To generate falling productivity from restrictive work rules it is also necessary to argue not just that inefficient work rules exist but that these inefficient work rules have been growing at a very rapid rate. Although

such restrictive union practices certainly exist, there
simply isn't any evidence that they have been growing.

Some have suggested the problem is caused by statistical weaknesses in the way in which construction productivity is measured. Productivity is simply inflation-
adjusted real output divided by hours of work. This
means that to measure productivity, current dollar
expenditures on construction must be deflated by some
price index to yield real output. Since construction
does not produce homogeneous output, however, inflation
is difficult to measure. If construction inflation was
being systematically overestimated, then construction
output would be simultaneously systematically underestimated, and construction productivity estimates would be
too low.

There is some evidence to support such a conclusion.
From 1954 to 1977 construction output was officially
estimated to have risen 58 percent, but the use of construction materials (tons of steel, concrete, etc.) rose
133 percent. Few believe that 1977 buildings took more
than twice as many materials as 1954 buildings. On the
other hand the government price index is basically an
index constructed from data taken from some major private
builders and buyers of construction. If government construction inflation estimates are wrong, then the analyst
must believe that major builders, such as the Turner Construction Company, and major users of construction, such
as the American Telephone and Telegraph Company and the
Bureau of Public Roads, don't know their own construction
costs. Few observers want to make such an assertion.

Alternatively, construction productivity may have gotten bogged down in shifts from simple to complex outputs.
Where the construction industry used to build simple in-
terstate highways across the wide-open spaces of Kansas
it is now building urban interstates, such as the proposed West Side Highway in New York, where millions of
wires and pipes have to be moved before construction can
even begin. Where the construction industry used to
build coal or oil fired electrical generating stations,
it is now building complex bogged-down nuclear generating
plants. Since construction output, in the case of electrical generating plants, is measured in terms of kilo-
watts of installed capacity, long drawn out flights over
safety show up in the form of fewer plants completed and
less output per hour of work in the construction industry.

Or the decline may be a straightforward case where
workers have gotten lazy and are simply doing less work
per hour than their fathers before them. Within the construction industry, most observers think that the decline
is real but perhaps exaggerated in the government numbers.

Construction productivity is a major part of America's productivity problem, but no one knows what really caused the decline or what can be done about it.

A GEOLOGICAL BLOW IN MINING

The reason for the decline in mining productivity are as clear as those in construction are mysterious. In 1983 mining productivity was 37 percent below where it was in 1972, but there was a simple explanation. Approximately 80 percent of the answer was found in oil and gas—the major mineral "mined" in the United States. The American oil industry is progressing up a rapidly rising cost curve because of geological depletion. There is a lot of oil yet to be found, but it is much more expensive to find it. Since output is measured not in feet drilled but in oil lifted out of the ground, productivity falls when production declines in old wells and when new wells yield less oil per foot drilled. Because of geological depletion it simply takes many more hours of work to produce a barrel of oil. In addition, any expansion of drilling, such as that which occurred after the first and second OPEC oil shocks, adds hours of work to the mining industry well before it adds more output—oil or gas lifted. In 1983, with a cutback in marginal drilling activities, mining productivity rose 15.2 percent. This did not completely offset the 22 percent decline that had occurred from 1977 to 1982, but it went a long way.

The remaining 20 percent of the decline in mining productivity is to be found in the other minerals mined in the United States. Here environmental protection and occupational safety (third grid effects) probably played a role—there is little evidence of rapid geological depletion of ore bodies. If open-pit mines have to be filled and the land restored to its natural contours, more hours of work are required to mine a ton of coal. If better ventilation and more tunnel supports are required to protect underground miners, more hours of work are necessary to mine a ton of copper.

To the extent that the productivity problem is caused by fewer accidents or a cleaner environment, the measured productivity problem is less of a problem than it seems. In the past fifteen years, deaths in underground mining have been reduced from three to two per millions of work. The air is better to breathe and there is less environmental damage than there used to be in mining areas. Neither of these is counted in conventional measures of mining output, yet they contribute to the well-being of America's citizens. If the benefits of such factors had been included in mining productivity, it would not have declined as much as it did. Such outputs are not counted, since no one knows how to weight the value of a life saved versus a ton of copper produced. Those interested

in environmentalism and mining safety may be faulted for
not finding the most efficient way to get the desired
results, but the heart of the productivity problem in
mining is not to be found in environmentalism or safety.
The measured effects are small, and even those small
effects are to some extent a statistical artifact of
defects in the way in which mining output is calculated.

If mining productivity had continued to grow at its
1948-65 rate of 4.3 percent per year, however, 6 percent
of the national productivity decline would have disappeared. Most of this 6 percent, however, is an uncon-
trollable geological blow from Mother Nature--fewer pools
of cheap oil yet to be found in the United States.

THE DEMAND FOR ELECTRICITY

Part of the national productivity decline flows from
gas, water, and electrical utilities, where productivity
growth has fallen from plus 6.3 percent per year to minus
0.9 percent per year. If productivity had continued to
grow at 6.3 percent per year in the 1977-83 period, 13
percent of the national productivity decline would have
disappeared. While causes of the decline in utility
productivity are crystal clear, clarity unfortunately
does not automatically lead to an equally clear solution.

Utilities employ most of their workers installing and
maintaining the distributing systems that deliver electricity, gas, or water to their customers. Relatively
few workers are employed actually producing electricity,
gas, or water. When the demand for the utility output
rises rapidly, productivity rises rapidly. Output is up
but more workers do not have to be employed, since the
extra output can be sold through the existing distribution system. Conversely when demand falls, productivity
falls. Less output is being produced but almost the same
work force is necessary to maintain the distribution system. As a result, utility productivity is a direct function of the rate of growth output. If output grows rapidly, as it did from 1948 to 1965, productivity grows
rapidly. If output grows slowly, as it did from 1972 to
1977, productivity grows slowly. If output falls, as it
did from 1977 to 1979, productivity falls.

The decline in utility productivity is in a class with
oil depletion or agriculture when it comes to public
remedies. There are none. If energy prices rise rapidly, energy consumption will fall and productivity must
fall with it. Since energy prices seem to have peaked
and do not appear likely to rise in the near future, one
would expect that the utility productivity would rebound
and continue to grow at the 3.6 percent rate of 1983 in
the next few years. Barring another OPEC oil shock, the
worst is behind us on the utility front.

Together mining and utilities represent the direct "energy" blow (a third-grid effect) to productivity. The decline in oil mining productivity is one of the reasons that energy prices are up, and higher energy prices lead to lower utilities productivity. When these direct effects are added to the indirect effect (industry has to devote a larger part of its investment funds to saving energy rather than raising labor's productivity), the energy shocks probably explain about 20 percent of the national productivity decline. This 20 percent, however, is not an additional 20 percent. It is simply a different way of viewing the decline in mining and utility productivity.

EXPANDING SERVICES

Services are the mirror image of agriculture. Agriculture was a rapidly declining low-productivity industry; services are a rapidly growing low-productivity industry. While agriculture's decline enhanced productivity growth, the expansion of services dampens it.

Services have been braking national productivity growth since World War II, but the brakes have been gradually tightening as service productivity falls farther and farther behind that of the rest of the economy. Back in 1948, when service productivity was 96 percent of the national average, moving a worker into services only lowered national productivity 4 percentage points. But by 1983 service productivity had fallen to 61 percent of the national average, and every worker who moved into services represented a 39 percentage point decline in productivity.

Services have been growing very rapidly, and from 1977 to 1983 they absorbed 65 percent of all of the hours of work added to the private economy. Of these 7.4 billion hours of new work, 36 percent went into health care, heavily into nursing homes, and 36 percent went into business and legal services (accountants, lawyers, consultants, etc.). In the economic expansion from 1982 to 1983, services accounted for more than 100 percent of the gain in full-time equivalent jobs in the private economy. A gain of 560,000 full-time equivalent jobs in services offset a loss of 144,000 full-time equivalent jobs in the rest of private industry. Within services, health and business or legal services accounted for a full 81 percent of the jobs generated in 1983.

Health care in many ways is like safety and environmentalism. Nursing homes account for a major share of the growth of the health-care industry; yet bathing, feeding, and caring for grandmother is intrinsically a labor-intensive, low-productivity industry. If each of us took care of grandmother at home, as the Japanese do, grandmother would not show up as part of the productivity problem. Taking care of grandmother in a nursing home, however, has some advantages in terms of the well-being of the children who do not have to time themselves to the care of an elderly sick person. Their well-being is not counted in conventional measures of health-care output.

The same problem exists in the rest of the health-care industry. Infant mortality has been cut in half over the last two decades and life expectancy at age sixty-five rose three years in the decade of the 1970s whereas it was rising at only a half a year every ten years in the decades of the 1950s and 1960s. Lower infant mortality rates and longer life expectancy are worth having. As productivity is measured, however, hours of work devoted to this end will show up as declining productivity. More hours are worked without producing more output, since health care output is measured in terms of treatments given rather than less illness or longer life expectancy. And even in cases where treatments fail, people feel better knowing that an effort is being made to save their lives. Such feelings have value even if they are assigned no value in productivity statistics.

When it comes to the growing army of American business and legal consultants, there simultaneously is and is not a measurement problem. Since consultants give advice, it is difficult to measure their output directly. If the quality of their advice is being underestimated in measures of service productivity, however, the unmeasured benefits will show up in higher productivity in the industries taking their good advice. The benefits cannot disappear. With an across-the-board slower rate of growth of industrial productivity, however, there is no evidence that consultants are having large positive effects which are incorrectly being attributed to industries other than their own. Legal and business services are being accorded a very slow rate of growth of productivity in the statistics, and they deserve it.

Legal services are, for example, mostly a zero-sum game which absorbs hours of work. Suppose you fall down on my unshoveled sidewalk and sue me. If you win you get to take some of my old output (income) away from me, but the process does not generate any new output that can increase the total income flowing to the two of us. But since the legal process requires hours of work, the economy's hours of work are up without any equivalent increase in the output, and productivity is consequently down.

As rapidly as the service industries are growing, such data underestimate the real growth of service workers. Many service workers are on the payrolls of manufacturing or other industrial firms and are not counted as service workers in the official statistics. If one looks at occupational statistics rather than industrial statistics, American payrolls are now almost evenly divided between 50 million office workers and 50 million factory,

service, sales, and farm workers who do everything else
that needs to be done in the economy.   If the office
workers are simply a dead-weight loss when it comes to
raising productivity, numerically it will be very difficult for America to break out of its productivity slump.

Paradoxically, while there is a genuine revolution
under way in information processing and office automation, these changes have yet to show up in gains in
office productivity. Quite the contrary. Between 1977
and 1982 real output rose 8 percent, yet at the same time
clerical employment rose 15 percent and total white-
collar employment 18 percent.   In contrast blue-collar
employment fell 2 percent.   The net result was a sharp
decline in white-collar productivity that completely
offset substantial gains in blue-collar productivity.

American banks illustrate the problem.   They have completely computerized their accounting systems and in
their automated tellers probably have more robots than
any other American industry, far outstripping the rise in
banking output, and productivity fell 2 percent per year.
In 1982 it took more hours of work to produce a unit of
output with computers and automated tellers than it used
to take in 1977 without them.

The U.S. Department of Labor has changed its occupational classifications dropping the distinction between
blue and white-collar jobs so it is not possible to compare 1983 with earlier years; but it is possible to compare 1983 and 1984. If one examines the rate of growth
of employment for different occupational categories and
compares it with the growth of real output (up 6.8 percent), precision production, craft, and repair workers,
as well as operators, fabricators, and laborers experienced productivity gains of 0.9 and 2.0 percent respec-
tively, while executives, administrative, and managerial
productivity was falling by 0.5 percent.   More and more
executives were producing less and less per unit of work.
In our most recent data, office workers were still a lagging sector when it comes to productivity growth.

To make offices into a leading productivity sector will
require changes not int he hardware of computers but in
the software of office sociology. Consider the different
options for using word processors.   One option is to
equip secretaries with word processors.   There is very
little productivity to be gained from such a shift.   The
secretary does exactly what she has been doing, and if
she was a good typist making few mistakes, the superior
speed with which mistakes can be corrected on a word processor makes little difference to her total productivity.

The other option is to equip executives with word processors and require them to do their own typing. A good
typist can type faster than he can dictate. Files can be
recalled with a personal computer in less time than it
takes to explain what files are needed to a file clerk.
By getting rid of personal secretaries and file clerks,

enormous gains in productivity are possible. The executive does his part of the task faster and other people
aren't needed to put his decisions and thoughts onto
paper. But this requires that executives have good key-
board skills. Traditionally, executives are too important to type. Standards of what important people do have
to change. Power and status have to be discarded. Executives must learn a new skill well. The needed facility
can only be acquired with practice and a transition period where executives seem clumsy. No one wants to appear
clumsy or incompetent in front of his or her subordi-
nates. As a result, word processors aren't used as they
should be used.

The same thing is true in accounting. Here again there
is a paradox in an explosion in the demand for accoun-
tants--employment up 41 percent from 1977 to 1984--at
exactly the same time that accounting is becoming computerized. Here again there needs to be a rethinking as to
what must be done and by whom.

With computerized accounting the line of least resistance is to simply order up all of the old accounts more
frequently and to add new systems of accounting that
could not previously have been calculated. Executives
now order up accounts on a daily basis that they used to
see only once a month or once a quarter. Tax accounting,
cost accounting, management information systems, inventory control--new forms of accounting appear almost daily.

Given these demands it is not surprising that firms
need more accountants along with the computerization of
accounting, but there is a real question as to whether
all of the new and more frequent accounts lead to better,
more efficient management. In all likelihood the answer
is no. Accounting becomes a form of defensive management
just a testing has become a form of defensive medicine.
Doctors order up every test they can think of, since they
don;t pay for the tests and they might come in handy in-
case they are sued for malpractice. In a similar fashion, managers order up every account they can think of,
since the costs don't come out of their salaries and they
may come in handy in defending what they have done. The
real problem is not to computerize a company's accounting
but to sit back and ask what accounts a company really
needs and how often. A little cost-benefit analysis
applied to accounting itself would not hurt.

In the end, office productivity will only flow out of
office automation if American white-collar workers are
willing to change what the office does and how it operates. Managers must become as willing to order themselves to learn to run a word processor as they now are
at ordering a blue-collar worker to learn to run a robot.
As yet few office workers seem willing to make need changes in office sociology.

To get American productivity growing again, white-
collar workers and service workers are going to have to

be at the forefront of the productivity revolution. Getting them there is going to be a management and sociological challenge of the first magnitude.

If service industries had not grown relative to the rest of the economy, however, 12 percent of the observed decline in national productivity would have disappeared. Alternatively, if service employment had grown but service productivity had held pace with that of the rest of the economy (stayed at 96 percent of the national average), 9 percent of the observed decline in productivity would have disappeared. If one adds in the growth of white-collar workers not on service payrolls, even more of the productivity decline could be attributed to the growth of white-collar support services.

Services illustrate the complexities of the productivity problem. Bathing and feeding old people may be intrinsically a low-productivity occupation, but every American wants to be bathed and fed when old. Lawyers may be a drag on productivity, but Americans are using them in prodigious numbers. Productivity statistics do not care whether you or some thief has your new stereo, but you care, and hire an "unproductive" security guard. In 1983, 602,000 private security guards (up 40 percent in the previous six years) were on some private American payroll. That is a lot of workers who in a more honest society could be productively employed making new goods and services rather than "unproductively" employed guarding old ones.

When the industry-specific first-grid effects from agriculture, mining, construction, utilities, and services are added together, they provide an explanation for slightly more than half the total slowdown in productivity growth. Where cures are possible, they need to be applied, but to a great extent America needs new offsetting sources of productivity growth that up to now have not yet been found. Much of the decline that has been identified is irreversible and none is easily reversed.

The American problem is not so much correcting old bad habits as developing new good habits. Old veins of productivity ore have become depleted; new veins will have to be discovered if America is to achieve the productivity performance it needs to match the international competition.

INFLATION, BABY BOOM, AND CAPITAL INVESTMENT: SECOND-GRID EFFECT

Inadequate investment in plant and equipment is a second-grid effect. Although Americans certainly invest too little, the problem is not quite as simple as it seems. consider the following puzzle: In the years from 1948 to 1965 when productivity was growing at 3.3 percent per year, Americans invested 9.5 percent of the GNP in

plant and equipment. In the years from 1977 to 1983 when
productivity was growing at 0.9 percent per year, Americans invested 11.5 percent of the GNP. Investment went
up 21 percent while productivity growth fell 76 percent.
Why?

The answer is to be found in the baby boom. The average American works with $58,000 (1982 dollars) worth of
plant and equipment. To reach average productivity
levels, new workers must be equipped with $58,000 worth
of plant and equipment. Implicitly the parents of the
baby boom generation were promising not just to bathe,
feed, and educate their babies but to save $58,000 to
equip each of their babies to enter the labor force
twenty years later as the average American worker. And
for every wife who entered the labor force the family was
implicitly promising to save another $58,000. These im-
plicit promises were not kept.

Investment was up, but the labor force was growing much
faster (up from 0.4 percent per year in the mid-1950s to
3.0 percent per year in the late 1970s). What was once
a rising capital-labor ratio is now a falling capital-
labor ratio, not because Americans are investing less but
because the labor force is growing much faster. With a
falling capital-labor ratio, stagnant productivity should
come as no surprise.

The amount of equipment per worker—the capital-labor
ratio-is one of the key ingredients in any model of productivity growth. New equipment allows labor to produce
more output per hour of work, but it is also a carrier of
new technologies. New knowledge without new equipment is
often useless. One cannot work with robots unless one
has robots.

The observed slowdown in the growth of plant and equipment per worker explains about 22 percent of the national
productivity decline.

The adverse effects of the baby boom were compounded by
two energy shocks and environmentalism. To the extent
that investments are made to control pollution or cut
energy usage, there are fewer funds left to raise labor
productivity. There are no hard official estimates of
how much of our plant and equipment has gone into energy-
saving investments since 1972, although it must be substantial, but about 5 percent of America's plant and
equipment investment has gone into pollution and safety
controls. If this investment is subtracted from the
totals, the slowdown in the growth of plant and equipment
per worker can explain something like 25 percent of the
total slowdown—perhaps a little more if one remembers
the role of capital as a carrier of new technologies.

The slowdown in the growth of America's capital-labor
ratio, however, was not due to stupidity or irrationali-
ty. It was a perfectly rational market response to the
economic facts of life. Firms invest to raise the
capital-labor ratio when it is profitable to do so.

Technical change brings about such investments, but they are also brought about by changes in the relative price of capital and labor. When the cost of capital falls relative to the cost of labor, firms find it cheaper to raise production by investing in capital than hiring more workers. With fewer workers and more capital, output per hour of work rises. Conversely, when capital becomes more expensive relative to labor, firms find it cheaper to raise production by hiring more workers and the capital-labor ratio falls. With less capital and more workers, output per hour of work falls.

In the aftermath of a baby boom, simple supply and demand predict that as the supply of labor rises, wage rates fall. With wages down, capital becomes relatively more expensive. Firms shift technologies, replacing expensive machines with cheap workers. Labor productivity falls. From the point of supply and demand the economy has been behaving precisely as it is supposed to behave. Economic signals have been calling for a reduction in the capital-labor ratio. Whereas the cost of labor (wages plus fringe benefits) was rising 1 percent per year relative to the cost of capital (a cost which includes the initial purchase price, the energy cost of operating the plant and equipment, and the interest cost of financing it) from 1948-1965, the relative price of labor was falling at an annual rate of 6 percent from 1972 to 1979. Where American workers were once becoming expensive relative to machines, they are now becoming cheap relative to machines.

Given such a sharp shift in the movement of the relative prices of capital and labor, it is not surprising that there was a decline in the capital-labor ratio. Business firms were doing exactly what economic incentives were calling for. One can imagine other offsetting factors (a sharp increase in the savings rate) which if they had occurred would have offset the impacts of population growth, but these potentially offsetting factors did not occur.

In some ways America is over the hump with respect to the baby-boom generation. Most of them are now at work, and the growth of the labor force will slow appreciably in the late 1980s and 1990s as the baby-dearth generations following the baby-boom generation enter the labor force. Female labor force participation rates are also rising to levels where the growth in female participation must slow down. Both energy prices and interest costs also seem to be mitigating. As a result, some of the decline caused by a slower rate of growth of the capital-labor ratio should disappear without remedial action.

Looking forward, the United States should enjoy a productivity rebound into the 1 to 1.5 percent range without doing anything. While better than that has been occurring, such a rate is not adequate. It does not come close to closing the productivity growth gap between America and its international competitors.

Even if the United States were living in a world by itself, 1 to 1.5 percent productivity growth rates would be inadequate if America is to absorb the baby-boom generation successfully. Regardless of the economic rationality of the causes, slow productivity growth is apt to produce unacceptable social and political results. With slow productivity growth, standards of living rise much slower than they have in the past. While Americans could get used to this new reality, the process of lowering expectations is not apt to be smooth. This is especially true for the baby-boom generation, which will end up with lifetime standards of living lower than those of both their parents and their children. (When older Americans bemoan the fact that their children will not be able to afford the house that they live in, this is precisely the problem to which they are implicitly referring.) A democracy only uneasily lives with what will see itself as a "deprived" generation.

Wanting a different result is a rational social desire but not one which can be implemented by simply liberating free enterprise. The market is giving America the market solution, but it is a solution that Americans don't want to live with and don't have to live with if they are willing to socially organize themselves to change the parameters within which the market works. If Americans, for example, were to save much more, then capital's relative price would fall and labor would once again find itself working with a rapidly rising capital-labor ratio. such changes don't happen automatically. Institutions and incentives have to be socially restructured to bring about the desired market results. One cannot fight the market, but one can channel it.

INCREASED PRODUCTIVITY REQUIRES HIGH-QUALITY INPUTS

Many of the factors that explain the decline in American productivity growth also explain the much smaller declines in the productivity growth rates observed in most of the rest of the industrial world. The same adverse factors are affecting everyone but to a lesser degree. While the flow out of agriculture is slowing in most industrial countries, some foreign countries such as France are still experiencing relatively rapid declines in their agricultural work forces. Countries without significant oil and gas industries such as Japan cannot suffer from declining oil and gas mining productivity. With different legal and health systems (The British spend just half as much on health care as the United States), services have not grown as rapidly abroad. Construction productivity has been falling in Europe, but at a slower pace than in the United States. Since most of America's in-

dustrial competitors already had high energy prices before the two oil shocks, they needed to invest less in
energy conservation, and demand fell less rapidly in
their utility industries.   The rest of the world also
ended up having a much smaller and somewhat later baby-
boom generation.

To see what must be done to catch up with productivity
growth rates of the rest of the industrial world, however, it is necessary to step back from detailed statistical analysis and look at the big picture. Catching up
with foreign productivity growth is simultaneously simple
and complex.

No one could build a high-quality economy out of low-
quality inputs just as no one can build a high-quality
product out of low-quality components. Yet whenever the
basic inputs--capital, labor, management, labor-management relations--going into the American economy are compared with those of the competition they just don't seem
to measure up.

Look first at the areas where hard comparative measurements are possible. In 1983 American gross investment (a
measure that includes investment in housing) was 17 percent of the GNP. At the same time the French were investing 20 percent, the West Germans 21 percent, and the
Japanese 28 percent. If Americans were to have kept up
with the Japanese in terms of plant and equipment investment per worker (and in the long run it must), it would
have had to have essentially doubled its investment to 30
percent of the GNP because of its more rapidly growing
labor force. In any one year such gaps make little difference, but compounded over a few decades they spell the
difference between success and failure.

In recent test of sixth graders in eight different
countries, science students in Sweden placed first,
Americans placed sixth. In geography the Swedes were
again first and the Americans fourth. In math Americans
were last, knowing only half as much as the Japanese.
Given such science and math scores it should come as no
surprise that Japan produces twice as many engineers per
capita as the United States, and that with twice as many
engineers on the payroll, Japanese products seem to be a
little better engineered.

In the late nineteenth and early twentieth centuries
when America was catching up with Great Britain, America
had the best-educated labor force in the world. It no
longer does. A second-class poorly educated American
labor force is not going to beat first-class well-educated German, French, or Japanese labor forces. America
invented high-quality mass public education; America is
going to have to re-invent it.

America's personal savings rate, 5 percent in 1983, was
the lowest in the industrial world by a factor of almost
three. Our neighbors, the Canadians, saved 13 percent,
the Germans 14 percent, the Japanese 21 percent, and the

Italians 23 percent. It does not take a genius to know
that Americans cannot compete on world markets saving
less than one-third as much as their competitors.

America's savings rates have not gone down. They never
were high. When America's per capita income was twice
that of the rest of the world, a 5 percent American
savings rate was equivalent in terms of generating
investment resources to a 10 percent savings rate in the
rest of the world. But that time is over. What was good
enough in the past will not be good enough in the future.

America invests less in civilian research and development than any of its major industrial competitors. Amer-
can civilian R & D spending runs at about 1.5 percent of
GNP while our competitors are spending 2 percent. Americans aren't smarter than the Germans or French. German
scientists with money will beat American scientists without money most of the time. In the 1950s and 1960s America spent more, not less, on civilian research and development than its competitors.

While it is not so easy to quantify, American management cannot escape its share of the blame. American firms
have undeniable problems with quality control.   When
asked to rate the quality of their cars, American buyers
listed only two American-built cars among the top ten.
Management is responsible for quality control. If American products are shoddily built then American management
is shoddy.

Neither can American government escape its share of the
blame.   American industry cannot be expected to eat
foreign competition if it must simultaneously cope with
repeated recessions, high interest rates, and an over-
valued dollar. Government has to do more than get out of
the way. American firms face foreign firms with local
governments in their corner. American firms need the
same help and support.

When it comes to that famous bottom line, each major
input into the American economy will have to be as good
as those of the competition if America is to be competitive. A world-class economy demands world-class inputs.
Converting existing American inputs into world-class
American inputs will not be an easy task, but it is also
not an impossible one. Other countries have done what
was necessary to make themselves competitive with America. Americans can do what is necessary to make itself
competitive with them.

8

The Quality Trilogy

Joseph M. Juran

Several premises have led me to conclude that our companies need to chart a new direction in managing for quality. These premises are as follows:

1. There is a crisis in quality. The most obvious outward evidence is the loss of sales to foreign competition in quality and the huge costs of poor quality.
2. The crisis will not go away in the foreseeable future. Competition in quality will go on and on. So will the impact of poor quality on society. In the industrialized countries, society lives behind protective quality dikes.
3. Our traditional ways are not adequate to deal with the quality crisis. In a sense, our adherence to those traditional ways has helped to create the crisis.
4. To deal with the crisis requires some major breaks with tradition. A new course must be charted.
5. Charting a new course requires that we create a universal way of thinking about quality--a way applicable to all functions and to all levels in the hierarchy, from the chief executive officer to the worker in the office or the factory.
6. Charting a new course also requires extensive personal leadership and participation by upper managers.
7. An obstacle to participation by upper managers is their limited experience and training in managing for quality. They have extensive experience in management of business and finance but not in managing for quality.
8. An essential element in meeting the quality crisis

    is to arm upper managers with experience and train-
    ing in how to manage for quality, and to do so on
    a time scale compatible with the prevailing sense
    of urgency.
9. Charting a new course also requires that we design
    a basis for management for quality that can readily
    be implanted into the company's strategic business
    planning and that has minimal risk of rejection by
    the company's immune system.

A company that wants to chart a new course in managing
for quality obviously should create an all-pervasive
unity so that everyone will know what the new direction
is and will be stimulated to go there. Creating such
unity requires dealing with some powerful forces that resist a unified approach. These forces are for the most
part due to certain nonuniformities inherent in any company. These nonuniformities include:

-   The multiple functions in the company: product
    development, manufacture, office operations, etc.
    Each section regards its function as something
    unique and special.
-   The multiple levels in the company hierarchy, from
    the chief executive officer to the nonsupervisory
    worker. These levels differ with respect to
    responsibility, prerequisite experience and train-
    ing, etc.
-   The multiple product lines: large and complex
    systems, mass production, regulated products, etc.
    These product lines differ in their markets, tech-
    nology, restraints, etc.

Such inherent nonuniformities and the associated beliefs in uniqueness are a reality in any company, and
they constitute a serious obstacle to unity of direction. Such an obstacle can be overcome if we are able to
find a universal thought process--a universal way of
thinking about quality--that fits all functions, all
levels, all product lines. That brings me to the concept of the "quality trilogy."
(Let me add parenthetically that my colleagues in Juran
Institute have urged me to let them call it the "Juran
Trilogy." Their reasons are purely mercenary. I have
yielded to their wishes. In Juran Institute we also need
unity.)
The underlying concept of the quality trilogy is that
managing for quality consists of three basic quality-
oriented processes.

-   Quality planning
-   Quality control
-   Quality improvement

Each of these processes is universal; it is carried out
by an unvarying sequence of activities. A brief description of each of these sequences follows:

Basic Quality Processes Planning

- Identify the customers, both external and internal.
- Determine customer needs.
- Develop product features that respond to customer
  needs. (Products include both goods and services.)
- Establish quality goals that meet the needs of
  customers and suppliers alike, and do so at a
  minimum combined cost.
- Develop a process that can produce the needed
  product features.
- Prove process capability; prove that the process
  can meet the quality goals under operating conditions.

Control

- Choose control subjects--what to control.
- Choose units of measurement.
- Establish measurement.
- Establish standards of performance.
- Measure actual performance.
- Interpret the difference (actual versus standard).
- Take action on the difference.

Improvement

- Prove the need for improvement.
- Identify specific projects for improvement.
- Organize to guide the projects.
- Organize for diagnosis, for discovery of the
  causes.
- Diagnose to find the causes.
- Provide remedies.
- Prove that the remedies are effective under operat-
  ing conditions.
- Provide for control to hold the gains.

Furthermore, these universal processes are interrelated
in that ways we can depict on a simple diagram.
The starting point is quality planning: creating a process that will be able to meet established goals and do
so under operating conditions. The subject matter of the
planning can be anything: an office process for producing
documents, an engineering process for designing products,
a factory process for producing goods, or a service process for responding to customers' requests.
Following the planning, the process is turned over to
the operating forces. Their responsibility is to run the
process at optimal effectiveness. Due to deficiencies in

Figure 8.1

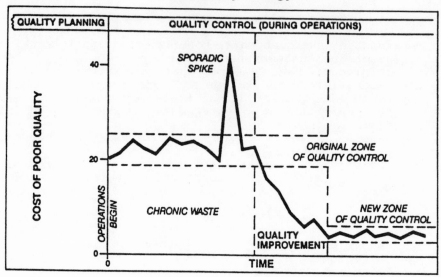

the original planning, the process runs at a high level
of chronic waste. That waste has been planned into the
process, in the sense that the planning process failed to
plan it out. Because the waste is inherent in the process, the operating forces are unable to get rid of the
chronic waste. What they do instead is to carry out
"quality control," to keep the waste from getting worse.
If it does get worse (sporadic spike), a fire-fighting
team is brought in to determine the cause or causes of
this abnormal variation. Once the cause(s) has been determined and corrective action is taken, the process
again falls into the zone defined by the "quality control" limits.

Figure 8.1 also shows that in due course the chronic
waste falls to a much lower level. Such a reduction does
not happen of its own accord. It results from purposeful
action taken by upper management to introduce a new managerial process into the system of managers' responsibilities: the quality improvement process is superimposed on
the quality control process, a process implemented in addition to quality control, not instead of it.

We can now elaborate the trilogy descriptions somewhat
as follows.

Process: Quality planning: the process for preparing to
meet quality goals.

End result: A process capable of meeting quality goals under operating conditions.

Process: Quality control: the process for meeting quality goals during operations.

End result: Conduct of operations in accordance with the quality plan.

Process: Quality improvement: the process for breaking through to unprecedented levels of performance.

End result: Conduct of operations at levels of quality distinctly superior to planned performance.

The trilogy is not entirely "new." If we look sideways at how we manage finance, we notice some interesting parallels, as shown below. (I have often used the financial parallels to help explain the trilogy to upper managers. It does help.)

Quality and Finance:
Parallels

Trilogy Processes
Quality planning
Quality control
Quality improvement

Financial Processes
Budgeting
Cost control; expense control
Cost reduction; profit improvement

In recent seminars, I have been collecting upper managers' conclusions on their companies' performance relative to the basic processes of the trilogy. The results are quite similar from one seminar to another, and they can be summarized as shown below.

Quality Process Performance
(Upper managers' ratings of their
companies' performance)

Trilogy processes	Good	Passing	Not passing
Quality planning	13%	40%	47%
Quality control	44	36	20
Quality improvement	6	39	55

These summarized data point to several conclusions.

1. The managers are not happy with their performance relative to quality planning.
2. The managers rate their companies well with respect to quality control, i.e., meeting the established goals. Note that since these goals have traditionally been based mainly on past performance, the effect is to perpetuate past performance--the very

performance that is at the root of the quality
crisis.
3. The managers are decidedly unhappy with their
    performance relative to quality improvement.

My own observations of company performance (during
consultations) strongly confirm the above self-assessment
by company managers. During my visits to companies I
have found a recurring pattern of priorities and assets
devoted to the processes within the trilogy. This
pattern is shown below.

Priorities for Quality Processes
Self-assessment

Trilogy **Prevailing** **processes** **priorities**	**By upper** **managers**
Quality planning Limited priority	Weak
Quality control Top priority, by a wide margin	Very strong
Quality improvement Very low priority	Very weak

As the above shows, the prevailing priorities are not
consistent with the managers' self-assessment of their
own effectiveness. That assessment would suggest that
they should put the control process on hold while increasing the emphasis on quality planning and especially
on quality improvement.

To elaborate on the need for raising the priority of
quality improvement, let me present several baffling case
examples.

1. Several years ago the executive vice president of
    a large multinational rubber company made a round-
    the-world trip with his chairman. They made the
    trip in order to visit their major subsidiaries
    with a view to securing inputs for strategic
    business planning. They found much similarity with
    respect to productivity, quality, etc., except for
    Japan. The Japanese company was outperforming all
    others, and by a wide margin, yet the Americans
    were completely mystified as to why. The Americans
    had toured the Japanese plant, and to the Amer-
    icans' eyes the Japanese were using the same
    materials, equipment, processes, etc., as everyone
    else. After much discussion the reason emerged:

The Japanese had been carrying out many, many quality improvement projects year after year. Through the resulting improvements they made more and better products from the same facilities. The key point relative to "ignorance" is that the Americans did not know what to look for.

2. A foundry that made aluminum castings had an identical experience. The foundry was losing its share of the market to a Japanese competitor, mainly for quality reasons. Arrangements were made for a delegation of Americans to visit the Japanese factory. The delegation came away completely mystified. The Japanese were using the same types of equipment and processes as were used by the Americans. Yet the Japanese results in quality and productivity were clearly superior. To this day the Americans don't know why.

3. A few years ago I conducted research into the yields of the processes that make large-scale integrated circuits. To assure comparability, I concentrated on a single product type--the 16K random access memory (16K RAM). I found that Japanese yields, were two to three times the Western yields despite similarity in the basic processes. It came as no surprise to me that the Japanese have since become dominant in the market for 64K RAMs and up.

4. My final example relates to the steel industry. The managers of American steel companies report that their cost of poor quality (just for factory processes) runs at about 10-15 percent of sales. Some of these steel companies have business connections with Japanese steel companies, and the respective managers exchange visits. During these visits the Americans learn that in Japanese steel mills, which use comparable equipment and process, the cost of poor quality runs at about 1-2 percent of sales. Again the American managers don't know why. Some of them don't even believe the Japanese figures. My own explanation is that the Japanese, since the early 1950s, have undertaken to improve quality at a pace far greater than that of the West. The slopes of those two lines (Figure 8.2) are an index of the rate of improvement. That rate is in turn dependent on the number of quality improvement projects completed. (A project is a problem scheduled for solution.) My estimate is that, in terms of numbers of improvement projects completed, the Japanese pace has been exceeding that of the West by an order of magnitude, year after year.

It seems clear that we must change our priorities with regard to the three quality processes. This change in

Table 8.2

World Competition in Quality

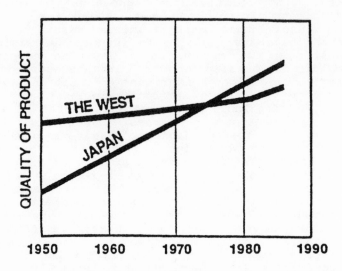

priorities represents a new course. Underlying this new
course is the quality trilogy. As a universal way of
thinking about quality, the trilogy offers a unified approach for multiple purposes. Let us look at two of
these purposes: training in managing for quality and
strategic quality planning.

With respect to training, many of our companies have
decided to break with tradition. In the past, their
training in managing for quality has been limited to
managers and engineers in the quality department. The
break with tradition is to extend such training to all
functions. Since this is a sizable undertaking, the
companies have set up corporate task forces to plan the
approach.

These task forces have run into serious obstacles due
to these same systems of variable mentioned earlier. It
is hopeless to establish numerous training courses in
managing for quality, each specially designed to fit
specific functions, specific levels in the hierarchy,
specific product lines, etc. Instead, the need is for a
universal training course that will apply to all audiences, but with provision for plugging in special case examples as warranted. The trilogy concept meets that need.

The training courses then consist of fleshing out the
three sequences of steps described earlier. Those sequences have been field-tested and proven to be applicable to all functions, levels, and product lines.

We have already seen that the trilogy parallels our
approach to strategic business planning. Our companies

are experienced in business planning; they are familiar and comfortable with the concepts of financial budgets, cost control, and cost reduction. We can take advantage of all that experience by grafting the quality trilogy onto the existing business planning structure. Such a graft reduces the risk that the implant will be rejected by the company's immune system.

The usual starting point is to set up a quality planning council to formulate and coordinate the activity companywide. The council membership consists of high-ranking managers and corporate officers. The chairman is usually the chief executive officer or an executive vice president. The functions of this council parallel closely the functions of the company's finance committee, but apply to quality instead of finance.

The council prepares a written list of its responsibilities. These typically involves the following:

- Establish corporate quality policies.
- Establish corporate quality goals; review quality goals of divisions and major functions.
- Establish corporate quality plans; review divisional and functional plans.
- Provide the infrastructure and resources needed to carry out the plans.
- Review quality performance against plans and goals.
- Revise the managerial merit-rating system to reflect performance against quality goals.

It is all quite logical, and some companies are already securing gratifying benefits from going into strategic quality planning. Other companies are failing to get results, however, and the main reasons for these failures are becoming evident. They relate to some areas that I will now discuss: goal setting; providing the infrastructure; providing resources; and upper management leadership.

Setting goals. Goal setting has traditionally been heavily based on past performance. This practice has tended to perpetuate the sins of the past. Failure-prone designs were carried over into new models. Wasteful processes were not challenged if managers had met the budgets, budgets that had in turn assumed that waste was a fate to be endured.

All this must change. Goals for parameters that affect external customers must be based on meeting competition in the marketplace. Goals for parameters that affect internal customers must be based on getting rid of the traditional wastes.

Infrastructure. Strategic quality planning requires an infrastructure to be set up. The nature of this is evident when we look sideways at the infrastructure needed for strategic business planning: a budgetary process; an accounting system to evaluate performance; associated procedures, audits, etc.

Much of this structure has long been in place to serve various local needs: division, functions, factories, etc. This structure must now be supplemented to enable it to meet strategic quality needs as well. This is especially the case in large corporations that traditionally have delegated matters of quality to the autonomous divisions. The quality crisis has caused some large corporations to revise this delegation. They now require corporate review of divisional quality goals, plans, and reports of performance. The new approach has required revision of the infrastructure.

Resources. It takes resources to carry out plans and meet goals. To date, companies have exhibited a selective response to this need. Let us look at several areas that require such resources.

-   Training. Here the response of companies has generally been positive. Companies have invested heavily in training programs for special areas, such as quality awareness, statistical process control, and QC circles. To go into strategic quality planning will require extensive training in the trilogy—how to think about quality. One can hope that the response will continue to be positive.
-   Measurement of quality. The quality crisis has required a major change in the basis for goal setting; the new basis requires measurement of market quality on an unprecedented scale. For example, some companies now have a policy that new products may not go on the market unless their reliability is at least equal to that of leading competitive products. Such a policy cannot be made effective unless resources are provided to evaluate the reliability of competing products.

Beyond the need to expand quality-oriented marketing research, there are other aspects of measurement that require resources: establishing the scorekeeping associated with strategic quality planning (the quality equivalent of the financial profit statements, balance sheets, etc.); extending measures of quality to the nonmanufacturing process; and establishing means for evaluating the quality performance of managers and fitting these evaluations into the merit-rating system.

-   Quality improvement. Here we have some puzzling contradictions. An emerging data base tells us that quality improvement projects provide a higher return on investment than virtually any other investment activity. Yet many companies have not provided the needed resources.

To be specific, that data base comes mainly from the companies that have presented papers at the annual IMPRO conferences on quality improvement. Those published papers and related unpublished information indicate that in large organizations (sales of $1 billion or more) the average quality improvement project yields about $100,000 of cost reduction.

The same data base indicates that to complete a project requires from $5,000 to $20,000 in resources. These resources are needed to diagnose the cause of the problem and to provide the remedy. The return on investment is obviously attractive. Nevertheless, many companies--too many--have failed to provide the resources and hence have failed to get the results.

To go into strategic quality planning will require companies to create a new role for the quality function, similar to that of the financial controller. In all likelihood this new role will be assigned to the quality managers.

In part this new role will involve assisting the company managers to prepare the strategic quality goals, the quality equivalent of the financial budget. In addition the new role will involve establishing the continuing means of reporting performance against quality goals. This role parallels the financial reporting role of the financial controller.

Collateral with those two new responsibilities will be others, also of a broad business nature:

-   Evaluation of competitive quality and of trends in the marketplace.
-   Design and introduction of needed revisions in the trilogy of processes: quality planning, quality control, and quality improvement.
-   Conduct of training to assist company personnel in carrying out the necessary changes.

For many quality managers such a new role will involve a considerable shift in emphasis: from technology to business management; from quality control and assurance to strategic quality planning. But such is the wave of the future. Those quality managers who choose to accept that responsibility, if and when it comes, can look forward to the experience of a life-time. They will be participating fully in what will become the most important quality development of the century.

9

The Pragmatic Philosophy of Phil Crosby

Philip B. Crosby

In 1952 I went to work for what was then the Crosley Corporation in Richmond, Ind. As a junior technician ($315 per month) in the quality department, I tested motors and set gear boxes. This was my first exposure to industrial life, and I really liked it. Here was this whole organization making things for people to use. This was the beginning of my life as a quality practitioner.

I wanted to learn everything I could about quality control so I could make it my career. So I joined the American Society for Quality Control, read every book I could find, and attended courses whenever I could talk the boss into sending me. Everyone else seemed to know so much more than I did. They talked about sampling, laws of probability, and standard deviations, among other things.

But I did learn clearly that the whole business rested on the foundation that it was impractical to try to do everything right and that a compromise had to be built into every situation. For everyone to do everything right the first time would slow things down so that nothing would get out.

Since nothing was ever exactly correct, I assumed that this was all in order. As I went to more conferences and talked with those more experienced in the field, I learned that quality was a desirable characteristic, that it was achieved through inspection and test, that the performance standard was "acceptable quality levels (AQLs)" and that quality should be measured by indexes.

It took me several more years before doubt set in. I began to realize that all of this was a self-fulfilling way of looking at things. We ordered material to AQLs and it came in defective; we sample inspected it, found it to have a limited number of problems, and put it into stock where it could be used to deliver a product that was not right either.

And, although I did not understand what management was all about, I began to recognize that quality was the result of policy. If we planned to do a lot of things incorrectly, it would work out that way.

The workers and other low-level people received the blame for lack the of quality, and the quality department was continually harassed by management when things went wrong. Quality managers came and went throughout the country. My years as one of them were very difficult until I learned to tell my management that if they had ordered something so big, it was going to come out so big. If they wanted it another size then they should change the requirement, not ask me to "be reasonable." The thought that I, as a quality manager, could sign things off whether I knew what was involved or not, was disturbing. But it was the practice.

It was not until nine years later, when I was at the Martin Company in Orlando, Fla., that it began to become clear to me. I had been writing and speaking about quality and was becoming quite adept at explaining how it was impossible for everything to come out right.

As the quality manager of the Pershing program, I had several hundred people in my department and the complete cooperation of management. Yet we continually had deviations, variations, and defects. The Department of Defense praised Pershing as the best they had and our quality operation as an example to all. Yet, as my boss pointed out to me, we continually let things slip past.

It was at this point that I realized that the policy of the company and the customer agreed with this result. In order to change that, I suggested that we get rid of AQLs and start concentrating on Zero Defects. This meant conforming exactly to the requirements instead of wasting time figuring out how far we could stray from them. We, I announced, were the problems, not the laws of probability.

It was here that I learned my first lessons about the futility of revolution. The company and the customer immediately pounced on the Zero Defects idea as a way to motivate the workers and boosted it nationwide. They did not bother to understand what I was thinking about.

The quality professionals, and the leaders of that group in particular, pounced on me as being impractical and uninformed. They also did not bother to ask me what I was thinking about. They were so deeply committed to the inevitability of error and the trade-offs that were called the "economics of quality" that they could conceive of no other way.

The only ones who made deeper inquiries were the Japanese. In 1963 several of them came to visit me and stayed long enough to learn that I felt quality was a result of management policy; that prevention was the way

to get it, not appraisal; that the costs of doing things
wrong were so enormous that they blanked out all the
conventional thoughts of "economics of quality." They
went back and made this concept the foundation of their
management policy.

People say that it was too bad that American management
did not listen to the quality control experts during that
period. What they do not realize is that management did,
in fact, listen. They installed quality control operations dedicated to the proposition that error was a normal part of business life and that we needed to learn to
cope with it. Nowhere in the literature of that day, and
rarely even now, is it stated that the customer should
receive exactly what was ordered.

In 1965 I joined the ITT Corporation as the Corporate
Director of Quality. This worldwide conglomerate offered
a marvelous laboratory. I was working with telephone
manufacturing, semiconductors, insurance, hotels, food,
and just about every other kind of business. Right off
the bat we established a corporate quality policy that
said, "We will deliver defect-free products and services
to our customers on time." Then I set up a school for
ITT quality professionals, and then for executives. We
proved that it was possible to manage quality by prevention.

In the mid-1970s I became alarmed about the state of
quality in the nation. I realized how bad things were
when I made a speech one day and the moderator, after
thanking me, said, "Now Mr. Crosby does not literally
mean that things can be done error free, of course." I
went back to the podium to say that I did indeed mean it,
and they were going to lose all their markets if they did
not learn to understand what had to happen.

I wrote *Quality Is Free* in 1977-78 with the idea that
I would publish it and, if anyone bought it, I would
start a consulting firm to help them improve. So in July
of 1979 I set up Philip Crosby Associates, Inc., in Winter Park, Fla. My idea was that I would write, speak,
and play golf. However, we were suddenly overwhelmed by
companies that were tired of paying ransom to the cost of
quality and that wanted to learn how to manage it. None
of these companies was in trouble yet, and they were all
profitable, but they were realizing what had to happen.
IBM, 3M, Milliken, Tennant, Celanese, J. P. Stevens,
Bendix, Honeywell, and many others became involved.
Since then we have had over fifteen hundred companies
from all over the world.

I realized immediately that the quality professionals
were not the ones to teach; they were not going to
change their minds. So I established The Quality College, which at the time consisted of a one-week course on
the management of quality. I taught at first with a
blackboard and chalk. Today we have films, dozens of
courses, and all kinds of supporting material--all

translated into seven languages and taught worldwide. We
do not deal with companies unless their top management
comes to class.
I broke the concepts down into what I call the "Absolutes of Quality Management." These were the comprehension blocks that were necessary to understand if one was
going to learn how to deal with quality.

1. *The definition of quality is conformance to re-
    quirements.* This means that management has to take
    setting requirements seriously, and then has to in-
    sist that they be met at all times. The problem
    has always been that every requirement was consid-
    ered negotiable. Now we are saying that if you
    want people to do it right the first time, you have
    to tell them what "it" is. This applies to product
    requirements as well as those in service and admin-
    istration. Conventional concepts say that quality
    is a matter of continual evaluation and re-evalua-
    tion. That produces a situation where no one knows
    what they are supposed to do.
2. *The system of causing quality is prevention.* Just
    as we deal with disease by vaccination and other
    preventive methods, so we have to learn how not to
    have the problems that cause nonconformance. Con-
    ventional concepts concentrate on examining the
    product when it is complete; what we want to do is
    work on the systems that produce the product or
    service of the organization.
3. *The performance standard for quality is Zero
    Defects.* Giving people standards that encourage
    them to believe that errors are a normal part of
    business life is counterproductive and insults
    their intelligence. The conventional concept that
    there is some overriding natural phenomenon requir-
    ing each of us to do a certain amount of things
    wrong is contrary to what we see about us. People
    do not plan to drop babies.
4. *The measurement of quality is the Price of Non-
    conformance.* What does it cost to do things wrong?
    In manufacturing companies it is at least 25 per-
    cent of sales; service companies spend half of
    their operating expenses. This is real money.
    Conventional reporting is aimed at defect levels or
    some index of that which encourages continually
    improving that result. Thus nothing ever gets to
    where it is defect free and management never knows
    when to get upset or excited.

As we began to work with organizations, their managements began to concentrate on taking requirements seriously. The employees appreciated the consistency that
was then produced. It was not a matter of writing a
whole batch of new procedures or specifications; it was

only a matter of working to meet those that existed. Many companies had never done that and had no idea if their output even worked. It is not possible to produce even more useful requirements until you know how the old ones worked.

Soon the client companies reported dramatic changes in costs, which made the financial people happy. But more importantly they found that everyone was beginning to understand quality that same way, and the customers were becoming very happy because they were receiving what they had ordered. Employee morale escalated rapidly, and absenteeism and turnover dropped in every case.

PCA was learning also. We developed films and other materials that would be taught to employees at all levels by their management. The films were like soap operas with real actors and situations. They have worked well. Now there are courses for everyone in areas such as supplier quality management, Statistical Process Control (SPC), corrective action, and many others. We took PCA public in 1985 in order to pay for the development of case history material and translations. We spent over $8 million dollars on that. As a result PCA operations, staffed by PCA employees, are located in London, Paris, Munich, Genoa, Toronto, Singapore, Sydney, Tokyo (the Japan Management Association), San Jose, Calif., Deerfield, Ill., and Winter Park, Fla.

We had to learn to take well-educated, experienced people and put them through a program for eight to 10 months in order to learn to become PCA counselors. They go on site to help the client company implement the process as required. They also do the majority of teaching in The Quality College. Their purpose is to guide the client company in learning to manage quality eternally. It is not our purpose to do it for them.

We see hundreds of companies in all types of businesses successfully learning to manage quality. They are turning it into an advantage for them, saving a lot of money, and dehassling the operation. It is not difficult, it does not cost much, and everyone gets to become a hero. The question is then: Why doesn't everyone do this?

The answer is that management still has the problem of bad information absorbed during their formative years. MBA schools, quality "experts," and conventional beliefs still insist that quality is a variable, that the employees are the problem, and that it is all a matter of change. They have not thought about this; they just are repeating the teachings of the past.

Actually quality is a choice. Organizations can make the decision to have it or not have it. There are several things involved besides understanding the absolutes:

1. All work is a process. The entire organization is responsible for the final output. Each individual's input and output can be measured by ordinary systems and understood by anyone.
2. People need permission to do things right. Employees at all levels need to be considered "chefs" who develop and document recipes, who can produce the same omelet each time on command, who know how to measure their work, obtain corrective action, and guarantee the process is defect free.
3. Management must serve as a continual witness to the commitment that the customer is going to receive exactly what we sold him. There are going to be no deviations, variations, or whatever. Quality is no longer some special thing that provides a marketing advantage. It is a uniform. If a company does not have a uniform, then it cannot play.
4. Organizations require a formal approach that keeps the quality process up-front. I listed 14 things that have to be done, but inside that list are hundreds of actions that the teams will figure out themselves

I have never determined why people insist on making quality so difficult by laying out technical roadblocks or structured techniques that have to be obeyed. If we as individuals want to be socially acceptable, we have to learn personal hygiene (clean shirts are not enough); we have to learn to keep all our promises (not just a select few); we have to pay our bills (not just those at our level). We, like our companies, cannot selectively comply with what is expected and ignore the things we find difficult or boring.

To repeat: quality is a result of policy, whether personal or organizational. If the policy is to make continual judgments about whether something is fit or not, then nothing will ever be dependable. In *Quality Without Tears* (McGraw-Hill, 1984), I laid out the profile of a quality-troubled company. It is easy to recognize such an operation:

1. They never deliver exactly what they have agreed to provide to the customer. There is always some difference.
2. They have a "fix-it" organization that helps the customer deal with the nonconformances and disappointments.
3. They do not have a clear performance standard. They talk instead about excellence, or quality, or something not specific.
4. They have no idea what all this costs. The price of nonconformance is not in their accounting system.
5. They think all of this is someone else's fault.

Companies can change quickly.   A big step toward
turning around can be made within a year.   In three years
quality can become normal practice and in five years no
one will remember the old ways.   But management has to be
serious about it.   Just setting up some complex techniques will do little to make the cultural changes necessary.

10

Building Excellence in Manufacturing

Steven C. Wheelwright

It is a pleasure to be with you this morning for at least three reasons. The first is that, as Lynn Wilson just mentioned, my background is in Utah. I went to the other state school down in Salt Lake, but hope that will not be held against me. This is the first opportunity I have had to be in Utah to speak. I lecture frequently and teach students from all over and occasionally have some Utah students in my classes, but it is a pleasure to be here with all of you.

The second thing is that I am flattered to be part of this Distinguished Lecture Series.

The third is that I am particularly pleased to be sharing the podium this morning with four friends and colleagues who will participate in the panel discussion following my lecture. These are executives who have demonstrated the kind of leadership needed in manufacturing-based organizations, which I will discuss. They have done much to help shape many of the ideas that I will discuss, and I appreciate their contribution.**

OVERVIEW

I would like to start by presenting some ideas and concepts and then demonstrate how those might be used. I would encourage you to write down any questions that you have as you are listening to my presentation and the

**Note: They include Hal Edmondson, VP-Dir. of Corp. Manufacturing, Hewlett-Packard; Leo H. Everitt, Jr., VP-Manufacturing, FMC Corp; Paul J. Kehoe, Vice Chm., Kellogg Co.; Dick E. Milholland, Senior VP, Chief Manufacturing Officer, Johnson Wax.

individual presenters on the panel.   Each of them will
make a short presentation to tell you something about
their organization, what they have been accomplishing,
and how they have gone about it.   Then you will have a
chance to ask all of us questions.

I would like to discuss several aspects of building
excellence in manufacturing.   I will start by providing
definitions in three areas--the concept of strategy, what
it means to have a manufacturing strategy, and what it
means to compete with manufacturing.   Then I want to discuss where I think U.S. manufacturing tends to be today.

Next, I want to describe what is possible for manufacturing.   I will discuss a couple of examples, but the
speakers who follow me will really demonstrate what is
possible.

Then, I want to identify some common themes among excellent manufacturers.   I think you will detect these
when you hear the four panelists, but it is useful to get
those out on the table so that we can examine them and
respond to them.   Finally, we will look at how a firm can
get started, again using the panelists as examples.

DEFINITIONS

Let me proceed with a few definitions.   The first I
want to discuss, levels of strategy, is based on how most
organizations are structured.   Figure 9.1 follows the
typical divisionalized structure of many U.S. companies.
Oftentimes if you are a smaller company, those top two
levels are probably merged.   If you are a big business,
such as one of the *Fortune* 500 companies, you may have
another layer in between the business and the corporate
level, such as a group or sector level or something like
that.

The notion of this first concept is that there are
three very distinct types of strategy to be developed in
an organization: corporate level; business level; and
the functional level (such as manufacturing, sales,
marketing, or design engineering).

Let me give some very simple definitions of the key
tasks associated with each of these strategies.   This is
important because understanding how the manufacturing
function relates to the rest of the organization is part
of the requirement for being effective in manufacturing.
At the corporate level, there are really two things that
are important: the first is deciding which businesses
you want to be in and which you don't want to be in; the
second is acquiring and allocating resources.   The way
the organization is structured is that generally they put
somebody in charge of each key resource, such as the
financial resource. Corporate development would generally be responsible for the human resource and might
include new businesses.   Frequently you also see a

corporate-level technical resource function. In fact,
Paul Kehoe has responsibility at the corporate level for
the technological resources of Kellogg's.

Figure 9.1. Organizational Structure

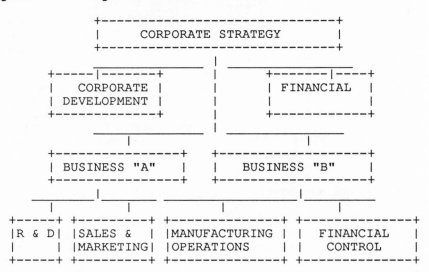

The second level is the business level. If you have
read Mike Porter's book, *Competitive Strategy*, you know
this is where he focuses much attention. It has to do
with how to compete as an individual business. For
example, if you are in Lynn Wilson's food products business, how are you going to get people to buy your products? What are you going to offer: higher quality,
lower cost, quicker delivery, more flexibility, and/or a
broader product line? These are some of the dimensions
on which you might choose to compete or obtain a competitive advantage.

At the business level, you also have to decide the
boundaries of your business or the segments to be served.
They can be geographical, by customer type, or by product.

It is important to do both of these together in the
business strategy, since you want to make sure you are
emphasizing something that the customers in your segment
care about. At times there are some tremendous mis-
matches between these. You may recall a few years ago
that Texas Instruments had this great vision of the home
computer--its segment boundary and the appropriate competitive advantage. Unfortunately, there was nobody in
the segment. After hammering away at it for many months,
they decided, "This isn't working. We didn't get the two
together. We better go back and rethink this." They

ended up writing off $700 million. What you normally
find is that the most successful companies are the ones
with the best match between these two things.
    The third level of strategy is the functional level.
That deals with how each of the functions--such as
manufacturing, marketing, and product development--
support what the business is trying to accomplish. So if
you are in the Wilson food products business, the manufacturing strategy addresses what manufacturing is doing
that makes a difference to the customer. Are they packaging the product a little better? Are they processing
it a little more efficiently, a little more precisely?
Those kinds of things are part of the functional strategy. In addition, since the functions are specialists,
you have to get them to work together. So in your functional strategy, you have to say something about "How do
your bring this all together?" The functions must interface and coordinate with each other.

COMPETITIVE ADVANTAGE

    The second definition I want to discuss is the notion
of competitive advantage. This is a concept that is
particularly important in today's world. There are six
generic characteristics that define a strong competitive
advantage. That is, if you looked at the companies that
are really successful over an extended period of time,
these are the characteristics they possess.
    First, they provide value to their customers. They do
things that are not done by their competitors that have
value to the customer. This means that they are externally driven. It is not what the company says that is
important, it is what the customer says that is important.
    The second is that your competitive advantage provides
leverage in the business. That is, a strong competitive
advantage makes a significant contribution to the success
of the business.
    Third, it is a unique match of your resources and op-
portunities, or it is a good fit. No two companies have
the same resources--the same people, the same equipment,
or the same distribution channel. Good strategy makes
the resources and opportunities fit together effectively.
    Fourth, it is durable and lasting. The short descrip-
tion would be that it is hard to copy. You want a
competitive advantage that other people cannot replicate
quickly.
    Fifth, you want it to be renewable. You want it to be
the basis for further improvement.
    Sixth, and a characteristic which often gets left out
of the equation, is that it needs to be compelling to the
organization. It must provide motivation and direction.
One of the reasons that quality as a strategy caught on

so quickly is because of this sixth point. Quality is
something that organizations and people endorse. Once
they know you are serious, they will go to great lengths
to accomplish it. That is why quality is a good element
of competitive advantage. There are other elements that
have that same characteristic.

The idea is that you want to have a competitive advantage that has all six of these characteristics. An
effective strategy is one that gives you all of these.
Strategy is thus a means by which you achieve distinctive
capabilities in areas that your customers care about. It
is based on getting better and better at what is really
important. It is not based on what you can buy, but on
what you can do.

One of the notions that has led many businesses astray
in the U.S., and I must say it leads many of my students
astray, is we confuse making money with a strong competitive advantage. I am a firm believer that if you have a
strong competitive advantage you will make money--if it
is an advantage that the customers care about and if you
provide capabilities that are hard to copy. But you can
make money lots of ways, and a lot of times people make
a lot of money, without a strong competitive advantage.

I remember talking with Bill Marriott one day as he
referred to a mutual acquaintance who had just made $430
million on a stock transaction in one day. He said, "You
know it's really discouraging to consider how many ham-
burgers I have to sell in my restaurants to make $430
million." I told him I thought he had a much stronger
competitive advantage than this other firm, and that it
would be much more lasting. I firmly believe that. So
this second definition of competitive advantage, and
pulling it together as a set of capabilities that make a
difference, is an essential element in competing in a
manufacturing business.

MANUFACTURING STRATEGY

The third definition is of the concept of a manufacturing strategy. This is a definition that some
colleagues and I have developed over the past few years.
The notion is that everybody has a manufacturing strategy
even if it is not articulated. It may be only implicit
in what you do. What it says is that a manufacturing
strategy is made up of all the decisions you make in
manufacturing. Here is a list of some of the categories
of these manufacturing decisions:

1. Capacity (Amount - Timing - Type)
2. Facilities (Size - Location - Focus)
3. Vertical Integration/Vendors (Direction - Extent -
    Balance)

4. Production   Technologies/Processes   (Equipment   -
    Automation - Linkage)
5. Work Force (Training - Pay - Security)
6. Production Planning/Materials Control (Centraliza-
    tion - Computerization - Decision Rules)
7. Quality Control/Product Assurance (Prevention -
    Testing - Problem Solving)
8. Product Development (Modification - Families -
    Projects)
9. Organization (Structure - Reporting Levels -
    Support Groups)

Every business makes decisions in all of these areas.
The idea of a manufacturing strategy is that you want a
consistent set of decisions that contribute to that
competitive advantage. Usually what makes a firm consistent, if it is a smaller company, is that it has had
someone who has headed up manufacturing for several years
and who has strong views on how the business ought to be
run. Every decision has his stamp on it and is generally
consistent.

There are other businesses where, because of the size
and the number of people involved in decision making,
some of the decisions may have a very clear pattern--such
as those covered by a corporate policy--but others may
have a random pattern.   The notion of a manufacturing
strategy is that it seeks to get this pattern of decisions to be consistent with what you are trying to
accomplish in business strategy.

THE REALITY CONCERNING U.S. MANUFACTURING

Using these definitions as background, we can now take
a look at what typically happens in U.S. manufacturing.
We need to understand not only what happens but why that
happens so that we can think about changing it.

Let me share some quotes with you that I gathered a
couple of years ago when I moved out to the West Coast.
I was all excited about manufacturing, but I found that
the West Coast was not. They were excited about lots of
things, but not operations. So I did a little survey,
asking, "What do people think of operations?" These are
some of the responses:

"R&D designs the product, marketing sells it, and
then manufacturing builds it."

"Everything is going well in manufacturing when you
don't hear complaints about it."

"In our top management meetings, marketing and R&D
dominate the discussion, with manufacturing being

'told' to produce it at the conclusion of the meeting."

"Manufacturing is supposed to make up engineering
delays and meet whatever promises are made by sales
and marketing."

The first one is kind of the euphemistic response. The
key word is "then." Manufacturing is at the end of the
line. I think the last quote is a much more accurate
description of how most manufacturing people feel. They
are supposed to make up engineering delays and meet whatever promises are made by sales and marketing. They play
catch-up. They are always fighting from a losing position. It is okay if design engineering slips on their
schedule, but manufacturing does not get to slip on
theirs. Or it is okay if marketing inadvertently says
they will ship an order and they know the plant is already fully loaded. Then manufacturing has to figure out
how to fix that, how to make it all happen. So the
typical view of manufacturing is that manufacturing is
the end of the line, an afterthought, playing catch-up.
    Let's look for a minute at why that tends to be the
case. I think there are four reasons. The first one is
that the manufacturing managers, and this is not meant to
be derogatory, do the impossible. That is, their role is
viewed as "can do/crisis management." The problem is
that they begin to thrive on it. Marketing comes in and
says to the manufacturing folks, "We need this," and the
first response is "That's impossible," and then 80 percent of the time they do it. Marketing gets reinforced
with the idea that our manufacturing folks can do the
impossible. So often you build in this kind of crisis
mentality in manufacturing.
    The second reason is that the organization's view of
manufacturing is that it is second rate. This comes
through in a couple of studies we have done recently. If
you look at pay rates in manufacturing and pay rates in
other functions, they tend to be systematically lower in
manufacturing. We looked at a very large semiconductor
firm, and the manufacturing personnel grade was three
levels lower than the equivalent engineering-grade level.
You are not going to get the best people into manufacturing, and those there are not going to feel like they are
equals, if in fact they are systematically lower in pay
and status than everyone else. One company decided that
this should be corrected and they raised 24 people from
manager level to director level because they said,
"You're right. These are all wrong. We have not considered these people as equals, and we should."
    The third reason is that I think top managers and their
staffs, particularly as the company gets larger and more
diversified, have a bias against operations solutions.
That is, they tend to opt for large projects with analyt-

ical solutions. The corporate office would rather worry
about spending big sums of money than working with 10,000
people in a quality improvement program. They are really
biased against incremental actions because what CEOs in
their right minds, sitting away from the plants, want to
have their success depend on all those people whose names
they do not know and whom they very seldom see.

A fourth and final reason is that I think in many
companies, major portions of manufacturing are treated as
swing factors. That is, if we have not quite made our
budget, it is manufacturing that has to ship more this
month. You might look at your own shipping schedule for
a month. Do you ship the same amount on day one of the
month as day five of the month, as day ten and day
thirty? If so, you are very uncommon. It is much more
common that half the volume of the month goes out in the
last five days. That's the idea of "Oh well, manufacturing, you know, they can catch up. They can make it all
work." After watching this happen in one company I was
studying, I said, "If I were a customer, the last thing
I would want, is to buy one of your products that was
shipped on the 30th of the month because I know right
behind it would come the field service engineers who are
going to finish the job on my site." That is the idea of
treating operations as a swing factor. We can make our
numbers, make it all work, and just kind of have manufacturing go up and down on a yo-yo string.

Now let me give you an example from one industry of
what happens when manufacturing is treated as second
class, as neutral, and as not very important. I'll start
with some older data based on a 1981 auto industry study.
This was when the U.S. auto industry was first waking up
to the fact they had a problem. The problem was that
Japan could make and deliver to the West Coast the same
car being made in Detroit, for $1,200 to $1,600 less than
the U.S. could. You can imagine the hand-wringing that
went on when they first started looking at this. This is
on a car that in those days wholesaled for $5,000 or
less. This is a big difference. When they looked at the
reason for the difference they found that half was in
labor costs and half in productivity. If you look
closely at those numbers, you find that the difference
stems from the fact that the U.S. industry said manufacturing was not important and the Japanese industry
said that manufacturing was important.

We hear a lot about Japanese labor being cheaper.
Figure 9.2 shows the labor cost differences. It is a
1981 study, using 1981 exchange rates. The first row
shows all manufacturing, which is the average full cost
to the company. That is, if a Japanese manufacturing
company hired an employee for a year, the cost including
bonuses, fringe benefits, and everything, would be
$22,000 to $26,000. In the U.S., on average, a company
paid exactly the same in that year. If you look at the

auto industry in Japan, they paid a 10 percent to 15 percent premium over all Japanese manufacturing. In the U.S., they paid a 100 percent premium. You cannot compete forever against people who pay significantly less than you do for the same work. (That is doubly true if you end up get-ting less from the workers than the Japanese were getting). That labor cost accounts for $600 to $800 of the cost difference per car.

Figure 9.2.   1981 Average Full Cost/Employee

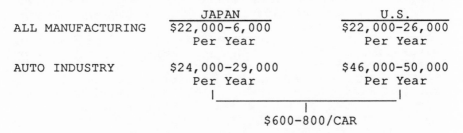

	JAPAN	U.S.
ALL MANUFACTURING	$22,000-6,000 Per Year	$22,000-26,000 Per Year
AUTO INDUSTRY	$24,000-29,000 Per Year	$46,000-50,000 Per Year

$600-800/CAR

   If you look at the productivity difference, that is where Detroit has had the most trouble. This is because the Japanese plants are no more automated than in the U.S. Probably the most automated plants in the world are a couple of plants in the U.S. and some plants in Germany. They are not the plants in Japan. So the productivity difference is not in Japanese automation. Instead it is in doing lots of little things in the factory. It is in the manufacturing management practices, the equipment uptime, inventory minimizations, closely linked processes such as just-in-time, and defect minimizations. That is where the other $600 to $800 comes from.
   Now the discouraging part is that Detroit has lots of money but still cannot correct the problem. If Detroit could close that gap by spending money, they would do it. In fact, GM has spent a lot of money. They have spent five billion dollars on Saturn. They have probably spent three-and-half billion dollars on Buick City. They have a number of other things going on that all involve a lot of money. Unfortunately if you compare the capital efficiency of the Japanese and U.S. auto industries the news is not good. If you look at replacement cost of capacity (what it would cost to build one vehicle of annual capacity), it turns out that in the United States it costs $4,700 per unit of capacity. In Japan it would cost a little less than half that amount. That is one of the reasons so many U.S. auto companies have gone to Japanese partners for their small cars. The U.S. is not competitive on variable costs nor on fixed costs. If you are in trouble on both, you are in serious trouble.

Let me give you an update on the auto industry using a
Ford study of 1984. Ford did their study based on a specific size car, the Escort or C car, as they call it.
They found that there was a $2,000 per unit cost differ-
ence. Again, half of that was in labor cost, and half in
productivity. The good news was that they felt that in
1984, the cost difference had leveled off, although it
had grown from that $1,200 to $1,600 up to $2,000. Ford
also did a study of prices. It turns out that the price
of an Escort-size car in Japan is $1,800 less than the
price in the U.S. You can imagine why the Japanese have
been selling so many cars in the U.S. Toyota makes over
80 percent of its profits in the U.S. selling probably 30
percent of its cars.

The U.S. is a very attractive market. One of the
things that I think we often forget about the U.S. market
is that for a company located in any country other than
the U.S., its most attractive market is the U.S. By contrast, U.S. producers see the most attractive market as
being our local or home market. Foreign producers see
the U.S. as more attractive than their home market because of its size and limited competition. So we end up
seeing the best of the world in our home territory. That
is certainly what has happened in the auto industry.

Now, the sad news for Ford is their five-year program
to reduce this $2,000 to zero by 1989. Let me just
outline its elements because it will give you tremendous
encouragement. The first one is, they have to get the
exchange rates between the yen and the dollar to shift by
one-third. You know Ford must be good because that has
happened. The second is, they have to make their labor
productivity increase by nine percent a year for five
years, and they have to make the Japanese auto industries
labor productivity increase by two percent a year. The
reverse had been true for 15 years. Since 1984 productivity is up to maybe three or four percent at Ford. It is
still at nine or ten percent in Japan. The third thing
is that they have to have the wage rates in the U.S. auto
industry stay unchanged for five years and the Japanese
wage rates go up ten percent a year. Obviously they
still have a long way to go. The limits on U.S. imports
have helped some by giving them a little breathing room
but it hasn't solved the basic problem.

THE POSSIBILITIES FOR MANUFACTURING

Do we have to have a manufacturing function that is
second class and reactive, or simply neutral at best?
Let's look at manufacturing's potential contribution.
Let me start by saying why I think the possibilities are
so attractive, particularly today. This is why my colleagues and I, as faculty members, have concentrated in
this area. The first reason is that manufacturing is

generally under-utilized as a competitive weapon. Most U.S. companies do not compete on the basis of manufacturing. They compete on the basis of product design, distribution, marketing, sales, and all other sorts of things. Therefore there is a tremendous opportunity.

The second reason is that manufacturing has the characteristics of a strong competitive advantage. If you build your advantage in part on manufacturing, it will be difficult for others to copy. The Japanese auto industry is one evidence of that. Another comes from a recent article in *The Wall Street Journal* about three German firms. Germany has higher wage rates than the U.S. and basically has permanent employment, paying 18 to 36 months severance pay for the lowest level employee discharged. Everything seems to be working against German firms, including a relatively small home market. Yet these German manufacturing firms are thriving. They are doing better than they have ever done because they have built an advantage that is hard to copy.

The third reason is that there are a number of new technologies and approaches that make manufacturing a very creative and dynamic field today. As an academic I have seen much more published on effective manufacturing in the last five years than the preceding fifty.

To understand what is required to realize manufacturing's full potential it is useful to consider the four stages of the continuum shown below: The stages represent different roles that manufacturing can take in a business.

STAGE 1 - INTERNALLY NEUTRAL
  "Minimize Manufacturing's Negative Impact"

STAGE 2 - EXTERNALLY NEUTRAL
  "Achieve Parity (Neutrality) With Competitors"

STAGE 3 - INTERNALLY SUPPORTIVE
  "Provide Credible Support to the Business Strategy"

STAGE 4 - EXTERNALLY SUPPORTIVE
  "Manufacturing as a Significant Contributor to the Competitive Advantage"

The first stage is internally neutral. In this stage, no news is good news. That is, if we don't hear from our manufacturing function we are happy, because the only time they call us is when they are late, when there is a quality problem, or when something has gone wrong. Stage one is when manufacturing keeps its head below the trench line so that it does not draw any fire, keeping itself from getting burned. Quite often this may work for the first year or two of a firm's existence but then it becomes concerned about the competitors making an end run

via manufacturing. This leads them to desire to keep up
with the industry, which brings us to stage two.
   Stage two is being externally neutral, or achieving
parity with competitors. In the case of the U.S. auto
industry, they defined their competitors as the other
U.S. auto companies and then institutionalized several
aspects of manufacturing practice, such as following the
same labor relations agreement, using the same manufacturing equipment, and visiting each other's plants to
make sure that one was not getting ahead of another.
They basically treated manufacturing as neutral. The
steel industry in the U.S. did the same thing, as did
tires. Lots of other industries in the U.S. have done
this, defining U.S. companies as the only competitors.
Stage two may work fine as long as everybody plays by the
same rules, but eventually someone looks at those rules
and decides that it seems silly to pay wage rates that
are double the U.S. average or to do some of these other
kinds of things. At that point someone comes in with a
different approach to manufacturing, and maybe the whole
business. In the steel industry it has been the mini-
mills--Nucor, Chaparral, and others--who came in and
said, "Look, there is another way to build a steel mill."
As competitive threats increase in stage two, companies
start thinking about stage three.
   Stage three is let us make manufacturing supportive to
our business strategy. It puts manufacturing in a
derived role. Manufacturing is not to define the business strategy, but rather to take the business strategy,
translate it into requirements for manufacturing, and
then deliver on those requirements. This is where I
think most of the business press is today. When they
talk about U.S. manufacturing and its challenges, they
are talking about going from stage two to stage three.
They are talking about manufacturing providing credible
support for the business.
   Stage four is something very different. It is the
notion of manufacturing making a difference to your
customers. This does not mean that customers have to
know everything that is going on in your manufacturing,
but it means there is something you do in manufacturing
such that if other things are equal, they would rather
buy your product. It also means that manufacturing works
as a part of the team. A requirement of stage four is
that you have to have all the functions working together
in stage four, not just manufacturing.
   The notion of all functions in stage four is one of a
team sport. Some say that the problem with Americans'
thinking of team sports is that we always think of a
relay race, especially in business. Americans think of
the product development function, marketing function,
manufacturing function, and the administrative function.
They think of this as a relay race where each one is a
specialist. The notion of coordination in a relay race

is handing the baton and then sitting down while someone
else runs the next leg of the race. A much better team
sport for the analogy is basketball, where all five
players are out on the court the whole time. Everybody
moves up and down the court with the ball, even if they
don't have the ball and are not shooting. That is the
notion of a team sport in business. I think that is the
right notion for stage four--all the functions working
together. It is not just someone deciding the business
strategy and telling manufacturing what to do.

Let me give you an example of a couple of firms that
have done this. The first one is the GE Dishwasher
Operation in Louisville, Kentucky. In Louisville, GE has
their major appliance headquarters, which consists of six
factories on one site. They formerly had about 15,000
employees, but now are down to about 9,000. The site has
a strong union contract. If one of the plants has a
workforce fluctuation, bumping occurs. Bumping means
that if you lay off somebody with any seniority in one
plant, they can replace somebody in another plant with
lower seniority on that site. Therefore, every time
Dishwasher hires five people, it would not necessarily
get five people off the street, but they would come out
of refrigerator, home laundry, and other areas. The
reverse is true when another plant has a workforce
fluctuation.

In spite of that tough environment, GE had the number
one position in dishwasher with what was largely a stage
two manufacturing operation. In 1979 Dishwasher management came to top management with a proposal to tune up
the product line a little bit and do some fixing of the
factory. They argued that for $18 million they could
maintain the position as industry leader with a third of
the market.

Somewhat to their surprise, they were asked some tough
questions when they came to top management. The sector
manager at that point was Jack Welch, now the CEO, who
has a reputation of asking rather tough questions. He
basically had them go back and do some more homework to
see if they could not improve GE's position. He said,
"If we are any good, why aren't we getting stronger?" He
didn't want just to keep the market position, anybody
could do that. His idea was to get stronger.

They went back and decided to see what they could do.
They came up with a proposal that required moving the
organization to stage four. This meant getting manufacturing, human resources, quality, marketing, and product
development involved. They came out with a new product
line called Perma-tuf C. It has a plastic tub and door,
made of a proprietary GE plastic.

Some of the results achieved in moving to stage four at
GE Dishwasher are shown in Figure 9.3.

Service calls are a big deal for GE, because up to one
quarter of GE's gross margin goes to service calls. In

fact, the performance of this dishwasher has been so
superior that they have had by far the lowest service
call rate of anybody. They came up with the idea that
what they needed was a TV ad. For example, they stated

Figure 9.3. Results of Stage Four Implementation

	1980/81A	1983A	1984E
Service Call Rate (Index)	100	75	67
Unit Cost Reduction (Index)	100	90	88
Number of Times Handled (Tub/Door)	27/27	1/3	
Inventory Turns	13	17	28
Reject Rates (Mech/Elec Test)	10%	4%	3%
Market Shares	33%	40%	
Productivity (Labor/Unit Index)	100	126	135

Other: 70 Percent Fewer Part Numbers, 20 Pounds Lighter,
Worker Attitudes (Positive 2X, Negative 0.5X)

that everyone had seen the lonely repairman on the Maytag
ad. Their ad would be a takeoff on that. It would have
two people sitting playing checkers, one a GE person and
the other a Maytag person. The telephone rings and since
GE stands for service, the GE guy dives for the telephone, picks it up, listens for a minute, and says to the
Maytag man, "It's for you." It turns out that the legal
folks didn't think that was a good ad.
    The real bottom line on this is the market share. In
1984, their market share was over 40 percent. Remember
this is not a market where Whirlpool and others roll over
and play dead. This business is an excellent demonstration of a stage four approach that integrates all the
functions. It wasn't just manufacturing, but all of the
functions.
    Let me discuss a second example, Chaparral Steel, a
business that is a lot like Nucor Steel. (Some of you
may know the Nucor Plant in Plymouth, Utah.) Chaparral
started as a mini-mill with a plant in Midlothian, Texas.
Midlothian is practically in the middle of nowhere. I
went to the plant on a research visit, and it turns out
that the closest place is the Holiday Inn 40 miles away.
They picked Midlothian because they said it has a strong
workforce, access to raw materials, and it is within 80
miles of Dallas.
    They built an organization where everybody is an equal
member. This organization has highly skilled labor,
group incentives, a president with three levels below
him, and hands-on managers. Everyone, including hourly
workers, goes out to visit competitors' plants. They
have a room where they have identified the ten best steel
plants in the world and they track their cost, quality,
etc. They have built much of their own technology,

including self-built casting lines, and are continually
enhancing them.   They also have advanced furnaces and
automated finishing.
   They started as a mini-mill, which is about 250,000
tons a year. They now are approaching 1 1/2 million tons
a year, the size of a small integrated mill.   They rep-
represent 1 1/2 percent of U.S. capacity in steelmaking.
They have the world's largest electric furnace, and they
have done phenomenal things.   The results are that they
are four times more productive than the U.S. integrated
mills, with sales of $320,000 per employee.   That is the
kind of number you might see for a pharmaceutical or
electronics company without much competition.   They are
very successful in a tough industry.   They have lower
costs than Japan and Korea.   In fact they have a very
simple rule which is: "If the shipping costs for one ton
of steel from Korea to the U.S. are more than our labor
costs, then we will be able to compete."   They now ship
steel from Midlothian, Texas, to 48 states.   They are
continually raising their quality, and now make bar stock
for forgings which is a high quality steel.

LESSONS FROM WORLD-CLASS MANUFACTURERS

   Let me draw some lessons from these by looking at some
common themes.   If you look across the companies, you
will find what I call four characteristics of the processes used by stage four companies like Chaparral Steel.
This describes how they run their firm.
   The first characteristic is that they have very clear
strategies, and people know these business strategies.
They also have articulated and consistently pursued
functional strategies.   There is not a lot of confusion
about what they are trying to accomplish.   All parts of
the organization understand what they are trying to
accomplish, whether it be the purchasing operations,
production planning department, development engineering,
or the product designers.   They agree on what they are
trying to do, and they are committed to accomplishing
that.
   Second, they have tremendous discipline and focus in
all aspects of the business.   They do not have knee-jerk
reactions to every competitor's move and everything that
comes down the pike.   They have thought about what they
want to do and how best to do it.
   Third, they integrate the functions. A good example of
this is new product development.   That is the area where
I am doing most of my research.   One of the things we
have found is that the time it takes from when you decide
you want a new product until the time that you are
delivering it to customers is a good indicator of the
degree of integration of your functions.   It is one of
those activities that involves not just production

designers, but also manufacturing, marketing, and everybody in between, to get that new product out the door. What we find is that the best companies do that very quickly. The faster they do it, the less it costs, and the better the products. They have really fine-tuned that capability.

Fourth, managers take the initiative and are leaders. They are not just managers who say, "Oh yes, I am taking care of the assets of the company in this part of the business." They are people who say, "I am building the assets of the company. I am doing something unique."

A study by one of my colleagues, who looked at managers who are pioneers and who really do bold new things, shows that they tend to have the following characteristics:

1. Strategic Thinkers
2. Systems View of the Business
3. Balanced Excellence
4. Dynamic Process Technology
5. Need For Order and Need for Learning
6. Consistency and Broad-Based Support
7. Intuition and Analysis

These managers are farsighted. A good test is to compare managers in a stage four company with those in a stage two company of the same industry. Review the job descriptions of their plant managers and there will be no comparison. Plant managers in a stage four company will see their position as involving working with marketing and product development, and interfacing with customers. They will define their job very broadly. On the other hand, in a stage two company, where manufacturing feels hard pressed in a kind of reactive mode, the plant manager will define the job as getting the product out the door by the end of the month: A much narrower definition.

Another characteristic particularly important is the need for balance. That is, these stage four managers understand that you must be able to justify what you are doing, but they also understand that sometimes you can't justify everything with the hard numbers. Sometimes you must say, "This is the right direction and we're going to move down this path." They then consistently pursue that.

A second of the four characteristic of these firms that I mentioned previously is that their resulting manufacturing strategy does a handful of things very well. It's very focused. I think one of the questions that's probably in the back of your minds is, "Gosh, if we're getting hammered in manufacturing, if we're not very competitive in manufacturing, don't we have to work on everything at once?" That is a basic question that I get asked by companies. The answer is that if you are bad at everything, yes. You'd better fix everything. Now you cannot fix everything at once so you pick the ones with the greatest leverage and start there. But eventually you have to fix everything. That will get you to stage three.

If you have parity and are competent in all areas of manufacturing, you can be a stage three company. If you want to be a stage four company, you have to focus on one or two things that you are going to be superior at, that you are going to do much better than anybody else. You don't find companies that have a twenty-year success record who are good at everything. They are certainly very competent at everything, but they are far superior at one or two things that are most important to the way they run their business, to their customers, and to their approach to the world. That is a characteristic of these stage four organizations. You have to build the organization and structure that supports it. Finally you have to keep enhancing those capabilities.

CAPABILITIES OF STAGE FOUR FIRMS

Let me tell you about some important capabilities in manufacturing. There are five of them that you tend to find in these stage four companies. One is that they develop the skills of their workers. Their workers are the most skilled in the industry.

The second is that they continually make incre-mental improvements in technology. That is, they get better and better at the technical side of their business. And they do things that the rest of us might say, "Well why are you doing that?" and they say, "Because it makes us stronger in terms of our capability."

The third is that they compete through quality. The winning companies really do have far superior quality to average companies.

Fourth, they get their workers involved over the long term, not just in the short term, but over the long term. They see worker involvement as a major part of what they are trying to accomplish.

Finally, they have internal manufacturing engineering for developing unique process technologies. That is, they actually make the machines run better than the average competitor. They may buy their machines from the same people, but they do something to them so that they get more out of them. They are the firms that tell the suppliers of equipment, "Here's what you ought to do on your next piece of equipment and especially on the next one you make for us." They are loaded with ideas on how to make the process run better.

This is a list of what they do not do:

1. Underinvest in capacity
2. Subcontract out core products and components

3. Train/require vendor to meet your requirements
4. Encourage vendor to expand
5. Pull business away in downturns or when vertical integration looks attractive
6. Hold up a price umbrella
7. Add product codes indiscriminately to match competitors
8. Subcontract new products

There is a lot of talk in the U.S. about, "Can we really fix manufacturing or is there another whole approach to this?" For example, can we subcontract manufacturing? The above list is one put together based on interviewing some very sophisticated companies who are worldwide competitors and this is their strategy in some of their businesses. The list says, we are unwilling to expand capacity as much as we need it, and so instead we are going to go to some subcontractors. We are going to ask others to provide some of this manufacturing investment. Then if we are a leading company, we have to train them to meet our standards, whether they are a Korean company, a Taiwanese company, or whoever. Then what we have to do is expand their capacity because we would like to give them more business. If the market turns down or if the business gets to a certain size, we decide to bring it in house and leave those suppliers without the business. Of course those suppliers will turn around and come into the business with their own products. They may come in with private label first and eventually end up taking a major chunk of the market with their own brand. We have certainly learned the names of a lot of Japanese firms who've done exactly this, and now we're starting to hear Korean names.

There was a recent *Business Week* article on the hollow corporation. I think this strategy leads to the hollow corporation. One of the top firms in the country has a phrase going through its management halls these days which says, "Own markets, not factories." The notion is that you can own a market, that is, you can control it competitively, without owning factories. I don't think there is much long-term evidence to support that. If you don't provide most of the value added to a marketplace, somebody else who does will take your place.

I was discussing the above strategy two weeks ago with a group of executives who were all from the same company. They were division-level folks and one of them pointed to a guy over on the other side of the room and said, "Bill, he's got your strategy. Right there." As we talked about it a little more, they added three more actions associated with this approach. One was holding up a price umbrella so that there is plenty of room for those suppliers to maneuver in. As you start feeling the competition from these former suppliers, the people you have put into the business, you start adding product

codes.   That is, you add more variety to get a broader
line.   And finally, you begin to subcontract new products, not just existing products.   It really is a recipe
for getting out of a business.

In conclusion, several firms are pursuing strategies to
achieve manufacturing's full potential.   Some have been
working at it for several years and have achieved outstanding results.   Their experiences are instructive in
learning how to get started and how to expand the
strengths of manufacturing.

11

Managing Change in Innovative Organizations

Rosabeth Moss Kanter

Yogi Berra said, "The future isn't what it used to be." That's a profound thought. We're in a world where change is so rampant that our views of a future unfolding logically from the past are no longer possible. And to continue the sports analogy, we're really playing very new games in business today. What it takes to win those new games is different from the skills and abilities and organizational systems that we used in the past.

MANAGING RESEMBLES *ALICE IN WONDERLAND* CROQUET

My favorite metaphor for the game being played in most businesses today is the croquet game in *Alice in Wonderland*. That's a game in which nothing remains stable for very long. Everything is changing around the players. That describes what it's like to manage today. Here is how it fits:

Alice tries to hit the ball, but the mallet she's using is a flamingo, and just as she's about to hit the ball, the flamingo lifts its head and looks in another direction. This is a good image for technology, for the tools we use. Just as people have mastered the technology, *it* faces in another direction, as the flamingo did, and there is something new to be learned.

Then Alice focuses on the ball, but the ball is a hedgehog, a living creature with a mind of its own, and just as she's about to hit the hedgehog, it unrolls, gets up, and moves to another part of the court. Just like our employees, our customers, our users, they're no longer lying down waiting for us to whack them. They too

have minds of their own. They will unroll, get up, and
move to another part of the court if they don't feel that
they're getting the treatment or the solution they need
fast enough. That's been true of employees for years:
growing rights-consciousness, career concerns, people
less loyal to their employers--accelerated of course in
this era of takeovers. It is true also of customers,
increasingly fickle, less "brand loyal," willing to shop
around and to demand quality service. It's certainly
true of the users of Management Information System
service, as anybody knows who tries to run a central
M.I.S. department and says to a user, "It's going to take
us a couple of years to get it all reprogrammed for you."
The user replies, "If that's the case, I'm going to do it
on my own P.C." The result is hundreds of different
systems, even in a small organization.

Finally, in that *Alice in Wonderland* croquet game, the
very structure of the game is in flux. Alice finally has
the mallet ready to hit the ball, but the wickets are the
card soldiers ordered around by the red queen, and every
once in a while, the red queen barks out another order to
have the wickets reposition themselves on the court. The
red queen could be the federal government barking out new
orders with respect to regulation or deregulation, and
suddenly industry structure changes or the company
reorganizes. There are other mini-red queens today: Sir
James Goldsmith, Carl Icahn, T. Boone Pickens, and other
corporate raiders who bark out orders to "Buy that
stock!" Suddenly there's the company restructuring again,
reorganizing to ward off the takeover because they have
been merged or acquired. The wickets increasingly are
even voluntarily repositioning themselves on the court,
as companies go into a nontraditional business and make
very unusual combinations that change the definition of
an industry--like Sears, a retailer, going into banking.

This is the new game: everything is in flux; technology
is changing at a rapid pace. Customers, employees, and
users are more demanding and willing to shop around, and
the whole structure of the industry is changing around
you. It's very difficult to win a game like that using
conventional methods. That's why innovation is so important. There's really only one way to win a game like
that--by using what I call the "Three F's," supported by
some "P's." The "Three F's" are the ability to be
focused, *fast*, and *flexible*, and the "P's" are a solid
base of partnerships. The winning organization befriends
all of those stakeholders in the business, with minds of
their own, who create change--the customers, the employees, the users, and even the regulators.

MASTERING CHANGE: THE NEED FOR FOCUS

I will discuss the environment that makes it possible for people to master change adequately, through using the "F's" and "P's"--the corporate culture to support winning the new game.

First, in order to win a game like *Alice in Wonderland* croquet it is important to be very *focused*, to concentrate on just a few things rather than many things. If you're trying to play a game where you have to watch things in constant motion, it's very difficult to be on top of all the things you need to do if you're distracted by too many demands, too many requirements, too many unrelated things. That's exactly why this idea of *focus* in corporate strategy is coming back into vogue. Twenty years ago the conventional wisdom on strategy was to diversify--keep many eggs in many baskets, have a large portfolio of many different businesses or activities, as a hedge against change. But conglomerates that did all sorts of unrelated things didn't necessarily make much money at it. The new wisdom says that too much diversification may not work, not in a rapidly changing environment. Business should be focused on just a few things that they know how to do very well, to build on competence and avoid being distracted by trying to keep up with too many things.

My Harvard colleague, Michael Porter, has new data that demonstrate this very well. He looked at the track record of thirty-three conglomerates in the *Fortune* 500 with respect to acquiring businesses that were unrelated to their core. Over a thirty-year period, those conglomerates divested an astonishing portion of all the things they bought. They eventually sold about 60 percent of all their unrelated acquisitions. It was interesting to look at who was high and who was low on that list. Lowest on the list were Johnson and Johnson and Procter and Gamble companies that have a very clear focus in their businesses. They bought the fewest unrelated businesses, and they tended to sell the fewest--under 15 percent of what they bought. At the high end were CBS and RCA that bought a lot of businesses and sold close to *90 percent* of all of them. Did this effort weaken the companies? Consider what's happened: RCA has disappeared into GE, and CBS has become part of the Tisch empire. On the corporate level, then, having just a few things that the business needs to do well makes a difference in winning a game where everything is changing and one cannot possibly master everything.

That's just as true inside a corporation. Successful departments cannot possibly do everything. They have a few clear strategic focuses, making it clear that "*this* is what we're going to concentrate on, and we'll keep those few goals in mind regardless of that flux around us."

MASTERING CHANGE: THE NEED TO MOVE FAST

But, of course, focus does not mean inflexibility. Organizations also need to change. So the second key to winning the game of *Alice in Wonderland* croquet is the ability to move very fast in today's environment. Organizations benefit from the "first mover" advantage: getting in there first before others do, to master an environment that's constantly changing--or you're always playing catchup rather than defining the terms of the game. The companies that are successful in this new environment are companies that focus on innovation, on being ahead of the competition, on using all of their skills to provide a new source of strategic advantage. Indeed, there are a number of ways in which information technology is now being used by companies to get that first mover advantage, to be in there fast and first, to nail down the customer, and to get the right location in a retail organization. Information technology is now a key.

One of the companies that is noteworthy in this respect is American Airlines. American Airlines used information technology to get a clear first mover advantage, the Sabre System which they placed in travel agencies to help them make reservations by computer: but naturally, American flights appeared first. American gained what can be called a "temporary monopoly," because they used information to be the first to give a service to their customers. (Later, this advantage was reduced by legal action.) American has been first in a number of areas, including frequent flyer programs.

By being first, you gain the opportunity to get in there, nail down the customer before the competition can, and gain the experience that helps you keep improving.

In contrast, consider Control Data, a much-admired company, but also a company that a long time ago bet on the fact that the mainframe computer was here to stay forever--not a bet that anybody would want to take today.   In essence, we need organizations that do think ahead and yet are always looking for the shorter-term, incremental competitive advantages. When a Sabre System is thrown out as a temporary monopoly, and you have to give just as much access to other airlines to get reservations on their flight, you've got another idea that you're ready to go with. That's what it takes to win the game today.

In order to do that, those organizations that are successful are making sure that there is a constant stream of innovative ideas coming up from their organization. They're trying to make everyone an innovator and finding ways to develop and build innovations out of the ideas coming up from the organization. I see strong companies developing a variety of systems and programs to stimulate ideas up from the ranks and even put people in charge of projects to run their ideas.

AT&T's new venture program shows how much potential is there to be tapped in an organization. Several years ago, just before the 1984 divestiture of local telephone companies, AT&T quietly put in place a program by which they would seek employee ideas. They would screen the ideas and choose a few that they would give big funding to for those employees to then run their own projects and, in some cases, run new business ventures in the middle of AT&T. They expected to fund a dozen or so projects, out of maybe fifty to one hundred ideas that would be submitted. They didn't give the program publicity; they just wanted to try it first. So without publicity and with the expectation that maybe there would be fifty or one hundred of these ideas for new businesses, extensions of existing technology, or other innovations submitted, they began the program. Over *2,500 ideas* were submitted in the first year. Similarly, Eastman Kodak has an Office of Innovation and a whole process for stimulating and encouraging people at every level to be thinking a little bit ahead. Innovation facilitators in every facility help people define a strategy for how they're going to take their ideas further. Those ideas that look like big ideas can get submitted to a venture board and get funding to set up a project or a line of business, a separate subsidiary of Eastman Kodak. Clearly, those companies that want to move fast and gain the advantage of innovation in order to win the new game are getting the ideas flowing and in operation everywhere.

In order to move fast, one also needs an organization in which information is shared broadly across all levels and across all ranks so that people know how to reorient and reposition quickly. In that sense, the M.I.S. function is not only one that needs innovation itself, but it also can be the foundation for innovation throughout the organization, because those organizations that seem best able to take advantage of innovation and move fast are also those organizations with open communication--without barriers or restrictions to the flow of information.

Open communication is expressed in all sorts of ways. One is in terms of the amount of data that is accessible to everybody at every level. For years I've wanted to rename the Management Information Systems Operation the *Employee* Information Systems Operation. Why only managers? In this new game, we're asking everybody to be able to reorient as soon as they see a new opportunity or learn something new or do something differently. That information has to get down the ranks to every level. They need the data as well.

In one leading company, several facilities are run by employee teams who manage that factory as though it were their own business. There is one job classification, and everybody's on the team, virtually without managers. It's a highly advanced system. In factories that are run

on that model, costs are half of what they are in a
conventional factory, quality is higher, and flexibility,
which I will consider shortly, is also much higher. The
company is sending technicians from those factories
around the country to train others in how to incorporate
new technology. One of the engines that drives that
system is information. Personal computers down at the
plant level enable everybody who works on a product to
find out exactly what's happening to that product, including its fate in the marketplace. The manufacturing
executives realized that unless production people can
know on a daily basis and have good data to look at, how
can they make sound decisions about what to purchase, how
much to produce?

Decisions increasingly are being decentralized in leading companies. And the thing that makes it work is information and communication. You can only give that responsibility to employee teams at the lowest level if
they've got the information behind it to make intelligent
decisions. Increasingly, the *information* is going to be
decentralized even if the information *system* isn't. Some
high innovation companies even take that communication
principle further; they make sure that nobody is restricted from finding out anything they need to know.
(Clearly there are some circumstances in which some
information has to be kept proprietary; but fewer and
fewer of those situations exist in major corporations.)

In a financial services company, one of the most innovative in the United States as leaders of a whole new
financial services industry, managers simply don't buy
the fact that if you have the wrong status you can't find
out certain kinds of things. They don't have fixed formal titles, they don't have status barriers, and they
don't even have written organization charts. All of
those traditional things are considered a barrier to
getting the right information into the hands of the right
people. Similarly, a leading bank, a bank that has bet
on information technology as one of its competitive advantages, was seriously considering eliminating all
titles. Now titles are sacred cows in a bank, where
"vice presidents" of various statuses abound. Instead,
they wanted to have the right people communicating,
getting information into the hands of the people who are
in the best position to make a decision. They wanted to
eliminate status barriers because one of the purposes of
status is that higher-level people get to know things
that lower-level people don't know. Power games that
managers play at higher levels of organizations are often
games that restrict information.

One telephone company that scored low in innovation, in
my research for *The Change Masters*, had lack of communication as a major barrier to innovation. The field
people would accuse headquarters of withholding certain
kinds of data. In retaliation, they would go out and

collect the data so that they could withhold it from
headquarters.

Communication is going to be one of the major ways that
organizations manage to move fast, take advantage of opportunities, redirect, reorient, and be innovative. In
turn, this requires a foundation of commitment. You
can't get people to move fast unless they're already
committed to the goals and to the organization, and unless they already feel a part of this organization.
Otherwise, they'll foot-drag, resist, find a million
reasons not to act on the new opportunity, not to do
anything. But if you've developed a system in which
people are committed to the leadership, believe in them,
trust each other, know that they've been involved in the
past and know that their needs are taken into account,
then when the time comes to direct change, they'll move.
A foundation of commitment in the organization to goals,
to the fact that my needs are being taken into account,
that I have been listened to, makes it possible to do all
these other things that allow organizations to move fast.

"Instant success takes time." All the things that
allow an organization to move very quickly are things
that in fact they've been preparing for years by laying
a foundation of trust, relationship, knowledge, and
information. This well-built foundation allows an organization to do something that becomes an "instant"
overnight hit.

MASTERING CHANGE: THE NEED FOR FLEXIBILITY

The third "F" that it takes to be effective in *Alice in
Wonderland* croquet is *flexibility*. Though focused on
just a few goals, organizations also need the flexibility
to keep bending and redirecting to take advantage of the
new opportunities that are arising in an environment of
constant change, where technology provides an opportunity
a minute.

In order to get that kind of flexibility, a company
needs an employee body that's broadly skilled and whose
assignments are broad rather than narrow. This is a real
change in the conventional wisdom about how to manage.
The conventional wisdom used to argue for narrow specialists, people who have a narrow job in which they know how
to do one thing that they do over and over again, to get
efficiencies of repetition. In this new environment, any
efficiencies of repetition are going to be wiped out by
the fact that there's going to be change, and people have
to do something new and different. In order to ready
people for change, for the fact that it's not going to be
the same tomorrow as yesterday, organizations need people
who think more broadly, who have more than one skill, who
have assignments that have been focusing on getting
results rather than just carrying out procedures mechani-

cally and routinely. In some high technology firms, a
common joke is that the typical job description for a
manager is "do the right thing." How much broader could
one get than that?

One of the problems that some telephone companies are
having as they try to reorient to the new competitive
marketplace is that for years people were measured on
working according to the rules, not asking too many
questions. Sometimes people didn't even know why they
were doing the things they were supposed to be doing.
Now a more broadly skilled group of people in touch with
more fields and disciplines, who see the big picture, are
going to be the success drivers for the organization in
the future.

In one case, the typical American way of doing things,
the narrow specialized job, bumped up against another
country's system. General Motors has a joint venture
with Toyota on the West Coast, New United Motors Manufacturing, Inc. One of the concessions GM had to get from
the union in order to do this had to do with a number of
job classifications. When GM ran this plant, there were
thirty-three separate classifications; Toyota for a similar plant had three. Consider the implications of
thirty-three different jobs versus *three* different jobs.
Toyota had people who thought more broadly, knew more
things to do, and therefore were more flexible when it
came time to change.

Educating everybody more broadly is one of the best
hedges against a game like *Alice in Wonderland* croquet.
So is teamwork across areas. If you need to redeploy,
develop a new project, take advantage of the new technology that's available, or reposition the company in the
marketplace, you need people from many different disciplines working together to do that. One of the key lessons about innovations is that innovation always takes
teamwork from more than one area. Unless it is very
narrowly focused on the concerns of only one function,
then innovation always cuts across areas and requires
more people to cooperate. Successful companies need an
organization structure that's oriented toward people
working across areas, in which people are comfortable
with project teams; care about ultimate results, rather
than just exercising their professional skills; and know
how to operate as task forces across areas.

One barrier to innovation is a myth I call "cowboy
management." Consider some images used in American
business: performance shoot-outs (as though it's high
noon at the management OK Corral); development of de-
liberate in-house competitions in which people slug it
out; writers who make a virtue of "ready, fire, aim" as
a guide to action; bootlegging the organization's resources to do a project; and wishing that headquarters
back East would go away. These ideas do get some temporary energy in the organization, but they also get

people focused on wiping out the competition in the next department rather than getting the overall results the company needs.

Setting up excessive competitions, where people focus on killing off other departments and areas to improve their own position rather than collaborating is a very bad way to succeed in *Alice in Wonderland* croquet. And one of the problems with performance shoot-outs are that somebody you need later may die of the wounds. Collaboration and teamwork is better strategy in organizations today than excessive competition, hostility across areas, turf-mindedness, and an attitude that we've got to protect our own rather than collaborating. Even if collaborating means departments may occasionally lose territory because they're part of a bigger entity, that's the attitude organizations have to encourage.

MASTERING CHANGE: THE NEED FOR PARTNER ORIENTATION

Behind all of the "3 F's" are the "P's" of *partnerships*. No one can win *Alice in Wonderland* croquet anymore by treating customers as adversaries, by treating employees as numbers, by treating suppliers as temporary conveniences. The best strategy is to befriend all the groups in the environment on whom the company depends, so that the whole network gains advantages together.

The new management wisdom for supplier-customer relationships is partnership-oriented wisdom. That's what American Hospital Supply was building when it put terminals in hospitals so customers could order supplies more easily from American Hospital Supply. That was a partnership with customers that involved giving them something that will help them do their business better while helping AHS do its business better. Security Pacific Bank could put terminals in car dealerships for processing loan applications instantly because of a close working relationship with those customers. A partnership means that customers or suppliers are willing to invest in the same kind of technology that you have.

Companies also cannot succeed without partnerships with employees who are willing to bend or even make concessions. Pacific Telesis has a remarkable labor-management partnership, which they call a business partnership with their principal union. The company realized that the only way that it was going to be able to put in a new technology was if the union worked with them on doing it, because it would cost jobs. They reasoned that if they worked as partners in planning the future, they could simultaneously provide job security and move on new technology. This would help them win the new game.

Manufacturers, especially, need partnerships with suppliers. It is impossible to take advantage of systems like just-in-time inventory unless suppliers feel there's

a longer-term commitment making investment in the technology worthwhile. That's what it's going to take to
make sure we have a competitive system so that we can
order across organizational boundaries. In fact, not
only do we all have to become partnership-oriented in our
attitude as a manager or an entrepreneur, but I think,
increasingly, as many of you who work in M.I.S. areas
already know, much of the technological development is
going to be developed across organizational boundaries.
It's going to be developed in joint development projects
with your customers or joint development projects with
your suppliers or with your users, rather than simply the
things we need in isolation. So those are the things I
think that it takes to win the new game.

NEED FOR INTEGRATIVE ORGANIZATIONS VS SEGMENTALISM

I have discussed the importance of "Three F's and P's."
They require a particular corporate environment. Stimulating innovation and entrepreneurship is a matter of
having an organization that I call *integrative*. It's an
organization where people pull together rather than
apart, where there might be some overlap across areas;
joint projects and joint development activities exist;
users and the central group are linked closely; communication and information knit everything together; and
shared goals and a focus for the business create unanimity of purpose.

The opposite of this kind of environment that destroys
innovation and change, I refer to as *segmentalism*. The
organization divides into pieces, into segments, and in-
structs every piece to operate totally independently,
governed instead by performance shoot-outs, hostility,
and rivalry. People are highly specialized just in one
segment, so they never get out and find out what's happening in the broader environment. Everybody focuses on
their territory only, without thinking about the wider
needs of the organization.

Segmentalism creates a totally rigid, inflexible organization. It is impossible to take advantage of a new
opportunity or mobilize that organization to do anything
differently. People are rigid; they protect their territory; they're inflexible; and they're narrow in their
focus.

RULES FOR STIFLING INNOVATION

This picture unfortunately describes too many organizations in America today. They operate as though
they prefer mediocrity and stagnation, as though they
were guided by a set of rules for remaining second-rate.
I call them the *rules for stifling innovation*.

First, be suspicious of any new idea from below because it's new and because it's from below. After all, if the idea were any good, we at the top would have thought of it already.

Second, insist that people who need your approval to act go through many other levels of the organization first. That way you can kill them off or discourage them. Or, if you're lucky, by the time they get back to you, you might be in a different job anyway.

Third, express criticism frequently, withhold praise, and instill job insecurity, because that keeps people on their toes. How else would they know you have standards? The "macho" school of management holds that people do their best work when they're terrified. Of course, it's the opposite of the foundation of teamwork and commitment and recognition of achievements that goes on in high innovation companies.

Fourth, decide to change policies in secret and reorganize unexpectedly and often. Because if you don't want innovation and change, you don't want people taking initiative. You want to keep them so off balance that they'll never be able to take initiative. They won't know what's going on; they'll be in the dark all the time.

Fifth, be control conscious. Count everything that can be counted; do it as often as possible. Because if you don't want innovation and change, you want things managed so tightly that you can never take advantage of new opportunities. There's no slack, there's no extra time to pursue anything new. People are too busy doing the things that are already being measured.

Finally, if you don't want innovation and change, you need attitudes that say that we already know everything that is important to know about this business. We've been doing it for a long time; why don't we just keep on doing what we've always done? This is not the right attitude if you're playing *Alice in Wonderland* croquet.

CONCLUSION

Companies that want innovation should reverse these rules: be more receptive to new ideas, get those idea flows going. Encourage faster approval, less red tape. Offer more praise and recognition for people, their talent, and achievements. Make sure there are resources that people can use to experiment. Provide advance warning of new plans, spread information so that everybody knows what's going on. Finally, foster the attitude that we're always learning, that we can learn from any level.

All this helps convert change from a threat to change as an opportunity. Change is always a threat when it's done *to* me, imposed *on* me, they're making me do it. But it's an opportunity if it's *my* chance to be a hero, if it's *my* chance to help us win the game by doing something a little bit innovative.

The real issue in managing change in an innovative organization is to create more opportunity for people themselves to take charge of change.

12

Challenge to America's Industrial Leadership

Armand V. Feigenbaum

It is a very great pleasure for me to join with you in this opening plenary session of this Thirteenth Annual Productivity Seminar. I have come to know of the importance of what you have been doing in the Partners Program at the College of Business in USU, and I have great respect for what you have accomplished.

BASIC CONVICTIONS

What I think brings all of us together this morning is our sharing of three basic convictions each of which I want to spend a few moments on: The first is that quality has become crucial to the industrial strength of the United States. Let me try to quantify this. Our data on customer preferences for the year 1987 indicate that eight out of ten buyers now make quality equal to or more important than price in their purchase decisions. Only three to four customers out of ten thought this way and bought this way in the year 1979. This 100-percent increase in buyer emphasis on quality in less than a decade is perhaps the most rapidly exploding marketplace trend in American business history.

The second conviction is that while American industry has made substantial quality gains, accomplishing the full job of international quality leadership still is a long way ahead. I spend a great deal of my time offshore in connection with our General Systems Company businesses, and in the countries which are America's major trading partners, I find that the prevailing judgment is that

a strong foreign manufacturer with a quality strategy
can't help but succeed in the U.S. market today--whether
the dollar goes up or down. What's behind this are three
widely held beliefs:

1. Some American companies have already given quality
    their best shot and haven't pulled it off.
2. Those who have won't stick with it when the quick
    fixes don't get spectacular results.
3. American trade policy is like a log floating down
    a river on which are thousands of ants each of whom
    thinks it's steering--a policy whose ambiguity
    minimizes long-term foreign concern about any
    genuine barriers to American market entry.

The Commerce Department estimates that nearly three-
quarters of all the products manufactured in the United
States are now targets for strong import competition; our
own studies as we work throughout the world indicate that
nearly all of American non-defense manufactured products
will have import vulnerability by the early part of the
decade of the 1990s. This means that to protect its
position in the U.S. market, an American company must be
able to design, build, and sell its major domestic product lines today with the potential also for supremacy in
the international marketplace--even though there isn't
yet much import competition or interest in exporting.
Murphy's Law, internationalized, says that if an American
company can get foreign competition today, it will get
it. Operating in international quality leadership terms
is the only way for a business to grow with Murphy rather
than be eroded by him.

The acceleration of quality improvement is equally
important in American service operations as in products.
This leads to the third conviction, which is that accelerating our rate of quality improvement is the single
most important competitive task facing all of us.   In
today's American market, when a customer is satisfied
with quality he tells eight people; when he's dissatisfied, he tells 22. That is the hard arithmetic of quality's effect on sales growth in the American marketplace.
Moreover, quality leadership can give companies a competitive advantage of five-cents-on-the-dollar, as much as
ten cents in some cases. For many companies, this can be
the best opportunity for improved profitability and return on investment, and one that our experience shows
will pay off early, with a sustained and growing return.

The acceleration of quality improvement is equally
important in American service operations as in products.
In some service processes, only one work product out of
ten goes through error-free. While much of the widely
publicized increase in service employment has come about
through market growth, some has been created by these
do-the-job-over quality problems. They are a principal
reason for the minimal productivity increase in services.

While it is not yet widely apparent, without significant quality improvement, some American service operations have the same vulnerability to foreign competition that affected manufacturing long ago. Our experience in the quality processes of financial service companies is an example. A telecommunications satellite is indifferent whether service operations of a financial institution or of a data-processing organization are located in Frankfurt, Tokyo, London, Paris, or New York so long as the operations are quality-effective. The industry is now moving toward this kind of quality-driven consolidation.

In my judgment, we have great capacity for achieving these necessary quality results in the United States. Several American industries continue to set the world quality leadership example--consumer--household durables, electrical equipment, diesel engines, aircraft, computer electronics, and agricultural equipment are just a few in my experience. Moreover, the total quality control improvement rate we've been able to achieve recently for some pace-setting American products has been much better than with some comparable foreign products.

WEAKNESS IN THE U.S QUALITY PROGRAM

Why then have so many American products been overwhelmed by foreign competitors? And why does there still seem to be so little serious attention to quality in the high profile programs and statements on America's competitiveness coming from both Washington and the top business community--even though clearly our challenge is to recognize that America's industrial strength is dependent on America's quality competitiveness? The reason is, sadly, that in some companies quality programs are still widely thought of as a sugar pill to help the organization swallow the really important improvement ingredients of technology and automation and financial restructuring. This sugar pill mixes fireworks displays of top management quality interest together with some corrective action projects, but without any managerial foundations that get at improving the basic business work processes which are really important to quality leadership.

In these companies, there can be a dozen different quality problem-solving systems, none of which is fully effective because they are inevitably blocked at some body's department wall. So additional task forces are formed to create still more quality-improvement schemes. Veteran employees are likely to view them as just more quality crusades that will die and be buried without autopsy like the seven or eight other crusades they have already seen come and go. Because there's no ingrained commitment to quality, 30 percent of all resolved customer complaints leave a dissatisfied customer. It's too

high a cost for producer, merchant, and buyer to pay--a
cost that continues to mount be cause of the network of
troubleshooters required to keep the constant stream of
buyer corrective actions on some sort of track.

LEVERAGE THROUGH QUALITY/AUTOMATION

There is a staggering difference between this and the
effective actions of the companies who are the quality
leaders I have mentioned. The approach of these companies is that quality is today's most powerful corporate
leverage point for achieving both customer satisfaction
and lower costs. Automation was once thought to give
that leverage but current experience shows that without
a quality foundation, automation merely generates more
bad products quicker than before.

There is a fundamental managerial difference between
basing quality results on robots as compared with basing
it on people-based organization-wide programs.   This
difference recognizes that the continually upward-moving
buyer demand for quality is the result of fundamental
economic changes in American businesses and basic social
changes in American homes.

The automobile industry is a major example of the vol-
atility of these quality trends. It is still not too
widely known that in the late 1970s, for example, several
hundred thousand Japanese cars were sitting in unsold
inventory on American docks when the Iranian oil crisis
and the consumer price explosion simultaneously hit the
market. Suddenly, the Japanese inventory evaporated and
the Japanese were rewarded for persisting in their quality strategy.

In 1987, the situation has once again changed. Recent
data showed a very large inventory of unsold Japanese
cars in the United States, up significantly from the
previous year. American car buyers who had been partial
exclusively to Japanese products are now actively shop-
ping for American cars again. This can be due as much to
the renewed emphasis on quality of American manufacturers
as to the higher prices of the Japanese products generated by the strong yen.

Future corporate results in this automobile market will
almost certainly continue to be governed by these trends
in quality. The recognized objective for some car manufacturers is that by the early 1990s, companies must
offer essentially perfect automobiles with the features
that buyers really want, produced at one-third less cost.
It is clear that those companies which meet this target--
whether American, Japanese, European, or Korean--will be
the ones to survive, perhaps even succeed, in the U.S.
car market. What is equally clear is that a major
acceleration in the existing quality-improvement rate of

some automobile and automobile supply companies is
required if they are to achieve this.

The automobile industry is just an example of the
changes that are sweeping across almost all other American markets. Summarizing these changes very simply, the
lifestyles of consumers and the work processes of companies now depend almost completely upon the reliable,
predictable operation of products and services with
little tolerance for the time and cost of any failures--
something very different from the past.

SEVEN BENCH MARKS FOR BUILDING COMPANY-WIDE PROGRAM

This is today's demand on the washer and dryer of a
large young family every Monday morning; on the new car
that serves as the family bus 14 hours a day, seven days
a week; on the telecommunications network that's a company's only data source; and, indeed, on the weapon system on which the life of a young airman, sailor, or sol-
dier may depend. The no-easy-backup products and services
we buy today explain quality's major influence on sales
and market share. They also explain why the old "we'll
always fix it for you" policy of many companies, while
honorable and important, is a horse-and-buggy, after-
sales service approach--a failure-driven policy instead
of one reflecting quality leadership. Quality is, in its
essence, a way of managing an organization today, a way
of managing that goes way beyond knowing all the right
buzzwords. It means knowing how to lead company-wide
programs which build on seven basic bench marks:

1. That quality is not a technical function nor
   department but instead a systemic process that
   extends throughout the company.
2. That quality must be organized to recognize that
   while it is everybody's job in the company, it will
   become nobody's job unless this company quality
   process is correctly structured to support both the
   quality work of individuals as well as the quality
   teamwork among departments. This is indeed the
   least well understood and least well implemented of
   the seven characteristics.
3. That the quality improvement emphasis must take
   place in marketing, in development and engineering, in manufacturing, and particularly in ser-
   vices--not merely in production for the factory
   workers only.
4. That quality must be perceived in this process to
   be what the buyer wants and needs to satisfy his
   requirements for use--not what the company needs to
   satisfy its requirements for marketing and production efficiency.

5. That modern quality improvement requires the application of new technology, ranging from quality design techniques to computer-aided quality management measurement and control, and is not a matter of periodic quality fireworks displays nor of dusting off a few traditional quality control techniques.

6. That widespread quality improvement is achieved only through help and participation from all the men and women in the company--not from just a few specialists.

7. That all of this comes about when the company has established a clear, customer-oriented quality management system throughout the organization, one that people understand, believe in, and want to be part of.

This is Total Quality Control for the 1990s as we practice it in the General Systems Company in our projects with companies in Europe and the world over, building upon the 35 years of application experience we have had throughout the world since we first originated what is sometimes called TQC.

Implementing this doesn't depend on geography or national cultural difference because quality has no nationality. What makes this work is a clear customer-oriented management process and work process throughout the organization--one that people understand, believe in, and are a part of.

COMPANY READINESS FOR STRUCTURING QUALITY PROGRAMS

What is the readiness among companies to succeed in structuring this genuine total quality improvement? There is a very wide variation.

While there are many fine examples of American companies with excellent quality programs, the quality programs of some other companies have traveled at best only 15 to 20 percent of the hard road to meeting the quality demands of today. In these companies, quality is still not a boardroom interest, still is thought of as primarily a technical job operating at secondary levels of organization. Quality is still not a mainline activity in development and engineering, where innovation is thought of as the basic drumbeat for technology, and quality work a much less challenging task. Nor is quality a mainline activity in the finance communities of these companies--even though accounting miscodes and billing mistakes can create more customer ill will than product returns. Nor is it mainline in marketing--where quality is thought of as what you have to sell to the customer even though the engineers and production people may not be doing it right. In these companies, high quality is still thought of as gold-plating requiring higher cost--even though experience clearly shows that higher quality means lower cost; that quality and cost are partners, not adversaries; a sum, not a difference.

QUALITY SYSTEMS REQUIRE MANAGEMENT FOCUS ON THREE AREAS

It takes relentlessly consistent and disciplined management leadership and methodology to convert all of this to a company quality program that matches the competitive strength of today's strongly quality-leveraged companies. We know from our General Systems experience in installing such total quality systems throughout the world that its implementation incorporates three primary areas into the practice of modern company management.

The first of these is to directly improve the quality process itself. To be successful in achieving quality leadership today, management must personally address the quality process or system in its own organization--to identify how it is presently operating, to determine the specific needs for strengthening its effectiveness on the hard road to quality excellence, and to lead in systematically accomplishing and maintaining these improvements.

This quality excellence-driven approach is a fundamentally different managerial task than the widely used approach that might be described as quality failure-driven, which merely sets in motion--within the existing and traditional quality process, strong or weak--one project after another to fix up quality problems, sometimes within some kind of overall improvement program which the organization recognizes is temporary. The hope here has been that, as a byproduct of their necessary purpose of providing specific quality corrective actions, these individual quality projects will also somehow bring about the repair and modernization of the quality process itself. Experience clearly shows that this does not succeed. The reason is that an inadequate quality process is likely ultimately to reject or to limit the application of the statistical controls and customer measurements and vendor cooperation steps initiated by the projects, which gradually die and are buried without autopsy. This is why quality reviews and statistics and other necessary techniques do not sustain themselves nor take permanent root in some companies and seem to require continual renewal and re-emphasis. The achievement of quality excellence is thus a far more demanding managerial task than emphasis only on some individual projects. The history of barriers between departments and the concept of quality as control and policing rather than prevention and self-steering remain deep and strong in many organizations, and are changed only by direct rather than indirect management time, attention, and leadership in the institutionalizing of a strong, modern, and fully oriented quality achievement process throughout sales, production, and technology in the company.

The second primary area of managerial attention is to make quality improvement a basic and continuing habit that is relentlessly pursued within the organization. The managerial purpose is to ingrain into the day-by-day detailed work of the company the actions which recognize that quality is a rapidly upward-moving target in today's market and that quality programs must be organized to recognize this. Traditional quality programs have instead been directed to the objective of establishing what was thought to be the single right quality level for a part and product and then directing all effort to meeting and maintaining that level--with improvements in the level only periodically examined. The management practice today, in contrast, must be oriented to the approach that when this so-called "right" quality level has been attained, progressive improvement must continue to more and more upgraded quality levels for the appropriate parts and materials as a way of life in the operating practice throughout the organization because this is what customers will demand and what international competition will call for.

For example, the more successful a product becomes, the higher the quality levels it must be programmed to achieve if it is to grow profitable. A 1-percent failure rate for a major integrated circuit-based consumer product with a production rate of 50,000 units a year places 500 failing units in the hands of customers. A ten-fold sales and production increase to 500,000 units with the same 1-percent failure rate places 5,000 failing units in customer's hands. This is equivalent, in the actual number of dissatisfied buyers, to what would have been the highly unacceptable failure rate of 10 percent at the earlier production rate.

Without a strong quality-improvement program, the company's success in achieving this higher volume could be a time bomb. The products that represent a high risk of customer dissatisfaction are not necessarily those with high failure rate percentages but instead those with high exposure to a large total number of dissatisfied customers. That's why, more than ever, the only way to compete with quality is with more quality.

The third primary managerial area is to establish the principle that quality and cost are complementary, not conflicting, objectives in today's company management decision-making. For many years, the managements of some companies routinely received recommendations from members of their organization that a choice had to be made between quality and cost--the so-called trade-off decision--because better quality inevitably would somehow cost more and would make production more difficult. Experience throughout the world has shown that this

simply is not true.   The reason is that good quality
fundamentally leads to good resource utilization--of the
work force, equipment, and materials--and consequently
means good productivity and very low quality costs in the
organization. Modern management must make clear throughout the company that what is expected is both quality and
cost--not one to the detriment of the other. The management thus does not give any opportunity for the old myth
that good quality is in some way more expensive to become
a self-fulfilling prophecy within the company.

Some of the world's most successful products are now
managed on this basis of the quality and cost partnership.   Let me use the example of large consumer durables
in the American market--such as household refrigerators
which were one of our very early total quality installations.   These household refrigerators are sold for
several hundred dollars--a price that has not significantly increased in several years in spite of some inflation in the economy. They are produced at the rate of
several million units per year. These products are subject to heavy stress by all family members from children
to grandmothers 365 days a year for at least the 10 years
that are a typical ownership cycle. Because of relent-
less quality improvement in what was one of the very
early total quality installations, the products of the
largest manufacturing companies in the consumer durable
industry now require little customer service and have an
extremely low failure rate--requiring a very low maintenance cost for the buyer--and very, very low quality cost
for the manufacturer. There is sufficient confidence in
the quality and cost of these products that, in this year
of 1988, these manufacturers now sell some refrigerator
models on the basis that the buyer will receive a full
return of all of his purchase money after months of use
if he is not completely satisfied.   With the refrigerator's already fine reputation, this very strong
additional confidence in its quality represents a formidable challenge to any foreign manufacturer. The business principle is that the way to compete with quality is
with more quality.

We have extremely strong resources in the United States
for this kind of competitive quality leadership--whether
in household durables or across a very wide range of
other American products.

RENEWING U.S. INDUSTRIAL LEADERSHIP

Re-igniting the explosion of our quality growth means
the restoration of quality to a primary role in American
management from the secondary role it has fallen into in
some companies. It means the redirection of technology
investments toward quality. It means the reemphasis of
the quality-mindedness of the American worker. It means

broadening quality improvement from production. It means genuine effectiveness in development, in finance, and in marketing, and it means the creation of a much greater role for our universities in providing strong educational support for our competitive objectives--particularly our business schools in which quality has, up to now, too often been a footnote at best.

Customer-oriented product leadership was developed in the United States and many American companies still excel in it. The application of technology to productivity and quality achievement characterized the industrialization of the United States from the 1920s onward. We are very strong in quality engineering and manufacturing engineering. Both are now crying out to be used.

The United States has the full potential to renew its industrial leadership, as more and more American managers return to personal leadership of strong and effective quality programs. This is not only in our national interest, but in the long run, for the benefit of people throughout the world.

Certainly, also, this pursuit of excellence leads to a greatness of spirit and action--adding a new and higher level of satisfaction to the work of all of us who are dedicated to continuing quality improvement for sound economic growth and higher standards of living both now and in the future of what is likely to be the demanding quality decade of the 1990s.

BUILDING WORLD MARKET SHARE THROUGH QUALITY AND PRICING

So far, I have emphasized that quality leadership has become a central factor in the economic strength of concerns as we approach the increasingly competitive decade of the 1990s. I would now like to discuss what international experience throughout the world indicates are key steps through which upper management should direct its competitive strategies to assure this quality leadership in both American markets as well as in world markets. Indeed, the clear business principle today is that a company must have international quality leadership if it is to retain quality leadership in its traditional American markets.

Let me begin by making clear that many of the world's most successful companies are achieving this result through building their market share growth around a deceptively simple business competitive strategy that fits the economic environment of the 1990s. This strategy, as we develop it in our General Systems programs, is a combination of competition in its highly visible and traditional form--that is, product versus product--together with a perhaps less visible but equally potent competition involving companies' effectiveness in quality management.

This has been the essence of Japanese export and acquisition strategy for a quarter century, as well as that of
some major American companies. The objective is to create market share through excellent quality and aggressive
pricing which, while built around discounts, nonetheless
provides profitability because of costs that are lower
and quality that is higher than competition realizes.
The Japanese describe this as the business approach that
is invisible to the West, although, happily, we have also
applied it in some American firms.

It continues to be a very effective type of blind-
siding competitive strategy for both Japanese and American firms. This is because some traditional managers
remain highly oriented to the visible side of product
competition--the steel, the iron, the circuitry, the
silicon--which was the approach many of us used in the
earlier years of our experience. It is where you try to
understand the competitor's cost and quality by counting
and analyzing the parts, which is no longer a good indicator. The key to the competitively high product
quality and deep cost reductions today is instead in the
effectiveness and quality of the systematic internal work
processes that produce the steel and iron.

Traditional management has been highly oriented to
product competition. Indeed, at the very highest levels,
the graduate business schools have taught it thoroughly
in their emphasis on marketing and finance, and some
engineering schools have been similarly oriented. Technology investments and developments have become heavily
product-directed and business and cost measurements have
been highly product-line oriented. So far as it goes,
this is all to the good--a business strength.

Until recently, however, quality and productivity were
thought of as essentially specialist activities that
belonged to some technical corner of the organization.
In many traditional companies general management planning
and reporting are accepted as routine in such areas as
finance, production, and marketing. But devoting such
personal top-level executive attention to quality and
productivity still raises eyebrows in many quarters,
still raises questions in some boards as to whether it
represents proper application of executive time.

Hence, many American managers, highly skilled in
competition among products, have been far less familiar
with personally leading the new and all-important form of
competition involving quality leadership. There can thus
be a tendency to reach for straws, a lack of personal
quality know-how, and an unsureness about investing at
levels that are routine in product terms, in the new
quality programs that are needed if their companies are
to remain competitive in national markets--let alone
world markets.

THREE PROBLEM AREAS IN MANAGING QUALITY

This lack of sureness of touch has led to what I call the three basic problem areas of traditional management quality attention. The first of the problems caused by lack of managerial know-how is that it has encouraged superficial quality programs in some companies. This includes such programs as periodic fireworks displays of top-level quality attention through management speech-- making, but with very little follow-up emphasis; or dusting off a few traditional quality control techniques and calling this the company quality program; or empha- sizing off-line programs of technical projects and motivational techniques, located at very low levels of organization and receiving very little operational support. These programs tend to be based on sloganeer- ing, superficial change, and single-sentence improvement formulas in place of the necessary emphasis upon consis- tent on-line implementation of the specifics of quality achievement throughout the organization, using all the modern methods needed to get the job done.

These superficial programs inevitably wither and dry up when touched by heavy production demands or economic fluctuations or budgetary pressures. This is why long-- service employees in some organizations will tell you that they are now going through the seventh or eighth quality improvement crusade in their careers, all the earlier ones having quietly died and been buried without autopsy. These employees want to know what is solid and different about the 1988 program that will really make it stick.

The second problem of lack of managerial know-how is that it has sometimes resulted in the industrial practice of some companies to think that it is possible to deal with competitive quality vulnerability by sending some local production abroad for later sale here, thus fight- ing engineering and manufacturing wars in foreign plants where quality and productivity are already competitively strong. While sometimes it may be necessary, this is again a partial solution which avoids the fact that the wrong production is likely to be sent abroad. It is likely to include the very components and products that should be improved locally right now to build the founda- tion for future competitiveness. Having someone else fight your quality and productivity wars starts an irreversible downward competitive cycle as the product experience of several industries will tell you.

The third problem is that we have sometimes approached quality programs as being primarily for factory workers and for mass production. This has completely missed the reality that the white collar and service areas are also one of the most crucial and overlooked areas for modern quality and productivity attention. It has missed the fact that both middle management in production and much of the development and engineering community require far more quality know-how help than it has received. It has missed the crucial point that the one-of-a-kind development and manufactured products have always succeeded even more in the application of total quality control improvement programs over the years than have the more visible mass production products.

FIRST STEP FOR QUALITY EXCELLENCE: MAKE QUALITY LEADERSHIP A GOAL

By comparison with this superficial approach to quality illustrated by these problem areas of partial quality control, the great business quality strength achieved by many successful exporting companies--whether the company operates in Japan, Europe, the United States, or Latin America--is the result of personal management skill and emphasis upon hard and unrelenting work in what General Systems calls the three fundamental areas of implementing total quality control. I think of them as the hard road to quality excellence, and I would now like to discuss this quite specifically.

The first step on the hard road to quality excellence is the major business decision to make quality leadership in the domestic and export market place a basic strategic goal of the firm. Unless the management of a company itself clearly defines to the organization the specific quality results that are required in quantitative terms rather than through vague generalities, and then budgets the specific resources for manpower, machines, and systems to meet these priorities, the quality results are not going to come about for the firm in its export markets.

Quality leadership today means a policy commitment to the engineering, production, and sale of products that consistently and with very low failure rates will perform correctly for buyers when first purchased and that, with reasonable maintenance, will continue to perform with very high reliability and safety over the product life.

Let me make clear that modern quality leadership is much more than product service or technical assistance. It makes heavier demands on an organization than the traditional policies of customer quality satisfaction that have primarily meant that product service and technical assistance from the firm will be readily available to customers. Because it is so important, let me repeat what I said earlier. The traditional assurance that a company "will always fix a product so that it will work again for the buyer" is honorable and important. However, it represents a policy of customer service to deal with product problems. The modern customer instead wants his product to work well for a long time without requiring any technical assistance.

Moreover, because it is so important, let me repeat what I said in my earlier remarks--that quality is an upward-moving target in competitive markets, and quality programs must be correspondingly dynamic. Let me give an example from our experience that shows why this is so important and how quality must be managed in dynamic, competitive terms.

General Systems Company divides consumer-product development into four stages of a product maturity cycle, each with a different marketing and engineering product quality approach to assure customer satisfaction.

Let's discuss the product maturity cycle of a popular product such as television. In the first stage of maturity the quality of the sets was dominated by *innovation*, which sold the product. Rough quality edges like unclear and wavy pictures, incessant static, and intermittent operation hardly deterred the consumer.

As market acceptance increased, the television set entered the second stage--*conspicuous consumption*. The tube was placed inside a handsome piece of furniture and became a console as well as a television set. Appearance is now a big factor in the consumer's perception of quality.

By the time the third stage was reached, television had become a part of the consumer's lifestyle. This is the *function* stage. The whole family uses the set for entertainment and the news. Quality--consistent product performance--determines the purchase decision.

The product enters the fourth stage of maturation when virtually everyone owns one and it becomes taken for granted. This is the commodity stage. Reliability and product economy are essential to quality acceptance.

Those television products that were handled as if the product were still in the appearance state were doomed to failure in the international marketplace. They were faced with internationally distributed products targeted to a successful company quality strategy which had dynamically been moved ahead to a function-and-commodity-oriented quality approach. This is where the consumers wanted to be. It was precisely this type of strategic management/quality decision that helped some international television product companies and their smaller supplier firms build major market share, as compared to the lesser success of the consumer-electronics products of other companies with less sharply focused strategic approaches to quality.

My second example of this step of business quality strategy has to do with a very popular electronics growth product, specifically the small computer. In one part of this small international computer market--the highest-selling computer peripheral product--the dominant product with the lion's share of market penetration sold at an average price of $4,000. After-sale costs over the product life added another $3,250--including $2,500 for maintenance and service which was 35 percent of the life-cycle cost for this product.

One traditional way to manage the quality strategy of a competitive company would be to engineer a product with comparable features and market it at a lower price. In this case, management of the competitive firm decided instead to bring out a product priced higher at $5,000, but engineered and produced to have after-sales costs (including only $500 for service) 7 percent of life-cycle cost for the product and one-fifth of the other product's service cost. Despite its higher selling price, product sales results of the new product are excellent. They are running four times greater than those of its competitor, and they continue to grow and dominate the market. The reason? The quality has been moved upward to meet the customer demand, rather than being permitted to remain at the earlier level.

The basic principle is that, for product success, it is necessary today to have a carefully organized quality strategy that fits the existing market situation and to have the program quality management and technology to implement it in depth effectively.

SECOND STEP FOR QUALITY EXCELLENCE: COMPANY-WIDE IMPLEMENTATION

Hence, the second step on the road to quality excellence demands that implementation of the necessary actions take place throughout the entire company, not just in the quality control department. Data show that 80 to 90 percent of quality problems requiring improvement are beyond the scope of the inspection and testing actions of traditional quality and reliability departments—effective and conscientious as they may be. This has caused corporate management to rethink, and frequently to fully restructure, quality management operations.

In the Far Eastern, American, European, and Latin American firms with successful quality programs, these quality implementation actions have been made part of the mainstream company actions throughout marketing, engineering, production, and service in the firm, as well as in the quality departments and in general man-agement itself. They are quality disciplines, if you will, to be applied by each function.

This is one dimension of the reason why I felt required to develop Total Quality Control as a structure of managerial and engineering technology to provide a practical, operational foundation for guiding a company in a systematic way through implementation of a modern quality program. In effect, quality is itself systematically managed and systems engineered, just as firms in earlier times learned systematically to manage their engineering, production, and sales.

How deeply such implementation penetrates is attested by the new relationship it makes between quality and productivity. There exists today in many companies what our General Systems engineers call a "hidden plant"--both in the factory and in the office--sometimes amounting to from 15 percent to as much as 40 percent of total productive capacity. This is the capacity that exists either because of the making of errors or the correcting of these errors.

This "hidden plant" is, in part, the direct result of the traditional industrial rationalization approach that I call factory-efficiency based--where productivity was conceived primarily as "more product and service output per unit of resource input."

This traditional approach creates very deep business quality problems because it includes as satisfactory production output such contributors to the "hidden plant" as products that can't be sold because they have defects, or that have to be recalled because they are unreliable or unsafe, or that have to be returned for product service too frequently. There is no greater waste of resources for companies and nations.

To correct this in General Systems, we today are using a newer and very different form of industrialization approach than many of the major companies of the world that I call quality-efficiency based. In productivity terms, we are changing the old "more product output per unit of resource input" to the new measurement of "more salable, good quality output per unit of input."

This approach recognizes that, in today's international marketplace, a poor quality product is of negative business value to the company that offers it, no matter how "productively efficient" the production process may have measured in the traditional sense. It is more the good product that is the meaningful national and international measure of productivity today.

The result of this change in productivity approach and measurement is very significant. We find that many production operations throughout the world, which were reported to their managements to be highly productively efficient in terms of the old non-quality-oriented factory-efficiency measurement--approximately 90-percent productively efficient, for example--are, in fact, at least one-third lower in true productive efficiency--approximately 60-percent productively efficient--when evaluated by more accurate and more realistic customer and market-oriented productivity measurements in quality-efficiency terms.

This one-third and more productivity deficiency has demonstrated to many companies one of the true causes of the persistent upward trends in their costs and expenses in recent years and their inability to be internationally competitive with using only the traditional factory-efficiency industrial rationalization approaches rather than the new total quality-efficiency approaches.

The quality-improvement contribution is very important to solve this problem today. In several of our General Systems operations, a significant proportion of the entire new company productivity increases, required in order to close this deficiency in productivity that exists for many companies, are now targeted and budgeted to come from the quality-improvement contribution of modern quality programs, and they are being achieved by these programs which now return productive efficiency to a true 90 percent or more.

THIRD STEP TO QUALITY EXCELLENCE: COMMITMENT AND TRAINING

This brings me to the third step on the hard road to quality excellence--continuous commitment, motivation, education, and measurement throughout the organization.

There are two requirements that make quality education and training effective for an organization. The first is that they have to be specifically job-related. Generalized philosophic training simply has not gotten the job done. What will help the general manager is understanding of quality strategic planning and how to manage total quality. What will help the design engineer is training in know-how to perform, for example, the quality-parameter design, an approach in which thousands of American and Japanese engineers have been trained for a number of years. What will help the manufacturing engineer is know-how to perform process-capability evaluations. This know-how, moreover, may help motivate his quality interests.

This leads to the second requirement for quality educational effectiveness, which is that it must be operated as an integral part of the total quality system rather than as an overlay that is hoped somehow to evangelize the organization on its own. The principle is that knowledge is power only when it can be used. To put the matter somewhat differently, our total quality system is the necessary foundation on which training and new approaches, such as computer quality aids, can operate effectively--it does not work the other way. This integration is the most important key to education's effectiveness. It succeeds only when management creates and documents and gets wide-spread employee understanding and genuine acceptance of quality-oriented operating conditions throughout the organization--the quality work rules and disciplines that we call total quality system procedures. For just one example, product design reviews really are organized to use such quality-education contributions as parameter-design results and process-capability demonstrations.

A primary goal of this is to assure positive managerial attitudes which are the keys to success for some organizations. A major task remains to develop these attitudes, the organization's quality culture if you will, required for a positive approach. The need for this is great at all levels of organization including the professional because due to deficiencies in our educational programs many in this present management and engineering generation--to put the matter bluntly--have not been conditioned to think of industry and business in primary terms of quality. Economics textbooks have usually dealt with technology leadership, price, production, and sales demand as the principal determinants of economic activity, with quality often touched on as of more incidental business interest. The more superficial forms of what has been called business strategic planning can all too likely automatically emphasize product function and features, and to treat specific customer quality use requirements only in a general non-quantitative way--thereby locking companies out of genuine modern quality leadership before product design has even begun.

The important function of research, development, and engineering is a particular example of the importance of establishing the correct quality mentality. As one of the important steps to establish today's product quality requirements with the required degree of realism, it is necessary that development and design engineers themselves talk and work directly with customers and users of the product. This is one of the strengths of smaller firms and is fundamentally different from the traditional tendency of some larger companies--and of some engineers themselves--that the engineer remain in his office and laboratory and be insulated by the company organization from continuing contact with the users of the products. Today, direct discussion with customers and users has become an organized and on-going engineering activity in the development of genuinely customer-oriented product specification, and in the testing of products in the quality programs of an increasing number of strong companies. The laboratory test and the professional test engineer--while important--are no longer enough, and research and engineering thinking must be oriented to recognize this.

ROI AS A MOTIVATION

So much for these three steps in the establishment of total quality control--strategic quality leadership, company-wide implementation, commitment and training. There is a strong economic reason to move in this direction. The motivator exists in the excellent industrial and business results that have come from a genuine

quality leadership policy in the international marketplace.

This begins in terms of the ROI, the return on investment, which for industry is an extremely important economic indicator.

Our experience demonstrates that the returns on investment from strong total quality programs in major firms
throughout the world today are excellent. They have
consistently exceeded the industry ROI pattern shown from
most other customary economic investments. This has been
a tremendous business benefit for these companies of
which some of their competitors are largely unaware.

To repeat what I said earlier, the essence of the
business management principle is that today, quality and
cost are a sum, not a difference--partners, not adversaries. This is very different from the incorrect business
myth during much of the 20th century that higher quality
means gold plating and somehow makes development and
production more difficult and more costly.

REASONS FOR IMPROVING ROI

There are three principal reasons for this outstanding
economic return on investment.

The first has to do with improvements in quality costs.
We have been measuring in our General Systems data base
the effects of quality costs on the income of firms since
we first developed the quality cost measurement approach
more than 30 years ago. This includes the full costs of
assurance--quality improvement programs, inspection
control, et cetera--plus the full costs of the failure of
this assurance--customer returns, rework, et cetera--all
systematically structured within the financial and
accounting system of the concern. These data for the
year of 1987 show that the true costs of quality through
many major manufacturing and service companies average
from 15 to 20 percent of sales.

The data also show that the quality costs of companies
which have had long-term systematic total quality emphasis were from one-half to two-thirds of this average
because they improved the prevention effectiveness of
assurance, were able to minimize inspection control, and
greatly reduced the costs of failure.

When you compare quality cost as a percentage of total
sales for recent years you find a significant cost savings trend over a two- to three-year period resulting
from the quality leadership programs of the firms. This
means that we have avoided continual cost increases that
would have characterized the continuation of quality
practices that no longer meet present market requirements. Such quality cost reductions have become a principal reason for the cost advantage certain major international companies enjoy in today's world marketplace.

These cost reductions have also enhanced positive cash flow for the balance sheet as well as profitability for the firm.

The second reason for the excellent economic results from total quality programs is productivity improvement. There is today no more effective way to improve productivity than for quality programs to convert the "hidden plant" to productive use. A significant proportion of the productivity increases of key international firms is now being achieved by quality programs.

The third reason is that higher sales result in today's market from the achievement of lower levels of quality failure and service costs. There is now clear evidence of the positive correlation between market share and market quality. Sales growth that favors products with high quality and low quality costs is becoming characteristic of the international marketplace. These results emphasize why the very strong, new relationship between competitive world leadership and total quality control has emerged as an enormously powerful new influence upon the management, engineering, and marketing policies of firms--both small and large.

CONCLUSION

The power, innovation, and continuity of strong total quality programs are thus becoming a major competitive strength for American business growth. The key is, in my experience, that the company has a systematic foundation so that quality is itself managed and systems engineered and motivated throughout the organization with the same thoroughness and depth that the product itself is managed, engineered, produced, and sold.

Certainly the favorable effect upon business growth of such total quality policies has many examples in American companies, whose strong businesses speak for themselves today. Leadership in this matter is one of the principal jobs of the manager in the company which intends to succeed in today's intensely competitive business environment.

This decade of the 1990s may well be described by companies and nations which maintain business strength as their "Decade of Total Quality Control Emphasis."

Finally, I should like to offer my thanks and congratulations to our Partners Program hosts for the excellence and high quality of their organization of this meeting, and to all present here for continuing success in your pursuit of quality leadership.

13

The Productivity Paradox Explained

Wickham Skinner

The theme of this conference is "Productivity Strategies for the 1990s." My approach may strike you as somewhat unconventional and contrary. I hope it doesn't strike anybody as disrespectful, because it isn't intended that way. In fact, my respect for an audience of this sort goes back to when I was at the Harvard Business School and was struggling to get people interested in productions operation management. I tried to convince them to work in factories and operations instead of going to Wall Street and dealing with second-order abstractions and pushing pieces of paper around. In *The New York Times* Russell Baker said, "It's only the Japanese and the Asians that manufacture. Americans merge, acquire, divest, and declare bankruptcy." This is an audience, I think, that is dealing with some of the most fundamental, difficult, and important problems in our society.

I want to propose an approach to productivity strategies for the 1990s that is quite different from what we have been doing in the 1980s.

For the last ten or eleven years, all of us practitioners and teachers in the field have been dealing with a very sick institution, which we all know and love, called manufacturing. We have prescribed very strong medicine for it. Has that medicine cured the patient, or do we need not only to build on what we've been doing, but also prescribe some different medicine? I think we need to change the prescription. The title that you have been given, "The Productivity Paradox," is kind of cute. My greatest detractors say, "Well, Wick, we seldom agree with your articles, and you don't say very much, but you sure are great at titles." I want to tell you what the title of this little talk really ought to be. It ought

to be called "Wallflowers at the Global Competition Ball"
or "Why Elephants Can't Dance."

I used to argue with my colleague, the great Bill
Abernathy. He wrote a book called *The Industrial Renaissance* in the very early 1980s. I said to him, "Bill, I
don't see the renaissance." Ladies and gentleman, I was
wrong! My great colleague, who died at a very early,
unfortunate age, is probably sitting up there saying,
"Wickham, I told you so."

In the last ten years we have seen a remarkable re-
industrialization effort. There has been the greatest
outpouring of energy, rededication, enthusiasm, and determination to turn this great institution around that I
have ever seen in my long career. I'll bet that history
will show that we have learned, re-learned, and tried
more in this ten- or fifteen-year period, and that more
people have become seriously, thoroughly, and enthusiastically involved in greater change recently, than has
taken place in almost any period in industrial history.
It has been an extra-ordinary period. Its purpose was to
try to regain our competitive ability. That's what got
us all going. It was absolutely essential to the American economy. We learned that manufacturing does matter,
that we can't survive and prosper on a service economy
alone.

After this fantastic Rip Van Winkle-reawakening of our
whole field, the results are a bit of a paradox and a
mystery. Productivity got off the 75-year curve of
roughly 2 to 5 percent a year in 1973, and stayed off
that curve for about 11 years. We are now back on that
curve. This is part of this extraordinary turn-around
that we have had. Look at what has happened in quality.
Sure, it isn't what it ought to be, but on a scale of ten
I would say we went from about a four or five to a seven-
just tremendous improvement. We all know it. Look at
the products you are buying. Look at what has happened
to the American automobile in this ten-year period.

WALLFLOWERS AT THE BALL

The data that come out of our factory operations say
that this effort has really succeeded. The question is,
however, have we really regained competitive ability?
You can pick certain industries and certain terrific companies and the answer is "Yes," but I'm going to tell you
that the overall answer is pretty clearly "No." We are
still struggling, we are still chasing. Have we stopped
imports? Of course not. Have we stopped the constant,
steady rise in imports? No way! Those imports are still
coming in, and they are still rising. If you look at the
curve, it has started to drop off a little bit. Imports
are now roughly 13% of our domestic market.

How about exports? We have finally started to export

a little, particularly in some commodity products, but our export picture is dismal compared to our Asian and Western European competitors. Our share of foreign trade, in total, has dropped over a ten- or twelve-year period to from about 21% to 14%. Our share of the world's manufactured goods is now down to 11%, while Japan has risen 50% over the last ten years. Global international trade is expanding and shooting up, the tempo is rising, and--to carry out my new title--it really is a ball. But sadly, we are like wallflowers at the ball. We are watching, we are trying to learn, we are trying to get back in the party.

We certainly are not there yet. But with the tremendous improvements we have made in productivity and in quality, even though we are not there, it is kind of surprising that we haven't done better. You also have to add to those terrific improvements what has happened to the value of the dollar. Look at different currencies; there has been a 20% to 60% drop. Why hasn't that done it for us, practically by itself? It hasn't. Look at falling unit labor costs. With the increases in productivity, our labor costs have actually declined on a per-unit basis. They have gone up in Japan. Look at the decline in union membership. We have had all these things going for us outside of the factory. Yet a surge in productivity still hasn't come off.

My conclusion is that the productivity and quality strategies that we pursued in the 1980s will not be enough in the 1990s. We have improved, but our competitors have improved even more. Look at the statistics in the auto industry. Ford has shown about a 40% improvement in the last six years, based on the returns to the dealer for any reason. Toyota has done even better; it is around 45%. General Motors is roughly 15%; Chrysler is about 12%. In other words, while quality in the American auto industry has improved, the Japanese have done even better.

When I was in Japan a couple of years ago I visited NDK Tapes, the giant manufacturer of video and cassette tapes tapes. We went through the most highly automated, unwasteful, absolutely gorgeous plant you have ever seen. I was taking a group of Eastman-Kodak people through it. There were about thirty of us. After we went through the plant we sat down in a conference room. Our Japanese hosts said, "What did you think of our facility?" It was a very bland and open-ended question. We all said, "This is the most extraordinary, fantastic, productive, high-quality plant we have ever seen." Our guide honestly looked really surprised. He said, "You really liked it?" We said, "Why are you so surprised?" He said, "We have seen the value of the dollar starting to change, and we predict that it is going to go that way for at least three years. We think the change against the yen is going to be large. We have decided that our plant

performance is about 45% of where we ought to be. We
will not survive in this business if we don't get that
45% up to 90 or 95%, and we think we have about a year
and a half or two years to do it." We said, "Well, what
sort of things are you going to do?" They said, "Well,
if you are really interested, let's change the schedule
and talk about this some more."

They brought in a lot of other people and got up the
vue-graphs. They had twenty-one projects--all the way
from cutting waste to improving quality even further;
things with vendors, scheduling, inventories, movement
between machines, information systems. We asked, "They
all look very good and potentially effective, but how are
you going to do them?" Then they showed us more graphs.
There were PERT charts on every single one of these projects with mileposts, due dates, specific achievement
targets, who had to do what, and who was responsible. It
absolutely blew your mind. With an already superlative
operation, they were planning difficult and demanding improvements. I have heard that they were successful.

In the meantime, we are struggling to get ourselves
back up on this productivity curve. The Japanese knew
the currency was changing. They hitched up their belts
and went to work. Don't mistake me. I am not saying
that we have wasted effort or that we have done the wrong
things. We absolutely had to do what we did. Have we
been barking up the wrong tree? Absolutely not! We have
to *keep* barking up it, but that is not enough.

Are these kinds of things, necessary as they are, going
to lead to competitive advantage? Those of you who have
studied Herzberg in organizational behavior know about
what are known as "hygiene factors," such as working conditions. If the working conditions are bad, that hurts
motivation and productivity. But if the working conditions are good, they don't motivate anybody. I think
productivity and quality are those kind of phenomena.
They are absolutely essential and critical, but is that
the way we are going to beat the Koreans, the other
Asians, and the Western Europeans? Everybody these days
can copy and learn from everybody else. We are copying
and learning from the great teachers of Japan, and we are
relearning from the great teachers of America like Mr.
Deming. He began writing his first papers in the 1930s
or 1940s, but he had to go to Japan to get people to
listen to him.

We are learning fast. We go to conferences like this.
We go to Japanese conferences and they come to ours. We
exchange literature. Everybody says, "Hey, hey, this is
what I just learned. Let me tell you about it." Competitors are even visiting competitors. We are in a totally
competitive world. My sense is that we are chasing and
chasing. Thank heavens, we can still see the leaders going over the next hill each time we come to the top of

one. We don't lose sight of them for long. We are with
them, and we are in the race. But I am not so sure we
are going to win the race in the 1990s the way we have
been doing it in the 1980s.

FACTS OF GLOBAL COMPETITION

What do we need to do? I think first we need to look
at twelve or so facts of global competition. You know
them all. What do we have to do in the 1990s? We must
deal with these facts of global competition. Decreasing
trade barriers are one. More big international companies
are producing everywhere.   They are moving, buying,
shifting, and trading across international boundaries.
There are more alliances, consortia, trading of information, partners, and technical exchanges.   Everybody is
going everywhere. Look at the Japanese coming in here;
look at us finally getting into Russia and China. A very
interesting thing is that low labor rates are rising. We
were worried about Japanese labor rates ten years ago. I
am a director of a medium-size company that has a factory
in Japan and a factory in Waltham, Massachusetts. Our
labor rates are lower in Waltham than they are in Japan.
Everywhere more small, aggressive, high-tech companies
are coming on fast, penetrating the market, and increasing employment and growth. Employment in *Fortune* 500
companies is actually declining, and this is happening
everywhere. This kind of competition is not just global;
it is big company/small company. It is competition coming from outside of your industry and blind-siding you.
Increasing management expertise is everywhere--much more
sophisticated management, and people who know and understand management. Over 60,000 MBAs are graduating every
year now (Heaven help us all!). We are getting swarmed
over with management expertise.   Some of it is pretty
bad, some of it is pretty superficial, and some of it is
very academic. But it does improve the rate of communication, exchange, and learning.
There is a more rapid flow and exchange of technology
products and techniques--Just-In-Time, TQC, MRP, and CAD/
CAM. Everybody is learning very fast. There is no monopoly on concepts and techniques. There is a great deal
more communication.   There are fewer secrets.   The response time to competitive change is being cut down.
It is rough, but I think this is all going to get
worse. We know about Korea, Taiwan, Singapore, and Hong
Kong--the dragons of Asia. Mexico is just getting good;
Brazil is very good in many, many fields. What is going
to happen in Indonesia, India, China, and, of course,
Russia? It is a very clear change. We didn't have to
worry much in the past about competing with the Communist
bloc. Very clearly, they are giving up much of their
economic philosophy. Those people are going to be com-

peting with us, as well as offering us more markets, very soon.

What does all of this demand of manufacturing, competitively, in the 1990s? I think the name of the game is changing from cost and quality--where everybody is getting so much better--to product development. It is changing to developing products that are targeted for specific customers, markets, and locations. The competitive game is changing to managing your new product development cycle much, much better. This change is going to require a lot more speed and flexibility, and the focus must be on time, time, time.

SEVEN PRESCRIPTIONS FOR PRODUCTIVITY

Let me step back once more to ten years ago. What were the formulas, the recipes, the medicine, if you will, that were being prescribed for us at that time?   There were six or seven things. One was that we had to get back on that productivity curve. Two, we had a tremendous amount of work to do on quality. Three, we needed more automation, more robots, more lasers, more flexible automation, and more computer-integrated manufacturing. Four, we needed to do a much better job with our people; there needed to be more involvement, more participation, and more teams. Five, we had to do a better and quicker job on new product development. Six, we had to do better on scheduling and inventories, including the whole field of procurement. And seven--Skinner Snake Oil--was manufacturing strategy, in which you stand back from operations, learn to focus your plants on limited tasks, and do those very well.

Just think for a second about those seven areas. How have we done? Fairly well in productivity and fairly well on quality. Miserably, in my opinion, on buying, introducing, testing, working out the bugs, and moving ahead with more automation and mechanization. We are doing better in human resource management, but how many of you can really say that you have tapped the spirit, energy, and creativity of your people?

There is fascinating literature on new experiments in human resource management. The data show pretty clearly that two out of three companies succeed for the first few years, but three out of four of them fail after that. There is a rubberband effect; we tend to snap back to the old ways of treating and handling people.

In new product development we are only a little past the old engineering attitude of "Do it, then throw it over the wall." Now manufacturing and engineering do it and throw it over the wall of production. All those walls add up. Any new product takes six or eight years to hit the market. A fascinating study was done by Kim Clark of our faculty, who visited all the major auto companies of the world. He collected data on new product development, showing that Americans take roughly one-and-a-half to three years longer than our Japanese and other competitors to develop a new model. In many companies that I have visited, that is a major competitive weakness. We haven't made very much progress.

As to production control and inventory control, who hasn't been through an MRP disaster? It has been tough and slow. I am not saying that we shouldn't do it. Just-In-Time has made some in roads. There has been some fairly good progress there. Skinner Snake Oil is still on the shelf, the prices are going down all the time, and there is a surplus. Companies talk about manufacturing strategy, but few have penetrated very far. My conclusion from these data is simply this: We have made only mediocre progress during the last ten years on the major ingredients required for improving competitive success. But why has progress been so slow? We knew what we had to do, but it takes too much time and talk and persuasion to get our corporate organizations to focus every element of the system on competitive performance in manufacturing. Many of you say, "I need a better accounting system. I am always arguing with those people in accounting. We still have old-fashioned accounting with everything based on direct labor, and I don't have much direct labor anymore. I have to get out of overhead costs, and the accountants really don't help much." You can also blame a lot of things on the finance people. The hurdle rates are so high, you can't get needed investments approved. I have seen company after company turn down investments with low predicted return rates, only to find themselves virtually out of business after six or eight years. We don't look at investments in a strategic way, so we have manufacturing companies that are not focused on manufacturing. Instead, each function has its own separate objectives and performance measures.

BASIC ISSUES FOR QUALITY PRODUCTIVITY

I want to leave you with three suggestions for achieving productivity quality at a basic level in the 1990s. First, there is a productivity paradox. It goes sort of like this: "If you go for quality you often get lower cost." If you go for efficiency, productivity, and lower cost per se, you often don't get it. You also often get worse quality rather than better. I see a kind of an obsession with "productivity". There is a backlash to this obsession. It can easily cause a reversion to the old-fashioned industrial engineering attitude of, "Scrimp and save, hire efficiency experts, cut and slice, and get out your stopwatch on everybody." A book entitled *The Uneasy Alliance* looks at the conflicts between achieving productivity and achieving innovation. It is interesting that technology and productivity aims often run headlong into each other. Furthermore, managers are often so preoccupied with working at the operating level or focusing on the short-term horizon that they fail to look at fundamental structural problems. There is no way to succeed with the wrong structure. I am talking about a manufacturing structure that starts with a make-or-buy decision, then goes to a capacity decision, then to the main choices of equipment and process technology, and then to the main infrastructure of operating systems. If those things aren't right, Heaven help you. If you have the wrong plant, the wrong size, the wrong location, the wrong equipment, or the wrong production control system, the best group of managers in the world can't succeed. I don't think that we think about those structural decisions enough.

Are our best management people going into production manufacturing and operations management? It used to be a struggle with our MBAs at Harvard, but last year the production operations management course at Harvard got the highest educational value ratings of any course in the first-year MBA curriculum. Even more interesting and encouraging was the fact that more students chose operations management/production manufacturing courses as second-year electives than any other area of the school. That includes finance, investment banking, and all the great, jazzy things of the day. Now, that is not because we are so smart and such good teachers. I am not there anymore, so I can't take any credit, but our students read the newspapers and have learned the importance of manufacturing excellence for survival. But the best of our management people are still not going into manufacturing.

I did a survey of twelve companies about four years ago. We said, "You pick out your comers. They should be five, six, or seven years at the most away from senior manufacturing and operations management positions." We then interviewed their "comers." The question was, are these young men and women really going to help turn American industry around and take us where we need to go? They were bright, energetic, marvelous people, and very impressive, but they worried me on three counts. First, they all had a very short-term operating point of view. Secondly, the engineering people generally had very little sense of the business. They could hardly talk about what was happening in competition, their division, their product group, or the company. Thirdly, there was a surprising lack of interest in the technology of their company, plant, department, and industry. Four out of five of them said flat out, "Technology is not important." I worry about whether we are getting the right people.

Let me close now with my third and final major concern, which I would urge that we think about and do something

about in the 1990s. This is the biggest problem of all.
American industry is organized on a traditional corporate
basis much more than are our competitors in Asia and
elsewhere. By that I mean a functional department struc-
ture--manufacturing, marketing, sales, accounting, finance, and personnel. The theory is that the job of top
management is to recognize that all of those departments
and functions have legitimate and professional objectives. The job of top management is thus to balance
among eight functions. I think that we have hung that
functional/departmental kind of organization on ourselves
for too many years, and it has become a very serious impediment to our growth, our learning, our adapting, and
our moving fast in the globally competitive world.

What can we do about that? In one sense, the biggest
problem for the 1990s is *outside* the factory. We have
done pretty well on improving the factory. We really
have gone to work on it with tremendous enthusiasm and
vitality. Now it is up to top management to get off our
backs and help us get things done with these other departments, so we aren't always fighting with engineering
on manufacturability, with accounting on getting a good
accounting system, with personnel to let us experiment
and rock the boat a little bit. We could easily say our
hands are tied. In some respects, American production
managers have been fighting with one hand tied behind
their backs. But the tempo in the global dance has increased.

Many of us in manufacturing are lions in the plant. We
are pussy cats when we get to top executive levels, try
to get some money, and convince other departments to see
things our way. We need to stop that. We have to insist, take charge, set up teams. We need to tell accountants and finance and personnel people what we need. We
have to experiment with new types of organizational systems. There is no reason why manufacturing--with 80% of
the employees, typically 90% of the assets, and an absolutely enormous stake and role in corporate survival and
manufacturing excellence in this decade--should have to
be just another one of those eight departments. Those
checks and balances are checking and balancing us into
oblivion.

What did we learn in the 1980? We learned that manufacturing excellence is absolutely critical to global
survival. We also learned something else: if you have
second-rate manufacturing, your strategic position becomes virtually impossible. We have got to continue what
we are doing in productivity and quality and do it even
better. But we have to do more. We have to get better
people in manufacturing, the best in the company. One
CEO, whom I admire tremendously (and who didn't come out
of manufacturing) said, as he thought about his manpower
planning problems, "I need the brightest people in the
whole company in operations." I said, "Why?" He said,

"Because it is so complicated, it requires the best minds." We need to think more about our structures and less about the short term. Finally, we need to get at these organizational barriers, take hold of them, take charge of them, and break them down.

To rebuild, manufacturing companies need to be truly focused on competitive superiority in *manufacturing*, rather than the collection of "professional" functional specialties we have now. We can't compete with the conventional "line and staff" form of organization described in management literature. This is the fundamental task before us if we are to answer the dilemma of the productivity paradox.

14

How Fast Response Organizations Achieve Global Competitiveness

Martin Starr

There is a lot of speculation about what makes one organization more competitive than another. Nobody knows the answer to the problem of how to become globally competitive next year or the year after that, because we are dealing with dynamic systems with changing rules and moving targets. Consequently, I can only tell you about the formula that successful companies seem to be following. Some rather interesting and unexpected elements emerge.

To begin with, I want to give you a feeling for the situation. Many of us have a strong desire to have everything perfectly categorized. Then we sit back and write notes in our little books and say, "I think I understood that. Now if I could only do it." Winston Churchill once said that he thought Lady Astor was a wonderful person, and that her only flaw was that she suffered from hardening of the categories. Relating Churchill's point to our situation, we must be very careful in how we divide up the world and to what elements and dimensions we attribute success, because it's a Rashomon-type story. Rashomon is a Japanese film classic in which several different characters give very different versions of the same occurrence as seen from their individual perspectives. The point is that one must be able to sort out error and discern authenticity.

In this regard, the following story is told about Picasso. An art collector in France bought a picture that he was absolutely sure was a Picasso. He went to a Parisian art dealer and asked him to authenticate the picture. The art dealer replied that he could do that, but it would take him a couple of months. The collector took the painting across the street to another dealer,

where he got the same response. He became so impatient
that he went to Cannes, where Picasso lived at the time.
He went into Picasso's workshop and said, "Dear Picasso,
I would appreciate it if you would sign this piece of
work and authenticate that it is yours." Picasso looked
at the painting and said, "It's a fake." The collector
said, "That's impossible; I saw you paint this myself!"
to which Picasso replied, "I often paint fakes."

WORLD-CLASS SYSTEMS

   World-class global systems--what categories can explain
a subject like that? Our Center for Operations at Columbia University in New York City has been doing research
on the behavior of foreign-affiliated firms in the United
States. At first we concentrated on Japanese-owned and
operated companies in the U.S., of which there are currently over one thousand. We have been studying them
since 1980. We have watched how they have altered the
basic management model that is used in Japan and how they
have adapted it to their U.S. operations, depending upon
where they are, what their industry is, and many other
factors.

   Our research team came back a short time ago from
spending a week and a half in Tennessee. While there we
interviewed representatives from five major Japanese companies to find out what was happening. One particularly
significant finding was that cultural factors are superficial surrogates for the real forces that account for
world-class performance. Successful companies, no matter
what part of the world they come from, are remarkably
similar in management style.

   In 1987 we added European companies operating in America to our study. We also began to visit European countries in an attempt to understand what is going to happen
in Europe in 1992. By using meetings, conferences, surveys, and in-depth interviews, we began to capture the
emerging characteristics of world-class competition in
Europe.

COMPUTER INTEGRATED MANUFACTURING

   The companies that are achieving and maintaining success are those that are using some form of comprehensive
information system such as CIM, the acronym for Computer
Integrated Manufacturing. I am not just talking about
off-the-shelf CIM software packages. Figure 14.1 illustrates the underlying concept of relational data-based
information architecture. At an even higher level of
systems architecture, we encounter the Computer Integrated Enterprise--CIE--but CIM is the more common
acronym.

The various concentric circles (or rings) of this diagram represent different levels of information in the firm. The outermost rings are the broad functions, which are all in communication with each other. Increasingly specific detail of the possible communications between the functional entities is represented as we move inward on the diagram. Each organizational function can be connected to every other one at all levels of detail. The information network and the rules for communicating are what is referred to as "integrated systems architecture." Each company has its own computer network and communication requirements, and so would have a unique ring diagram of its system's architecture.

Figure 14.1   CIM "Wheel"

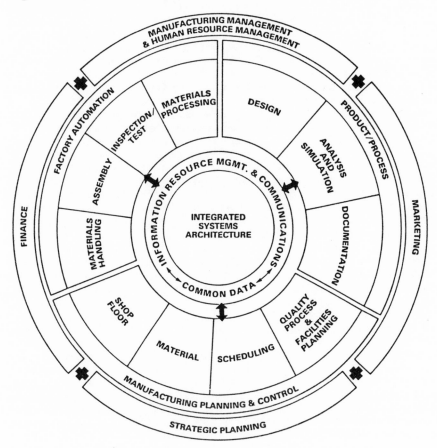

CIM "Wheel" Developed by the Technical Council of the Computer and Automated Systems Association of SME (CASA/SME) © 1985 CASA/SME, Second Ed., Revised 11/5/85.

Relational data bases, which radiate their communication potential between all functions, are crucially important. They do not have to be formal data bases. They must, however, be designed to enhance communication between all the fundamental players who share data in the system. If two people don't talk to each other because one is on the eighth floor and the other is on the fourth floor, or they really don't like each other, or they are vying for the same position in the same firm, or if they actually give each other misinformation, the ring is broken and the concept becomes non-operational.

We have entered a new era in which companies are dealing with elements such as design information while simultaneously communicating about factory processes. Other interactive information elements in the ring include engineering design, costs, and quality. Successful companies view all of these things as interrelated by the flow of information within and outside of the firm. This helps managers reach decisions about what to do next, whether it is implementing quality improvement programs or designing new products. Good decisions depend upon a good information framework.

If the system is even halfway working on a relational basis, it makes you pretty close to world class. This simplifies the traditional dimensions of success. First of all, everybody in business talks about low cost. It is a *sine qua non*. Even if you argue that high quality is most important, most people will agree that when push comes to shove, it boils down to a question of cost. We keep alternating between wanting the highest quality and the lowest cost.   Successful firms strive for both, because multiple objectives and criteria are part of the notion of CIM and data-relational systems.   Trade-offs are part of their architecture. You don't give up on quality and say, "I'm going for cost only," or whatever comes first on the list. Low cost, high quality, on-time delivery, and service: together these factors make up the interdependent package that the producer supplies and the customer buys.

But there is something of great importance that is often left out of the package. What is it? It is the performance parameter *time* that increasingly has become a differentiating factor of successful companies. Our surveys show that companies that use *time-based management* principles are more likely to be successful in penetrating new markets and sustaining global competitiveness.   They use domestic, local, regional, and international information data bases to speed decisions and accomplishments.   They are constantly extending their data bases, which keeps them well-informed and minimizes their surprise at competitive moves. Their managers are conscious of the knowledge required for change: how long it will take to move from where they are to where they

want to go.   The crucial dimension is the time-response
factor.

FAST RESPONSE ORGANIZATIONS

The title of my presentation is "How FROs Achieve
Global Competitiveness."   FRO is the acronym for Fast
Response Organizations.   FROs are not the same as high-
speed organizations, where a frenetic management is
geared to "putting out fires."   In fast response organizations, managers do not wait for something to happen
before they take action.   Part of time-based management
involves Preplanned Fast Response capability, which has
also been called the Anticipatory, or Corrective, Fast
Response ability.   Fast response managers are prepared to
create new situations, to visualize and respond to likely
scenarios, and to defer action until the time is right.
Thus, they are acutely aware of *timing* as well as *time*.
Delays in lead time, lag time, think time, communication
time, etc., are continuously being cut down and compressed
significantly.   Within organizations all over the globe
as diverse as Brunswick, Hewlett-Packard, and Honda, we
have found that faster-response business units are more
successful than their slower-response competitors.   Often
some units are FROs while others within the same organization are not.   CEOs of companies such as General Electric
and Hewlett-Packard are using successful FRO-type business
units to set the pace and then cloning or replicating them
elsewhere in the company.   This approach looks good; it
works.   In other words, you set up a pilot unit showing
how the system can operate.   Then you export the successful pattern to other business units.
An FRO pilot system is an artificial entity that creates
interface problems for the organization bureaucracy.
While pieces and parts of it may be studied, it's not a
functional reality until the normal organizational setup
is totally altered.   FROs will not operate in the traditional organizational framework.   Why is that true?   Traditional organizations emphasize *tactics* and tend to ignore the fast-response aspects of *strategies*.

STRATEGIES AND TACTICS

Most organizations have gone a certain distance with
respect to tactics such as just-in-time, minimization of
work-in-process, getting rid of waste, and improved quality (reduced defective) in their processes.   In other
words, they are *doing things right* before *doing the right
things*--those that are strategically correct.   Global
competitors believe that everyone should be *continuously*
involved in doing strategically right things.

A lot of organizations are concentrating their efforts on the tactical aspects of operating without looking at the strategic aspects. That approach dooms them to failure. It just will not work in the long term, because FRO-type global competitors start with "strategizing" and move through "tacticalizing" (as show in Figure 14.2).

Figure 14.2   FRO Issues

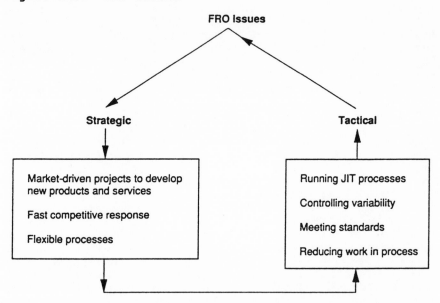

The ability to have a reactive informational structure disseminated throughout the organization creates rapid decisional support capabilities. It adds the time parameter to the MIS functions: it keeps track of things, but it also moves fast. If it is used only for tactical purposes, such as production scheduling and inventory, then the system cannot operate at the upper-corporate level with respect to market-driven projects. Tactics alone do not address the key issues: What should we be doing, what are the products, and what are the services?

A variety of manufacturing companies are finding out that strategic-level service is a part of their business. They need to be able to respond to customer requests quickly. They must also be able to act flexibly if a competitor comes out with a new strategy for products or services.

Our studies indicate that most companies in the United States are well along the way tactically. Japanese companies in the United States consider these tactical problems--such as JIT, zero-defects, and the way in which vendors are made part of the system--as solved or steadily solvable. A minimal number of vendors, strong trust relationships, keeping things moving, no waste, nothing on the loading platform, maintaining the highest quality-- these are typical of tactical things that the Japanese take for granted. They may not have achieved perfection, but they keep trying.

It is interesting to note that American workers in Japanese-run plants in the United States seem to thrive under Japanese management, whereas American managers are more at odds with their Japanese colleagues. The American managers find it hard to deal with fast-moving, fundamental changes and continuously higher standards. Vendors in the U.S. find it difficult to work with Japanese companies for the same reasons. A lot of the Japanese companies are disappointed at their inability to develop highly reliable trust relationships for fast-changing product and service arrangements with American vendors.

American companies are doing fine with the tactical issues, such as getting rid of waste, making quality improvements, and bringing about continuous tactical chance. They are learning to pay attention to detail and to leave nothing to change These priorities all come from survey statements by companies operating on the tactical side. Who's going to knock tactical FRO improvement, which, it has been shown, can double your productivity, reduce costs by 20%, and allow growth three times faster than the rest of non-FRO industry? This is accomplished by getting rid of stuff just waiting around, thereby increasing the percentage of total time dedicated to value-adding operations. But the underlying power of FRO will be missed if only the tactical benefits are pursued. Although strategic benefits are harder to measure than tactical benefits, they are essential for survival in a fast-response competitive environment.

COMPETITORS AND SUPPLIERS IN THE TOTAL STRATEGIES-TACTICAL CIM LOOP

Global competitors are bringing suppliers onto the strategy side of the CIM loop, making them a privileged part of their interactive information system. In some companies customers are also part of the strategy side of the CIM loop. There are now big companies with equally big customers hooked into their information systems by terminals directly connected to the producer's computer. They are sharing information about established and start-up products. Orders that used to arise suddenly (or so it seemed from the outside) have become schedulable, albeit with short lead times. For example, the sales managers of a large chemical company felt that they had to keep six carloads of a particular plastic outside their customer's plant on a railroad siding. By using a CIM-

type information tie-in, the company has cut its rail-
siding inventory down to one boxcar because it knows when
the customer's orders are coming. What seemed sporadic
has become logical as both parties jointly anticipate new
product start-ups, special orders, last-minute orders, and
even changes in long-standing orders. The key to success
requires putting all of the players inside the same informational system.

Such success stories illustrate the savings that can be
made using tactical CIM concepts. Strategic CIM capabilities, on the other hand, are not cost-oriented, but are
strongly related to survival. Figure 14.3 depicts the
total set of organizational activities that should be
supported by the CIM system.

The major emphasis in the figure is on the strategic
components that operate through the PROJECT MGMT box. The
importance of the suppliers' roles is very evident.

The cycle to note in Figure 14.3 is: find-design-build-
ship. To get this cycle working, you need to have an

Figure 14.3   CIM System

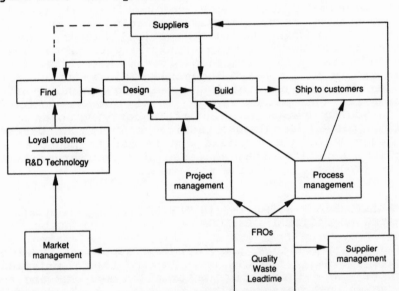

awareness of the FRO capability with respect to project
management (strategic), as well as process management
(tactical). Our research indicates that the leverage
today goes to the company that is concenating on *project*
management rather than *process* management, except when the
project is dealing with changes in process.   Project
management style is where global competitiveness seems to
be emerging on a tremendous scale. Leverage is on the
side of those who know what to design, build, and ship,

and know how to do this continuously. In this cycle, design, marketing, and production are joined together in a new organizational form.

ORGANIZATIONAL CHANGE

Marketing, R & D, production, development--all of these functions and others as well, are connected by the inter-active information network. When these functions are forced to talk to each other on a constant, ongoing basis, the organization changes.

Organizational change is absolutely essential. To know what changes to make requires the collective intelligence of the entire organization. The flexibility of the pro-duction processes determines the ability of the organi-zation to deliver the variety of outputs demanded by cus-tomers in the marketplace. R & D and production managers have to become aware of market research and market systems dynamics. Designers of products, services, and processes in the fast-response companies whom we have interviewed sit down with market researchers and jointly endeavor to find out how people are using their products and what they might prefer. That is not a typical U.S. approach.

ORGANIZATIONAL SIZE AND LEARNING

It is critical that the organization be small enough to ensure that the communication linkages between all of the functional entities are in place. Successful organiza-tions can be part of giant companies, but they use *decen-tralization* to keep the information system of workable size.

The bureaucracy of large organizations is intended to constrain information flows. This is entirely counter-productive from the FRO point of view, which strives to employ individuals to take whatever actions are needed then and there. FROs require reasonable decision autono-my. Between 300 and 500 employees is the number that seems to emerge over and over again as the optimal size for FRO-oriented companies. As soon as an entity within the business unit grows larger than that, the Japanese decentralize it. American companies such as GE and Ford Motor say they are doing this as well.

"Is the business unit too big?" You can't get these CIM systems working until you have a viable communication network. One of the basic principles I have already stated is that these organizations cease to be managed in the traditional way. They are *learning* organizations in which you are really managing *intelligence* rather than *information*. Managing intelligence--rather than data or materials or schedules--is the critical orientation that emerges for successful companies in this era of global competitiveness.

CONTINUOUS PROJECT MANAGEMENT

Finally, let us turn to the continuous, ongoing project management that supports this system. What does the project plan (organization, system, team, unit) responsible for change look like? First, every employee in the business unit becomes part of a project management group. Not only are they responsible for the everyday affairs of production, marketing, and so forth; but they are now also part of one or more project teams. Although they have a variety of jobs to "keep things running," they must also get involved in project assignments to change products and processes.

Second, there is no "Start" or "Stop" to these projects. The "PERT" model constrains creativity by requiring the total replacement of an old system with a new one. Those with major vested interests in the old system naturally resist disfranchisement. Such "PERT" project management destroys the possibilities of working cooperatively to improve, rather than replace, an existing system. The new kind of incremental, continuous, ongoing project management seems to be working well for the companies that are using it. It takes a complete modification of traditional organizational arrangements actually to achieve continuous project management systems.

We have examples in the U.S. of FROs that are successful in both strategic and tactical modes, though many more of the latter. Some companies that have seriously addressed this issue are: Allen-Bradley/ Rockwell International Corporation, American Honda, Brunswick, General Electric, Hewlett-Packard, Northrop, Prime Computer, Inc., and Tandem. The same applies to European and Asian firms, and more companies are trying to enter the business Olympics all the time. The combination of knowledge and will is surfacing, and where it is happening the project organizations are unique, cooperative teams. They are responsible for shaping the future, for determining emerging global leaders.

Time is the dimension that business leaders use for leverage. They minimize time to innovate (not just reduce it) by continuously innovating. They use innovation to provoke general customer dissatisfaction with existing products. This destabilizes the marketplace and permits entry and re-entry opportunities. These business leaders strive to upgrade quality standards to make obsolete the production investments of their competitors, and to supersede skill levels that formerly sufficed.

What is the message of this presentation? It is that the old, traditional, bureaucratic organization can no longer prosper--or even survive--in the present global business environment.

PART III

Corporate Leaders on Productivity and Quality

15

Introduction

Y. K. Shetty and
Vernon M. Buehler

Though the quest for leadership in productivity and quality continues, many American businesses have not yet fully recaptured the reputation for productivity and quality excellence. A recent study conducted by the American Society for Quality Control showed that even though corporate executives believe quality and productivity are the most critical issues facing American business, many do not know how to achieve it.

Major corporations throughout the United States are vigorously addressing this challenge. Companies that are known for productivity and quality leadership have lower manufacturing costs and higher profit margins, and thus capture sustainable competitive advantage. Who are these productivity and quality leaders? What can others who are trying to improve their competitive advantage learn from these companies? Even though there is no consensus on who America's productivity and quality leaders are, some companies have been recognized as such in journals such as *The Wall Street Journal*, *Business Week*, *Fortune*, and *Forbes*. Furthermore, studies have also identified companies as productivity and quality leaders. Peters and Waterman's research, published in *In Search of Excellence: Lessons From America's Best-Run Companies*, confirmed that companies such as Hewlett-Packard, IBM, Procter and Gamble, Johnson and Johnson, Maytag, Dana Corporation, Intel, Texas Instruments, Digital Equipment, 3M, Caterpillar, Delta, Marriott, McDonald's, Dow Chemical, Exxon, Xerox, and General Electric are consistently productive and provide quality products that are ranked among the top in their respective industries in financial performance over a twenty-year period. Respondents to

the American Society for Quality Control survey were also
asked to name five companies, excluding their own firms,
that they associated with high quality. Companies listed
include: IBM, General Electric, Ford, GM, Hewlett-Packard, 3M, Boeing, DuPont, Xerox, Procter and Gamble,
Kodak, Digital Equipment, Exxon, Maytag, Johnson and
Johnson, Caterpillar, McDonald's, Motorola, Honeywell,
and Texas Instruments. Many of these companies are also
listed in the *Fortune* reputation survey in the category
of Outstanding Quality of Products and Services.

This section contains papers by executives from selected companies with excellent reputations for productivity,
quality, and competitiveness, and who have participated
in USU's nationally recognized Partners Program. They
describe company efforts to improve productivity and
quality in achieving competitive advantage. Ideas for
developing and implementing quality and productivity
improvement programs are suggested, as well as descriptions of their experiences in applying those ideas for
optimal advantage.

JOHN YOUNG

John Young's paper, "Responding to the New Realities of
Global Competition," discusses the symptoms of declining
competitiveness in the United States and identifies the
underlying problems. Then he moves to examine some of
the policy choices for improving these conditions. The
balance of his paper discusses how information systems
are used at Hewlett-Packard to enhance its competitiveness by: improving the execution of business activities;
improving quality and productivity; managing assets;
tightening supplier relationships; shortening product-
development cycles; and working across geographic and
organizational boundaries. He concludes by stating that
productivity is absolutely the key to winning in the
marketplace, and that technology, along with partnerships
between business and academic institutions, can play a
major role in preparing companies to compete fully in the
changing global business environment.

A strong case is made by Julie Holtry in her paper,
"Total Quality Control: A Breakthrough Approach to Teamwork," for creating the "Juran" environment of shared
visions, teamwork, and continuous quality improvement.
She describes H-P's Total Quality Control (TQC) as an
approach for creating this environment that promises the
competitive edge needed in global markets. TQC is a
management philosophy that views every aspect of the
business relationship with the customer--internal and
external--as a process that can measured and improved
through scientific methods. Thus, quality means customer
satisfaction with documentation, sales interaction, shipment, and billing, as well as with product reliability

and durability. Perfection is the goal using a methodology that requires universal participation and teamwork. Results from their TQC teamwork include: (1) reduced manufacturing cycle time from three weeks to four days; (2) inventory reductions from four months to one month resulting in a $542 million savings; (3) reduced product repair turnaround time by 25%, and (4) reduced overdue receivables providing a $152 million savings.

LEWIS C. VERALDI

Lewis C. Veraldi's paper, "Ford's New Business Ethics: Quality is Job #1," discusses the efforts of Ford Motor Company in achieving world-class quality and improving productivity. Back in 1980, Ford's image for quality was not very good and that caused the company to examine its existing design process, which was sequential in nature: design-engineering-manufacturing marketing. Under this system each group of specialists operated in isolation from one another. Recognizing the problems involved in the traditional process, Ford replaced it by a simultaneous "team" approach in their new cars. This approach is designed to promote continuous interaction between design, engineering, manufacturing, and marketing, along with top management, legal, purchasing, and service organizations. Overall, coordination or direction is by a car product development group or by a program manager whose primary function is getting all of the team to work together.

This approach was a major factor in the success of Taurus and Sable. It has helped Ford to improve its product quality enormously--over 60 percent since 1980. The future is going to see this team approach in all new Ford Motor products. For six years in a row, Ford has been first in quality among all domestic auto manufacturers.

In "Ford's Major Transition in Continuing Improvement," William W. Scherkenbach discusses his company's massive management changes that will enable it to compete successfully in world markets. Ford uses six guiding principles based on W. Edwards Deming's fourteen obligations of top management to promote continuing improvement. They are:

1. Quality comes first: This principle applies to all elements of Ford's business and requires defect prevention rather than defect detection.
2. Customer focus: Products must meet customers needs and expectations at a price they are willing to pay.
3. Continuous improvement: There is a potential for continuous improvement in each step that companies take to create products and services.

4. Employee involvement: This is the company way of life, creating an environment in which all employees can solve job-related problems, identify improvement opportunities, and realize job satisfaction.
5. Surpass competitors in overall performance: The company intends to set the industry standards for excellence in product quality and technology worldwide.
6. Partnership with suppliers/dealers: Ford recognizes the need for joint, long-term relationships with customers and dealers, and encourages them to adopt the philosophy of continuing improvement in quality and productivity.

Scherkenbach believes that all these principles must be pursued at the same time. Ignoring or over-emphasizing any one of them will reduce the likelihood of making the transition continuous for improvement in quality and productivity.

ED FINEIN

"Xerox Gains from Productivity Innovations," by Ed Finein, discusses the experiences of his company in improving productivity to meet the challenges of the worlddwide competition. To confront the competitive challenge, Xerox in 1980 started to assess its corporate strengths and weaknesses. The company found that it took too long to develop new products its products cost too much; and it did not fully satisfy customers' requirements. The company recognized that in order to overcome these problems and to eliminate their competitors' advantages, it had to engage in an internal revolution in product design, production, and distribution.

Specifically, company renewal efforts were based on reducing product development time by one-half, reducing product development manpower by one-half, and improving unit manufacturing cost by 50 percent—an aggressive productivity improvement target. In order to achieve these targets a number of actions were taken, such as the use of customer need-based product planning, co-locating design engineers and manufacturing, and encouraging continuous supplier involvement. As a result of these actions, Xerox's engineering productivity has more than tripled. Along with productivity, the company has taken measures to improve quality, mainly in the area of process control and automation. Finein feels that Xerox has made the most progress in the area of quality for competitive advantage.

Paul A. Allaire's inspiring paper, "Quality: A Competitive Strategy," lists the dramatic results that were achieved from major changes made in the way Xerox develops, manufactures, markets, and services its products: (1) reduced manufacturing costs by 20%; (2) cut time for bringing a new product to market by 60%; (3) substantially improved product quality and market share; and (4) reduced defective parts from 8% to 3/100 of 1%. This amazing reversal of their downward slide is credited to the involvement of people in problem solving and quality improvement, which was based on these assumptions: (1) management does not have all the answers; (2) all people have ideas on how to do work more efficiently; (3) people closest to the problem often have the best answers; (4) employee involvement taps an unlimited source of knowledge and creativity; and (5) people want to share thoughts and help with solutions. He concludes with this counsel: (1) senior management must be committed to change; (2) commitment by union leadership must match that of management; (3) be prepared to make an initial investment in training; (4) patience and discipline are required; and (5) the quality process is continuous.

DOUGLAS N. ANDERSON

The comprehensive quality process at 3M is described in Douglas N. Anderson's insightful paper, "Quality, A Positive Business Strategy." 3M's quality philosophy has five parts: (1) quality is consistent conformance to customers' expectations; (2) measurements of quality are through indicators of customer satisfaction, rather than indicators of self-gratification; (3) the objective is consistent conformance to expectations 100% of the time; (4) quality is attained through prevention-oriented improvement projects; and (5) management commitment to lead the quality process. Anderson traces the implementation of this philosophy through training, removing roadblocks, creating teamwork, and providing incentives. He concludes with some successes, ranging from dramatic dollar savings to minor procedural changes that improve morale and the work environment.

WAYNE R. PERO

Wayne R. Pero's chapter, "Dow Chemical's Quality and Productivity Improvement," describes the four key elements of his company's Quality Performance Improvement Process. This process is simple and starts with the customer. The second element of the process is having a good working relationship with the suppliers. The third element is focused on the process and the recognition that continuous improvement comes from working on that process, and that the process is under management's control The focus here is on identifying, through the use of statistical tools, which processes are in control and which are not. Then everyone in the organization works on reducing the variability to bring the processes under control. The fourth element of the company program is the need to measure. These measurements, to be effective, should reveal how well the customer requirements are being met, how well the suppliers are meeting company requirements, and how well the key processes are running.

One challenge, Pero says, was to develop training programs that would help the managers and employees implement goals. Dow used a "Toward Excellence" program that rests on the fact that most successful companies have an obsession for quality products and services, and the customer is where it all starts and ends.

The next challenge was to develop a training program to make quality and productivity a way of life at Dow. This program, "Quality Performance Workshops," emphasizes dissatisfaction, vision, and application to create the change in attitude that is necessary for quality and productivity improvement. In simple terms, this training program works as follows: (1) to foster dissatisfaction with the current situation, (2) to create a vision of a better way, and (3) to encourage application of the concepts, tools, and techniques that will result in change for the better. The business teams that have gone through these training programs report significant cost reductions and quality improvements. One team claims savings of $17 million in the first year. In another, the company found ways to save $2 million in the first year.

F. KENNETH IVERSON

In his paper, "Effective Leadership: The Key Is Simplicity," F. Kenneth Iverson provides some background on Nucor Steel, a nationally recognized company that is known for its successful competitive strategy, and outlines his views about what makes a good manager in business.

Nucor used a low-cost competitive advantage by employing a more efficient mini-mill technology. The prices of their products have been equal or less than the price of the same products produced by foreign steel companies. The company has been highly profitable and in a number of years its return on stockholders' equity exceeded 20 percent.

When many of the U.S. steel companies are regularly losing money, why has Nucor been successful? Nucor's success is directly related to its ability to achieve a low-cost advantage largely resulting from its organizational structure and employee relations program. Following Iverson's "lean management" philosophy, only four levels of management separate Iverson from the hourly employees. Nucor is a decentralized corporation and managers make day-to-day decisions that determine the success of the company. It also has very few staff personnel because of top management's great confidence in operating personnel.

Nucor is also known for its employee relations program. A major part of the employee motivation system at Nucor is its employee incentive system. Many workers earn very attractive wage and this has made the company appealing to job seekers. The company has never laid off or fired an employee for lack of work in the past fifteen years. In addition, the company maintains an open communications system, so that employees are familiar with the company's plans and problems. It provides attractive benefits to employees in its management practices. What is the result of this type of program? The result has been a very productive organization. The average integrated steel company in the United States last year produced about 350 tons per employee. Nucor produced about 980! The company prides itself on being the most productive steel company in the world.

In short, Iverson's message is simple: even in a highly competitive smokestack industry, it is possible to achieve high productivity and compete successfully. The ingredients of success are modern technology, highly motivated employees, and an enlightened environment.

RODNEY J. FALGOUT

Rodney J. Falgout, in "Monsanto Upgrades QC Teams to Second Generation Work Teams," describes the evolution of a strategic human resource perspective in one division of his firm. Experiencing limited success with quality circles and other human resource programs, Monsanto recognized that it needed something more to combat the pressures of an increasingly turbulent environment. It developed a business strategy that included specific provisions for managing human resources. This strategy was communicated to all employees and was augmented by other changes in organizational structure, compensation, and training programs. Thus far, this integrated effort has improved productivity dramatically and helped the division to remain competitive.

ANDREW S. GROVE

"Human Resource Profession: Friend or Foe?," by Andrew S. Grove, CEO of Intel Corporation, provides a chief executive's perspective of the human resource function. Grove questions how well the human resource function in general has managed its task to help the firm achieve competitive advantage and bottom-line success. He challenges human resource professionals to assume more leadership in (1) "laying the track for the management systems" that guide line managers and (2) "greasing the skids" so that line mangers can perform well. His basic message--human resource practitioners must practice what they preach to help their companies to gain competitive success.

DALE P. ESSE

In "Kodak's Copy Products Quality Program," Eastman Kodak's Dale P. Esse, manager of product quality, describes their Quality Improvement Program for the Copy Products Division. The characteristics of this program, which has the active, continuous support of upper management, include: (1) strong emphasis on teamwork and communications; (2) decentralization of responsibility for quality to operating units; (3) replacement of in-process quality inspection with a final product quality assurance audit; and (4) re-directed focus on customer-perceived quality. Gains in quality and cost include: (1) 90% reduction in non-conformities; (2) major reductions in staff and unit costs for quality assurance; and (3) major reductions in rework costs. Continuous improvement is encouraged and rewarded and is becoming an essential part of Eastman's culture.

THEODORE A. LOWE

Theodore A. Lowe's essay, "Excellence in Manufacturing at GM," explores the experiences of General Motors Truck and Bus Group in improving quality. GM in this division uses the concepts from three major quality experts: W. Edwards Deming, Joseph M. Juran, and Philip B. Crosby. The company tries to understand and integrate the three approaches in order to accelerate its quality improvement journey.

Major commitment to quality improvement was initiated in 1982-1983 by providing Deming Process training to management. Since then, a series of actions has been taken, including Juran training, establishment of a Quality Council, Crosby training, union involvement, and continuous employee awareness and training initiatives. After outlining the process involvement initiatives, Lowe reviews his company's experiences in applying the approaches of experts.

Lowe feels that Deming's philosophy challenged the company's past practices and helped to introduce the statistical thinking in managing quality. The company learned from Deming and Juran that 85 percent of the quality problems are management controllable. Therefore, it is management's job to initiate action in the system to correct the common causes of variation and improve the process capability of operation.

Whereas Deming's fourteen points are more of a road map, Juran provided an assortment of problem-solving tools. In addition, Juran recommended four major thrusts in the quality improvement process:

1. Establish annual quality improvement goals.
2. Establish hands-on leadership toward quality improvement.
3. Establish an executive steering committee to lead the quality improvement process.
4. Establish a vigorous education and training process.

To accelerate the company's quality journey further, it needed to achieve an awareness and involvement of the entire work force, from top to bottom. Philip Crosby's program provided the mechanism for transforming the quality of the whole company. Crosby's fourteen steps gave the company guidance for building a quality improvement attitude throughout the organization. Lowe feels that the ideas of Deming, Juran, and Crosby are complementary. For example, the Deming process is reinforced by the Crosby fourteen-step process to assist management in transforming the organization. It also needs Juran's breakthrough process as a framework for applying statistics. The effectiveness of Juran's problem-solving approach is enhanced by the application of statistical tools that the Deming process promotes. By integrating the three approaches, the company has made tremendous advances in its quality improvement efforts.

ROBERT A. COWIE

"Dana's Five Steps for Improving People Involvement," by Robert A. Cowie, focuses attention on the measures the company has taken in linking human resource management with its strategic plans. The company goal is to be the low-cost, high-quality supplier in selected markets worldwide. This means that the company must have high productivity, a fast response, and a bottom-up orientation, and also be customer-driven. To accomplish these objectives, Dana uses a number of human resource management practices, such as open communications with company employees, employee involvement, job rotation, and promotion from within. These activities are geared to promote identity with Dana and eliminate excessive controls on employees.

H. DON RIDGE

In "IBM Profits-from-People Programs," H. Don Ridge notes that all IBM managers are held responsible for two things. First, they are responsible for getting things done. Second, they are responsible for managing the people who report to them. As a result of this approach, line managers, and not human resource professionals per se, are the key human resource managers in the company.

Key features of IBM's human resource programs include an appraisal program, identified as PPCE (performance planning, counseling, and evaluation); merit pay philosophy, which emphasizes superior performance; equal opportunity; employment security; open communication with employees; and an extensive educational program. Ridge attributes IBM's successes to it recognition that people are its most valuable resource.

JOE C. COLLIER, Jr.

In his paper, "Quality: America's Path to Excellence," Joe C. Collier, Jr., formerly Senior VP of Florida P & L and now president and CEO of Central Maine Power Co., describes how Florida P & L--the first company outside Japan to compete for Japan's coveted Deming Prize--instigated its QIP (Quality Improvement Program). This came after visiting Japan's Deming Prize-winning service-oriented firm, Kansai Electric Power Co., a user of Total Quality Control. Collier discusses the key to QIP--determine customers' valid needs and mobilize the entire firm as part of a culture change to meet those needs--and its four principles: (1) focus on customer satisfaction; (2) apply the PDCA (plan-do-check-act) cycle to all jobs; (3) manage by fact; and (4) respect people. The program involving 1700 Quality Improvement Teams has reduced service unavailability from 70 to 48 minutes, lowered unavailability of fossil units from 14% to 7%, reduced lost-time injuries to zero, and cut complaints by 75%.

BOBBY INMAN

The next paper is "Exploiting Technology to Regain Markets," by Bobby Inman. As a retired admiral with a distinguished record in the intelligence field, Inman, now a corporate leader in speeding the commercialization of new technology, traces the role of technology in the growth of the United States and suggests actions to improve the creation, application, and marketing of technology. To protect our leadership in creating technology we must increase the use of government grants for graduate studies in science and engineering, and reinstate the R&D tax credit policies. To speed the application or commercialization of technology, he suggests: (1) reducing the barriers to commercializing government-funded technology by streamlining regulatory processes and shortening the procurement cycle; (2) facilitating the flow of technology from university labs by better patent policy and reduction of bureaucratic rules; and (3) increasing private sector collaboration in the precompetitive phase of research to ensure getting a critical level of sustainable effort, for industry must have a constant focus on time and quality as well as cost. To improve the marketing of technology, Inman is persuaded by the Japanese experience that we must focus on quality and understanding foreign cultures. His conclusion is that, to be a global competitor and maintain our standard of living, the United States must focus on time, quality, and cost.

ARDEN C. SIMS

As one of only three winners (along with Motorola and Westinghouse), of the coveted Baldrige National Quality Award--the highest quality honor in the United States-- presented by President Reagan in 1988, Arden C. Sims, the president and CEO of Globe Metallurgical, a small producer of specialty alloys, describes the actions taken to achieve the quality turnaround after recounting the problems facing Globe. Actions included: (1) train all employees and suppliers in quality techniques; (2) establish QEC (quality, efficiency, and cost) committees at all organizational levels; (3) communicate the advantages of quality to employees; and (4) determine the quality needs of customers. Among the results of Globe's quality efforts was recognition including: Ford Motor's Q! and Total Quality Excellence Awards; Utah State University's Shingo Prize for Manufacturing Excellence; and the Baldridge National Quality Award. Sims concludes with these steps for maintaining and improving quality: (1) recognize that quality improvement is a continuous daily process; (2) keep communications open to employees, suppliers, and customers; and (3) capitalize on your quality recognition and keep striving for more achievements.

RICHARD S. SABO

In his timely paper, "Linking Merit Pay with Performance at Lincoln Electric," Richard S. Sabo describes the key elements of that firm's widely recongized and very successful compensation system. The steps to ensure fairness and honesty in accomplishing this difficult task are outlined, followed by an enumeration of these benefits: (1) helped maintain the firm's position as the world's largest manufacturer of Arc Welding products for 53 years; (2) low employee turnover rate; (3) high quality products with minimal rejection rates; (4) no union strikes; and (5) no company debt with an unbroken record of dividend payments.

JOHN R. BLACK

John R. Black's essay, "Boeing's Quality Strategy: A Continuing Evolution," provides an overview of the quality improvement process within the Boeing Companies. The formal efforts to enhance quality started in 1980. The company goal is to deliver products that meet its commitment to excellence--to make Boeing the recognized standard for the quality, aftersales support, and for technical and economical performance for those products. As a part of the program, Boeing made a comprehensive attempt to change company culture. Along with it, the company established a quality improvement program. It focused on developing a comprehensive and cohesive strategy for implementing employee involvement.

The quality circles process is a part of the employee involvement program and is responsible for systematically locating and solving problems. One half of the projects provided cost savings, while the other half resulted in improvements that are highly significant, but are not easily convertible to dollar figures. According to Black, Boeing expects to achieve significant results in the future. They expect to have (1) all employees trained in the use of statistical tools, (2) a pilot project on self-regulating work teams, and (3) layers of management reduced. The company is also planning to use suppliers that have their processes under statistical control.

The process of continuous improvement, to which Boeing is committed, is not one that can suddenly be realized in a company. Every company must make it its own. Top management must be committed, employees must be involved, and the process must be locked in for the long term. Only then will the program achieve the most results.

CLIFFORD J. EHRLICH

The paper, "Marriott Benefits by Linking Human Resources with Strategy," by Clifford J. Ehrlich, describes the driving forces for strategic human resource management and the methods used at the Marriott Corporation to link human resource management to strategic planning.

Ehrlich believes that two factors have magnified the issue of linking human resources to strategic planning: the ascending importance of strategic planning in the management process and the increasing scarcity and costliness of human resources. Marriott attempts to achieve a linkage between strategic planning and human resource activities in several ways. First, the vice president for human resources reports the president and chief executive officer, and the human resource executive for each division, in turn, reports to the general manager of the division. This results in the human resource staff being present when important company plans are discussed. A second linkage occurs in the budgeting process, in which the human resource activities are closely scrutinized on the basis of how they contribute to the achievement of specific strategic objectives. A third linkage is simply the result of the awareness among the human resource executives of the company's strategic direction. This linkage has helped the company develop a staffing plan to meet the growth needs of the strategic plan and to improve the compensation program aimed at encouraging the company's growth plans.

MARK SHEPHERD

"Current Challenges for American Industry," by Mark Shepherd, Jr., analyzes the massive changes taking place in U.S. industry and makes a number of recommendations for improving its competitiveness. While the United States is struggling to regain its competitiveness, the nations of the Asia/Pacific Region have skillfully exploited their labor-cost and productivity advantages to increase steadily their share of world markets.

Productivity is the key to the country's competitiveness. Lower productivity growth in the United States has contributed to reduced profit margins, flat production, downsized capacity in terms of both capital and labor, and an increasing loss of market share to imports. America's competitive strategy however, should not rely on forcing our trading partners to give up their legitimate advantages. Instead, we should develop a strategy that builds on America's strengths to tip the competitive scales in our favor, says Shepherd. To this end, he suggests:

1. Balancing the financial scales between the United States and its international competititors. This would necessitate actions aimed at: increasing the availability of capital, reducing its cost, and reducing the distortions in exchanges rates.
2. Improving the basic skills of the work force. Technical manpower shortages should be remedied through encouraging more students to pursue engineering and science education.
3. Accelerating the development of advanced manufacturing processes that facilitate the transition from R & D prototype to full-scale commercial production. The government should encourage R&D--

and help provide firms with the cash flow necessary
to develop advanced manufacturing technologies.

Shepherd believes that in these changing times our
traditional ideals of freedom, patriotism, and spirit
must be blended with new values: a zeal for winning; a
firm belief in fiscal responsibility; a determined effort
to tilt our nation's resources toward productivity and
investment; a revival of the American work ethic; and a
firm determination to manage our destiny. It is time for
American ingenuity to come to bear on the problem of
international competition.

SUMMARY

In summary, these insightful papers by America's outstanding achievers in quality and productivity provide
much hope for a renaissance in U.S. competitiveness.
Their strategies for improving competitiveness generally
deal with the use of human resources, technology, product
development, quality, and productivity. Stress was
placed on the need for continuous incremental improvement
in quality and productivity. In this increasingly
competitive global marketplace, it was emphasized also
that products must be developed that are targeted for
specific customers, markets, and locations. Speed and
flexibility are essential in producing for these niche
markets. Finally, these papers show that the US is
making encouraging progress in the competitive race by
improving productivity and quality, applying new technologies, and increasing employee involvement and teamwork.
But there is no room for complacency!

16

Responding to the New Reality of Global Competition

John Young

Having to compete in the world environment is a new idea for most Americans. We have taken being competitive for granted during most of our nation's history. That can no longer be safely assumed.

Today I think we need to start with an assessment of where we stand, and then I'm going to try to leap from global competition to information systems, if you can believe that. I'm not going to postulate information systems as the savior of our national competitiveness, but I think I can make a credible case for its playing an important role. In fact, a partnership between a lot of the academic work and a lot of the practitioners' work in companies might be the best way to bring about that renaissance.

RESPONDING TO GLOBAL COMPETITION

I'd like to talk about responding to this reality of global competition. As I indicated, it's a subject that I have spent an awful lot of time on. I did chair this commission for President Reagan, and gave him our report in January of 1985, just about three years ago. I learned that the fate of many commission reports is to go directly to the Smithsonian without passing through either very many heads or hands.

I discovered that there's also a reason for that. You know, there's no owner for some report like this. You don't clear out your desk and clutch this new idea to the number one of your overall agenda. So I formed this organization, the Council on Competitiveness, to provide

some continuing emphasis, and that's what we're doing.
We're looking for those windows of opportunity, particularly in the public policy area, where we can advance our
competitiveness agenda. Incidentally, we just completed
a project of assessing the competitive statements and
postures of all 13 presidential candidates.

Let's start by reviewing the changing environment that
causes us to have to rethink that taking for granted of
our ability to compete. In 1960 we had less than 5 percent of our gross national product involved in any way in
international commerce. That's up close to 25 percent
today, and we are deeply linked by a whole variety of institutions with the world trading environment. World
trade itself has grown dramatically, by a factor of
seven, since 1970, faster growth than most nations'
economies. So the international marketplace is a real
area of opportunity.

There are new competitors. We mostly grew up in this
country thinking about Europeans as our natural trade
allies. Facts are that by 1991 or 1992 we will do two
times the trade with the Pacific Rim countries that we do
with all of Europe. And that rate of increase is diverg-
ing at a very rapid rate. So we have to understand who
those new competitors are. The so-called NICs--newly
industrializing countries on the Pacific Rim--have made
concerted efforts to nurture specific, high-growth industries. They have taken advantage of some national targeting strategies, things that are well understood by the
Japanese and were perfected by the Japanese. These
strategies include closing the home market, building a
base of capability, assembling the technology in today's
very mobile technology world, and then developing export
markets.

These targeting strategies constitute new rules of
competition to which governments--and other firms--have
not yet responded. They work like a charm, and you do
that with a very different cost base and are able to
catapult your economy ahead in a dramatic way that has
never quite been accomplished before. Real GNP growth
rates of 5, 6, 7, 8, 9, 10 percent per year.

With the growing trade of things like intellectual
property, there are whole new rules of the road. Non-
tariff barriers to trade have grown up at a dramatic
rate, and despite four rounds of improving GATT--the
Tokyo round, the Kennedy round, and others I'm sure
you're familiar with--the real barriers to trade have
grown, not decreased. A lot of that has to do with the
character of trade. It's no longer just manufactured
goods, it's intellectual property. The most important
things we own fit on a roll of tape. Yet, you can buy
that roll of tape for a floppy program with Lotus 1-2-3
on it at any vendor stall in Hong Kong for $1.50. That's
the cost of the floppy. What's on it has no recognized
value by a very large fraction of the trading world.

These are all issues that are before us that we have to think about in considering what's going on.

Let's start with an agreement on what competition means. You have to get your mind out of what it means as a company and start thinking about a country because we're talking about a nation. Competitiveness is the degree to which a nation can, under open and fair market conditions, produce goods and services that meet the test of international markets while simultaneously maintaining or expanding the real incomes of its citizens.

That means not marking down your goods by cheapening your currency, like we are doing today to clear our inventories. The challenge is to meet that international competition under open fair, conditions, doing it in a way that enhances our standard of living.

Note that competitiveness isn't an end in itself. It's a means to an end, and the desired goal is a rising standard of living. For individual people, that means rising real wages. Those high wages don't come automatically; they must be earned in a world economy. For nations, a rising standard of living provides the means of achieving other national goals--at least any that require money from tax receipts.

SYMPTOMS OF DECLINING COMPETITIVENESS

We've got some symptoms that we are not doing as well as we might in meeting that competitiveness test. I distinguish symptoms from the real root causes. I'm going to talk about both, but first let's look at some of the symptoms:

1. Massive trade deficits
2. Declining rates of return in manufacturing
3. Loss of world market share in high tech
4. Stagnant real wages
5. Failure of the economy to create new jobs

A merchandise trade balance is an indicator, a symptom, it's not an end in itself. After all, I think last year Uganda had a positive trade balance. but you wouldn't argue that was a total proxy for affluence in the world market. So this taken apart from everything else is just an indicator. It's one of several ingredients I think you have to look at. Yes, our trade imbalance has been exacerbated by the strong currencies in the 1980s. But you can see we began having our problems well over a decade ago. We had a positive trade balance every year this century until 1970. It began really changing over the 1970s and 1980s and even at times when the currency was cheap. So that's an issue.

Real returns on capital. What kind of pay-back do you get from investing in manufacturing assets? You can look at the industrial bond yields as a kind of a proxy for

the market rate of return for that kind of not-too-risky
a return, compared to equity returns, the investments,
and real manufacturing assets. We can see again a long-
term trend line of declining returns. In fact, in recent
years you could have made as much money on passbook savings as you could have made in investing in industrial
American assets. Again, this is not too persuasive a
picture that we in fact are competing effectively as a
nation.

Some people say, "Okay, big deal. Most of the stories
you hear about industrial America, the so-called rust
belt, don't matter. Those industries were last year's.
High tech is what it's all about, and they are going to
save us from this problem."

Well, if you define high technology simply as those
industrial sectors that spend more than 5 percent of
sales, on an average, on R & D, you can look at that set
of industrial sectors, and you will see by world market
share comparisons that in only three cases has our market
share even stayed the same or grown. In most cases it's
dramatically declined. In fact, if I looked at the statistics for 1986, the only year that we have complete, we
see that the trade deficit with Japan for electronics is
greater than it is for automobiles. There's a partnership between the technology and traditional manufacturers
that's quite real.

One of the tests we said we had to meet was maintaining or increasing our real standard of living. A lot of
people know in their hearts and in their pocketbooks that
we, in fact, are not doing as well as we have done over
a lot of years. We crested in the early 1970s and we are
about 8 percent below that level today. That's why there
are so many working spouses, two-income families, and
other arrangements that have gone on to allow consumers
to continue some of their historic growth patterns, which
have happened for some different reasons than the output
per hour really being improved.

FACTORS DETERMINING COMPETITIVENESS

With some of these symptoms, then, let's move to the
next step and see what these underlying problems are and
what policy choices there are for thinking about improving some of these activities.

First of all, we said trade policy was one of those
underlying causes.

In theory, the way it works is this. It only works
this way in the United States. The U.S. trade representative (USTR), Clayton Yeuter, negotiates trade policy,
but the total enforcement mechanism is in the Department
of Commerce. That sounds a little crazy, but it turns
out it doesn't matter because they don't have the power
anyway. All of the real key decisions are made by either
the State Department, for reasons of political interest,

or by the Department of Defense to enhance national
security issues. Time and time again, over our postwar
history, we have traded away, subordinated, and otherwise
given short shrift to our trade issues for other national
policies.

That was great after the war when we had such an enormous influence in world policies. Today, that is no longer the case. We really have to have a very different
understanding of, and enforcement of, our trading system.

There's a kind of a blind response among so many in the
current administration that free trade is the answer to
every problem, which simply doesn't recognize the realities of life that there are so many non-market economies,
so many mixed and planned economies, so many developing
countries who use different rules than are covered by the
rules of the road, that it simply doesn't map out the
reality of today's world marketplace. The world's trading system has inadequate rules for trade in intellectual
property, and there are as yet no remedies for many
"non-tariff" or hidden trade barriers. The upcoming GATT
round and many changes in this area are absolutely
critical to maintain the integrity of the world trading
system.

Likewise, the instability of world financial markets
calls for better coordination of fiscal and monetary
policy among the world's most active trading nations.
Capital issues are fundamental. Cost of capital is an
ingredient that grows across parts of our country. Our
savings rate is abysmally low. It's the worst among all
of our trading partners, and of course you can't invest
what you don't save, and that means our cost of capital
is high.

The Commission on Industrial Competitiveness assembled
more than 30 economists to give testimony on our nation's
cost of capital compared to our major trading partners.
We got our greatest surprise: They agreed with each
other! Now they didn't agree on how to compute it, but
the answer was clear. Cost of capital is somewhere between two and four times as large in the United States as
it is for our Japanese competitors. A very fundamental
ingredient, savings rate, is much higher even in Germany.
But if I add the newly industrializing countries'--Sing-
apore's, Korea's, and so forth--you would find savings
rates up in that 40-percent band. It's just a dramatic
reinvestment climate.

These first two factors--trade policy, and savings
rates and capital costs--should motivate business leaders to get more actively involved in public policy issues, to which only government leaders can provide the
solutions.

The currency ratios, a subject of very great debate and
discussion in the newspapers of the United States, I
think, is interesting to take a moment to talk about. I
claimed at the outset of this section that these were the
root causes, but I want to tell you that despite what

many people think and say, I do not think myself that
currencies are a cause. Currencies are a dependent
variable. They're an outcome of many other activities.
If we're incurring a trade deficit, we're paying for
those goods that come in, let's say from Germany, in
dollars. But if we're selling less to them, we're not
generating as many marks as the Germans are paying us.
So if you go home to Germany with this sack full of
dollars, you cannot spend dollars in Germany. You've got
to convert them into marks to have something that's
useful to you. So there are more dollars to be converted
into marks, and you would see the dollar then tending to
go down, not up.

That's the textbook scenario, but in reality it's going
exactly backwards from what logic would tell you would
happen. Why? I puzzled about that for months, and I
finally discovered the answer. There are so many dollars
in the world today. It is the international currency of
exchange. If I went to New York this morning, and today
was a typical day in New York at the New York Fed that
clears dollars, you would find that about $1 trillion
will change hands in New York today. You compare that
with our $4.5 trillion economy and you see that's a lot
of dollars. It turns out that the financial transactions
in dollars are about 50 times larger than the trade
transactions.

If I take some actions that get the financial aggregates out of balance, the resulting transactions over-
whelm trade. So what happened? The trade imbalance was
going as we just described, but we currently created this
giant fiscal deficit. We drove up the interest rates
that had every portfolio manager around the world thinking in dollars, moving that money around to take advantage of these higher returns in dollars. So we've
created this trade situation out of fundamentally a
fiscal imbalance problem.

It's really important to understand the differences
between the real root causes and some of these symptoms.
No amount of trade bill activity, no amount of legislation aimed at that problem is going to really solve the
root cause. It's so important that our Congressmen
understand that, and we keep working to make that point.

Let me move to another factor in competitiveness--
technology. Commercial technology. If you eliminate
defense, we're being dramatically outspent by our competitors. You can see those growth rates; they're just
dramatic. Probably 75 percent of our productivity growth
rate in the United States has been influenced by technology. You can just look at those curves and get a sense
of what's likely to happen.

Productivity is a fair competitiveness factor. This is
probably the summary judgement. Yes, an absolute level
of output. We're still pretty good. But these are rates
of change, and all of those competitors have dramatically
better rates of change and are closing in at a very rapid

rate. So our real wealth per person--our standard of
living--fundamentally goes back to getting more output
per person. You see a rather discouraging spot when
you're even below the UK. I could have picked any period
of time, and we could have gotten that same answer.
We'll get the same answer no matter what.

WHITE COLLAR PRODUCTIVITY

We're starting to head now more toward some other
issues that end up at the management of information systems. When we look at the goods-producing sector, we see
that total output per worker from the mid-1970s to mid-
1980s went up, for all workers, roughly 11 percent. If
I take a look at only production workers, people whose
job really is production, we see that despite a lot of
criticisms about productivity, they haven't done that
badly. They have a 20-percent increase in output per
person. Let's take a look at another category of employees, roughly called knowledge workers--that is, people
who work with information. That's roughly half of the
jobs in the country. Here we find a rather interesting
story. Their lack of productivity, or negative productivity growth rate, has in fact offset half of the growth
from the real production workers.

The information sector has a much different job mix
than the goods-producing sector, and output per worker in
the information sector is so low--those service economy
productivities are so bad--that it's really ruining
America's productivity situation. This, mind you, is
happening in spite of huge investments in high technology
equipment.

THE PUBLIC SECTOR AGENDA

I think about competitiveness by thinking about a
public sector agenda and a private sector agenda, because we are really partners in this country. Companies
don't make trade policy. They don't set fiscal policy.
They don't deal in monetary policy. They don't set the
investment levels for technology, and so forth. But how
well that's done indelibly sets the framework within
which competition takes place. If that is not done well,
I don't care what kind of a genius manager you are,
you're not going to win in today's world marketplace. So
that's the public sector agenda. A lot of things we've
been talking about have to do with that set of issues.

A SHARED AGENDA

We have a couple of areas in which we are real part-
ners--education and technology. About half of the R & D

dollars, $125 billion last year, are spent by the private
sector and half by the federal government. It's a real
partnership. Of course, a lot of that gets spent in
universities and other educational institutions, which
brings us to the other partnership--K through 12 as well
as the university. That's public money. Yet for companies like Hewlett-Packard, one of our largest investments
is in training and retraining employees. Young people
entering the work force today are probably going to have
five different careers. They will need to be retrained
five times in their working lives. It's a very major
investment to acquire and maintain those skills.

THE PRIVATE SECTOR AGENDA

For the private sector, being competitive is only their
responsibility; no government can do it for them. If
government could, of course, the Concorde would be the
world's most successful airplane, having been legislated
into existence and supported. Of course, that is simply
not the case. So the private sector has to do its job
well.

That's all I'm going to say about public policies. It
was more of a way of getting into this information idea,
and I'm going to use our own company as a proxy for the
private sector, not that it truly is, but it's one that
I know enough about to credibly discuss. Some things
we've been working on, particularly how information ties
to a competitive renaissance in American private sector
competitiveness, are quite relevant.

So let me just go on to some of the things we have been
working on in our own company. This is about the same set
of issues that our Commission identified that people
ought to work on.

First, increased international presence. You just
can't export things from Logan, Utah, when that's your
only base of operation. You have to have a real international understanding, a presence in many countries.
Many U.S. companies have not made that effort. Our Commission determined that about 25,000 more companies could
export than do today. We are so horizon-bound as to not
see the potential. For Hewlett-Packard, half of our
business comes from outside the United States and we have
major manufacturing and marketing locations in almost 50
countries around the world.

Second, shortened product-development cycle. With the
mobility of technology today, time to market is everything. Mobilizing your resources to take advantage of
flexible manufacturing and some of those other things
that have been the issue for the last ten years--I think
time to market is the issue for the next ten years. It's
really incumbent on companies to understand the full implications of what that means. So reduced manufacturing
costs, getting a team, fielding a team of employees,

getting rid of those cultural barriers--all these are a
critically important set of issues.   This includes
simpler, easier-to-build design, total quality control,
standardization and consolidation of key manufacturing
processes, and closer relationships with suppliers.

Third, focusing on real customer needs sounds obvious,
but it's honored in the breach many times.   Customer
needs should dictate strategy and structure. HP has just
completed a major overhaul of its computer platform.

Finally, using information systems to create this
competitive advantage.   We're going to see in a little
bit of detail of how we have approached this problem.   HP
is running at about a $10 billion rate this year.   We are
active in measurement and computational products and very
active particularly in distributed computing.   That business direction mirrors our own use of computers inside of
HP.   We have about $200 or $300 million in expenses for
our business information systems.   It is up to 3.6 percent of sales and not an insignificant investment level
for sure. We run our company on about 850 of our HP 3000
computers, all networked together.   We have 82,000 employees.   And for the business needs, not engineering,
but the business of Hewlett-Packard, we have about 65,000
terminals and personal computers for those 82,000 people.
We have perhaps the most information-rich environment
that I know of in any company, and we use it as a very
real strategic asset in our business.   It's a way of con-
necting people to the critical issues we are trying to
improve in our company.   Managing information is considered an integral part of running the business at HP.
Our information strategy is set and managed by our
Management Council--the company's key operational committee. Each functional area--manufacturing, R & D, marketing, and so forth--defines the information needs for its
activities.   This approach means that the applications
and systems implemented really match the strategic needs
of our business partners.

At HP we've identified which information flows need to
be managed on a uniform, global basis and which ones can
be adapted a bit more to meet local needs.   There are
five global systems that gather information from HP's
more than 375 sales and service offices and its more than
54 manufacturing facilities. The global systems are controlled from the corporate level.   However, there are
many other local or "shared" systems that have been adapted to suit the operational needs of different HP entities. To ensure that we can still gather data from these
local systems and amalgamate it in a useful way, we've
defined 30 different basic business codes.   These are
items that must be uniquely identified on a companywide
basis--such as employee, customer, or part number. These
codes enable us to centralize the information without
centralizing the activity.

USING INFORMATION AS A STRATEGIC RESOURCE

What kinds of issues have we pursued, given our agenda?
First, the better execution of our business activities.
Second, improving quality and productivity. Third, managing our assets. Fourth, tightening our supplier relationships. Fifth, shortening our product-development
cycles. Finally, working across geographic and organizational boundaries.

This last one is an interesting one to think about,
organizationally at least. Most of the real payoffs of
CIM, computer integrated manufacturing, could often be
described as the automation of cooperation.

What are some of the payoffs we've seen from our investments in information systems? Well, let me just list
a few of those most easily quantified:

1. HP's sales in 1987 were $8.09 billion. If our
   inventory were still at that level of 20.5 percent,
   we would have had a total of $542 million in
   working capital tied up in inventory.
2. Similarly, we've reduced our accounts receivable by
   $146 million over the same time frame. We achieved
   this by using our distributed information systems
   to improve the accuracy of our order processing.
   Since we installed this system, we've cut our costs
   to process a dollar's worth of orders by two-
   thirds.
3. At the beginning of this decade, we began efforts
   to reduce our field failure rates to one-tenth of
   their 1979 levels, and we're well on our way toward
   achieving that goal. Our total quality control
   efforts deserve the credit, but information systems
   have played a key role. For example, we're able to
   provide our suppliers with very accurate quality
   data, and we've used it to help them reduce incom-
   ing defects by 90 percent since 1982.
4. Finally, we've provided our sales force with
   portable computers, which has enabled them to
   reduce time spent in meeting and information
   gathering and to spend more time with customers.

How did we achieve those results? Well, working on
quality has been one of the major drivers. I set a goal
for our company of cutting the failure rates of the hardware products we make by 10 to 1 over the decade of the
1980s. There's no question we're going to achieve that
objective. And if you plotted out what that meant today
we would be a factor of 6 better than in 1979, and that's
exactly where we are. There's been a terrific pay-back
in a variety of ways. Certainly customer satisfaction is
a big intangible, but there's some very major tangible
benefits of reduced costs. In analyzing our manufacturing costs it's not just the 1-percent warranty cost that
we have that is affected by better quality. Around a

third of total manufacturing costs are incurred because you do not do things right the first time. That's what's there to be gained.

Inventory savings are another. Most of your inventory is in place to fix failures. Inventory really is a stock-stockpile to fix the mistakes. When you stop making mistakes, suddenly you don't need that inventory. In fact, that turnover ratio is down significantly, it's a half a billion dollars in inventory we don't have. That is more than the total profit price of every computer at retail value we own in our company. Out of assets substitution alone, we have gotten back that total information system's investment just in inventory.

Things like accounts receivable savings simply prove that quality works in information as well as in products. Amazingly enough, you send a customer a bill that looks like what he ordered, they send you a check. But if you send them a bill that doesn't match what he thinks he ordered, they assign the newest clerk they hired to spend at least six weeks wrestling that problem.

Let's look at sales force productivity. We did a total quality control analysis of this process-oriented discipline. We found out that, by putting a portable computer in the hands of every salesman, we could change the way they work. We have increased the time in front of our customers by 35 percent measured data. That's a dramatic improvement in productivity.

TECHNICAL BARRIERS TO USING INFORMATION

There are a lot of technical barriers to using information. HP's product strategies have been aimed at eliminating these technical barriers:

1. Slow support for standards
2. Hierarchical and proprietary networks
3. High cost of ownership for computers
4. Inability of PC users to access data located on corporate systems
5. A bewildering variety of "unfriendly" computer user interfaces

In short, HP understands what technical barriers have prevented people from using information as a competitive resource. I won't give you a marketing pitch, but I can assure you that our product strategies have the goal of eliminating those barriers. And I'm proud to say that the list is getting shorter every day.

MANAGEMENT BARRIERS

There are some further management barriers to using information. Information people started in that funny

glass room that was temperature-controlled and had that
100-horsepower chiller out there to keep things from
burning up. Computer gurus talked funny languages and
they never got integrated into the fabric of the company.
They weren't accepted as real strategic partners.   Consequently, operations people do not appreciate, in every
case, what information they need or could better help
what they do, and the information people are often
isolated from the real strategy in the company.   This
kind of a separation presents a pretty serious problem.
     There's also a narrow view of the strategic potential
of information systems and their investment returns.
I've heard CEO after CEO say, "How do we get our information systems costs down?"   They don't ask how they can
get the value up or what they can do to take advantage of
their information resources. If you don't take a lot of
care in looking at cause and effect relationships, you
don't see those potential problems.   A third management
barrier is the lack of company-wide information flows.
One even more cynical than usual CEO remarked to me the
other day, "Why should I spend all this trouble getting
my computers to talk to each other when our people don't
talk to each other anyway."   Well, I think he had a
point.   In his case it may be hopeless, but it's a sad
commentary on the kind of teamwork that it takes to win
in that new global marketplace we're talking about. There
is no room for the "them and us" or the half-hearted
effort.   It's got to be a dedicated team environment and
you need to work across these boundaries.   And those
organizational cultural barriers to change are very real.

A VISION OF THE FUTURE

     A vision of the technology has begun to emerge that
will make it possible for business and technical decision
makers to gain access to useful information and to use it
to competitively differentiate their firms.

-    Computer customers will be able to choose from a
     wide variety of applications and systems provided
     by different vendors and to integrate them into a
     companywide network that makes it possible to ex-
     change information.
-    Computing Technologies will become more specialized
     for particular functions such as database manage-
     ment, design automation, and so on. These special-
     ized resources will be distributed on the network
     and available to a broad set of users. "Smart"
     networks will automatically select the computing
     resources on the network that are the most appro-
     priate and available for a given task.
-    Software tools (for instance, data reduction tools)
     will be available to search for the information,

translate it into a usable form, and display it in
a way that complements decision making. Artificial
intelligence will play a role here.
- User interfaces will be intuitively simple and consistent across all applications, allowing the user
to communicate with the system in a very natural
way. Artificial intelligence "agents" will enable
users to automate complex tasks.

CONCLUSION

My conclusion to all this is as follows: Tough competition is here to stay. This is not a one-time aberra-
tion of suddenly the Japanese showing up selling cars on
our shores. The mobility of technology today is dramatic. It is not going down, it is going up, and you'll
find increasing numbers of the world's countries with far
lower cost bases than we with access to the most modern
technical tools, manufacturing processes, and know-how
that you can imagine.
We have a joint venture with Samsung Corporation, one
of the very large corporations in Korea. On my first
trip there some five years ago, I was touring their facilities. I saw them making televisions sets and sitting
at PC monitors. I watched them ramp the VCR lines with
all these control charts and all these processes--very
sophisticated. I saw a lot of automated equipment. I
asked these guys, "You're paying these people on a production line $.40 an hour. How come all this automa-
tion?" They said it would be crazy to start a world
business today depending on cheap labor. They need the
quality; they need the repeatability. They need to do it
right. I said, "Where do you get these control charts?
Every one of these wave-solder machines has defect den-
sities on how things are going. Boy, that's pretty
elegant. I don't see that very often in the best plants
anywhere." They said, "Yes we have to keep control." I
asked where they had learned to do this. They said they
took advantage of an anomaly in the Japanese social
system. You know, they require all of their key people
to retire at age 55. So they just went to Japan. They
got all the retiring production managers and they brought
them over here to Korea. And six months later, they were
close behind the cutting edge of how it's done in the
world today.
Productivity is absolutely the key to winning. You
have to face the simple reality of that $.40 an hour
labor. We have to earn our standard of living every day
in the world marketplace, whether we like it or not.
That is the reality of it. We do that by being better at
what we do and having to regroup our forces and get our
productivity turned around. A lot of our white collar
workers, our knowledge workers, are at the core of our

productivity problem. We could really solve a lot of the
problem with better information management systems.

Some of the barriers to using information are technological. Vendors and academic institutions working with
them really have to aim at eliminating those. But the
most significant barriers I think are managerial. While
academic institutions such as the business school here
can have, I think, a major role through symposia such as
this, I think a lot of us who run major businesses have
to go back and take personal responsibility for relooking
at our programs and making sure that we are preparing our
companies to fully compete in the very changed world
environment we find ourselves in today.

17

Total Quality Control:
A Breakthrough
Approach to Teamwork

Julie Holtry

Dr. Juran has certainly impacted Hewlett-Packard's approach to quality improvement. He has taught us many things. But he has particularly helped us to focus on driving cultural, attitudinal changes in our environment: changes which facilitate quality improvement.

ATTITUDINAL & CULTURAL CHANGES

Juran says, "Before anything will be done, there needs to be a "breakthrough in attitude"--a belief that improvement is possible. And even after someone has figured out how the improvements can be achieved there is still the task of convincing everyone involved that the new method is worth a try--a breakthrough in cultural patterns." He is making an important statement to corporate management today and has reaffirmed a conclusion that we have reached at Hewlett-Packard.

Managers have a new job today: creating attitudinal and cultural changes in the workplace. Perhaps this job is the most important job of the coming decade.

Why do I say this? What is happening in business today that warrants such a conclusion? It's becoming quite clear that the world has become one very interdependent marketplace, and global competition has become increasingly fierce. Companies are being forced to change the way they do business with their customers.

This competition has even changed the way nations govern themselves. For example, you can't open a newspaper today without reading about legislation that's intended to address our import-export imbalance. And

many of you are aware of a U.S. law recently enacted to
emphasize quality. This is the National Quality Award
established for the purpose of encouraging American
businesses to practice effective quality control. The
first awards will be presented in November of 1988.

The fact is that competition is demanding much more
from us--and quality is becoming a key differentiator,
and a strategic issue which must be used as a competitive
advantage. In order to do this, quality needs to be managed differently today. Managers need to make breakthroughs in cultural patterns in our current workplace.
They must create a revitalized environment where a shared
vision becomes the driving force for quality improvement,
and teamwork is used to effectively execute these strategic visions.

We have found an approach which is helping us create
this kind of environment and achieve results in quality
improvements--results that can give us the kind of competitive edge we need to compete in global markets. The
approach is called Total Quality Control.

But before I get into this topic, let me put my remarks
in some kind of context as to our company. I am not certain how familiar many of you are with Hewlett-Packard;
who we are, what we do, what we look like. Hewlett-
Packard is headquartered in Palo Alto, California. HP is
an international manufacturer of measurement and computa-
tion products and systems used in industry, business,
science, health care, and education. HP equipment is
used in many different ways. An HP financial calculator
can help you figure out the financing for a new home. An
HP electronic test instrument helps car makers check for
vibrations so the car you drive will have a smooth ride.
An HP analytical instrument can measure the chemicals in
suntan lotion to make sure it protects you from sunburn.
An HP desktop computer helped design the fuel system for
an airplane that you might have flown in. And if someone you know ever has a heart attack, an HP medical
electronic product can help revive that person quickly.

HP sales in 1987 were $8.1 billion. From 1977 to 1987,
the company's net revenue grew at an average annual rate
of more than 20 percent. HP has 82,000 employees worldwide, a network of 410 sales and support offices and dis-
tributorships in 78 countries. Besides U.S. plants, we
have research and manufacturing facilities in Europe,
Japan, Canada, Latin America, and Southeast Asia.

First, I think it's important to review a little of our
quality history. What we know of quality management
today certainly reflects our experiences from the past.
Then I want show you how we've adapted the philosophy and
methodology of TQC to a key management process--the process of strategic planning and implementation. It's
through this process that we have attained the greatest
breakthroughs in creating the "Juran" environment of

shared visions, teamwork, and continuous quality improvement.

HP'S EXPERIENCE WITH QUALITY

Looking at our early history, I can honestly say that focusing on quality isn't really new to HP. We've focused on providing product quality excellence since the company was founded in 1939. But our perception and understanding of quality today is certainly much different than it was then. In fact, it's much different than it was just a few years ago.

Quality began moving to the forefront of company concerns at HP in the late 70s because, like many other companies, we were feeling the increased demands of competition in the marketplace. Technology was becoming more of a commodity. It wasn't enough to be making a superior product anymore. One calculator can only be so much better than another; we had to lower our prices. In order to do that we had to lower our own internal costs of doing business.

So in 1979 we conducted some cost of quality studies. In every case, we found that our costs of not doing things right the first time were from 30 percent to even 50 percent of our revenues. It was in response to this finding that our president and CEO, John Young, set what he calls a "stretch objective" or what we call 10 percent. He challenged us to improve the reliability of our hardware by a factor of ten in ten years--by 1990.

Why a factor of ten? To force us to change our basic approach, our "same old way" of doing things, and to change our expectations about what is possible. Had he asked for just a 30 percent improvement, we probably wouldn't have been motivated to try fresh approaches to our tasks.

To respond to this challenge we sent study groups to our joint venture in Japan Yokogawa Hewlett-Packard, or what we call YHP. YHP had made astounding gains in quality improvement through their adoption of Total Quality Control (TQC). They began their efforts in 1977 and in only five years these were their results:

- manufacturing cost down 42 percent
- R & D cycle time down 52 percent
- failure rates down 79 percent
- productivity up 120 percent
- market share up 193 percent
- profit up 244 percent

REDEFINING QUALITY

So all these experiences, the forces of competition and cost of quality, YHP successes and the 10 percent goal, helped to shape our current understanding of quality and actually led to our redefinition of quality.

At HP, we have found that our customers are actually redefining the quality of our products today. Quality no longer just means hardware or software reliability or durability. It now means customer satisfaction for the "total business relationship" with the customer--the quality of our documentation, the quality of our sales interactions, the way we ship the product, bill our customer, etc.

And we found that not only was quality the route to customer satisfaction but it was also the path to improved productivity. Where we found areas of high quality, we found high productivity. Where we identified areas of low quality, we identified unproductive areas. And so, pursuing quality became critical in the way we managed our business. In 1980, HP launched a company-wide TQC effort.

TOTAL QUALITY CONTROL

Before I give you some concrete examples of our results, let me take a moment and tell you how we are defining TQC at HP. It is probably not much different from how many of you have studied it or how other companies are defining it.

TQC is a management philosophy and a way of operating totally committed to quality that focuses on continuous process improvement. TQC views every aspect of the business relationship with the customer as a process which can be continually measured and improved through the use of scientific methods. Perfection is the goal. The methodology requires universal participation and a teamwork approach to problem solving. The results are "customer satisfaction."

The "customer" concept applies to both external and internal customers, and requires every person and every unit in the organization to regard itself a both a producer and a customer, and insist on receiving and delivering products and services of perfect quality at each stage of the process until they reach the end user. Thinking of colleagues as customers produces a subtle, but powerful change in people's attitudes. It helps foster the cooperation among departments and divisions that is so essential to a decentralized company like HP.

The bottom line to TQC is that it makes you ask seven very basic questions. Who are my customers? What do they need? What are their measures and expectations? What is my product or service? Does my product or ser-

vice meet their needs and expectations? What is my process for providing their need? What corrective action is
required to improve my process?

Searching for the answers to these questions fosters a
shared vision. Mapping out the direction of a group's
activity helps everyone agree on what they are actually
doing or should be doing and how to measure their performance. And when a group reaches consensus on how to measure the success of their efforts, you've gone a long way
toward building a unified team.

TQC RESULTS IN MANUFACTURING

That is enough theory. Let me briefly describe some of
our recent results and give you some examples of the way
TQC forges teamwork. In the early 1980s our manufacturing facilities were the first to follow YHP's lead. For
example, within two years our business computer manufacturing operations were able to reduce manufacturing cycle
time from three weeks to four days. Inventory went from
four months to one month. And they were able to accomplish this with 20 percent fewer people.

After we gained experience in manufacturing, we turned
our focus to other production environments. The use of
TQC in the product repair centers has enable our U.S.
support organization to reduce their repair turnaround
time by 25 percent without increasing the size of the
work force.

TQC RESULTS IN CREDIT CONTROL

Let's look at how TQC helped our accounts receivables
performance. We have an operation that, in essence,
serves as our catalog sales division. They book about 25
percent of all our orders each year, most over the telephone. Most of the sales are small.

In 1984 our overdue collections in this division were
$652,000. Management was unhappy, as were the customers
whose shipments were put on "hold" because they weren't
paying their bills. As the HP credit people dug into the
problem via TQC methodology, they turned up some surprising and embarrassing facts. In many cases, customers
weren't paying their bills due to our errors—specifically, delivery to the wrong address, wrong product, wrong
price, etc. HP improved their internal processes, dropping overdue receivables to $218,000 within two years.
That's $434,000 less invested in the business in the form
of uncollected funds.

The aggregate results of these kinds of effort throughout the company are large. Overall company-wide inventory savings have been $542 million and a natural spin-
off of this has been floor space savings of $200 million.

Companywide accounts receivable savings have been $150 million.

TQC ENGENDERS TEAMWORK

These accomplishments hinge on the kind of teamwork that TQC engenders at HP. Let me tell you another story that illustrates TQC teamwork in action. This is a case where it would have been easy for the situation to deteriorate into a finger-pointing session between divisions of HP, but it didn't.

We have an operation in Roseville, California, called Computer Support. It's responsible for supplying repair parts and exchange assemblies for all our computers worldwide. Until recently, they had a less than enviable reputation with their customers, who are HP's field sales representatives. Their delivery time just wasn't fast enough. So they used TQC methods to analyze thoroughly their own repair process and identify what slowed things down.

Their information showed them that 80 percent of their delivery delays were caused by waiting for just 20 percent of the parts they needed (Juran calls this the vital few), and that those parts, in turn, came from other HP divisions. They didn't point an accusing finger at the guilty divisions. Instead they put on an educational roadshow that they took around the company. It mapped the entire process of repairing customer orders (or end user orders)--from the customer, to HP customer engineer in our field organization, to SMO (the Roseville computer support operation), to the supplying HP division, back to computer support, and then back to customer engineers when repaired.

This broad, informative picture--and its focus on internal and external customers convinced the other divisions that they were an integral part of a very broad and important process. They are now much faster in sending parts to Computer Support, because they understand better how their own actions affect customer satisfaction. They see themselves as part of the same team.

USE OF TQC IN STRATEGIC PLANNING

I want to spend my last few minutes talking about an application of TQC that has perhaps the greatest single potential for achieving breakthrough results at HP--TQC applied to strategic planning and implementation, or what the Japanese call "hoshin kanri."

The word "hoshin kanri" is actually derived from two Chinese characters--"ho," meaning direction, and "shin," meaning needle as in a compass. "Kanri" means policy.

So the literal translation of hoshin kanri is "direction of policy" or what we call strategic planning.

There's a little story behind how we adopted hoshin. One day, a renowned Japanese quality consultant was visiting one of our divisions. He asked the general manager if he could see his annual plan. The general manager responded, "Sure, I have it right here in my desk." He reached into his desk, brought his only copy out, dusted it off, and presented it to the consultant. The consultant lifted it up to his nose, took a little sniff, and said to our general manager, "This annual plan smells a little musty. Smells like it doesn't get out of the drawer very often." On another occasion, in another division, after receiving the general manager's annual plan, this same consultant very nicely turned to him and said, "This is a very nice one hundred year plan, extolling perpetual virtue."

Well, it wasn't too hard to see his point. Some changes needed to be made in our planning and implementation process. As you may know, Juran places a great deal of importance on planning. We needed to make our annual plans living documents. We needed objectives that were clear, realistic, could be completed within an annual time frame, and could be measured. In addition, we needed implementation plans that were truly capable of driving a change throughout the organization.

So we began to implement a structured objective-setting process where objectives, strategies, and measures are all hierarchically linked together, spanning all functions of the business. This is the hoshin process. It is not my intent to walk you through this process in detail, but our planning is a process--a continuous cycle with no beginning or end. It really starts with an annual review--an analytical review of the previous year's objectives and accomplishments. Key issues are identified and analyzed from the bottom up to determine how much improvement or change is required in the next planning cycle, say one year. Extensive detailed and structured planning follows with a plan deployed at each level linked with all other plans being developed.

Here's how the plan's deployment works. A strategy and measure at one level of management will become an objective and goal to the next level down: "how" a manager wants to accomplish an objective (or his strategy) becomes the "what" that has to be done by the next level down (their new objective).

Finally, the strategies come to life through detailed implementation plans. Essential to the implementation process is periodic review. Built-in progress checks and reviews verify that the strategies were correct, the implementation is progressing, and the goals will be met. And if not, course changes are required. Of course, getting through this process is not the ultimate goal:

the ultimate goal of hoshin is improved performance. And
we are getting results!

Hoshin kanri fosters a shared vision and creates
changes in people's attitudes--employees are motivated
because they belong to a general movement in which they
are directly participating and contributing to the a-
chievement of the strategic issue.   Managers are motivated because they can be assured that the objectives
they are working on are directly tied to key customer
concerns and are aligned with their boss's priorities.
Juran, as you may know, calls this kind of participation
one of his Rules of the Road for implementing change.

We are obviously sold on the effectiveness of TQC.   We
feel it is a very important tool for our managers as they
face difficult challenges today.   Assuredly, the adoption
of TQC underscores the value of achieving breakthroughs
in teamwork to enable us to gain a strategic foothold in
world markets.   Thank you, Dr. Juran, for helping us see
the light!

18

Ford's New Business Ethics: Quality Is Job #1

Lewis C. Veraldi

Today, I would like to share with you what we at Ford are doing to achieve world-class quality and improve productivity. But, to understand where we are today and where we are going, it is necessary to understand where we have come from.

WEAKNESS OF SEQUENTIAL DESIGN PROCESS

Traditionally, Ford and other automobile manufacturers developed new vehicles in a "sequential" design process. What do I mean? Basically, throughout the design of a vehicle, each activity does its thing and then hands off to the next activity.

The designers do their thing--design--and then turn that over to the engineers. After the engineers do their job, manufacturing is told to go mass produce the product. And marketing is then told to go sell it. That's an oversimplification, but it dramatically points out the flaws in the traditional system. What you have is each group of specialists operating in isolation of one another.

Moreover, what someone designs and styles may be quite another matter to engineering, and by the time it reaches manufacturing there may be some practical problems inherent in the design that make manufacturing a nightmare. The people who actually build the vehicle haven't been consulted at all, and marketing may well discover two or three reasons why the consumer doesn't like the product and it is too late to make any changes!

As in football, sometimes the ball is fumbled during
the hand-off.

The result of this traditional process was a lack of
teamwork, poor quality, redundancy of effort, and extreme
inefficiency.

TEAM APPROACH REPLACES TRADITIONAL SEQUENTIAL PROCESS

What caused us to change the way we do business? Back
in 1980, Ford's image for quality was not very good. In
addition, we were in the process of losing over $1 bil-
lion two years in a row. In this climate, we were beginning to plan a replacement for our mid-size and large
cars. Of course, these replacements would become today's
Taurus and Sable. The investment was estimated to be $3
billion and we knew the old ways of doing business would
not work.

In their class, Taurus and Sable were to be designed to
compete with anything in the world--foreign or domestic--
in fit/finish, ride, handling, and vehicle ergonomics.
In short, they were to be designed with world-class quality and provide customers with a compelling reason to
once again shop and buy American.

As vehicle objectives were defined (and re-defined), we
knew upstream involvement and employee commitment were
essential, and that the existing organization wouldn't
support our needs. Therefore, the sequential organization was replaced by a simultaneous "Team" approach, TEAM
TAURUS.

Team Taurus's organization is designed to promote continuous interaction between design, engineering, manufacturing, and marketing, along with top management, the
legal, purchasing, and service organizations. Overall
coordination or direction is by a car product development
group or program manager whose primary function is getting all of the team to work together. All these groups
work simultaneously to bring our new car to market. Instead of being last to be involved, for example, manufacturing is involved some fifty months prior to producing
the first vehicles. The "downstream" people were fac-
tored into the program as early as five years ahead of
introduction. Thus, all activities had an equity and an
equal opportunity for simultaneous participation throughout the entire program.

To insure that the best ideas of the people who would
be designing and building the car would be considered,
our engineers developed a comprehensive "want" system.
We visited the Atlanta Assembly Plant and spoke to the
hourly and salaried personnel who eventually would build
the car. We asked them to tell us how to design a car
that was easy to build and would avoid the design problems that had led to poor quality in the past. We
visited the plant fifty months before Job #1 so that we

could incorporate their suggestions in the basic design of the product. Their suggestions, along with those of other groups, resulted in more than 1,400 wants being identified. Over half of these were incorporated into the product.

To illustrate, the assembly workers told us that to achieve consistent door openings and tight door fits, a one-piece bodyside was necessary. So we reduced the number of components on the bodyside from twelve components to two. The doors are also one piece for improved quality and consistent build.

SUPPLIERS TREATED AS PARTNERS

Just as important is the early involvement of our suppliers. In today's automobile industry, the suppliers are very critical members of the team. They are our partners and their early involvement is essential to achieving our world-class quality objectives.

On Taurus and Sable, we initiated two supplier programs:

- Early sourcing
- System sourcing

Early sourcing identifies component sources early and brings them upstream in the design process. The supplier is responsible for the fit and functioning of his components. System sourcing is a process where components that must be coordinated both in color and fit are sourced to one supplier.

An example of early sourcing is the Taurus subframe, which supports the engine and transaxle. It was sourced to A. O. Smith three years in advance. This allowed the engineering and manufacturing team to make 137 design revisions to improve the variable cost, reduce weight, and achieve an automated assembly.

By bringing suppliers into the process early, we could take advantage of their expertise. Prince Corporation, who supplies some of the sun visors, suggested several features that were added to the Taurus. These features included a dual visor system, a new pull-down visor mirror, and a new dome light which will not shine into the driver's eyes at night. Masland Carpet, the supplier of the station wagon load floor carpet, suggested a method to insure the carpet nap all ran in the same direction. The result is a uniform appearance for the load floor.

Early sourcing has another advantage. Prototype vehicles, which are built from components supplied by the production source, allow early resolution of fit and finish problems.

On a limited basis on Taurus, we initiated a process of system sourcing. The station wagon interior garnish moldings were all sourced to O'Sullivan. They were responsible for coordinating the fit and color match of all the interior garnish moldings.

Another aspect to system sourcing was the sourcing of the die models and tools for the interior garnish moldings to one supplier, Pro-mold. By having one tool supplier, we could evaluate the fits and coordinate revisions much more efficiently. The result--better fits and better quality.

ATTAINING PERCEIVED QUALITY OBJECTIVES

Several new engineering processes were developed during the Taurus program. By far, the most extensive program to involve engineering was the Best-In-Class Expanded Image Program. The intent of the program was to focus more attention on details that affect the perceived quality of the vehicle, including the interaction between the vehicle and the driver/passenger.

To determine our objective, the team sought out the best vehicles in the world and evaluated more than 400 characteristics on each of them to identify those vehicles that were best in the world for particular items. These items ranged from door-closing efforts, to the feel of the heater control, to the underhood appearance. The cars identified included BMW, Mercedes, Toyota Cressida, and Audi 5000.

Once completed, the task of the Taurus Team was to implement design and/or processes that met or exceeded those "best objectives." I am proud to report that as we went into production, we had achieved Best-In-Class status on 80 percent of these 400 items. And that was accomplished with teamwork and paying attention to the details.

Finally, we continually asked ourselves the question "WHY BUY TAURUS?" In other words, why should someone cross the street to shop in our store? We asked customers, dealers, buff magazine writers, service people, insurance companies, and professional drivers like Jackie Stewart, early in the program, what features they wanted. By the time we introduced Taurus and Sable, this translated into a feature list thirty-two pages long! These features included flush side glass for reduced noise, polycarbonate bumpers for rust-free life, and first-class seats for long-distance riding comfort.

PROGRAM MANAGERS IMPLEMENT TEAM CONCEPT

Enough history! Where are we going today? As you can see, teamwork was a major factor in the success of Taurus and Sable. Early and dedicated involvement by all members of the team was key.

The future is going to see the TEAM TAURUS approach taken to all new Ford Motor Company products. It has already been put in place and endorsed by the top management of the company who have signed a pledge of support for our new way of doing business. The team concept has been designated as the "Program Management" organization. We have identified "Program Managers" who are putting their teams together to take new cars from concept to customer the same way Taurus and Sable were brought to market.

The program managers' assignment is to provide leadership for the planning, design, engineering, sales, manufacturing, quality assurance, and service for their products. I said "their products" because it is *their product*." The objectives for each vehicle will be the basis for measuring the performance for all members of the team.

The program managers have the responsibility for the "WHAT" and "WHEN" decisions of a program and for working with the line activities who retain authority for "WHO DOES IT" and "HOW THE JOB IS DONE." The program managers have the further responsibility of involving the line people as early or as far upstream as possible--in effect making them part of the team from the beginning and involving them in the decision making.

This upfront commitment by all activities is reflected in one of the tools we have developed for the program managers, a timing discipline chart. The purpose of the chart is to get a commitment from all activities as to what tasks are required and when they must be performed. Each member of the team signs the chart. The chart allows each member of the team to see how his activity impacts other activities. For example, one area of the chart shows the design events that must occur twenty-six months before production begins. In addition, management can use the chart to assess how the program is proceeding. If these key events are performed late, we know they will affect the quality and timing of the launch of the new product.

The program manager's scope encompasses all aspects of the program and all activities. Each activity--design, manufacturing, sales, etc.--identifies one representative to work on the program manager's team. Each representative is responsible for coordinating the activities of his or her component and ensuring that the objectives of the team are achieved.

Well, what kind of person are we looking for as a program manager? I have a long list of personality traits but let me mention a few. He should be results-oriented, self-confident, product excellence-oriented, decisive, have a broad view of the organization, and, maybe most important, have a sense of humor.

IMPROVING AMERICA'S COMPETITIVENESS

Now, let me shift gears for a moment. We have made
great strides at Ford by changing the organization and
initiating new processes but people are the most important element. Our colleges and universities have a role
to play in helping us achieve our world-class objectives.
First, we need more generalists. Technical specialists
should be exposed to all facets of the business. All
disciplines need a better appreciation of the roles of
others.

Second, we need courses designed to improve America's
competitiveness. Students need a better understanding of
how quality is achieved, such as through statistical process control or quality function deployment. Continuous
study is required to identify ways to help the American
worker be more productive and efficient.

If America is going to be competitive worldwide, we
must improve our manufacturing productivity and increase
our level of engineering technology. At Ford, the results of our new process are already being realized. The
quality of Ford products has improved over 60 percent
since 1980. For six years in a row, we have been first
in quality among all domestic manufacturers. While we
are pleased with our progress, we are not there yet. The
Japanese quality is still better but the gap is closing
quickly. There is much that remains to be done. We are
developing new processes to reduce the length of time to
develop new products, improve the flow of information,
and increase the role of the supplier to include participation in product design.

In closing, let me note that the latest result of our
team effort is our new Continental to be introduced in
late 1987. The Continental is equipped with a unique
combination of hi-tech features not found collectively on
any other luxury car in the world. You'll hear more
about the Continental in the coming months.

At Ford we have a single goal and that is to be manufacturers of cars and trucks that are responsive to our
customers' wants and exhibit world-class quality in every
segment in which we compete. With the Taurus and Sable
we are starting to see it. And this is just the beginning. The sparkle in the oval is getting brighter year
after year.

19

Ford's Major Transition in Continuing Improvement

William W. Scherkenbach

I want to share with you some of the changes taking place at Ford that will enable us to compete successfully in world markets on a continuing basis. We really are in a new economic age, and just getting back to basics is not good enough anymore. This chapter deals with the "transition in continuing improvement" and the resulting implications of a massive structural change in the way we do business.

Ford Motor Company is a multinational enterprise engaged primarily in the design, manufacture, wholesale, and financing of cars, trucks, parts, and accessories. Other activities include a tractor business, aerospace and communications businesses, nonautomotive financing, land development, and outside sales of products made by automotive-supplying divisions.

To this end, the company is in business to provide:

- High-quality products and services that satisfy customers' needs and expectations
- Employment that enables people to develop and use their full abilities
- Protection of our shareholders' investment

In pursuing this mission the company must maintain mutually beneficial relationships with dealers and suppliers. It operates in ways that meet legal requirements and merit the support, trust, and approval of its many constituencies.

Mission statements are easy, although a lot of time is typically spent in developing them because every word is significant. Top management in many companies might com-

municate the mission and never realize that it is also
their responsibility to provide the beginnings of that
road map in the form of six guiding principles, which are
based on W. Edwards Deming's fourteen obligations of top
management for continuing improvement.

FIRST PRINCIPLE: QUALITY COMES FIRST

Quality comes first at Ford Motor Company. This
principle applies to all elements of our business and
requires defect prevention rather than detecting problems
after they occur. I will explain the difference between
defect detection and defect prevention later, but right
now I cannot overemphasize the phrase that quality applies to all elements of our business. Every one of us
in this company manages processes. Every one of us has
customers and suppliers, and we all affect the quality of
what the customer ultimately purchases.

I will explain a bit further: A process is a blend of
equipment, material, people, methods, and environment
from which a product emerges. This product may be paperwork, hardware, service, or a myriad of other possibilities. The product is typically sorted through mass inspection, and the good product is sent onward, while the
bad product is scrapped or reworked. Depending on the
results of the inspection, the process is adjusted to
compensate for the bad product. Many people place emphasis on the fact that the feedback to adjust the process
is rather slow. This is usually the case, but speed is
not the distinguishing difference between detection and
prevention. Automatic compensating machinery has extremely fast feedback but is usually the epitome of a
detection system. This is because it typically does not
adjust statistical signals, and this is the major difference between detection and prevention.

In a prevention system the same five types of in-puts
blend to produce an output, but instead of depending on
mass inspection of that output, the prevention system
focuses on measurement of the process as well as the output. These techniques balance the economics of looking
for trouble when none exists and not looking when it does
exist. There will always be the need to measure or verify the quality of the output, but the costly and unfound-
ed dependence on mass inspection is eliminated.

SECOND PRINCIPLE: CUSTOMER FOCUS

Customers are the focus of everything we do. Our products must meet their needs and expectations at a price
they are willing to pay. Concern for customers begins
with product planning and extends through delivery and
service after the sale. Each discipline and level should

learn the needs of their customers and the limitations of the suppliers. Management often stresses the importance of communication between engineering and manufacturing, learning one another's problems and working together as a team. Of equal importance, however, is the teamwork between marketing and sales, and product planning and engineering. Marketing and sales have got to know the customer's needs and then pass this usable information on to design and engineering for translation into something that can be produced.

THIRD PRINCIPLE: CONTINUOUS IMPROVEMENT

Continuous improvement is essential to our success. There is potential for improvement in each step that we take to create products and services. This is a strict departure from traditional practice that some level of control or performance is good enough. An excellent example of this difference in the manufacturing aspect of our business is our historical acceptance of the fact that meeting the engineering specifications was the best one could do in providing a quality product. We're now in the new economic age, and our competition is showing us that just meeting the engineering specifications is not good enough anymore if we are to consistently meet our customers' needs. Instead, we must continually reduce the variability of our products and services, thus obtaining the highest quality at the lowest cost.

Management Reviews Every System. One of the key elements of this principle is the responsibility of management to lead in the examining of every management system and operating precedent now in effect to determine whether it supports or inhibits continuing improvement in quality and productivity. Some of the systems and operating precedents are obvious, such as work standards, training, hiring and firing. But there are a host of other systems that are not so obvious that may inhibit continuing improvement. Mr. Petersen, Ford's president, has requested and received a list of inhibitors that can be changed only at the corporate level.

Let me explain further the shortcomings of these inhibitor systems and give you a look at some of the possible changes taking place at Ford.

Performance Appraisal Systems Destroy Teamwork. There are at least four major reasons why traditional performance appraisal systems are inhibitors to continuing improvement. The number one reason is that they destroy teamwork. American businesses are functionally oriented with purchasing, engineering, marketing, manufacturing, and so forth. Each discipline is evaluated on meeting some objectives that are, again, functionally oriented. For instance, high on purchasing's list is the lowering of negotiated costs. High on manufacturing's list is

that they get the tools they need to reduce their total
manufacturing costs, so purchasing might not meet their
objective of negotiating lower and lower cost because
right now better tools cost more. There is some cooperation, but it is in spite of the system, not because of
it. I might cooperate with you because we have grown up
together in the company for the past twenty to thirty
years or for whatever reason. But this cooperation only
goes so far, because my career, my family's security, my
bonus, my whatever depends on my meeting my objectives.

Performance Appraisal Systems Reduce Initiative. Another reason that traditional performance appraisal
systems inhibit continuing improvement is that they reduce initiative or risk taking. They are attribute-type
systems. That is, you either make your objective or you
do not make you objective. Because of the penalties for
failing to make objectives and because they are typically
negotiated, we end up with objectives that don't have
much "stretch" or are relatively easy to achieve. This
is a situation in which a company cannot long compete.
Another factor that contributes to lack of stretch is
fear of the unknown. A person may know of ways to achieve an 8% savings in one year. He is required by his
objectives to attain a 5% savings each year. What happens by the end of the first year? He shows a 5% savings. He effectively is banking the additional 3% for
next year so that that objective can be met. It is what
I call an Alexiev mentality. You may recall that Vassily
Alexiev was a Russian super heavyweight weight lifter.
He was paid a sum of money for each world record he
broke. Not being a dumb person, he broke a lot of world
records. But he did it a few grams at a time. We need
business systems that will foster continuing improvement,
not stifle it. The problem isn't the people--it's the
systems. People learn to play the system. And you can't
blame them for trying to survive.

Performance Appraisal Systems Overlook Nonhuman Inputs.
Traditional performance appraisals do not distinguish
between the people and the rest of the system. As I
mentioned earlier, people are just one input to a process. Other inputs include the methods, environment,
equipment, and materials. The main assumption in rewarding or punishing people is that they are solely responsible for the results of the process. Yet we know
that the outcomes are the result of blending all of the
inputs. Certainly we see differences in accomplishments,
but are those differences caused by the system or the individual? I have had the opportunity of talking with
quite a few senior executives in both government and industry, and many of them relate stories of how they were
able to ride the system at one time or another during
their career. At those times other inputs had a greater
effect on the outcome than they did. Others who followed
in that position were not as fortunate. The system over-

shadowed their best efforts, and they did not meet their
objectives. Former General Motors Chairman R.C. Gersten-
berg said of even his job, "I am like an ant on the front
of a log heading downstream toward a treacherous bend and
all I can do is stick my foot in the water to try to
steer us clear and yell 'whoa you SOB, whoa.'"

Performance Appraisals Systems Increase Variability.
Traditional performance appraisal systems increase the
variability of performance of people. This is because of
the implied preciseness of the rating schemes. What I am
going to state here will not be obvious to those who do
not understand variability, but I will do the best I can
to explain it. Traditional systems try to differentiate
performance levels. As a result, we end up with such
categories as outstanding high, outstanding low, excellent high, excellent, excellent low, satisfactory plus,
satisfactory, satisfactory minus, unsatisfactory, and so
on. This implied preciseness or ranking, it is felt,
lets people know where they stand and makes it easier for
management to determine rewards. The criteria for those
awards revolve around the assumption that we will reward
those who are above average or perhaps in the upper 1% or
5% or 10% and in the most positive light, encourage those
in the lower half or bottom 90% to do better. The reason
we will reward these categories is that we feel that the
differences in people really come from the other elements
of the system. The same system that put a person above
average one year might put him below average the next.
Because nobody really likes to be classified as below
average (and the way management has been avoiding their
responsibilities, below average now is "excellent"),
people try to emulate those who are ranked above average
or otherwise change what they are doing to get a better
rating. Because about half of the people are trying to
change to become above average, the variability of the
outcomes of the organization can increase to twice what
it would be if they would have just continued what they
were doing. Businesses cannot consistently meet their
customers' needs with a system that fosters greater variability. Even if those who are below average do not try
to change, they may be devastated by the stigma of being
below average. Until they recover from that shock, their
productivity and quality will suffer. We cannot do business today with that kind of waste.

*Performance Appraisal Systems Should Encourage Employee
Contribution.* I've stated what is wrong with present
systems, now I want to address the issue of what a system
would look like that was supportive of continuing improvement. The principal purposes of an appraisal and
development system should be to nurture and sustain individual employee contribution to the continuous improvement of the company (as a team) and to provide an assessment or evaluation of performance for the employee
and management. The system must be based on a deep re-

gard for people and recognize that employees are the company's most important resource. The system should contribute to the development and motivation of the company's most important resource. The system should contribute to the development and motivation of all company employees. This tenet will require a continuous effort in counseling, coaching, and honest, open communications between the employee and the supervisor, supported by opportunities for enhancement of professional, managerial, and interpersonal skills.

In January of 1984, I visited with executives from ten Japanese companies to find out what systems they were using to develop and evaluate their employees. I found that although they have borrowed Western-style evaluation systems, they apply Eastern criteria. I observed that while performance was the main criterion for raises and bonuses, teamwork was the main criterion for promotion. All of the companies said that their management spends a considerable amount of time (around 25%) on people-related activities. In fact, I was introduced to a people-related system that has immediate application. It is known as nomunication. The word is taken from the Japanese word *nomu*, which means to drink, and the English word communication. The practice involves workers and supervisors meeting after work at a bar to discuss opportunities for improvement! Not entirely for the above reason. I returned from Japan very enthusiastic about what I had learned. What I learned was that this is an area in which we are not ten years behind them. If management acts now to change our system, we can better develop our human resources, which will enable us to be more competitive.

They also spend considerable time on training in a wide variety of subjects. Much of the training emphasizes teamwork as well as skills development. The emphasis on training can be better understood in analyzing the two business approaches. In Japan the emphasis is on hiring the best possible people. Much effort is put into the interviewing and selection process. Once the best people are hired, they are trained in ways to meet the company's customers' needs. In the United States, certainly we want the best possible people, but our real emphasis is on our business systems.

What I am proposing is a rating system that recognizes the fact that most people should be performing within a system. That is, if management has done their job of selecting, training, and developing their people, and if you are performing within a system, there can be no further distinction of being above or below average or the top or bottom 1%. The same system that produced the top 10% produced the bottom 10%. The next time you measure, the position might be reversed. Part of the rating system then would reflect the fact that there are only three possibilities of position: outside the system on the low

side, in the system, and outside the system on the high
side. We also want to encourage and foster continuing
improvement in our employees. The company cannot continually improve unless its people do. A second tier assessing declining performance, stable performance, or
increasing performance should be used to modify the
first-tier assessment. This is important, because you
should promote people on their potential to handle the
next job, not as a reward for the past. You do not
necessarily promote the person who is ranked first in the
group. You do promote the one who is best suited for the
job.

Daily Production Reports Overstress Quantity. Another
inhibitor to quality and productivity is rather innocu-
ous. It takes the form of the daily production report.
These seemingly informative documents quantify the number
of whatever is produced the previous day and may also
give measures of productivity. What is not realized by
management is that they place undue pressure for sheer
quantity. The reports go daily to God and country. If
production is down one day, there had better be an explanation. Because of the distribution of reports, the
phone calls cascade down from the front office to the
plant manager and beyond. Because of this, the plant
will salt away some production so as not to look too bad
on the daily report. Likewise, first-line supervisors
will bank output to protect their hourly short-falls.
The waste is obvious. The pressure on quantity compro-
mises quality as well as productivity. Much of the waste
can be eliminated by giving the appropriate wheel base to
the plant manager (or any other manger) to recover from
the day-to-day problems that will occur. One way to mit-
igate the daily pressure is to distribute the five daily
reports to upper management weekly instead of daily.
This gives operating management more time to take appropriate action and not just quick-patch to get it out
today.

Financial Management Systems Short-Term Focus. The
financial management system can also be an inhibitor to
continuing improvement. It can be too restrictive and
focus on the short term. By too restrictive I mean that
management does not have the flexibility to trade off resources, because in some corporate cultures if you miss
one budget line item, you have failed. By focusing on
the short term I mean the emphasis on "What have you done
for me this quarter or this year?" Anyone can show a
short-term profit if he cuts out maintenance or training
or R&D. What we are piloting in North America is a three-
year plant operating budget that also gives local management the flexibility of managing and reallocating their
resources. Budgets have already been established for the
next two fiscal years and are being discussed a year beyond that. Previously, with new model adjustment, we
often didn't have a plant operating budget until halfway

through the first model year. Our people were tied up in
negotiations rather than getting the job done. The
three-year budgets allow people to spend their time on
meaningful improvements.

Continuous Training Essential. Changing company systems alone will not assure continuing improvement. We
must recognize a continuing training and education commit
ment to all employees. To put it in perspective, our
Japanese competitors provide at least one year of training before they assign anyone to job responsibilities.
This training goes a long way to ensuring that the employee fully understands his total job, the policies of
the company, as well as his customers' and suppliers'
needs. The focus of this training is not statistics:
that is covered elsewhere. I recently talked with
Genichi Taguchi, a distinguished statistician and Deming
Medalist, about training. He stated that the Japanese
plant manager has flexibility in many areas, but the one
area he cannot reduce is his training budget, because
training and education are the cornerstones of greater
consistency.

As processes change, we must institute appropriate job
retraining to qualify employees for new job opportunities
and utilize attrition for reduced work force requirements
whenever possible. Our change to continuing improvement
cannot be made unless we make it clear that we are not
asking people to work themselves out of a job. They will
be working themselves out of an assignment, but not out
of employment.

**FOURTH PRINCIPLE: EMPLOYEE INVOLVEMENT/MANAGEMENT
PARTICIPATION**

*Employee involvement and participative management are
our way of life.* These processes create an environment
in which all employees can solve job-related problems,
identify improvement opportunities, and realize job
satisfaction. Central to the realization of this principle is management's ability to reduce fear in their
organizations. This principle must be one of the first
to be implemented, because if people cannot freely
recommend and do what is needed, no statistical or any
other management tool can help. One of the most important accomplishments of the Ford/UAW Employee Involvement
effort has been the recognition by all employees, from
the chairman of the board to the newest worker, that we
each have something to contribute and can do so in an
atmosphere of mutual respect. As this trust is realized,
employees will be more apt to take the initiative in
situations where the system had previously prevailed.

Improved efficiency is gained by encouraging everyone
to identify and help resolve problems throughout the
organization. Teamwork here pays great dividends. While

the majority of problems are system problems and are the responsibility of management to correct, other employees are sometimes in a better position to recognize these problems and opportunities, and should pass this information on to management for action.

Part of creating the environment for continuing improvement is to provide all management people with a broad understanding of statistical thinking and statistical methods. These are powerful tools in helping identify action opportunities for continuing improvement. Management needs these tools to effectively train and supervise their organizations. Some of the basic tools include:

- *Control charts.* These are obviously the backbone of the defect prevention system. Before any decisions affecting the future are made, what they are being made on should be predictable, should be in control.
- *Ishikawa, or cause-and-effect diagrams.* These are extremely important, because they force people to explicitly think about the specifics of their process as well as their suppliers and customers. Once this is done, problem solving and improvement is greatly facilitated.
- *Histograms.* These are only truly effective on data that are in a state of statistical control. This must be the case when assessing the capability of a process. The histogram then can give valuable graphic information on the distribution of individuals.
- *Pareto charts.* These are another basic graphic aid used to focus problem solving on the vital few versus the trivial many.
- *Scatter diagrams.* They are extremely useful in examining the relationship of paired data. This relationship, however, has nothing to do with cause and effect.
- *Check sheets.* They make it easy to compile the data and in such a form that they may be used easily and analyzed readily.
- *Graphs.* They can greatly improve management's productivity. Instead of poring through reams of tables and numbers, management can quickly see the trends or other information with graphs. Even if they insist on the implied precision of tables and numbers, augment them with graphs.

Not only management, but everyone in the company must be able to think statistically. It is a fundamental tool in problem solving. The Japanese require one week of statistical training for all upper management, two weeks for middle management, and four weeks for all others. Since virtually all managers in the past twenty years have come from within, they have at least two months of initial statistical training, which does not include the continuing education and training each receives.

FIFTH PRINCIPLE: SURPASS COMPETITORS IN OVERALL PERFORMANCE

Long-term success requires surpassing competitors in overall performance. Worldwide, we intend to set the industry standards for excellence in our products, quality, and technology. In setting the standards, we must be innovative in developing products, services, and technologies that satisfy customers' needs. We should allocate resources to focus on the long-range primary goals of the company. Short-term objectives should be completely consistent with long-term objectives. Most companies do have the long-range goals: Ford certainly does. But that really is not the issue. The problem is that there usually exist company systems that force decisions and initiative to focus on the short term rather than the long term, and this must be changed. Also, in order to satisfy customers' needs we must first know them. This is usually the weakest link in any business operation. We assume we know what is best for the customer when in fact we oftentimes don't.

SIXTH PRINCIPLE: PARTNERSHIP WITH SUPPLIERS/DEALERS

Suppliers and dealers are our partners. Our actions contribute to their success. We need to establish joint, *long-term* relationships with suppliers, encouraging them to adopt the philosophy of continuing improvement in quality and productivity. We should choose suppliers based on quality of product and services as well as cost. Suppliers should be able to provide evidence of sustained statistical control, so that in the long run, higher quality will cost less, not more as it does now. Deming has stressed that not only does higher quality cost less, but it also fuels the economic cycle to provide more jobs for our people.

CONCLUSION

The point of my going over these six principles is to put into proper perspective the role of any of the constituent parts of the process of continuing improvement. People typically focus on SPC (statistical process control), which is really only a small part of statistical methods, which is again only a part of this total process. Training is another area to which people commonly give their sole attention when in fact each of the six principles must be implemented. To put it relatively simply, I have found that a company must balance training, consulting, and removing inhibitors if it is to have a chance at transforming its organization with this philosophy. In other words:

- We must see to it that everyone in the company, our supply base, and our dealer organizations, is trained in ways to continually improve. As I stated before, this training is far more than just SPC. But training is not enough.
- We must remove the inhibitors to never-ending improvement. Whether they are management systems, management styles, operating precedents, or technologies, if they stand in the way of continually meeting our customers' needs, then we must change them.
- We must also identify and take action on opportunities for improvement at every level.

All of these elements must be pursued at the same time. If we ignore any of them, or if we overemphasize any of them, we reduce the likelihood of making the transition to continuing improvement.

20

Xerox Gains from Productivity Innovations

Ed Finein

I'm delighted to be here today to share with you our experiences in improving Xerox's productivity to meet the challenges of the 1980s. Xerox today is a company that is confronted with significant worldwide competitive pressures in all aspects of its business. I hope our experience in meeting those challenges will provide some insight into what it takes to be a world-class company.

PRODUCTIVITY BACKGROUND

First, let me discuss the issue of productivity and its impact on Xerox. It's no secret that in the United States, growth of real wages has declined and productivity, as measured by output per worker, lags behind many industrialized countries. Current head-lines reflect the frustration felt by Congress, industry, and the American consumer with our ability to compete on a worldwide basis.

Much of what has happened to industry is the result of arrogance and complacency. Americans, in the past, felt they could produce anything, their products were the best, and they could sell whatever they made, at home and abroad. At the same time, foreign competition was felt to be inferior in quality, performance, and value.

By the 1970s, we faced high levels of inflation, oil shocks, and significant foreign competition capable of meeting the needs of the marketplace. By the end of 1986, we faced a situation where real wages were equivalent to their 1969 level. Industry has fought back by closing plants, cutting wages, and exporting jobs. While companies may have achieved short-term improvements, these actions may slash individual living standards in the long term. The real culprit has been declining productivity.

Since 1973, output per worker in the United States, as defined by gross domestic product per employee, has been growing less than 1 percent per year compared to a rate of 2 percent in the 1960s. That statistic places the United States as twelfth among the leading industrialized nations of the world for the period of 1981-1985. The lag in productivity is clearly a significant factor in America's declining competitiveness.

Today we face a world of open markets, rapid technology transfer, and shortening product life cycles. To compete requires more flexibility than shuffling financial assets or moving jobs, production, or technology overseas. We live in a world economy where technology, information, and money can move across borders with the speed of light.

The company that can play--and win--in this complex environment must be fleet of foot and efficient to the extreme. It is my feeling that any company that is not already engaged in an internal revolution of seeking productivity in all aspects of its business--product design, production, and distribution--could well find itself assigned to slow but certain decay.

Having said this, let me say that many--if not most-- American companies are woefully behind the curve in recognizing, let alone implementing, what it takes to continually improve their productivity to a point where they can successfully compete on a worldwide basis for the long term. We need to capture the innovative spirit that used to be reflected in our products and focus it on new ways to improve the management of productivity throughout the business.

XEROX IN PERSPECTIVE

Xerox, like many other companies, suffered from arrogance in the 1970s. Xerox created the plain-paper copying industry in 1959. That was the year we introduced the Xerox 914 copier. Prior to that, you'll recall, the most popular office copying techniques were relatively messy--either wet processes or carbon papers.

The 914 changed all that. It transformed the Haloid Company of Rochester, New York, into the Xerox Corporation. For the next fifteen years, we were, in a way, victims of our own early triumphs. The company's--and the world's--first plain-paper copier, the 914, was one of the most successful, if not the most successful, new product ever introduced in corporate history.

We had such a stranglehold on the copier market throughout the 1960s and early 1970s that we hardly paid attention when IBM and Eastman Kodak began marketing high-speed copiers, the most lucrative part of the market.   Nor did we worry when the Japanese began to offer small inexpensive copiers in the mid-1970s, an area we ignored until recently.

The Xerox of the late 1970s was a bureaucratic company in which one function battled another, and operating people constantly bickered with the corporate staff. Disputes over issues as relatively minor as the color scheme of machines had to be resolved by our CEO.   The result was painfully slow product development, high manufacturing costs, copiers that were hard to service, and unhappy customers.

In the mid-1970s, as I've said, the Japanese camera makers entered the low end of the market.   They used aggressive pricing to gain a foothold there, facilitated by lower cost, and proceeded to own a sizable market share.   Their strategy was similar to the one they used so successfully in automobiles, cameras, home appliances, calculators and watches.

The Japanese strategy worked well.   Through the late 1970s, we saw our market share erode at an alarming rate. But the problem was masked for awhile because the industry was still growing.   Xerox continued to place more units and the company's revenues and profits continued to rise, peaking in 1981.   In spite of this, the problem had become readily apparent by 1980. We had to rapidly improve our productivity to deliver products to the customer if we were to effectively compete with our competitors in the global market.

It has been said that "self-reflection is the school of wisdom."   If so, Xerox got quite an education during those few years.

The courage and willingness to be introspective is a prerequisite for any organization that aspires to carry the banner "world-class." The nineteenth-century philosopher, James Russell Lowell, said: "No man can produce great things who is not thoroughly sincere in dealing with himself." I believe that same holds true for companies.

We began in earnest in 1980 by assessing our corporate strengths and weaknesses.   Many of the problems we identified relate to points I mentioned before.   We found, for instance, that it took Xerox too long to develop new products.   Our products cost too much, and that did not fully satisfy our customers' requirements.   In fact, we were horrified to find that the Japanese were selling their small machines for what it cost us to make ours.

After an in-depth study, we recognized the need to overhaul the very way we managed our business.   We found that to play--and win--in the new competitive market, we had to be efficient to the extreme.   We had to engage in an internal revolution in product design, production, and distribution to eliminate Japanese competitive advantages.

COMPETITIVE BENCHMARKING

Let me first talk about competitors. Here we began to
understand and evaluate our problems through a process
called competitive benchmarking. Benchmarking in Xerox
is a tool to identify industry cost and performance standards and to set goals. It also provides us with insights into how these cost and performance standards can
be achieved or exceeded and to develop internal action
plans. Most importantly, benchmarking is an ongoing
learning experience, both for the people involved and for
the company as a whole. It defines the productivity improvements we need to compete effectively.

Forms of benchmarking have been used in industry for
years. Early in the twentieth century, for instance,
Walter Chrysler used to tear apart every new Oldsmobile
that came off his competitor's assembly line, to determine precisely what went into the car, how much it cost,
and how it was made. Armed with this information,
Chrysler had a better sense of what he was competing
against.

At Xerox, our competitive benchmarking looks both inside and outside the reprographics industry. In the
beginning, we visited and studied several leading-edge
American and Japanese companies. We visited Japan and
studied several of our competitors there--Canon and
Ricoh--toured factories and visited R & D facilities, and
reverse engineered our competitors products. Our studies
revealed the need for at least some change in virtually
all phases of our business, from product design to sales
and service.

CREATING PRODUCT DELIVERY TEAMS

One of our problems was the way we were organized. We
had a matrix management structure in our Product Development Organization. That meant that any one development
effort had to flow through separate functions--product
planning, design engineering, manufacturing engineering,
and service engineering--each, essentially, operating in
a vacuum. There was then no individual clearly responsible for the end product. The reason this structure was
created in the first place was to prevent errors. But it
had the unintended effect of almost preventing product
delivery.

With so many different organizations involved, there
were costly overheads and inevitable slowdowns. There
constantly was need to review and gain concurrence across
various groups, necessitating program management and
time-consuming committees to address cross-disciplinary
issues. Virtually all issues were cross-disciplinary and
fell victim to this process. The cycle was so long, in
fact, that product develop-ment programs sometimes became

obsolete in mid-stream because of changing market needs. To address these problems, we were forced to improve the productivity of our product delivery organization. The first thing we did was to disassemble the matrix organization I described a moment ago and we created Product Delivery Teams under one person, called the chief engineer. The chief engineer is totally accountable for a product development project in total, including quality, cost, and schedule. The chief engineer manages all the design teams, the model shop, and pilot plant. He has complete authority to modify the development schedule and to make go and no-go decisions along the way.

I am happy to say that nowadays the bureaucracy-- and much of the corporate staff--is gone. In their place are entrepreneurial "product-development teams" and "problem-solving teams."

PRODUCTIVITY TARGETS

Using the competitive benchmarking techniques, we also set very aggressive targets for ourselves in all areas of product development from product planning to product development cost, schedules, unit manufacturing cost, product quality, marketing, service, and customer acceptance levels.

Specifically, our renewal based upon industry benchmarks called for nothing less than reducing product development time by half, reducing product development manpower by half, improving manufacturing quality by 90 percent, and reducing unit manufacturing cost by 50 percent; clearly aggressive productivity targets!

REDUCING PRODUCT DEVELOPMENT COSTS

In addition to these objectives an equally critical challenge was to insure that we fully satisfied our customers. Accomplishing that was contingent upon understanding a customer's existing and latent requirements.

The process begins at the product planning stage. We identify market trends by conducting focus groups and customer surveys. In essence, we have our customers "build" their ideal machines. They make their own trade-off decisions. For instance, sacrificing a little speed for an additional paper-handling feature. In the end, we're able to pair appropriate technologies with customers' requirements.

In product development, many of our competitors were using only one-fourth the labor we required for the same level of engineering output. Matching this was essential to our goal of accelerating our rate of new product introductions and of reducing our product development costs.

To pare down those costs, we took several important steps. First we took a page out of the Japanese book and began promoting the concept of the engineering generalist, or multi-functional engineer. Generalists are capable of handling a greater variety of tasks. Engineering specialists, on the other hand, constantly pass pieces of projects from one to another throughout a development cycle, causing delays and adding cost to the process.

Another action we took was to co-locate design engineers and, where possible, manufacturing. Putting the entire design team responsible for a product under one roof facilitated communication among the team members, saving time and enhancing the creative process.

A seemingly simple and obvious action was to stabilize design goals. In the product development process, changes frequently force retooling, which is expensive and time-consuming. Whereas Xerox routinely used to change about 50 percent of the parts over the course of a design cycle, that figure is now down to 20 percent—still not good enough, but it is better.

We have had a reputation as a technological innovator, so it should come as no surprise that, in reassessing our product development process, we decided to incorporate the latest technology. Xerox now uses state-of-the-art computer-aided design systems, which reduce the amount of time it takes to bring a design concept to prototype stage.

Another idea we've borrowed from the Japanese is continuous supplier involvement. Xerox encourages its vendors to share their expertise, not just sell us their product. In this way, they become more than suppliers to Xerox. They become strategic partners in the design process. Many of the suggestions they make directly improve parts quality or availability, impacting the product's manufacturing cost and deliverability.

And finally, Xerox—an office systems vendor—is practicing what it preaches in the area of office automation. Many of our people have used the ethernet local-area network for several years now, and they wouldn't give up their electronic mail for anything.

As a result of all this, our product development schedule is 20 to 50 percent shorter than it used to be. Engineering productivity has more than tripled since we began our efforts nearly five years ago. Specifically, on our recently introduced 1065 copier, we have been able to cut the development time by at least 20 percent, our development resources by one-third, and in the process have reduced our unit manu facturing cost by half! And all of this has not come at the expense of product performance either. Our field testing shows that the 1065 is meeting all critical customer expectations in terms of reliability, copy quality, features, and productivity.

CUTTING MANUFACTURING COSTS

In parallel with our progress in reducing our product development costs, we also moved to reduce manufacturing costs. As I mentioned earlier, our goal was to reduce Xerox manufacturing cost by at least half to match or improve on competitive levels.

Our early supplier involvement program has paid dividends in this area as well. Also contributing to lower manufacturing costs have been partnerships with the union; reduced manufacturing staff and overhead; multinational sourcing of materials; and automated materials handling techniques.

While reducing manufacturing costs, Xerox did not sacrifice quality. While before, budgets and schedules were two key criteria for deciding bonuses and promotions, now product quality and customer satisfaction are just as important. In fact, we took a number of measures to improve product quality, mainly in the area of process control and automation. We have perhaps made the most progress in the area of quality.

LEADERSHIP THROUGH QUALITY

All of what I've been talking about relates in some way to products--how we develop them and how we build them to compete in the world marketplace. But product is just one part of a much larger question, which is, how do we recast the COMPANY--the entire organization--to succeed in the global area?

This larger question deals with quality, not only in manufacturing, but also in how we think, how we conduct our business, and how we relate to each other and to our customers. We have addressed this through a program called "Leadership Through Quality," which our chairman, David Kearns, personally began and fostered throughout the company.

This program has encouraged every Xerox employee to identify and satisfy customer requirements for his output, whether the customer of his effort is another Xerox employee or a marketplace customer. One of the things this process has emphasized is a concerted employee involvement program. We are attempting to bring every Xerox worker at every level of the organization--from Senior Management to the hourly paid manufacturing people--into the problem-solving process.

The program has been very successful. In one case, a team in our high-volume business unit worked for nine months to reduce the cost and delivery time of a copier

part. What had been a $70.00 part with a thirteen-week
schedule was whittled down to $30.00 and a ten-week
hardware delivery.

What makes the accomplishment so gratifying is that the
team members represented a variety of disciplines and
worked well together to solve a problem that no individual could have tackled alone. It took people from design,
engineering, the model shop, and administration--with
their collective knowledge and ideas--to make it happen.

In another case, a team in our low-volume business unit
took an infant technology and evolved it into a production design, meeting all the customer requirements for
product functionality AND driving down cost from $12.00
to $5.00 per unit. Again, the sense of ownership of a
problem by a group of employees encouraged them to
surmount it.

There are more than 600 problem-solving teams like
these within the Xerox Reprographic Business Group today.
Some 70 percent of our people are involved in them. Each
person receives forty hours of classroom training in
problem-solving techniques and statistical quality control, to enable him to help solve problems in his immediate work environment. We have made the investment in our
"human capital." Our employees are our most valuable
asset.

Our "Leadership Through Quality" religion has also
emphasized giving the customer what he wants. We sample
each of our customers--at least once every eighteen
months--to survey their satisfaction with our products
and services. The output of this survey is used to
restructure our products, services, and, in fact, corporate priorities.

Our efforts in meeting customer requirements have paid
dividends. Our surveys show that, in many market segments, we are now the reprographic industry benchmark.
If the new corporate approach sounds similar to that of
the Japanese, it is no coincidence. We have gone to
extremes to study our Japanese competitors. Our successful Japanese subsidiary, Tokyo-based Fuji Xerox, helps us
keep tabs on the Japanese. In fact, we visit Japan
annually to recalibrate our competitive benchmarks.

SUMMARY

This is a summary of what we have been doing for the
past five years--developing the strategies, and putting
in place the systems, to become a world-class company.
To accomplish that required redefining the way we do
business and achieving productivity improvements in all
areas. I think we have done what a few other American
industries have done. We have significantly narrowed the
advantage that such formidable Japanese competitors as

Canon, Sharp, Ricoh, and Minolta had enjoyed, thereby stemming their advance in our market.

But for all our efforts, there is more to be done, especially since the competition is hardly standing still. To remain competitive in a worldwide market is a never-ending process. We may no longer be the company we once were, but we are not yet the company we want to be. We are a company in transition.

21

Quality: A Competitive Strategy

Paul A. Allaire

At the outset, I would like to commend the College of Business at Utah State for sponsoring this series of seminars. Bringing representatives of business together with distinguished faculty members and students to focus on key business issues and concerns is a much-needed part of the process of keeping American business competitive in a global economy.

I don't believe I have to remind any of you that America is locked in a battle for global economic supremacy. Let me give you just a few facts to make this point.

Fact Number One: As recently as 1960, the Japanese accounted for only *2* percent of the world's economy. Today they account for *10* percent.

Fact Number Two: When I graduated from high school, America controlled some 35 percent of the world economy. Our portion today is about 20 percent.

Fact Number Three: Since 1984, we have gone from being the largest creditor nation in the world to the largest debtor nation.

These are fundamental issues for American society, with enormous impact on our way of life, our standard of living, and our ability to create meaningful employment.

The causes of America's economic decline are varied and complex. Each of us probably has our own favorite version of what went wrong. Almost all of us have pointed the finger of blame at someone else. We complain about the cost and interference of government regulation. Or the lack of management leadership. Or the high cost and the low productivity of the American worker. Or some mythical attribute of "Japan Incorporated."

There is some truth in each of these, I suppose. But in my judgment, the root cause of our trouble is that we became arrogant and complacent. Because America was on the top of the economic pile, we assumed it was our birthright.

Although I don't always like to admit it, in many ways Xerox is a microcosm of what happened to much of American industry. The students are too young to remember, but I'm sure many of the business people here today remember the Xerox 914, the first plain-paper copier. We introduced it in 1959 and it quickly created an entire new industry. Some people have called the 914 the single most successful product ever made. It launched Xerox into an era of feverish growth and success.

But with two decades of success, we became complacent and took our eyes off both the customer and the competition. We saw the Japanese coming at the low end of the market, but we didn't take the threat seriously.

We went on continuing to believe we would always be successful, even as our market share began to shrink. After all, we told ourselves, this was our industry. We created it. We built it. And we owned it.

Fortunately, Xerox reacted in time. In the late 1970s we started to take a good, hard look at what we were doing at Xerox and how we run *our* business. And we started to take a good, hard look at the competition and how they run *their* businesses.

We were startled by what we found out. One of the first things we realized was that our costs were too high--and not just a little high. In fact, the Japanese were *selling* their small machines for what it cost us to *make* ours. We assumed that because they were low cost, they were poor quality--we were wrong! Then we tried to convince ourselves that they could not be making money. Wrong again! They were profitable.

That woke us up in a hurry and we went to work in earnest to begin closing the gaps.

We realized that to be a world-class competitor in the 1980s and 1990s, we had to challenge everything we had done in the past. We had to change dramatically --from the way we develop and manufacture our products to the way we market and service them.

We've been at the process of changing the corporation for about six years now and although, we still have a long way to go, the results are gratifying. Let me give you just a few examples:

- We have reduced our average manufacturing costs by over 20 percent despite inflation.
- We have reduced the time it takes to bring a new product to market by up to 60 percent.
- We have substantially improved the quality of our products. In fact, Dataquest rates our products as number one in five out of six market segments.

-   We have decreased our defective parts from 8
    percent to less than three-hundredths of 1 percent.
-   We have improved our market share in the past few
    years--perhaps the first American company in an
    industry targeted by the Japanese to do this.

I'm also proud to tell you that we did it without
closing our factories or moving our manufacturing offshore.   I tell you all this not to boast, but to illustrate that there is nothing inherently wrong with American business. We lost our way in the 1970s, but we have
found it again.

People sometimes ask me how we are doing it at Xerox--
how we have reversed our slide and begun the long tough
road back. Believe me, there is no magic formula.   We
are doing it by involving all of our people--union and
non-union alike--in problem solving and quality improvement.   The entire management team has a deep and real
commitment to employee involvement. Our incentive is a
powerful one--survival as a successful business entity.

You've all heard a good deal about quality recently.
We define it at Xerox as "conforming to customer requirements," pure and simple.   It's an axiom of business
that's as old as business itself, yet many of us lost
sight of it.

And when we speak of quality, we mean more than just
product quality. We take the view that every person in
the company has a customer for the work he or she does.
For many people, the customer is someone inside the
company--the person we type reports for or the person to
whom we deliver parts.

It follows from this view of quality that it must work
its way into the entire organization--into manufacturing,
sales, service, billing, training, finance, and so on.
Our quality policy sums it up well.   It says simply:

Xerox is a quality company.   Quality is the basic
business principle for Xerox.   Quality means providing our external and internal customers with innovative products and services that fully satisfy their
requirements.   Quality improvement is the job of
every Xerox employee.

Xerox is hardly alone in this approach.   Scores of
corporations are finding that employee involvement in
quality improvement is a powerful way to improve business
results. And some of these companies are not in manufacturing.   In fact, one of the leaders in quality is
Florida Power & Light--the major electrical utility in
the State of Florida.

The movement has spread to government as well.   We
recently hosted a meeting on quality specifically for
representatives of the federal government.   It was
attended by senior executives of not only the Department

of Defense, but also a wide variety of service organizations, including the Internal Revenue Service, the FBI,
and the Social Security Administration.

This heightened interest in quality is not surprising.
The Japanese have realized for years that you don't have
to sacrifice quality for cost. In fact, quite the reverse is true.

A focus on quality--on satisfying the customer and
meeting customer needs--actually drives cost down. That
clearly has been our experience at Xerox!

The focus on quality that we initiated four years ago
was built on some very fundamental assumptions about the
American worker:

-    That management does not have all the answers;
-    That all people have ideas about how their work can
     be done more effectively;
-    That people closest to the problems often have the
     best solutions;
-    That this almost unlimited source of knowledge and
     creativity can be tapped through employee involve-
     ment;
-    And that people are willing and eager to share
     their thoughts and participate in developing
     solutions to business problems.

Those beliefs have paid off handsomely. Today more
than 80 percent of our work force is involved in more
that 4,000 problem-solving and quality improvement teams
around the world. We still have a long, long way to go,
but I am convinced we can do it. When I look back on
where we've been and where we are going and ask myself
what advice I would give to others, I come up with five
specifics:

First, senior management has to be committed to change.
Without genuine, hands-on commitment, all attempts at
quality improvement and employee involvement are doomed
to failure. And that commitment must take the form of
action, not rhetoric.

Our expression for that at Xerox is that managers must
"walk like they talk." In other words, their actions
must demonstrate that they are willing to listen to the
ideas of employees; they are sincere in their efforts to
change the work environment; and they are serious about
their drive toward quality improvement and customer
satisfaction.

*Second, the commitment of union leadership must be
every bit as strong as that of management.* That certainly has been and still is the case at Xerox. In fact,
quality circles were a part of our manufacturing operations before we launched a company-wide strategy of quality improvement and employee involvement.

Credit for that goes to the strong and enlightened leadership of the union that represents most of our hourly employees--the Amalgamated Clothing and Textile Workers Union. They understand that we must be competitive and that our union workers can provide significant help in that struggle.

The Sloan School of Management at M.I.T. has looked at our experience and summed up our success in one sentence:

> The high level of trust built up over the years between labor and management in Xerox was clearly the instrumental factor in the company's success in employee involvement.

Third, it takes some initial investments. At Xerox, for example, we give every man and woman in the corporation six full days of training in problem solving, quality improvement, and team building. For us, that meant training 100,000 people worldwide. That's an investment equivalent to twenty-five-hundred man years.

It's a significant investment in both financial and human resources. But we're convinced it's one of the best investments we've ever made.

Fourth, it requires patience and discipline. Our experience has been that results don't come as quickly as we would like. There are some false starts. There are parts of the organization that lag behind others. There are teams that don't initially work on real business problems. There are managers--particularly middle managers--who see employee involve-ment as a threat.

One of the Japanese experts on quality and employee involvement likens the need for patience and discipline to that of the bamboo farmer. Once the bamboo seed is planted, the farmer must water it every day. He does that for *four years* before the tree breaks ground! But when it finally does, it grows sixty feet in ninety days.

That's true also of employee involvement. It takes time. It takes nurturing. It takes patience. But when it finally takes off, its power is tremendous. We, like many other American companies, are proving this. It's a very powerful concept that can energize the total organization.

And fifth, the quality process is continuous. That's because as we improve, two highly dynamic forces are at work. First, as we get better, so does our competition. Second, as we meet the requirements of our customers, their expectations of Xerox also increase. What we see is an upward and never-ending spiral of increased competition and heightened customer expectations.

If you had told us that six years ago, we would probably have been discouraged by the thought of running a marathon race with no finish line. Today we find it invigorating. The pursuit of quality has taught us that as good as we are today, we must be better tomorrow.

That's a new concept for many of us in the West.   I
recently read a book called *Kaisan*, by Masaaki Imai.
Imai says that in the Western world we have an expression, "If it ain't broke, don't fix it."   In Eastern culture, the philosophy is, "If it isn't perfect, make it
better."   That's a powerful concept for all of us to
emulate.

As you can probably tell, I have a great deal of
confidence in the ability of American business to compete
successfully in the global marketplace.   I don't sub-
scribe to the conventional wisdom that our foreign
competitors are superior.

We still have the world's greatest financial resources,
industrial capacity, and distribution system.   And we
have one other asset--the American people, with their
immense resilience, strength, and creativity. Our people
can win, as long as the competitive environment is fair
to all.   That means that government, labor, and industry
must support one another.

Conferences such as this play an important part in
helping to keep America competitive.   Thank you for
inviting me to participate.

22

Quality: A Positive Business Strategy

Douglas N. Anderson

The 3M company began in 1902 as a manufacturer of a single product--sandpaper. Today this highly diversified company markets more than 50,000 products world-wide. Our growth and expansion into new markets are attributable to several key elements: attention to customers, dedication to product and service quality, and encouragement of innovation.

The first 3M laboratory was established in 1916 to develop products that would meet customer requirements and contribute to the company's growth. Masking tape was one product invented to meet customer needs in body shops, a product that led to hundreds of others for the automotive industry.

Over the years, the company has responded to customer needs through a proliferation of technologies into new products and markets. We have adapted to changing markets, economic situations, and competitive pressures with a consistent management strategy--the ability to manage change.

In this age of rapid changes in technology, competition, and economics conditions, however, the challenge for maintaining growth and success has taken on even greater dimensions. To stay competitive we must keep our products competitive. Quality must go beyond products and innovation; it must become the sum total of everything the supplier delivers, as well as what the customer expects to be delivered and how much the customer is willing to pay.

This focus on total quality has become a critical strategy for managing change in 3M. The following summary describes the 3M Managing Total Quality process, the methods we have used to operate it, and the milestones we have achieved in implementing it in our operations around the world. Finally, we offer a vision for the future, using the total quality process as a business strategy to achieve and sustain leadership in a highly competitive global marketplace.

On the surface, quality improvement appears to be a dynamic new business tool. However, a closer look shows that "Total Quality," the involvement of an entire business organization in a process of customer-driven, continuous improvement, has been with us for more than 30 years.

Until recently, Total Quality was considered by many a Japanese concept. The Japanese clearly have shown the significance of quality as a competitive strategy. Japanese companies have become dominant competitors in such industries as steel, automobiles, cameras, electronics, and more, through dedicated application of Total Quality Improvement.

Today, companies all over the world are learning to implement a total quality process. If we have learned one thing from Japan, it should be that quality improvement depends on a systematic approach in the entire organization. There are no quick solutions to quality. There must be a permanent management process that examines all products, procedures, and processes on a contin uous basis for constant improvement.

Summarizing the concept is simple. Defining and implementing the process is a complex task.

3M'S BEGINNING WITH TOTAL QUALITY

The 3M company first committed to the Total Quality process in 1979 under the leadership of Lew Lehr, then CEO. In 1980, we established a Corporate Quality Department, responsible for defining quality objectives and designing a strategy to implement continuous quality improvement throughout the corporation.

We began by defining five Essentials of Quality as the basis or 3M's new quality philosophy.

1. *Quality is Consistently Meeting Customers' Expectations.*

Quality has been defined by many quality management experts in terms such as "fitness for use," "meeting specifications" or "meeting the customers' requirements." Our experience has been that these definitions fall quite short in meeting the true wants and needs of the marketplace.

The 3M definition represents three key components of quality: "consistency," "expectations," and "customers."

Consistency implies doing it right every time instead of just doing it right the first time.

Expectations move the process from a static focus on requirements to the dynamic process of continual improvement to meet the changing needs and desires of customers. It also leads us to the understanding that customer satisfaction is strongly influenced by many non-product service and innovation issues. When we speak of fitness for use or meeting requirements, we have found that most people want simply to document the specifications and resist changing them. Using expectations as part of the definition involves people in sales, marketing, billing, shipping, accounts payable, accounts receivable, purchasing, and other staff support functions in the quality improvement process.

The importance and interrelationship of each function within our organization is underscored by our definition of the customer. We understand that our external customers are provided with quality products and services through the efforts of a series of internal "customers," each receiving the work or product of another internal person and passing it on.

A secretary, for example, is a supplier, delivering a multitude of services internally. In turn, the secretary's customer is a supplier who passes on the service to others. Each person is responsible for determining the expectations of the internal customers and identifying specific areas to improve in meeting the external customer's expectations. In this way, each person and function with in 3M influences the quality of our products and services, no matter how far removed each is from the final product delivered to the user.

2. *Measurements of Quality Are Through Indicators of Customer Satisfaction.*

Companies often get caught up in measurements of certain activities that can make them look good on paper, yet show little significant information on how well they are competing on the basis of quality. These are measurements that management, owners, and stockholders like to see that indicate that their investment is being productively employed. Examples of these measurements are profit, annual sales growth, number of acquisitions, number of sales calls per day, and number of daily/weekly/monthly reports turned out by a company department.

At 3M, we have expanded our traditional measurements to include measurements of attributes most important to our internal and external customers.

We are using customer satisfaction indicators to measure our business: Are we delivering products that are reliable and on time? Are employees empowered and given the skills to meet the changing needs of the customer?

At 3M we use cost of quality as a measure. Early in the total quality implementation process, however, we found that concentrating on only this measure as the driving force leads to compliance rather than continual process improvement.

By focusing on customer-oriented measurements, such as employee and customer surveys, we get a more accurate picture of our customers' level of satisfaction with our products and services. When customer and employee needs are satisfied, growth will occur and in turn satisfy the profit objectives of management and owners.

3. *The Objective Is Consistently Meeting Expectations 100% of the Time.*

This concept is perhaps the most difficult to understand and accept. Traditionally, we had set performance standards with the attitude that errors are inevitable. This attitude implied that to err is human; we condoned a defect level, for example, 5 percent. This attitude carried over to many product operations, which fostered an acceptable quality level. In this way, a certain failure rate was projected before an operation was begun and allowed to become an acceptable form of management.

The issues is not one of perfection; the issue is reaching an agreement with the customer on expectations and then meeting those expectations 100 percent of the time. Implementing a quality improvement process based on prevention and 100 percent conformance to the agreed standard eliminates problems and errors.

4. *Quality Is Attained Through Prevention-Oriented Improvement Projects.*

In 3M's Total Quality process, causes of non-conformance are identified and corrected, which benefits both the customer and the balance sheet. We adopted systems for identifying causes of errors and implementing projects to change the process, procedure, or materials to prevent errors from recurring. This system of prevention replaces the system of inspection, which identifies mistakes after they have occurred, and places quality at the source.

The American Society of Quality Control estimates that errors due to rework, retest, or reinspection of rejected units accounts for anywhere from 15 to 40 percent of production capacity. The same holds true for work done in the professional areas, such as marketing, finance, and administration.

5. *Management Commitment Leads the Quality Process.*

The final and most important quality concept that 3M has adopted is management commitment. This commitment starts at the top of the organization, where it must be recognized that quality improvement doesn't just happen. It has to be planned and actively managed like every other aspect of the business if it is to become a way of life.

Experts believe that only 15 percent of all errors are attributable to the work force; at least 85 percent are related to management-defined systems. Errors are often the result of misinterpretation by those who must work within systems and of management's unwillingness to solicit or listen to new ideas. The result is organizational discrepancy in system interpretation, which can be corrected only by management.

To achieve system uniformity at 3M, our senior management replaced policies with values and business objectives, using customer expectations as a measure of success.

At 3M, quality improvement is a people process. Management takes a leadership role in demonstrating commitment and cultivating that same attitude in every employee. Management's role is to provide training, to define expectation, and to prevent problems. The critical challenge is to create an environment through-out the organization that encourages individual involvement in decision making and personal ownership of the improvement process.

Our overall corporate improvement process is guided by a corporate Quality Steering Team. This team includes 3M's senior management: the Chief Executive Officer and Chairman of the Board, the Executive Vice Presidents of our business sectors, the Vice President of Finance, and our Senior Staff Vice Presidents.

Together, the members of our Quality Steering Team have defined corporate values and overall business objectives. Each member works closely with the individual organizations to integrate quality measurements into their business evaluation systems.

QUALITY IMPLEMENTATION STRATEGY

Translating our corporate values and objectives into operational activities is a major undertaking, complicated by 3M's size and diversity. Our individual business units and staff departments are each unique in function and they operate in diverse parts of the world. It became obvious that the best way to implement the improvement process was to provide guidelines and methods that can be adapted and modified to suit the cultural needs, problems, and personalities of each operating area.

Formal training for all supervisory and management personnel worldwide became our first step in institutionalizing the quality process. Initial training involved a "Quality Workshop" covering the five Essentials of Quality and eight implementation elements.

Implementation begins with management working through an awareness stage to gain an understanding of quality as

it applies to their individual environments. It begins
with establishing the vision for the organization: what
we want the organization to look like without the problems of today. This vision includes a plan for taking
advantage of opportunities; it is a proactive approach
for designing the organization's future, with three to
five-year goals.

Next, management develops measurements for the evidence
of success. These are indicators developed to help us
quantify our achievements in moving toward our vision.
They are measurements of how we are meeting customer,
employee, and owner expectations.

After defining our vision and measurement system, we
begin the journey of achievement with a quality action
plan, to be reviewed and updated annually. The Quality
Steering Team of each business unit has the responsibility for identifying major improvement opportunities and
developing a specific action plan to achieve them. Improvement teams are also created in each area of operation to work on the improvement projects and to act on
specific problems more closely related to their own
areas. It is important that all parts of the organization, from top to bottom, have a voice in updating the
plan. This is achieved with the team process.

The cycle is then ongoing. Quality improvement becomes
a continuous process of identifying errors, establishing
measurements, and setting goals to prevent errors.

MANAGEMENT TRAINING

Training is conducted for the management group of each
business unit. This has helped to identify specific problems and to stress the need for teamwork in achieving
quality improvement.

Initial training exposes management to a new awareness
of quality and promotes a changed attitude in evaluating
the business and it operations.

Concurrent with Quality Workshop training, the Corporate Quality Services Department provides several levels
of service to help 3M business units interpret and
implement quality in their organization. Tools are used
to survey quality improvement opportunities, customer
satisfaction levels, waste and rework percentages on
jobs, and employee reaction to and involvement in the
improvement process. Quality Services consultants also
facilitate groups in developing teamwork and problem-
solving skills and assist them in focusing on the task.
In addition, these internal consultants help business
units and staff groups defines customer expectations and
identify service improvement opportunities.

The focus of all data gathering and workshop activity
is to help employees at all levels understand how they
affect the customer with their products or services.

Through these kinds of training support, we learn to determine such things as how many times the phone rings before it is answered and how many days it takes us to handle complaints. Then we can identify areas where we can improve our responsiveness to internal and external customers.

ROADBLOCKS TO QUALITY

It would be ideal to say that after completing the Quality Workshop training, each unit can immediately and completely implement the new quality philosophy to solve problems and take advantage of opportunities for improvment. Although we certainly see success demonstrated in a variety of areas, we also meet a wide range of roadblocks, some expected and others that come as a surprise. Some relatively frequent obstacles and the methods we employ to remove them follow.

Quality Outside the Factory

Since most of the successes by the Japanese have been achieved and documented within factory or production environments, it is not surprising that 3M also experienced many of our early improvements in this area. Historically, a factory has functioned within a wide range of standards, measurement methods, and well-defined processes, more so than any other business operation. Applying programs for improvement in the factory was much easier than in other areas; the opportunities were more obvious and the indices for measurement were frequently already in place.

Implementing the process was more difficult in less rigid areas, such as marketing, R & D, administration, and staff support groups. Often, the "product" produced in these environments is so interrelated with other functions or so poorly defined that it was extremely difficult to identify the problem, let alone break it into manageable segments for improvement. Applying traditional indicators further complicated the process because specific dollar measurements were never applied or the costs were hidden in a myriad of other categories.

It became quickly obvious that to extend quality improvement beyond the factory we needed additional techniques and methods. We developed a training package that includes a wide range of statistical and analytical technique to promote brainstorming, data gathering, data analysis, presentation of information, control, and prioritization. We have also developed an extensive selection of internal measurement tools for improving our services and determining customer satisfaction.

Some of the more successful techniques being used to overcome barriers in the improvement process are process analysis, functional analysis, flow charts, the Ishikawa cause-and-effect diagram, and nominal group technique.

Functional analysis, as opposed to process analysis, is a means of identifying the functions of a particular job, the internal and external customers, and the "products" produced in each function. Each individual completes a Functional Analysis for his or her job; the manager then combines the data for a department or area of the organization.

Flow charts are developed to identify each step in the process if the "product" involves multiple phases or travels through several areas before completion. Flow charts streamline the analysis, facilitating the study of problem areas and potential opportunities.

Having identified the products, customers, and processes, an action team can rate the products on the importance to the operation and evaluate how well the product meets "customer" expectations.

Ishikawa or fishbone diagrams can then be used to identify the potential causes of the problem and the action steps needed to correct them.

Nominal group technique can be used in both the evaluation and brainstorming steps to ensure the involvement and participation of everyone.

Other tools that we use in the analysis and identification process include Pareto diagrams, histograms, scatter diagrams, control charts, Gantt charts, and check sheets, in addition to process dissection, capability studies, and probability plotting.

All of these methods greatly improve our ability to isolate hard costs associated with non-production activities, such as order entry and marketing.

Rather than train every person in all techniques, our strategy is to tailor this training to suit the requirements of each individual area. Corporate Quality Services consultants work closely with business units to determine the most appropriate tools applicable to the specific problems being addressed.

Teams

Analyzing "products and customers" emphasized the importance of team efforts as never before. It became obvious that quality objectives could not be achieved without having first, personal commitments to quality, and second, group commitments to work together for improvement.

Teamwork, however, is not a natural working method in our society. It must be learned. Like most American companies, 3M has systems in place that stress and reward individual efforts and achievements more than group accomplishments. Undertaking quality improvement projects on a team basis needed new insights into group behavior, from top management through quality teams below the supervisory level.

Using our own Human Resources Department as well as outside services, we provided a multitude of courses and techniques on group processes, dynamics, and motivation to increase understanding of group activity. We then tied group training and management techniques, such as performance management, to tangible programs that are quality related. These strategies have accelerated the integration of teamwork within the company.

Today, more than 2,000 registered and many additional quality improvement teams are actively solving work-related problems. These teams, made up of employees at all job levels, have not only yielded dollar savings, but have also gone a long way in promoting quality awareness throughout the corporation.

Plateaus

It is not uncommon to see a business unit make tremendous headway on several quality projects, then start to flounder in trying to establish a next goal. Solutions to this dilemma range from the Quality Steering Team surveying employees and identifying reasons for lack of interest, to trying new techniques available or simply recommitting to quality as a group.

As a corporation, 3M constantly interfaces with outside companies and experts to identify other tools and ideas to expand our scope and ability to assist improvement.

Time

The most common barrier encountered in quality improvement is time--the time needed to involve already-busy people, to identify areas to improve, and to implement prevention and corrective action.

There is no question that allocating time for quality improvement requires management's belief and commitment that improvement will reduce costs, increase productivity, and ultimately provide more time for productive uses. Firefighting, or the effort spent resolving crises, can be reduced as the causes are identified and eliminated forever. Once a group achieves its first success, it is much easier to gain time commitments for further projects. For this reason, it is important to keep initial goals realistic and attainable.

The 3M company has overcome the time issue by integrating the quality process with our business strategy. We have found that it is critical that a quality vision, measurements of success, and quality improvement plans be directly related to the company's mission and objectives. In this way, quality is viewed not as additional work, but as a framework and methodology form which we approach our jobs. Quality becomes focused on achieving our goals, on why we are in business. This is a concept that has had to be understood particularly by middle managers, who are responsible for making quality a part of operational plans as well as of performance appraisal, so that

every employee understands his or her role in implementing quality.

We have evolved in this process of using quality to
make the best use of our time. We have made specific
corporate programs measurable, with each business group
participating in improvements and reporting on its functional area: manufacturing, R & D, marketing, and administration.

Also, we are evaluating and modifying our reward and
recognition systems. Employees can expect to be evaluated quarterly. We are testing and piloting gain share
programs in many of our business units.

Quality improvement--in our goals, measurement systems,
action plans, and recognition programs--has become part
of our daily business operations, not a separate function
to be allocated special time.

Attitude

It would be naive to expect that a group of more than
80,000 individuals will accept and internalize a new
philosophy at exactly the same pace or in the same
manner. And, that has not happened at 3M.

The success of those who have been active in the improvement process has had a snowball effect. Continued
internal promotion and awareness of those successes,
ongoing training in improvement techniques and support,
and direction of top management have all had a dramatic
impact on creating the necessary attitude change.

SUCCESSES

The 3M company has found that if we focus on customer
expectations, ultimately production will increase, costs
will go down, and market share will grow. The objective
is to create profit because customers are willing to buy
and buy again.

Our customers buy when they are satisfied by quality
and cost. We raise quality and create savings with our
improvement process. We look at effectiveness--how well
we interpret and translate what the customer wants--and
efficiency--how well and consistently we meet that expectation.

Our divisions, staff organizations, and overseas sub-
sidiaries are each independently implementing the quality
process, with a very broad range of success. In the few
years since we began the Total Quality improvement process, achievements have ranged from dramatic hard-dollar
savings to minor procedural changes that improve morale
and the work environment.

In a 5-year period, for example, we achieved a $2.5
billion dollar increase in sales with 10,000 fewer employees. Improvements resulting from our quality award
nomination projects alone are saving the company over

$200 million a year, and these are just the highlights of ongoing accomplishments by improvement teams. Other evidences of success range from a substantial reduction in credit adjustments due to order entry error, to an improved transportation system that cut transit time in half while reducing freight cost and overcharges as well. We have demonstrated that we can reduce the time it takes to complete an administrative process or to manufacture a product by as much as 50 times. Despite the scope of individual successes, each is recognized as an important contribution.

Our company is actively involved in developing ways to identify and recognize success. Our own corporate quality surveys are conducted regularly to evaluate quality improvement programs in the organization and to identify additional improvement opportunities.

We also participate in the development of national and international standards and recognition systems. The U.S. government sponsors a National Quality Award to recognize quality achievement in manufacturing organizations, service industries, and small companies. The major criterion is how customer satisfaction is measured and followed up. New stand-ards of quality excellence are also being promoted worldwide through systems such as the International Standards Organization 9000 Series for the European Common Market.

The 3M company is the "living laboratory" for our quality process; our learning is ongoing. Most importantly, we are able to bring what we have learned to our customers. We are sharing our successes.

The 3M Quality Management Services group, formed in the mid-1980s, works with businesses, organizations, and government agencies around the world to implement quality improvement. Using our internal quality process as a model for Managing Total Quality, we are helping others to implement a continuous improvement process so that they can better manage their businesses.

WHAT IS NEXT?

Building on our quality essentials, 3M has positioned Quality Vision 2000 as a framework to define the future. This allows us to establish an overall goal to focus on, a goal that is part of the quality process model. We are taking action in a number of ways to bridge the gap between our current profile and our vision for the future. This translates into quality improvement plans at all levels, plans that address the major issues defined in our vision.

Issue: Global competition will significantly increase, and the Total quality process will be an increasingly important strategy for achieving success in the global marketplace. As such, quality will not only be part of the overall strategic business plan, it will also be strongly positioned as a sales strategy. We will become even more proactive in our effort to understand our customers, developing aggressive strategies that address customer expectations for all our services.

Issue: Technology will force shorter product and service life due to obsolescence, and the demand will be for shorter new product and service development time. Quality and innovation will become even more important, along with the strategy of doing right things right.

Issue: Customers will increasingly make their purchasing decisions based on perceived value. Such concerns as service quality, product quality, life cycle cost, delivery quality—all key ingredients of perceived value—will become more important. We will continue to develop programs to quantify customers' perceptions of key buying criteria for both products and services. We are also using systems to benchmark how our customers perceive us and our competitors. Continued measurement of customer perceptions at all levels helps us to stay on top of custemers' changing needs.

Issue: Partnership between buyers and sellers will eventually become a requirement for doing business. Industrial manufacturers will be proactively positioning certification programs for their suppliers as well as seeking proactively to be certified and preferred suppliers to their customers. We are working to develop partnerships with our customers, which helps us to begin at the product development phase better to meet their expectations with innovative products and services in exchange for long-term business relationships.

Issue: Customers will expect 100 percent—in product and service performance as well as responsive and friendly transactions. We must strategically translate customer wants and needs into design, manufacturing, and service specifications and procedures. We will continue to use and develop methodologies to establish service improvements as well as product improvements. Developing partnerships with our customers will foster this goal.

We feel that the future of quality improvement involves an even more intense focus on understanding our customers. Additional customer-focused tools, such as Quality Functional Deployment, will be used for increasingly more products and services. More and more, product quality will be taken for granted and service quality will differentiate suppliers. 3M is only one choice available to our customers. We recognize that we must participate more aggressively in their decision making.

QUALITY—A POSITIVE BUSINESS STRATEGY

Quality has become more than a business opportunity to impact growth and provide a competitive edge in the marketplace. It is a tool for survival. Commitment to quality has become essential for maintaining leadership in this rapidly changing, highly competitive, global market.

A quality strategy provides customers with the products and services they expect. In addition to product performance, the competitive edge will include service and all interactions with the customers before and after the sale.

In positioning quality as a positive business strategy, we have built quality into our business. We have incorporated quality into our corporate vision for continuous improvement in all businesses and support services to achieve and sustain global leadership in our chosen markets.

Adopting quality as a positive business strategy requires a willingness to change, to create the environment for change, to provide training, to demonstrate support, and to reinforce progress. The quality process must be ongoing and never-ending to keep up with customer and market changes. This requires a continuous flow of training, new techniques, and teams to keep the competitive edge strong. Total quality leadership is hard work. There are no substitutes or shortcuts.

Quality--the ability to respond to and manage change--will be the key ingredient separating the leaders from those who falter in the global market.

23

Dow Chemical's Quality and Productivity Improvement

Wayne R. Pero

Most of my career with Dow Chemical has been spent in manufacturing. I have worked in several of our plants in the United States and have spent a couple of years overseas. Even more recently, I was fortunate to have the experience of managing our Denver sales office. In that job, I became very aware of the need to pay close attention to all customer requirements, not just product quality. I saw firsthand how difficult it can be to make a sale when up against a tough competitor.

You might say I've been around the block once or twice. I'm old enough to have watched the U.S.A. go from the enviable leader in quality and productivity to a nation struggling for survival in industry after industry. I am pleased, though, that I am young enough to, hopefully, see this country regain that leadership position in quality and productivity--because I'd like to see my kids and their kids enjoy the same standard of living and opportunities that my generation has enjoyed.

RESPONDING TO WORLD COMPETITION AT DOW

About the only way this is going to happen, though, is if companies--and individuals like you and me--make quality and productivity a priority. Everyone--at every level in American businesses and in American schools--must actively and enthusiastically pursue quality and productivity improvement. Being world competitive must be a strategic intent--in other words, a first consideration in everything we do, not just a passing fancy.

Dow has that strategic intent, and we're making the
changes that quality consciousness demands. The changes
have not come easily, but the reward for this change has
been finding a training program that helps the organization change.

But, before I tell you about our successful approach
to quality and productivity training, I'd first like to
tell you a little bit about Dow. It is truly a multinational company.

- One-half of our sales are in the United States,
- One-half of our new capital is spent in the United
  States, and
- 53 percent of our people are based in the United
  States.

About half of our products are what we call basic
chemicals--products like chlorine, caustic solvents, and
plastics such as polystyrene, polycarbonate, and polyeth-
ylene. These products are generally sold in high volume
and, more than likely, are upgraded or used in the upgrading of other products before you and I see them on
the shelf or in the store window.

The other half of our products are specialties. These
products are usually sold in smaller volume on a performance basis for specific end uses. For example, ion exchange resins are used in water purification or to remove
metal from water. You'd find epoxy resins in can coat-
ings, in microchips, and in circuit boards. Latexes are
used in paper coating, and in carpet backing and adhe-
sives; and METHOCEL* cellulose ethers are used as thick-
eners for a variety of food products such as ice creams.

There is still another group of specialty products that
go directly to the shelf for you and me to buy. These
include pharmaceutical products like NICORETTE* and
SELDANE* antihistamine, consumer products such as SARAN
WRAP* and HANDI-WRAP* plastic films, and ZIPLOC* plastic
bags. We also produce herbicide and insecticide products
for specialty agricultural uses.

Our products are extensive and varied. Worldwide, we
employ 51,300 people to develop, manufacture, and service
them. Incidentally, we hire an average of 400 to 600 new
college graduates per year in the United States.

Over the years Dow has recognized the importance of
good people management. The fact that we have paid close
attention to this most important resource in the past has
made it easier to put a process in place for continual
improvement.

- We have good working relationships between managers
  and employees, and between hourly and salaried
  personnel.
- We try hard to create a work place that allows
  total involvement, as well as the opportunity for

everyone to contribute and receive recognition for good performance.
- There is a real place for the individual and the freedom for this individual to feel part of the management process.

Although we are mostly a salaried organization, we have good relations with bargained-for employees and the several unions who represent these employees. Teamwork is a common thread.

I make these special points because good human relations is the key to any quality and productivity management process. Managing people to create the desire for continuous improvement is the core of any quality and productivity program and must be the focus of any learning program.

As with most companies, Dow recognized the need to change in the early 1980s. We realized then that all the things that made us successful in the 1960s and 1970s were not going to work in the 1980s and 1990s. World competition was demanding a change. That change would take a major training effort and a fulltime commitment by management to lead the change.

The U.S. Area Operating Board started this change with the announcement of a Quality Performance steering committee in late 1983, a move that led to the creation of my job. This steering committee created a road map that laid out for the organization what the management process was, exactly. This steering committee decided that the process must be customer driven, it must involve everyone in the organization, and it would require continual improvement through the elimination of waste. As you will see, the process is built around those three points.

ELEMENTS OF QUALITY IMPROVEMENT PROCESS

With that background on Dow I would like now to describe the key elements of Dow's Quality Performance Improvement Process that our training is built around. I will include the steps we've taken to implement this management process.

First, we have found that this management process always works. It is making our businesses better—a whole lot better. It is making so much difference that we can see why those companies that do it will survive and those that don't will not.

The quality improvement process is simple. So simple, in fact, we have, over the past decade, overlooked the obvious—the focus. The process starts with the customer. It is, and needs to be, customer driven. That is why we exist. This applies to companies, to teams, to functions, and for individuals. We learn daily through surveys and meetings with customers that we do not always

clearly understand which requirements are most important
to them.   And, the closer we get to the customer, the
more we find areas where we can improve.

The second element of the quality performance improvement process is having a good working relationship with
the suppliers.   Suppliers should have well-defined requirements and should be held accountable for their performance based on those requirements.   Suppliers should
be selected on performance, not just on price.

The third element of the quality performance improvement process is to focus on the process.   Continual improvement comes from working on the process, not the
people.   The reason this is a management process is
because only the managers can fix the process.   The workers work in the process and know where the waste is, but
only the managers can change the processes to eliminate
the waste.   Unfortunately, we have found that the managers do not see the waste as clearly as the workers.   The
higher up the line the managers are, the further they are
from the waste and the less they see it.   Managers see
waste at 3 to 5 percent, while the workers will say 30 to
50 percent.   The manager's job in the new process is to
break down the barriers so the workers will openly talk
about the waste without fear of reprisal or loss of jobs.

In the new process, the focus is on identifying,
through the use of statistical tools, which processes are
in control and which ones are not.   Then, everyone in the
organization works on reducing the variability to bring
the processes into control.   Everyone works on centering
the output of the processes so the aim point meets the
customer requirements all the time.   This may sound
simple, but we have found that most of our processes are
not in control statistically.   We have even found that
some of our more sophisticated manufacturing processes
under computer control can be out of statistical process
control.   For sure, most of our non-manufacturing processes do not have the predictability that we want.   In
fact, we see most of our improvement opportunities in the
non-manufacturing areas such as accounting, order entry,
invoicing, and planning, to name a few.

The fourth element of the quality performance improvement process is the need to measure.   These measurements,
to be effective, should measure how well the customer
requirements are being met, how well the suppliers are
meeting our requirements, and how well the key processes
are running.   Are they in control?   Do they have the
right aim point?   As basic as these measurements are, I
will bet that most companies are the way Dow used to be.
We had tons of measures but few that answered these very
important questions.

TRAINING PROGRAMS

Our challenge was to develop a series of training programs that would help our managers and employees work in this new culture. Our first training challenge was to launch an effective program that would help us focus on quality and the customer. We used the "Towards Excellence" program, put together by Zenger-Miller for Tom Peters, the co-author of *In Search of Excellence*. "Towards Excellence" draws out the fact that most, if not all, successful companies have an obsession for quality-- in the form of quality products or services. The customer is where it all starts--and ends.

The "Towards Excellence" program was very suc-cessful, as it helped break down barriers between the different functions. As we focus more on the customer, and our thinking becomes more oriented to our business groups, we continue to build trust between the functions and even within functions, because there is more sensitivity to internal customers as well.

Our next challenge was to develop our own training to make quality and productivity a way of life in Dow. We looked closely at all the quality gurus--Deming, Juran, Crosby. We also visited other companies to see what was working for them. The conclusion of all this research was that, because it was a management process, each company had to tailor its own training to fit its own personality. So that we did.

The product of this research and internal development was the Quality Performance Workshop. It is not only the content, but also the approach to training that has made this workshop successful. The Quality Performance Workshop was originally designed for our commercially oriented management teams that are made up of research and development, manufacturing, technical service and development, and sales personnel. The workshop has since been modified for use within the various functions, including the administrative functions.

The structure of the workshop incorporates the key elements of any formula for training. First, training has to bring about dissatisfaction with the way things are being done. Then it has to provide a vision of what the new comfort zone is to look like.

And, finally, the training has to help the participants take the first step in reaching that new plateau. In other words, application has to be an integral part of the process. These three elements constitute the formula for training: Dissatisfaction + Vision + Application = Change. Throughout our Quality Performance Workshop, we have built in these three elements--dissatisfaction, vision, and application--to create the change in attitude that is necessary for quality and productivity improvement.

Early on, we learned that training in numbers often does not work because a critical mass is not established in the work place. So, we made it imperative that only natural work groups--in other words, teams with a common purpose of business, job, or functional responsibility--would participate in the workshops. For instance, with our commercial teams, we request that the business team be part of the same workshop in which their market management teams are participating.

We also recognized that it is critical that managers, as well as employees, be equally involved in the training. Since the manager is part of the natural work group, the manager is automatically part of the training.

MODULE FOR QUALITY PERFORMANCE WORKSHOP

So, what is this Quality Performance Workshop? It's an extensive two- or three-day seminar. The length depends on the exposure the teams have previously had to the key elements of the quality management process.

The workshop is designed to systematically progress through these six basic training modules:

1.   Introduction or What's-In-It-For-Me (WIIFM) Module
2.   Mission Statement
3.   Visions of the Future
4.   Cost of Waste
5.   Simple Problem-Solving Tools
6.   Measurements

In each module, the teams will accomplish specific goals and they'll learn from each other. The skills taught in the Quality Performance Workshop are ongoing, dynamic, and intended to change thinking and actions.

A key to the success of this training is the fact that less than 15 percent of workshop time is spent in lecture. Ten percent is allowed for question-and-answer sessions, while the participants spend the rest of the time--75 percent--making decisions and working on their very real problems.

Time is allotted for team presentations at the end. In these presentations, the teams summarize what they have accomplished in each module. They also outline how they, as a team, are going to use the quality management process in the future to address the real problems they face.

In the first module, the WIIFM Module, the training concentrates on creating dissatisfaction and shaping the vision. Through team workshop exercises, lectures, and video presentations, the group is introduced to the quality improvement process, which they spend time examining. As the work groups diagram and understand the quality improvement process, they become more comfortable with the

need to change. They see that what they have been doing
is not necessarily wrong, and they begin to see the huge
potential for improvements; they begin to imagine a better system.

In the second module, the teams spend time preparing a
mission statement that applies to their own specific work
situation. They identify who they are, who their customers are, and what their customers' needs are. They learn
that a common mission is important to the team's success.

In the next module, the teams, through group interaction, practice divergent and convergent thinking and,
through this interaction, create visions of the future.
What will it look like when they are successful? It is
in this module, the third, that they create what we call
process quality statements.

In the fourth module, the teams learn more about the
cost of waste. They discover that waste has been building up for years and that we've gotten used to tolerating
waste in all forms. This waste exists in the form of
waste of time, capital, materials, and lost business, and
it can range from 15 percent to greater than 50 percent
of cost of sales. The teams start out thinking of waste
in the 5 to 10 percent range, but by the end of the module, they learn how to identify the things that are barriers to the realization of their visions.

Teams are taught the skills and techniques in the fifth
module that will enable them to take the complicated
problems and break them down into solvable units. They
learn to use simple tools and techniques. Fishbone diagrams, block flow charts, run charts, and histograms are
just a few of the powerful tools that the groups learn to
use to identify and solve their specific problems.

Through simple problem-solving techniques the teams
learn where to work on waste, thus bringing the element
of application into the equation. As part of the training, they again practice divergent and convergent thinking, learning how it provides a powerful mix of creativity and conformity in the team environment. Statistical
process control techniques--SPC--are also introduced in
the context of problem solving, and teams begin to be
comfortable with these methods of pinpointing and controlling variability in processes.

As the final step of the Quality Performance Workshop,
the work groups learn the performance measurement techniques that will enable them to keep track of where they
are and where they are going. Measurements, they learn,
are what convert a program into a process, and measurements are needed to identify processes or parts of processes that need improvement. Work groups are shown how
to use measurement techniques such as indexing to chart
progress toward their own particular goals.

The final stage of the workshop agenda--as I mentioned
earlier--is for the work groups to summarize what they
have accomplished in each module. They conclude their

presentations with an outline of ways they are going to apply the concepts and techniques to their job functions in the future.

RESULTS FROM WORKSHOP TRAINING

That should give you a pretty good idea of the way our quality and productivity training works. In a nutshell: we foster dissatisfaction, create a vision of a better way, and encourage application of the concepts, tools, and techniques that will result in change for the better. And we strive to get everyone urgently and relentlessly pursuing quality and productivity improvements. However, we don't stop there. We do it over and over again--continual improvement--and we never stop looking for ways to be better.

Is it working? Well, to date, over 80 percent of the commercial teams have gone through the workshop. In all cases it has had an impact on how the teams are approaching their businesses. For example, one business team and the market management teams reporting to it credit savings of $17 million in the first year to the implementation of workshop techniques. Another business team credits the workshop with significant cost reductions to the business and, even more importantly, the development of different market strategies.

The process does work. One team in Georgia worked with a customer to reduce product variability to well below previously accepted industry standards. And they're shooting for even further reductions. One of our customers, an industry leader, says we revolutionized their industry in less than six months. In another business, one that we should know how to run because we've been in it over forty years, we found ways to save $2 million in the first year.

We know we will have work yet to do to establish the complete cultural change we're aiming for, but to date, we're pleased with the progress we've made with our quality and productivity training. Building a quality culture across America is going to take the efforts of every one of us--you and me included. For America to be world competitive and recognized as the quality and productivity leader in the 1990s will require a return to the work ethic our parents and their parents practiced. It will require a national strategic intent to build quality into our products and to be the best at what we do. It will take management and workers working together, not against each other. It will take industry, government, and academic co-operation, not confrontation.

I sense a real awakening in America. I know you recognize your part as evidenced by your attendance at this conference. I know Dow recognizes what it has to do and knows there is nothing more important than our total com-

mitment as a nation to the need to be the global quality
and productivity leader.

24

Effective Leadership: The Key Is Simplicity

F. Kenneth Iverson

Nucor is a manufacturer producing steel and steel products. We operate seven steel mills on four sites. We produced, last year, about 1,700,000 tons of steel. We have a capacity of 2,000,000 tons, and we're the ninth largest steel producer in the United States. What sets us apart?

NUCOR'S TECHNOLOGY AND PROFITS

All of our mills use the latest steel technology. One hundred percent of our steel is continuously cast. In the United States even today, only 50 percent of the steel is continuously cast, whereas in Japan, over 90 percent of the steel is continuously cast. For more than fifteen years, the price of the products we produce, FOB our plants, has been equal or less than the price of these same products produced by foreign steel mills dockside USA. Also, for the last fifteen years we have not laid off a single employee for lack of work.

We operate profitably. Since 1965, when I became president, this company has never had a loss quarter. My predecessor resigned because the company had defaulted on two bank loans, and I got the job because I happened to have the only divisions that were making money at the time. We will have sales this year of about $800 million. In a number of years, our return on stockholders' equity exceeded 20 percent.

NUCOR'S ORGANIZATION STRUCTURE

Certainly, most of the success of this company is due to its organizational structure, and to our employee relations programs and policies. One of the things that we believe in very strongly is that the best companies have the fewest number of management layers. We think that the size of a company is not determined by its sales but more by the number of management layers. The fewer you have, the more effective it is to communicate with employees and the better it is to make rapid and effective decisions.

I attended a lecture one time by Peter Drucker. He brought up the fact that the number of management layers is one of the factors that determines how well a company does. He mentioned that sometimes companies get so many management layers they become unmanageable. Somebody in the audience asked him, "How many management layers is that?" He said, "Nine effective layers." Someone else then said, "Why?" He said, "For two reasons. One is that when you start a memorandum out from the top with a CEO and come all the way down through nine management layers, it can't in any way resemble what it started out as." He said, "Secondly, a young man in his whole career can never really effectively work his way up through nine management layers." In the next sentence he said, "The U.S. Army has nine management layers."

We have four management layers, the first one being the foreman. Above the foreman is the department head, who would be our manager of melting and casting, manager of rolling, division controller, or sales manager. There are about five or six department heads in each division. They report directly to a general manager who is a vice president of the company, and he is the only one who reports to our corporate office.

We're very much a decentralized corporation. These general managers make the day-to-day decisions that determine the success of the company.

The other point that we believe in is to reduce the number of staff. Staff people in marketing, engineering, or purchasing, in many cases, do not help you make better decisions nor do they accelerate decisions. Perhaps we carry it to extremes. With $800 million in sales, our corporate staff consists of a total of seventeen people, including stenographic and clerical help.

DECISION MAKING AT NUCOR

We do have in this company a very strong feeling of loyalty to our employees. We believe that there are two successful ways to manage in relationship to employees. That is: Tell them everything or tell them nothing. Both ways can really be successful, except we happen to believe in telling our employees anything they want to know about the company, unless it happens to be proprietary or it has to be secret for some reason.

We try to impress upon our employees that we're not King Solomon. We use an expression that I really like, and that is, "Good managers make bad decisions." We believe that if you take an average person and put him in a management position, he'll make 50 percent good decisions and 50 percent bad decisions. A good manager makes 60 percent good decisions. That means 40 percent of those decisions could have been better. We continually tell our employees that it is their responsibility to the company to let the managers know when they make those 40 percent decisions that could have been better. Because if they tell us, and if we examine them and agree that a bad decision was made, we will change it. Over the years we've gotten the employees to the point where they don't hesitate to tell us when they think we've made a poor decision.

The only other point I'd like to make about decision making is, don't keep making the same bad decisions. Unfortunately, over the last twenty years, up until recently, that's what we have done in our steel industry. I have a story to illustrate this. We have people in the Nebraska plant who love to hunt. We have a group that goes moose hunting every year in Canada. A couple of fellows from that plant went up last year. The plane flew them in and, when it left them for a week of moose hunting, the pilot said, "Now remember that this plane will only carry one moose." So, they went out on Monday. Tuesday they shot a moose. Since they're not the type who sit around and drink around the campfire and do nothing, they went hunting on Wednesday, Thursday, and Friday. On Friday, they shot another moose.

The plane came back on Saturday and the pilot said, "You have two moose. I told you the plane would only carry one." They said, "Aw, that's what the pilot said last year and we put two moose on the plane." The pilot said, "OK" and he tied one moose to one pontoon and the other moose to the other pontoon and he took off along this lake. He got up about 400 feet and couldn't climb anymore and began to lose altitude. Finally, he crashed into a group of pine trees. As the pilot was pulling himself out from the wreckage he said, "Where are we?" One of the hunters said, "Just about the same place we crashed last year." Don't keep making the same mistakes.

INCENTIVE SYSTEM

All of Nucor employees have a significant part of their compensation based on the success of the company. The most important incentive system we have is our production incentive system. We take groups of about twenty-five to thirty-five people who are doing some complete task, such as making good billet tons, good roll tons, or good finish tons. We have more than seventy-five groups of this type in the company. We establish a bonus that is based on a standard. If the employee group exceeds that standard in a week, they receive extra compensation based upon the amount of increased production over the standard. Very simple. There is no maximum. It is never changed unless we make a large capital expenditure that significantly changes the productivity opportunities for the employee.

The bonus is paid weekly, and in our steel mills today it is not unusual for that bonus to run 150 percent of the base pay. All we do during that production period is take the base pay plus overtime, multiply it by 150 percent and give it to the employee. The average hourly employee at the steel mill here in Utah averaged about $40,000 last year. They earn every bit of it.

What's the result of this? The result is that the average integrated steel company in the United States last year produced about 350 tons per employee. We produced about 980. The mill here in Utah produced over 1,000. Our total employment cost per ton is about $60 per ton including fringe benefits. The total cost for the integrated producer was about $135 a ton. It's no small wonder that when we, or other mini-mills who have comparable types of programs, get into a product, the integrated producer moves out of that product.

NO LAYOFFS

We have not laid off or furloughed a single employee for lack of work for more than fifteen years. There's a reason why we have that policy. Most of our plants are located in small towns and rural areas. We think the rural part of the United States has great untapped labor resources. People don't want to go to the cities particularly. They go there in order to find jobs. Big corporations go there because that is where the people are. Actually, if you establish manufacturing facilities in rural areas, you find that there is a flood of people who apply for work. We put a steel mill in a town of Jewett, Texas, that has 435 people. People said, "Where are you going to get the 300 people to run this plant?" There were only 12,000 people in the whole county. We had more than 2,000 applications from people in Houston and Dallas who didn't want to live in Houston and Dallas. They wanted to live in this nice rural community that's about mid-way between the two. Under those conditions, of course, we have to accept our social responsibilities, because we are generally the largest employer in the area, and in many cases almost the only employer in the area. Accordingly, we can't just lay people off, because they have no place to go. So if we have a slow economic period, everybody works four days a week instead of five. But everybody still has a job.

The other thing I firmly believe in is, you don't get good people if you lay off half of your work force just because one year the economy isn't very good and then you hire them back. If you do that, you aren't going to get the best people in the area. That's why we will not lay off people.

EMPLOYEE BENEFITS

We do have a number of unusual benefits for our employees. For example, we pay $1,500 a year for four years of college or four years of vocational training for every child of every employee in the company. We have at present about 380 to 420 children of employees enrolled in about 180 different learning institutions in the United States.

In case you should think that we are overly paternalistic, we also have some very tough rules. If you're late, you lose your bonus for the day. If you're late more than thirty minutes, or you're absent for any reason including sickness, you lose your bonus for the week. We do have four forgiveness days. We have some people who take those forgiveness days in January and February, and we have some people who haven't taken any for five years. I'll tell you a true story about this that happened a couple of years ago. We had an employee who came into the plant in Darlington, South Carolina, and said to the head of melting and casting, "Bill, Phil Johnson (one of our melters) has had an automobile accident and he's out by the viaduct holding his head." Bill said, "Why didn't you stop and help him?" He said, "And lose my bonus?"

We try very hard to eliminate as much as we can any distinction between management people and anybody else in the company. We all have the same group insurance program, holidays, and vacations. We all wear the same color hard hat (green). We have no company cars, company airplanes, company boats, executive dining rooms, assigned parking places, hunting lodges or fishing lodges, and everyone travels economy class. We think it is very important to destroy that hierarchy of privilege that is so prevalent and pervasive in many corporations in the United States.

MANAGERS MUST BE ADAPTABLE TO CHANGE

While I'm talking about that, let me mention some of the things I think make a good manager. One of the most important things is that a good manager must be adaptable to change. He must, in this day and age, readily accept

new technologies as they develop. Because of the mobility required of executives, he also has to be able to
adapt rapidly to geographical and cultural differences.
Children do this very well, but you find as we get
older, it's much more difficult. You have to focus on
the fact that "I am going to do it. I am going to make
a change."

In 1962, I moved from New Jersey to the little town of
Florence, South Carolina. My son was in the fifth grade.
I was going to the plant the first day and he said, "Dad,
I don't want to go to school." He had already been to
one day of school. I said, "Mark, what's the problem?"
He said, "Well, the other kids all have a hook with their
name on it to hang their coats." He said, "I don't have
my name on any hook and I'm not sure I can find one. I'm
not sure I can find the chair that I'm supposed to sit
in." Then the tears started to come, and he said,
"Besides that, I can't understand what the teacher is
saying."

About two weeks later he came home and said, "Dad, do
you know what a 'purd' is in a sentence?" I said, "No."
He said, "A 'purd' is what you put at the end of a sentence." A month later he came home and said, "Do you
know that the Great Lakes are filled with salt water?"
I said, "Mark, we lived in Michigan for seven years and
you know the Great Lakes aren't filled with salt water."
He said, "Well, I've got a teacher in fifth grade that is
teaching all the students that the Great Lakes are filled
with salt water." I said, "Well, why didn't you speak up
and say something?" He said, "You don't tell Mrs.
Singletary anything." (Just like some managers.) But
the real point of my story comes in the fall when he
started into the sixth grade. He said, "Dad, do you know
that fellow from Michigan who bought the Chevrolet
dealership in Florence?" I said, "Yeah, I know him." He
said, "He's got a son in my class and gosh, does he talk
peculiarly."

COMMUNICATIONS

We run a survey in our corporation about every two
years or so. We survey all employees about what they
think of the hospitalization program, what they think of
profit sharing, and a lot of other questions. It takes
about an hour for them to go through all the questions.
The one thing that's interesting about it is the fact
that with each survey the average hourly employee has
said he wanted better and more communication from the
foreman. I think that, in American business, that probably is one of the most important things we don't do
well; that is, teach our foremen to communicate with the
employee. You don't make an employee a foreman because
of his communications skills, you do it because of his

technical skills. So you end up with a foreman who may
be very good technically, but he really cannot communicate effectively with the employees, who have all kinds
of questions.

I am reminded of a story about a personnel man who went
out in a plant. This story is to make the point that the
training sometimes takes a long time. The personnel man
spotted a foreman who had an employee by the arm and he
was shaking him. He said, "Listen. We are going to get
the yield up in this plant by the end of the week or
you're fired." The personnel man went over and said,
"That's not the way we do this nowadays. That's not
really good human relations." The foreman said, "Why
not? It's management by objective. I told him what the
goal was, and I told him the consequences if he failed to
reach the goal." The personnel man said, "We have a
course in human relations in this company that we'd like
to send you to." The foreman said, "I'd love to go." So
the foreman went away for two weeks of training in human
relations and then came back. The next day, the personnel manager was out in the plant. The foreman had the
same guy by the same arm and he said, "Now listen. The
yield in this plant is going up by 2 percent by the end
of this week or you're fired. How's your mother?"
Unfortunately, in many cases, that's exactly the way we
do it.

Communication is terribly important. I really think it
ought to get more attention in business schools. But
it's not only communication, it's the quality of that
communication. Certainly, a big part of communication is
learning how to listen as well as how to say something.

I have a story on the point of quality communications.
We have a plant in Fort Payne, Alabama. Before the in-
terstate was put in, I'd fly into Chattanooga and then
I'd wind down through Lookout Mountain until I finally
got down to Fort Payne, Alabama. One day, I was making
that trip and as I rounded the mountain, a woman came
around the corner. She went so far out on the road, she
almost made me go over the side of the mountain. As she
went by, she rolled down her window and said, "Pig!" And
I rolled down my window and said, "Cow!" And I went
around the corner and ran right into a pig. The quality
of communications is vital.

PLANNING

Like any executive making a talk of this type, I really
want to say a few words about planning. I think that in
some companies, it's absolutely ridiculous, unrealistic,
and sometimes almost fanciful. For example, consider the
objective by a corporate office that says this company or
this division is going to grow by 25 percent per year.

That's really not planning, it's pearls cast before swine.

The short-term plans in a company, such as the year's budget, the year's production, etc., should always be a bottom-up type plan. In Nucor, we say that we want a 60/40 percent probability. We want 60 percent probability that you can make that plan and 40 percent that you won't. It's not a bit unusual for us to have a division come in with a budget for the year that projects the earnings to be less than they were the year before. It doesn't concern us one bit because there may be some forces at hand. We may be past the top of the construction cycle. There may be some basic reasons why that's going to happen.

Long-range plans are different. Long-range plans, I think, really should be the work of a corporate office putting together all of the projects that are underway and all of the projects they think might develop in the company. It's a guidebook. It's a guidebook of places the company might go. It also helps prepare you for what might be some unusual crisis in people resources or in financial resources. It's not a Bible. It really helps you avoid difficult areas. I've never met a five-year projection in my life and I never expect to. It's always different from the plan.

It does prepare you for the unexpected, as shown by this story. There was a fellow out hunting in North Carolina in the 1920s, a farmer, and he was looking to shoot a bear to feed his family. He hunted all day and didn't get a bear. So about sunset, he dropped down on his knees and he said, "Oh Lord, I am a good Baptist. I go to church and I pray, and you have answered my prayers. I'm out here looking for a bear to shoot to feed my family this winter. Please help me." He got up and he went around a corner of a rock, and there was the biggest bear he had seen in his life standing up on its hind legs with its paws outstretched. He aimed his gun and fired and the gun misfired. He dropped down to his knees and said, "Oh Lord, let this be a Christian bear." The bear dropped down on his knees and said, "Oh Lord, bless this food of which I am about to partake."

PRODUCTIVITY

My remarks would not be complete, of course, without some reference to that super buzz word "productivity." I want to give you just a few brief thoughts.

One is, there is no quick fix. You can't decide you might want to put in quality circles and really have a more productive organization, necessarily. This is evidenced by the fact that about 60 to 70 percent of the firms that put in quality circles have abandoned them. There has to be an overall culture and an overall philosophy in a company to really get the type of productivity that you are interested in. The Japanese system won't work here. There are certain elements of it that we can accommodate and incorporate. But basically, we're a much more heterogeneous society, and workers in this country have different expectations and different goals than Japanese workers. But let there be no mistake. Our workers today have a different attitude than did our grandfathers and even some of our fathers. Work was a place that they spent eight hours a day. They built most of their lives around their community, family, or religion.

Workers today expect more out of their jobs. They expect the job to be meaningful; they expect to be able to advance; they expect to participate, particularly in those decisions affecting their work place; and they expect to understand how the company operates, where it's going, and how it expects to get there. If you don't develop programs that satisfy those needs and those interests of workers, you can be assured, in the long run, your company will not be successful.

We do have, in this country, some problems at the moment. It's been blamed on a number of reasons, one of them being the lower cost of labor and more productive labor outside the United States. I had a friend recently who is in the wire rope business. He went to Korea since he was getting beaten badly by the Koreans on the price of wire rope and he wanted to find out why. He took his worker foreman along with him. They were going through a plant in Korea and they found a worker who spoke some English. He said, "Do you like working for this company?" The worker said, "Oh, it's a marvelous company. They give us lunch, and they pay us well." He asked, "How many holidays do you have?" The worker said, "We have fifty-four holidays." He said, "What in the world are the fifty-four holidays?" The worker said, "We get Christmas, New Year's, and every Sunday." That won't work in the United States. It's not acceptable to management, and it's not acceptable to the workers.

Well then, what is the answer? Certainly the answer is that we have to automate. We have to develop our processes to the point where the lower labor cost in the final sales price for competitors outside of this country is more than offset by the higher costs of shipping their products into our marketplace.

As I travel around this country, I am concerned by the attitude of many businessmen who seem to feel they cannot compete with foreign suppliers. Certainly, it's not only textiles or automotive, it's steel, farm implements, etc. They blame it on government subsidies, lower labor costs, or better technology, and then what happens? They reduce their capacity, source offshore, eliminate product lines, and pressure government for protectionism. My real concern is that they are making bad decisions. They are making decisions that are bad for their business and bad for our economy.

We do have, in this country, the people, the ingenuity, and the skills to compete against foreign manufacturers in almost every single area. I'm completely convinced of it. What we need is a dedication to some new management styles. We certainly should not accept at face value the management practices of the past, because many of them haven't worked. We need to try new ideas, we need to make new mistakes, and we need to be quick to accept new technology. If we do that, we can compete with manufacturing facilities anywhere in the world.

25

Monsanto Upgrades QC Teams to Second Generation Work Teams

Rodney J. Falgout

I'm delighted to be in Utah, a state whose history is rich in the struggle for personal freedom, to talk about American industry's struggle to give its employees the freedom to excel. We're all familiar with the need to help employees, but how do we translate that philosophy into reality? How do we change a culture that took decades to develop, and how do we change it quickly enough to have a positive impact on profit and employee morale? I'd like to share with you how we did that at the Fibers Division of Monsanto Chemical Company, an operating unit of Monsanto.

In his book, *Managing in Turbulent Times*, Peter Drucker writes, "In turbulent times the first task of management is to make sure of the institution's capacity for survival, to make sure of its structural strength and soundness, of its capacity to survive a blow, to adapt to sudden change and to avail itself of new opportunities."

Today, I'm going to address the latter part of management's task--indeed responsibility--to avail itself of new opportunities, to maintain or establish a competitive manufacturing base.

QUALITY CIRCLES PROVIDED FOUNDATION

By the late 1970s and early 1980s, Monsanto's fibers plants were beset by the same problems common to much of American manufacturing--eroding profits, foreign competition, rising costs, and seeming inability to do much about any of it. We responded at the time in much the same way as the rest of American industry. We divested or eliminated businesses that no longer fit our long-range business direction. The remaining businesses were restructured resulting in sizable reductions in the work force.

We felt a need to involve our employees in this transition and in 1979 we successfully launched the first of a series of successful quality circles. Like other companies, Monsanto found the quality circle approach worked to break down barriers between managers and wage employees. And, like many other companies, Monsanto eventually realized that the very characteristics that made quality circles attractive--being voluntary, operating parallel to the cultural structure, and functioning temporarily-- also limited their value. Quality circles, while part of the solution, weren't the total solution.

That led us about two years ago to decide to take a harder look at how the philosophy that spawned quality circles could be expanded to become a much broader, much more integrated part of our business.

First, let me set the stage. At that time, 1985, the pressures on our fibers business were pretty severe. We knew we had to do something to relieve them. We also knew that whatever we did wouldn't work unless we had the wholehearted support of *every* employee in our organization, not just wage employees this time and not just those who chose to volunteer to participate, but everyone. Our challenge was to develop a strategy that would competitively position our business for the 1990s. This challenge assembled a consolidated effort that developed a strategy or direction for manufacturing referred to as the "plant of the '90s."

INTEGRATING HRM INTO THE BUSINESS PLAN

Our human resources offer us a significant opportunity to improve our competitive position. Today I will share with you our direction for managing our human resources in the 1990s. I will:

-   give you a perspective of how we began;
-   review the evolution of major events;
-   tell you about the planning process we used to develop the human resource management plan for the 1990s;
-   define the issues that need resolution;
-   review our desired benefits; and
-   conclude with results to date.

Competitive challenges caused us to reassess our basic and traditional ways of managing our resources. That reassessment pointed to the need for change. One major change needed is in the management of our human resources. Today we have many human resource programs operational in the fibers business, but they are programs. They lack strategic direction and need to be integrated into our business plans. We recognized the need to de-

velop a plan that focuses on integrating our human resource management process into our business direction.

Our plan required the need for culture change. Culture
is a word used frequently today. Its meaning varies as
it is applied in different situations. We define culture
as what we do, and how we do it.

Before discussing the culture change needed for the
plant of the '90s, I would like to take a few moments to
review major events that occurred in the evolution of our
directional plan. Employee involvement began in 1979 in
fibers when the direction toward increased productivity
and employee involvement was begun with the implementation of the quality circle concept in all of our locations.

In 1984 the Fibers Division emphasis was on plans to
strengthen our businesses with aggressive three-year
goals to improve productivity and return on capital. In
1985 the Fibers Division went through major restructuring. It was a very traumatic year when decisions were
made to exit certain businesses. Two early retirement
programs offered during the year provided us with opportunities to accelerate productivity plans and goals set
in the previous year by not replacing people associated
with ongoing businesses.

The transition from the quality circle concept to total
involvement began in our plants. This transition began
the integration of our human resources to support our
business direction.

Let's review the Planning Process for HR Management
used in the development of the human resource management
plan defining the direction needed to bring about the
culture change for the plant of the '90s. Our goal is to
achieve a competitive advantage in the 1990s. To accomplish that goal we recognized the need to reassess the
traditional methods used in managing and operating our
plants.

A team commissioned by myself, made up of personnel
superintendents from our locations, was given the objective to develop a plan to change the culture for the
plant of the '90s. The plan defines the direction we
will take to change our culture. It consists of two
major components: a mission statement and a strategy to
achieve our mission.

Our strategy focuses on key areas that will have a
major impact in accomplishing that mission. There is a
need for our employees to understand our business direction. We found that communicating to employees the direction we want to take them is important to making the
changes we want to make now and in the future.

A mission statement was developed to accomplish that
objective. It will serve as a consistent foundation to
move us into the 1990s.

SELF-MANAGED WORK TEAMS

Let's review the key areas that will have major impact
in changing our culture. The first is organization. As
we look to the plant of the '90s, we see an organization
design that places responsibility, authority, and decision making lower in the organization through selfmanaged
work teams focused on product line results. (A self-managed work team is a natural work group of seven to twenty
employees, focused on achieving defined goals within
defined parameters without a first-line foreman.)

Jobs and organization structure will need to change to
accomplish this direction. These changes will evolve as
we move toward the plant of the '90s. We've already made
organizational changes. For example, a business unit in
our South Carolina facility, composed of about 250 employees, operates with no first-line foremen. They operate with self-managed work teams.

At our Texas facility, we now have our maintenance organization administratively reporting to our production
units to create a team effort to accomplish product line
results. Job responsibilities have also changed.

At some of our locations, production operators are performing maintenance work and maintenance technicians are
performing production work. Production operators are assuming more responsibility in analyzing product quality,
giving them more control over the entire process utilizing statistical process control.

WORK ENVIRONMENT IN THE 1990S

As we look at work environment in the plant of the
'90s, we see it as being a lot more flexible than it is
today. There will be more freedom for employees to do
what is needed to accomplish defined business objectives
and goals. Each unit will have specific key business
goals defined that are simple, understood, and measurable. Self-managed work teams may establish their own
work practices to enhance their unit results within certain defined parameters.

As we move to the plant of the '90s, we see the evolution of the self-managed teams and compensation systems
that focus on performance, skills, knowledge, competitive
rates, and profitability. Benefits will be designed to
minimize the difference between wage and salaried employees. Other forms of recognition will be developed to be
compatible with the achievements of the work teams, such
as achievement awards and bonuses.

A major area that needs attention as we move toward the
plant of the '90s is communications. We feel communications should promote ownership and partnership concepts
in our locations. Employees need to understand the goals
and objectives of our business. They need feedback on

how we're doing against those goals and objectives. They should be aware of how customers feel about our products--the products they're producing. They need to understand how the plants are evaluated as well as the competitive environment we face in our business. And they should definitely know our direction, our long-range plans for the future, and our communications should be timely and direct.

The management style in the plant of the '90s will see the boss/subordinate role replaced by the facilitator role. The new style will promote employee involvement in accomplishing results at all levels in the organization and promote partnership/ownership. The style will increase responsibility and accountability at the lowest levels of the organization.

Training will be vital to help us make the changes needed for the plant of the '90s. Areas for emphasis are (1) the development of skills and knowledge to implement and maintain advanced systems in the plant of the '90s, (2) developing team skills in problem solving and conflict resolution, and (3) the retraining of people for new job skills will be essential as we move forward. Integration of job responsibilities will become commonplace. We must also develop leaders versus supervisors by training our managers in a different style as they work with people.

As we developed our plan, these issues were identified:

- Corporate benefits
- Compensation practices
- Job security
- Accounting/audit considerations
- Enrollment
- Legal aspects
- Fibers division coordination
- Changing management style

Some of these issues have been resolved and plans are being developed on others.

DESIRED BENEFITS/RESULTS ACHIEVED

We feel key benefits, such as the following, will result from our direction:

1. Reduced costs by operating with fewer people;
2. Improved communications through fewer levels of supervision;
3. A multi-skilled work force which will result in the need for fewer resources;
4. Improved commitment to results. We're seeing that happen already; and

5. An improved utilization of our human resource skills, knowledge, and experience base.

Our results have been extremely successful to date. Not only have we achieved a 50 percent productivity improvement that seemed out of reach a few years ago, but we have replaced the adversarial relationship between management and wage employees with a feeling that we're all on the same team working toward the same results.

At some of our plants, it has meant the difference between mere survival and outright financial success, and those results have been achieved with a minimal amount of disruption, physical or emotional, and with a fraction of the supervisory foremen we worked with before. We were able to reduce 35 percent of our first-line foremen in the last eighteen months with further improvements expected in the near future.

Why have we been successful?

First, a foundation was laid with quality circles. That earlier success allowed implementation of the self-managed work teams to be seen as a gradual transition, a natural evolution.

Second, the change took place at the same time as other cultural shifts--major reductions in a work force that had been relatively stable and major changes in a marketplace that suddenly was more demanding.

Third, the changes were institutionalized throughout the business. Every level of employee, every product line, every plant, and every part of the business was involved.

That doesn't mean there haven't been problems and obstacles that needed to be overcome. There was scattered employee resistance to suddenly being thrust into a decision-making role after the security of being given explicit instructions. And there was resistance from managers to sharing information and responsibility with other employees.

But on the whole, our direction has been extremely successful. Supervisors say morale and productivity are up, employees are taking more active roles in making decisions and solving problems, and our sites are producing more and better quality products with fewer workers. As one spinning operator at our Greenwood, South Carolina, plant put it, "I want to be challenged. I want to find out what I'm capable of achieving. Without the opportunity to test myself I'll never know what I'm really able to do."

Our plant of the '90s program has given employees the opportunity for greater self-fulfillment. It has given the company the opportunity to remain competitive. That's an unbeatable and successful combination plus a testimony to the power of trust and a greater stake in our business. With it, we all win.

26

Human Resource Profession: Friend or Foe

Andrew S. Grove

Before I start, since I have a subject entitled "Friend or Foe?" I would like to find out who in the audience works in the human resource profession? There are enough of you so that I have some trepidation to proceed. Trepidation comes from the fact that when I first developed this talk with this title and gave it to our human resource manager at Intel, he said, "Why do you put the question mark at the end of the title? You know the answer darn well."

It is not that simple. What I am really talking about you might have gleaned out of the introduction. I am an operating manager. I manage a company. I am responsible for a very specific financial and product output. Yet, of course, human resource issues of management are a part of any operating manager's job, whether or not they explicitly recognize it. But conflicts constantly arise regarding the role of the human resource profession in the opration of an output-oriented enterprise such as Intel.

PERFORMANCE DEPENDS ON EXTERNAL/INTERNAL FACTORS

I am going to try to put the subject in some sort of a perspective. Basically when we are running an organization--the organization could be a government organization, a financial organization, or a university--that organization is there to generate some type of a desired output, an output that society considers valuable. How we as operating managers perform depends on two types of factors: external and internal. I will put this in a two-by-two matrix, courtesy of the Harvard consulting group. I will put the external conditions on top and the internal performance of the organization on the bottom.

What are external conditions? External conditions are all those things that corporate managers never recognize in the annual report when results are good, and always hide behind when the results are bad. For example, when oil prices go up, we cannot help that, so our performance goes down. When oil prices go down, we do not mention it. That is the best way to understand what I am talking about. These are the things that we cannot really control too much; nevertheless they have a profound effect on our performance, good or bad. If I could paraphrase a famous saying, "It is the tide that raises or lowers all corporate boats at the same time in the same way."

Our task as managers of organizations is to make the most of whatever external factors affect the performance of the corporation or the organization. If the external conditions are unfavorable, and we fall asleep at the switch internally, we go out of business. If the external conditions are favorable, we succeed even with poor performance. When all is going well for us such that the conditions on the outside are good and we do a good job, we get a gold medal for our performance.

Now what is internal performance? That is where human resource professionals come into play. A lot of things are involved. First among these is being at the right place at the right time and with the right product. When it comes to that, quite frankly, it is best to be both lucky and smart. But the second best is to be lucky. I will give you an example of this. If I asked you what company was responsible for the invention of the personal computer, what would you answer? The personal computer was actually introduced by a little-known company called Mitz. That was about three or four years before Apple. They had this weird-looking box that no one knew how to use. It was a good product but the world was not there yet. The software that was needed was not there, and the world's computer awareness that was needed was not there, so it died. A year or two after it died, Apple arrived with a very similar product, but at that point the product was right for the market. So being at the right place at the right time with the right product is the best of all these things.

Second is being in a position to ride the tide. A perfect example is Chrysler. They were bailed out by the federal government just before the arrival of restrictions on Japanese imports. Chrysler was alive and therefore when the tide came in that lifted all automotive boats, they were able to ride it.

The third is that we have to constantly and doggedly pursue, sustain, and renew the performance of an organization. This is the hardest of all types of corporate activities. Product planning and the like is easy, particularly when you are lucky and you cannot do much about external performances. But nagging your organization into better performance, a bit at a time, is what we are all about. It is hard and most excruciating and, quite frankly, the least romantic and least publicized activity that involves all managers. So, who is involved in it? The middle management is the part of the organization that is involved with pursuing, sustaining, and renewing the work of the organization.

Another very important element is to constantly keep an eye on the output. It is very important for us not to be so mesmerized by the daily work and activity that we forget what the organization is supposed to do. The university exists to educate students and not to give papers. Companies like Intel exist to generate profits by serving customers and making electronic products. To do all that, it is very important for us to have management systems.

NATURE OF MANAGEMENT SYSTEMS

What are management systems? Every company has them. We have systems for planning, whether it is a formal system run by a corporate staff with forms and computers, or whether it is done in the old way, by scribbling on the back of envelopes. So, there is a system, implicit or explicit, that all corporations use. All organizations have systems for goal-setting. Some companies have very formal management-by-objectives systems, while in other companies somebody sets goals by barking out orders.

There is always a system of performance assessment, good or bad. It really exists and is well defined, even if you cannot describe it readily. And, of course, there is a system of promotion, compensation, and termination. Likewise, there are systems of training and development, formal or informal, ad-hoc or systematic.

There is a communication system wherever you work. It may be well developed and technologically advanced, or it may be that employees find out what is going to happen in the company only when they pick up the daily newspaper. It is whatever system you have.

There is a way in which your organization maintains, promulgates, and hands down the culture of that organization. Maybe it is through the use of colossal reports, role models that are very well defined, or folklore. There is a system in which we do that.

The main point is that all organizations have management systems. Not all of them describe the systems explicitly. Sometimes management systems are just what is in the air. A most important point is that very few organizations actually describe their management systems in the way that they operate. For instance, the U.S. government has a voluminous, well-defined system for performance assessment. Yet you all read about whistle blowers

that are removed from their jobs for speaking up. Which
is the real system? The one that is described explicitly
or the one that disposes of the whistle blowers? Ford
Motor in the last decade had a very well-developed career
planning system, but when you read Lee Iacocca's book you
get quite a different perspective on how it actually
worked. There is frequently a duality of the system that
is described and the system that actually lives.

It seems that in every organization, both management
and the human resource people have an image or notion of
what their management systems should be like. What they
then describe is what they think it should be rather than
what it is. That is a very crucial point and a stumbling
block in the workings of organizations.

MANAGERS OWN MANAGEMENT SYSTEMS; HR MAKES SYSTEMS WORK

Who owns these management systems? Not the human resource professional. Operating managements own them since
it is the management structure that is responsible for
developing and delivering the product. They are the
people who own all of these systems that we have talked
about.

On the other hand, we pay the human resource people in
our organizations presumably because, in some fashion,
they add value to the workings of the organization, they
bring something to the party. In my view what they bring
to the party, when it comes to the organization's management systems, is to lay the track for the management systems so that operating management has a track on which to
proceed and perform its work. It is for them to set up
a performance assessment system, describe it, and teach
operating management how to use it. It is for them to
set up a performance bonus system. It is for them to
figure out the appropriate way of systematic communication between management and lower-ranked employees. It is
for them to grease the machinery of all this so these
things will happen: performance gets assessed, bonuses
get administered fairly, and information proceeds back
and forth between various levels of management.

To draw an analogy that is perhaps more accepted and
more traditional, look at the finance profession. The
profit and loss statements of every organization are the
responsibility of the operating management. I wish that
I could have blamed Intel's 1986 profit and loss on our
finance organization. I could not. I am responsible for
that as operating manager. But finance developed the
system by which the game is played. It spells out how
inventories are valued and how reserves are calculated.
Finance lays the track by which the whole process of
inventory is counted and how all of that trickles down
through the system and gets added up. This is the
analogy. Management owns the profit and loss and the

management systems of the company. Finance greases the
skids for the profit and loss to work. The human resource profession greases the skids for the management
systems to function.

HR STAFF PERPETUATES CHARADE; SAY ONE THING, DO ANOTHER

The question is how well has the human resource profession, in the gross generality of American industry, performed its task.   Intel, probably like all your companies, has performance assessment categories such as
"superior," "exceeds requirements," "meets requirements,"
"marginally meets requirements," and "does not meet requirements." The best phrase to assess human resource
performance is that it "meets requirements"; not "superi-
or," nor "exceeds requirements," but just "meets requirements."

Why is it not better? I come up with two factors: the
first is what I call the Pollyanna syndrome and the
second is the problem of the shoemaker's children. (It
has been pointed out to me that I should call the first
one the PollyDonald syndrome, or something like it, in
order to even out the sexist connotation.)

The Pollyanna syndrome basically says that when we,
operating managers, say one thing and do another, the
human resource profession acts like nothing is amiss.
Operating managers have a hard time looking at reality
and seeing reality. The reason is that it, reality, is
full of worms. Reality is generally not pretty. We say
we have a meritocracy, but it is hard to implement and
enforce meritocracy. Assume you have a 4 percent budget
increase and I tell you to apply meritocracy. You cannot
give poor Joe nothing, so you have to give him something.
You cannot give him 1 percent or 2 percent, so by the
time you rationalize your plan for poor Joe, who really
should not get anything, you give him 3.5 percent. This
means that you will not have enough money to give the
people who really make things work in your company any
better than 6 percent. So, meritocracy has turned out to
range from 3.5 percent to 6 percent. That is not meritocracy. Then you start arguing that Joe has been here
for twenty-five years and all of a sudden the whole idea
of meritocracy has gone out the window.

We tell it like it should be, not like it is. The
human resource profession should be our conscience, but
often they turn the other way and participate with us in
perpetuating this charade. Some of the worst euphemisms
come from the human resource profession. For example, I
have described Intel's categories of performance assessment. You have no idea how many battles I have had with
our human resource people who are aghast by the phrase
"meets requirements." They say that is not good. It does
not make your people feel good about themselves. But I

cannot help the mathematical fact that half of our people are below average! But if I say that, I get crucified, and the first nail comes from the Human Resource Department. It is very difficult for operating managers to face the facts and the reality. We need help; help to prod us to face reality, not to talk us out of it.

I will give you an example. I write a weekly column for a newspaper. People write to me about work problems, kind of Ann Landers-style, and I try to give them advice. This is a recent question:

I have been working at a bank as a temporary, part-time new accounts clerk. This position offers no benefits and minimal pay. Although in theory I am a part-time employee, I have routinely been working forty hours per week. Also, since I had worked at this bank in the past as a teller I am often asked to work in that capacity at no extra pay. In fact, I often work next to brand new tellers who make more money than I do. I have talked to the personnel director about this situation but he offered no help, because the bank's policy did not allow the use of temporaries in teller positions.

So, it is okay for a bank to use a temporary in the teller position when you cannot pay the teller salary because of the policy that does not permit the use of a temporary in the teller position. It's Catch-22 coming from the personnel profession.

I think the simple rule that I would like to leave with you and that we all ought to try to live by is that, whether you are on the human resource side of the fence or the operating management, if it is too embarrassing to say, then do not do it. If you are doing it, then steel yourself to be able to say it exactly the way you do it.

The second phenomenon is the problem of the shoe-maker's children. Basically, the human resource organizations have typically been the worst in following management systems. When it comes to performance assessment, they have a tendency to be non-meritocratic. When it comes to training, typically the human resource people train themselves less rigorously than the other professionals in an organization.

A particular weakness of the human resource people is careful execution of the details. I have faced innumerable human resource people who complain to me that they do not have time to do their work because of their paper work. The paper work that they are complaining about is the performance review and the related compensation work for the people in their organization. They do not have time to do their work because they have to attend to the paper work. First of all, the system of the paper work was generated by them. Second, that piece of paper, which is administrative trivia to the person who complains, is the annual performance assessment of an employee in the organization. It is the change in his/her compensation as a result of an annual performance assess-

ment. If that is not their work, what is their work?
Typically I found that the quality of execution of this
kind of thing is much worse than the way we process sales
orders, production scheduling orders, and the like. These
deal with inanimate objects. By contrast, the paper work
the human resource people complain about, the administrative trivia, concerns the lives of fellow employees.

So, this is another factor. You can all make up your
own reasons why it has come to be that way, but it is a
very unsatisfactory situation when the organization that
is expected to be the promulgator of the human resource
systems, and the conscience of all the rest of operating
management, does not provide a proper example.

BEWARE OF FADDISH HR APPROACHES

I have one last thing that I would like to discuss concerning other ways that the human resource profession can
be more helpful and less of a hindrance. *Try to resist
the lure of fads*. There is a $25 billion training and
development industry in the United States. (When I first
heard that number, it was almost as big as the semiconductor industry worldwide. It is now bigger than the
semiconductor industry.) It is a huge industry. Now
these people have products to sell, and just like the
retail stores at Christmas, they must come up with new
products. They cannot sell the same thing over and over.
So each year we have some new acronyms, such as MBO one
year, MBWA the next, and then corporate cultures. Now
the human resource departments buy the products of this
$25 billion industry and bring them home. But it doesn't
work that way. Pursuing, sustaining, and renewing is
grubby work, day in and day out; these hard tasks include
assessing performance, doling out compensation, training
people, setting objectives, and all these other
things. The new fads are really distractions that, like
the diet of the day, offer a simple answer when there is
nothing but hard work that can truly give you results.

HR CAN HELP RESTORE U.S. COMPETITIVENESS

In my view, which is colored by the fact that I am in
a badly beleaguered industry that is in a recession, the
manufacturing industries of this country are in deep
trouble. We have lost the strong competitive position
that we had worldwide in the decades following World War
II. We have become just *one of the* leading industrial
countries rather than *the* leading industrial country.
For us to hang onto the standard of living that we are
accustomed to, we need a renaissance of performance, of
corporations, public organizations, the people who manage
these organizations, and the people who work in them.

The human resource profession has the potential for a major "added value" in all this.   As I mentioned, the added value comes in laying the track for the management systems and in greasing the skids so they can   perform well.

I am not asking for the human resource profession to do this task on their own.   I am asking for this to be done in partnership with operating management.   The key thought that I would like to leave with you, the key that is missing very often and should *never* be missing, is to bring the utmost intellectual integrity to the job. Simply put, say it like it is, and if it does not feel good to say it like it is, then change what *is*, rather than what you say.

27

Kodak's Copy Products Quality Program

Dale P. Esse

ABSTRACT

An integral part of any successful quality improvement project is the active, continuous support of upper management. Their positive attitude and active involvement foster a dynamic, team-oriented environment which transcends all working levels. To maximize achievements in this type of atmosphere, new philosophies must take root and continuous improvement must be encouraged.

This paper describes the Quality Improvement Program implemented at the Copy Products Division of Eastman Kodak Company, a program which utilized the above philosophy to effect significant cost savings and quality improvements. Characteristics of this improvement program that will be detailed include: a strong emphasis on teamwork and communication, assembly's ownership of quality, the replacement of in-process quality control (QC) inspection with a final product quality assurance (QA) audit, and a redirected focus on customer-perceived quality.

BACKGROUND

Since the start of Kodak's Copy Products Division in 1975, traditional 100 percent inspection had been used throughout the assembly process. In recent years, however, copier competition, both foreign and domestic, threatened to replace Kodak's share of the marketplace with similar high-quality products at lower costs. In 1983, a newly appointed Copy Products QC management recognized many drawbacks of the 100-percent inspection system, such as:

- 100-percent inspection is not 100 percent effective.
- 100-percent inspection is essentially a sorting process of good product from bad.
- 100-percent inspection is not cost-effective.

In addition, assembly had little responsibility for quality and no apparent incentive for building it right the first time. QC inspection acted as a "police force," enforcing corrective action after the product was assembled (defect detection, not defect prevention). The accepted philosophy to improve quality was to increase the frequency of inspection. Acknowledging the "proof of the need," a management team of recognized leaders from assembly, quality control, and manufacturing engineering started discussions to develop a plan that would reduce QC inspection from 100 percent to sampling. A strong resistance to change the traditional 100-percent inspection system was quite obvious and due, primarily, to the fear of changing the long accepted social positions of QC and assembly. That is, the QC "empire" would be significantly reduced and assembly would be forced to accept the responsibility for building a quality product. These concerns and many others were addressed by the management team, and a three-phase quality improvement plan was formulated that would change phases as quality improved and stabilized.

The Phase I, II, III Quality Improvement Plan was implemented late in 1983 on all KODAK EKTAPRINT Copier/Duplicator products. The use of statistical sampling principles was required for each phase of the plan to maintain an acceptable outgoing quality limit (AOQL). However, applying these principles to a highly complex, low volume product, such as the EKTAPRINT Copier/Duplicator, proved to be a formidable challenge. The AOQL number derived for each assembly area had to be *estimated* based on histogram data of the actual average nonconformities per unit for that area. This histogram data would determine where each assembly area would start:

- Phase I (100-percent inspection with controls)-- where product quality was poorest and required all phases of the step-down process.
- Phase II (Lot Sampling)--where product quality was better and Phase I was not required.
- Phase III (Continuous Sampling)--where product quality was best and Phases I and II were not required.

Major characteristics of the Phase I, II, III Quality Improvement Plan included:

- Management presenting the plan to the copy products community in an attempt to educate a majority of the people prior to implementation.
- Management demonstrating their commitment to the plan by holding weekly roundtable discussions with assembly, QC, and manufacturing engineering to address problems and concerns.
- Establishing acceptable control limits that were realistic.
- Distinguishing between a major and minor defect, with a major defect having priority for corrective action over a minor defect.
- Shifting phases or lowering control limits only on the consensus of QC, assembly, and manufacturing engineering.
- Implementing a formal failure analysis system to insure management-controllable problems would get resolved.
- Using the Pareto Principle in failure analysis to enable QC and manufacturing engineering to utilize their time on the critical few problems.

PHASE I

Phase I was the continuance of 100-percent inspection, but control limits were added that defined the maximum number of nonconformities on an inspected unit which assembly should not exceed. To establish the control limits, a team comprised of assembly, manufacturing, and QC engineering evaluated those inspection criteria that were important to the product's function and then categorized each inspection check as major or minor. A major is defined as a check that, if nonconforming, would cause the Equipment Service Representative (ESR) to correct it during installation, cause noncompliance to regulatory agency or safety requirements, or result in a service call at a future date. This could be due to a numerical value which significantly exceeds its specification or a condition that would decrease reliability.

The team then reviewed histograms of the past nonconformity data for the specific assembly area in order to establish control limits. A minimum of one month's data was reviewed with only major nonconformities being considered. If an inspected unit did not exceed the established control limit, the unit was accepted, repairs were made by assembly and reinspected for subject repairs only by QC. But if an inspected unit exceeded the control limit, assembly was required to repair, reevaluate, and resubmit that unit to QC for 100 percent reinspection. The detainment of product due to assembly's re-evaluation and QC's re-inspection provided assembly with an incentive to build it right the first time. During operation of the plan, results were continually reviewed by assembly and QC, and the control limits were systematically tightened (lowered).

Once assembly minimized the number of operator-controllable errors, a need was recognized to formalize a system that would address the management-controllable errors. The system developed, called the Failure Analysis Plan, generated a Failure Analysis Form (FA) for each major nonconformity found during inspection. This form served a dual purpose. First, it acted as a tool to initiate specific corrective action. A Failure Analysis Team comprised of a representative from manufacturing engineering, assembly, QC supervision, and QC engineering was contacted to collectively analyze the specific nonconformity and, where possible, establish a corrective action sequence. Where immediate corrective action was not possible, the FA Form was held "open" until corrective action was complete. In areas where a high number of FA Forms were generated, it was necessary to apply the Pareto principle. In this manner, analysis was done on the significant few versus the "trivial" many. Secondly, the Filure Analysis Form served as a data reporting tool to be entered into a computerized central data bank. Reports could then be extracted on a routine or special basis to assist in determining those problems that should be addressed. Examples included yield reports, high runner reports, and overall nonconformity reports.

When a particular assembly area achieved and maintained a previously agreed upon control limit goal, Phase II was implemented.

PHASE II

This phase utilizes the lot concept wherein assembly formed lots of a predetermined size and inspection evaluated a random sample from the lot.

Phase II used the same major nonconformity criteria as Phase I. The same team that set the control limits under Phase I established a control limit which was the basis for the acceptable sampling criteria for Phase II. As the assembly area progressed through Phase II, the limit was continually reviewed and tightened.

In most assembly areas, a lot size of five units was used which maintained both good product flow and minimal statistical validity. When assembly informed inspection that a lot was ready for audit, inspection verified lot integrity and selected the sample unit(s) forming the lot utilizing a random sample selector (common die). Inspection completed the entire inspection procedure and noted all major nonconformities found on the sampled units. When a noncomformity pre-vented checklist completion, on-the-spot repairs were made, with those nonconformities still counting towards the total. Upon completion of the checklist, all non-conformities were verified by both assembly and inspection supervision.   If the number of major nonconformities exceeded the established control limit, the entire lot failed and was returned to assembly for correction (i.e., all uninspected units were checked for the nonconforming conditions found on the inspected units).   After repairs were made, all units were subjected to a screening operation by assembly.   This previously established screening checklist insured that all units could pass inspection on the second submittal.   The screening procedure was modified and updated by assembly, as necessary, to serve this purpose.   The entire original lot was then resubmitted to QC for reinspection.   A random sample was taken which may or may not have contained the previously inspected unit(s).   The same procedure applied as on initial submittals except tightened (lowered) control limits were established on reinspection.

Several unique reports were used under the lot plan. One was a yield chart that showed in percentage the daily progress of initial sampling and resubmittals.   This chart also acted as an indicator: high consistent yields indicated that the control limit could be tightened.   In addition, a weekly lot sampling report was issued which included both the above data and a running list of nonconformities.   These reports were used at weekly roundtable discussions which covered the positive as well as the negative results encountered.

During Phase II, when assembly firstline supervision recognized the benefits of improved (faster) product flow, they became very proactive for quality improvement and this resulted in significant quality gains.   This enabled assembly to reach the goals required to implement Phase III sooner than anticipated.

PHASE III

In Phase III, we continued using the same major nonconformity criteria and Failure Analysis System as used in Phases I and II.   The initial step was to establish the control limit, average outgoing quality limit (AOQL), and the inspection sampling rate.   This step determined the type of plan used and was accomplished by reviewing the nonconformity data for the specific assembly area for at least the past four weeks.   The plan began by inspecting a specified number of units in a row at 100 percent. This value was dependent on the particular average outgoing quality limit and inspection rate chosen.   Once the value was achieved, a unit was randomly selected for inspection upon the completion of the assembly process. This random selection process was accomplished through the use of a random sample selector.   Once selected, the unit was subjected to a complete inspection.   If the number of major nonconformities found during inspection

did not exceed the established control limit, the unit
was accepted, repairs, if necessary, were made and inspected by QC, and continuous sampling continued per the
specified sampling rate.

If the number of major nonconformities exceeded the
established control limit, the unit was returned to assembly, repairs were made and reinspected by QC. The
next four units which completed the assembly process were
then subjected to 100-percent inspection. The concept of
inspecting four units in a row was necessary to maintain
the AOQL that was chosen. If the four unites met the
control limit, sampling resumed according to the specified rate. If any of the four units exceeded the control
unit, 100-percent inspection continued until the specified number of units in a row successfully passed inspection.

In addition to the timely and accurate nonconformity
reports used throughout all three phases, a status sheet
and yield chart were also utilized. The status sheet was
used by inspection to keep track of the number of units
inspected and not inspected so that they could accurately
monitor the specific stage of the plan they were in. The
yield chart was similiar to that of Phase II except that
sampled units were plotted instead of lots.

OVERVIEW OF SUCCESS OF PHASE I, II, III

The Copy Products Phase I, II, III Quality Improvement
Plan was very effective in reducing nonconformity rates
and significant cost savings resulted. The plan also
proved that product schedule did not have to be sacri-
ficed for good quality. Also, there were large assembly
savings in rework, scrap, and overall product costs such
as reduced work in-process and reduced floor inventory,
resulting in faster through-put.

The increased awareness towards the Phase I, II, III
Quality Plan also brought about many changes in attitude
and philosophy. The antagonistic feelings that once
existed between assembly and QC evolved into a productive, team oriented relationship between the two groups.
Assembly acquired a strong incentive to build it right
the first time and recognized the need to assume responsibility for quality. Overall, the copy products community saw the need to be cost effective to remain competitive and to take a closer look at the customers' needs
and how the customer perceived the quality of our machines.

To meet these needs and our mutual goal of zero defects, a plan had to be devised that went beyond the
Phase I, II, III Plan and would give total responsibility of in-process quality to assembly and enable
inspection to make the transition from controlling in-
process quality to controlling final product quality.

QA OF THE FUTURE

By 1985, quality had substantially improved (primarily due to assembly's ownership of quality) and QC inspection became a redundant process. Once again, the management team devised a step-down plan not only to reduce QC inspection but to eliminate it entirely from the building process. In Phase I, II, III, QC inspection audited product based on design specifications (i.e., assembly set-up specifications), but the QA of the Future Program focused on realistic standards (i.e., quality as the customer perceived it). Inspection transitioned from in-process quality control (QC) to final product quality assurance (QA). As an area met a control limit of zero major noncomformities 90 percent of the time, QC inspection was withdrawn from that area and assembly assumed full responsibility. The QA auditing of the final product was based on input from our customers (marketing and the customer equipment service personnel).

The QA of the Future Program received total management commitment, and because of this continued support, quality gains were significant with all inprocess QC inspection systematically eliminated in less than one year. In addition, feedback from within the factory and from the field indicated the quality levels continued to improve.

The QC inspection group has been reduced significantly since 1983. With this elimination of QC inspection, assembly has had to implement plans to hold the quality gains. One of these plans (detailed later) evaluates and compares actual assembler performance. Other plans implemented in the QA of the Future Program include a final product acceptance audit and a ten-level conformance audit of packed units. These audits focus on one main theme: audit the product based on functional performance, not on assembly set-up specifications.

FPAA (FINAL PRODUCT ACCEPTANCE AUDIT)

Final Product Acceptance Audit (FPAA), implemented in early 1986, is a random sampling QA audit of the final product and is based on customer-perceived quality. Various major definitions include:

- Control limit (C) is the number of major nonconformities allowed per unit and is based on previous data.
- Modified control limit (Cm) is a tighter control limit than "C". Initially, Cm is 75 percent of control limit but as quality improves and stabilizes, Cm is reduced to 50 percent of control limit.
- Major nonconformities have been split into two categories, A and A'. An A' is a nonconformity

that would be adjusted by an Equipment Service
Representative (ESR) as part of the normal machine
installation, therefore not added into the total
nonconformities that are charged against the
control limit (provided that assembly can demonstrate that the condition can be adjusted within
acceptable limits). A nonconformity would not be
adjusted by an ESR as part of the normal machine
installation and would require additional time to
adjust it to acceptable limits.

-   A product engineering organization was formed at
    this time which combined in-process QC engineering
    functions with the manufacturing and design engi-
    neering functions to more effectively support the
    production process.

-   All nonconformities are verified by a team repre-
    senting product engineering, assembly, QA supervi-
    sion, and QA engineering, and classified as A, A',
    or minor (low priority) nonconformity. The pur-
    pose of this is to provide immediate feedback to
    the assembly line and prompt product engineering
    for any necessary corrective action.

Initially, a specified number of completed units are
audited per the FPAA checklist and the data compiled.
The control limit is determined from the data and sampling begins by randomly selecting a completed unit for
audit prior to shipment. For example, if the sample rate
is 1/3, an average of 33 percent of all units is chosen
for auditing over a period of time.

Several improvements have been incorporated into the
FPAA plan to make it a "user-friendly" plan and increase
its chance of success. One feature is the modified control limit. This is an early warning indicator that the
quality of machines has worsened and that there is a high
potential for exceeding control limit if the problem is
not addressed. Screening of units by assembly is one
option that has been used to improve and stabilize process quality. Other modifications have been incorporated
which easily identify the quality of the assembly process
at any given time.

Another improvement of the FPAA plan is the use of the
rolling average. In Phase III (continuous sampling) each
unit inspected was plotted against the control limit.
This resulted in many large "spikes" on the chart for
nonconformities per unit. A rolling average of nonconformities per unit tempers the "spikes" and allows assembly time to stabilize the process before it goes out
of control and exceeds the control limit. For most Copy
Products applications, a five unit rolling average has
been used successfully (i.e., each point plotted represents one audited unit with its number of nonconformities
averaged with the number of nonconformities found on the
previous four units audited).

Other key programs have been implemented to aid assembly in the transition from assembler to assembler/inspector. Two of these plans are summarized in the following sections.

CPM (CRITICAL PARAMETER MONITORING)

CPM is a variable screening process audit performed by assembly as inspection is removed. The purpose of CPM is twofold:

- The primary purpose is to provide the assembly supervisor with a tool to guarantee acceptance quality levels in his/her area.
- The secondary purpose is to allow the supervisor to take a closer look at individual assemblers on a frequent basis.

The assembly supervisor for each assembly area is responsible for monitoring critical parameters on their assemblies before they shift to the next assembly area (their customer). The critical parameters are defined by each assembly supervisor with input from product engineering. The basic guideline for defining critical parameters is: A critical parameter is one that, when not set up properly, could directly affect machine performance, customer satisfaction, and/or final product acceptance audit.

The length of the CPM checklist, the percentage of units monitored (a minimum of 10 percent of the production schedule is required) and the frequency at which each assembler is monitored (a minimum of two audits per assembler per week is required) are determined by the assembly supervisor and reviewed, where appropriate, with product engineering to maintain consistency. The data generated from CPM Audits (distributed once a month) help to determine possible assembly processes that drift with time, prioritizes problems for corrective action, reduces risk of floor line purges, clarifies assembly procedures, and identifies potential problems with specific assemblers.

ADR (ASSEMBLY DISCREPANT REPORT)

The Assembly Discrepant Report is a reporting system of all problems found during the assembly build process or CPM audits that need further engineering analysis. A failure class is assigned to each non-conforming condition such as: parts-mechanical, assembly area responsible or under investigation. The name of the person designated for implementing corrective action and target dates for completion are also recorded on the ADR. Meetings

are held bi-weekly (chaired by the assembly general
supervisor) to update the status of each ADR to insure
proper follow-through to completion.   All ADRs are
recorded into a central data base for retrieval at any
time.

CONFORMANCE AUDITS

Copy Products has enhanced the product audit testing by
implementing a 10-level conformance audit that confirms
the unit is fit for customer usage by auditing all possible customer environments.   The operating procedure
states that every four weeks, a specified number of units
(2 percent of the shipping schedule) must be removed from
the packaging area prior to shipment.   They are unpacked
and set up in the factory per installation procedure used
by our field service personnel.   These units are then
audited at certain "levels," such as high altitude, environmental, regulatory, or customer usage.   By the end of
a four-week period, these units will have been audited on
at least one of the ten "levels."   The results of the
conformance audit testing provide management with timely
information on product early life performance, reliability, and conformance to specifications.

CONCLUSION

Until 1983, Copy Products Division operated on principles that proved to be not only costly but essentially
ineffective in achieving and holding any real quality
gains.   Our products cycled their way through an elaborate maze of queues, waiting to be inspected, repaired,
reinspected, and moved to the next queue.   This operating
philosophy failed to keep pace with modern aspects and
advantages of active Quality Improvement programs.   Today, the Phase I, II, III and QA of the Future Quality
Improvement plans have shifted full responsibility for
in-process quality from quality assurance to assembly.
This transfer of responsibility has been accomplished
without any significant amount of added cost to assembly.
In addition, inspection has changed from its former
role of in-process sorting to its new role of auditing
final product based on the customer's needs.   The gains
in quality and cost reductions include:

- An overall average major nonconformity per unit
  reduction of 90 percent on all *EKTAPRINT* products
  since the implementation of the quality improvement program.
- A 70-percent reduction of QA personnel with a
  direct labor savings of nearly three million
  dollars since 1985.

- A 50-percent reduction in QA unit cost.
- Significant reductions in rework costs (e.g., from 12.5 percent to 8 percent on one product alone).

The social consequences of assuming new responsibilities have been overcome and a more productive environment has evolved. As continuous improvement is encouraged and rewarded by management, the gains to date will not only be held but exceeded. Continuous improvement must become a part of a company's culture, taught and practiced at every level. The Copy Products Division of Eastman Kodak is well on its way to achieving such a culture.

28

Excellence in Manufacturing at GM

Theodore A. Lowe

I would like to start my presentation with an old Buddhist parable.

It seems that three monks were having a long and fruitless argument over some matter. . .and they decided to present their views to the wise old master. The first monk spoke long and well, supporting his case with illustrations from the life of Buddha. The master listened and said, "Why you are quite right." The second monk presented his arguments, and they were truly eloquent, and when he finished, the master told him, "You, too, are right." Now, a third monk had been following all this and he became very troubled; "These two men were in complete disagreement, surely they both can't be right." The master turned to him and said, "And you too are right."

This presentation will make the point that we must be like the wise old master and use the concepts of all of the gurus in developing a quality improvement process.

BACKGROUND FOR THE QUALITY JOURNEY

On our journey to world-class quality, we will need to follow the directions of three leading quality experts: Dr. W. Edwards Deming, Dr. Joseph M. Juran, and Philip B. Crosby.

While others have debated what's lacking in the direction from either Dr. Deming, Dr. Juran, or Phil Crosby, we looked for the right things from each. It was our position that they were 90 percent common in philosophy and that they complemented each other. Therefore, we tried to understand and integrate the three approaches. By using the strengths from Deming, Juran, Crosby, and others, we believe that we have been able to accelerate our quality improvement journey.

Before I highlight some of the most valuable directions and the lessons learned from the masters along our journey, let me provide you with the background for the quality journey at General Motors Truck and Bus Group. This, headquartered in Pontiac, Michigan, is responsible for the planning, designing, engineering, manufacturing, assembly, and marketing of General Motors trucks and buses worldwide. As a result of consolidating all of GM's truck and bus operations in mid-1982, the truck and bus group has become one of the largest and most important parts of GM's worldwide business.

In 1982-1983, commitment and involvement in quality efforts were begun by providing Deming Process training to management, SPC training to production people, and we established a groupwide SPC council.   In February 1984, Juran training was initiated.   In March 1984, an executive quality council was established, and in October, the quality improvement process was launched at an off-site with over one hundred of our senior managers.   In 1985, we established our quality improvement structure--which included   forming   customer   satisfaction   improvement teams--and we also initiated Crosby training.

In early 1986, we took strong action to involve the union in our process--a major step forward.   In July of last year, we believe we came to a real turning point. With union involvement, we jointly redefined the quality improvement process and developed a quality road map. The process consists of seven elements, each with a tenet, a vision of where we want to be regarding our quality culture, and initiatives to be taken to attain our objectives.

To continue the quality improvement process momentum, the executive quality council has designated 1987 as the year of employee involvement, application, and achievement.   We have spent the last four years in building awareness and commitment, and providing training.   Now we need to apply the lessons learned from the masters if we are to achieve world-class quality, but what are the lessons that we learned from Deming, Juran, and Crosby? Next, I'll review our experiences in applying the approach of each expert, look at how and why we integrated the three approaches, and conclude by summarizing the lessons learned.

APPLYING THE DEMING APPROACH

We were well into the Deming Process when the old GM Truck and Coach division was merged into the Truck and Bus Group in September 1982.   In fact, our first Deming overview for our executive staff was titled "Deming's Ten Points."   A few months later, when Deming came out with his fourteen points, we were hard-pressed to explain how we had missed four points. One of our first initiatives in Truck and Bus was to provide Deming Process overviews to all of our plant managers and staff heads and their staffs and to initiate SPC training for the work force. Later we added concepts from Myron Tribus and others to reinforce the training.

Dr. Deming triggered our quality renaissance. His new philosophy challenged our past practices. While many of us were not very comfortable in confessing our sins in public, Dr. Deming's denunciations gave us the license and courage to question our traditional practices in the open. In addition to sparking the renaissance in thought, Dr. Deming gave us a way to get at "truth"--through statistical thinking.

We learned about variation and the difference between common and special causes. We learned to use control charts to separate the special causes of variation from the system problems.

We learned from Deming, and later Juran, that 85 percent of the problems are management-controllable. Therefore, it is management's job to initiate action on the system to reduce or correct the common causes of variation and improve the process capability of an operation.

To understand whether our processes were stable, capable, and on target, we learned to use statistical tools, starting with seven soft tools of Ishikawa and progressing to the Taguchi and other designs of experiments techniques. We're still learning how to apply these tools.

To spread our experiences and efforts, we established an SPC council. We learned from each other's experiences in training and applying the Deming Process.

Dr. Deming emphasizes the need for ongoing improvement. His fifth point tells us to constantly and forever improve the system of production and service. This concept is illustrated by the Deming circle, which symbolizes the problem analysis process. The plan, do, check, analyze, and act circle also serves as a model for the quality improvement cycle of a company--planning and designing a new product, making and selling it, checking customer satisfaction, and acting to further improve customer satisfaction.

Dr. Deming's principles helped us establish a learning environment, which in turn gave a boost to the effectiveness of the training from the other experts that followed.

However, not everybody was ready or willing to learn. Many managers turned away because of the criticism of their past practices and others were put off that Dr. Deming focused more on what needed to be done than on how to do it. Deming himself scoffs at the type of executives that ask for the recipes--there is no instant pudding.

Dr. Deming warned us not to jump into SPC training for the masses until we had removed the roadblocks to quality. We did not listen, however, and we learned the hard way that plants that trained selectively with a purpose were more successful than those that trained everybody top to bottom and were done with it.

The use of SPC was more difficult to apply in our assembly plants and staffs. The journey in these areas was certainly tougher than in traditional manufacturing plants as there were no documented experiences or directions to follow. Often we faced the response, "How can I use it, we're different," from people in functions that used little variable data.

The implementation of the Deming Process and SPC in general was more successful at the lower levels. The workers and quality engineers could make use of the SPC tools. So, even though Dr. Deming directs his fourteen points at management, the Deming Process at Truck and Bus became a grassroots movement, centered around SPC training and application.

But we feel the grassroots movement was successful for us. If we revisited the fourteen points today, we would be amazed as to how far we have addressed his roadblocks. Dr. Deming triggered the reaction by helping to establish a participative and learning environment and by providing a means for getting at the truth, through the use of statistics.

APPLYING THE JURAN APPROACH

Whereas Dr. Deming's fourteen points are more of a final destination than an actual road map, Dr. Juran provides a more specific systems approach to quality control, improvement, and planning for all parts of the organization.

We learned from Dr. Juran about this more scientific approach to quality management. We learned the value of a project-by-project orientation and the application of the "Breakthrough Sequence." Dr. Juran provided an assortment of problem-solving tools in addition to SPC. With his quality spiral and "fitness for use" definition of quality, Dr. Juran gave us a strong orientation to meeting the customer's expectations.

When Dr. Juran addressed our top eighty executives for the first time in November 1983, he recommended four major thrusts in our quality improvement process:

1. Establish annual quality improvement goals.
2. Establish hands-on leadership toward quality improvement.
3. Establish an executive steering committee to lead the quality improvement process.

4.   Establish a vigorous education and training pro-
      cess.

We acted aggressively on his recommendations, starting
with the creation of our executive quality council and
the implementation of Juran training.

Dr. Juran's education process is structured around the
Juran trilogy of quality planning, quality improvement,
and quality control. Quality planning focuses on creating a process that will from the start have a very low
cost of poor quality. Quality improvement strives to
lower the cost of poor quality in existing processes, and
quality control's intention is to hold the gains and keep
the process in control.

"Juran on Quality Improvement" is a training process
that is based on a project-by-project approach, with
project being defined as a problem scheduled for solution. It addresses the *vital few*. Many of our plants
continue to use the "Juran on Quality Improvement" video
tapes to facilitate floor-level project teams.

"Juran on Quality Planning," on the other hand, facilitates projects that are processes scheduled for improvement. Because systems are responsible for 80 percent of
our problems, "Juran on Quality Planning" helps address
what Dr. Juran calls the "useful many" and what we at GM
call the "significant many." We participated in the
field test of this training program and plan to use it to
help staff project teams improve the quality of their
processes.

Dr. Juran stressed the need for establishing the
problem-solving machinery required to achieve improvement. The third step in his Breakthrough Sequence is to
organize for a managerial breakthrough in knowledge by
creating problem-solving steering arms and diagnostic
arms. The steering arm guides the overall problem-
solving effort by establishing the direction, priorities,
and resources to accomplish the task. The diagnostic arm
is the work group with the investigative skills and mobility to follow the trail wherever it leads until the
root cause is identified.

Dr. Juran divides the problem-solving effort into two
journeys--a journey from symptom to cause and a journey
from cause to remedy. He states that the most difficult
journey is from symptom to cause because it is not clear
where the responsibility lies.

To steer our quality improvement efforts, we established customer satisfaction improvement teams in 1985,
for each one of our product lines. The teams, which include representatives from all key disciplines, focus on
increasing customer satisfaction. They have assessed our
current quality position, established objectives, and developed plans and projects to accelerate our rate of improvement. The customer satisfaction improvement teams

operate on a project-by-project approach and have effectively addressed many of our *vital few* problems.

Dr. Juran urged our management to establish an annual
quality improvement program, setting objectives and
seeing that specific projects are chosen, year after
year, with clear responsibility for action. His approach
conformed readily with our five-year business planning
process. Dr. Juran advised us that our quality objectives must be set according to the marketplace. They
should not be limited by elements outside our immediate
control or by what we think can be realistically achieved
with our current resources.

He told us that after our upper managers set the broad
improvement goals, it is up to the middle managers to
establish the teams, resource requirements, measurements,
and projects to meet the goals. To support our commitment to becoming a customer-driven organization, our
executive quality council has established the broad overall objective of reducing the discrepancies in our processes and problems experienced by our customers by at
least 25 percent in the 1987 calendar year. In this
regard, we are asking all plants and staffs as well as
our customer satisfaction improvement teams to align
their goals, plans, and efforts with our group quality
objective and cascade the objective and strategy downward
to cover all functions and levels in the organization.

APPLYING THE CROSBY APPROACH

Dr. Juran's direction accelerated our knowledge and
also got more members of our organization involved in our
quality process. His training proved to be most valuable
to the managers and quality professionals responsible for
implementing and managing the quality improvement process. With his total comprehension of quality management, Dr. Juran and his material served as our teacher.
To further accelerate our quality journey, we knew we
needed to achieve an awareness and involvement of our
entire work force, from top to bottom. The principal
strength of Philip Crosby's program is the attention it
gives to transforming the quality culture of the organization.

By stressing individual conformance to requirements,
Crosby involves everyone in the organization in his
process. His fourteen steps, a "how-to" for management,
provide an easy-to-understand, structured approach to
launching the quality improvement process and starting
the journey to world-class quality. Although there were
pockets of the organization that were well on their way,
the Crosby Process helped us to get almost *everybody* in
the organization started on the journey. The fourteen-
step process provided a very explicit and structured approach to implementing a quality improvement process--a

common road map for everyone to follow. It also gave guidance for building a quality improvement attitude throughout the organization, and for establishing a uniform quality vocabulary.

In following step two of Crosby's fourteen-step process, we implemented a group quality improvement team, as well as plant and staff quality improvement teams, to run the quality improvement process. The quality improvement teams manage the "soft" or non-product areas covered in his fourteen steps such as awareness and communication, quality education, cost of quality, and recognition. The fourteen-step process provided us with the most defined, simple-to-follow road map for our quality journey.

Like Deming and Juran, Crosby starts his process with management commitment.   But we were more successful achieving management commitment with the Crosby Process. Perhaps it is because these four absolutes of quality required by Crosby to achieve management commitment also provide a new philosophy and a breakthrough in attitude that Deming and Juran require in their approaches. An example of the commitment from our management is our executive quality council visit process to our plants and staffs. These visits, which occur twice each month, are solely for quality and for discussing progress and any obstacles to the quality improvement process. The theme for these visits is "How Can I Help?" Crosby also asks for a management commitment to quality training and awareness for all levels and functions. It does not go into the depth of Juran's training but it provides broader coverage.   Whereas Dr. Juran's project-by-project approach attacks the vital few problems, Crosby's error-cause-removal step and emphasis on conformance to requirements have helped us address the category of problems that Dr. Juran calls the "useful many."

We have used the Crosby training to help everyone focus on the quality of their business process and to understand their internal customer/supplier relationship. We all have individual products and customers. How do our personal customers perceive the quality of our individual products? And what are their requirements for us?

We also have internal suppliers who provide us with products and services that we use to complete our tasks. What are our requirements for our suppliers? How do we provide feedback to them on the quality of the work they provide for us? This understanding of the customer/supplier relationship helped to further crystallize the concept of quality in our staff functions.

INTEGRATING THREE APPROACHES: BENEFITS/PROBLEMS

In adding the Crosby Process to the previous focus on Juran and Deming, it was important for us to overcome the perception by some parts of the organization that the

Crosby Process was only a means of cheerleading workers
to achieve zero defects. In that regard we were fortunate to have the depth of knowledge gained from Deming
and Juran so that we were prepared to get the train
accelerating quickly once Crosby helped us finally get
almost everybody on board. The quality management practices and problem-solving techniques that we learned from
Juran and the statistical techniques and management principles that we learned from Deming increased the effectiveness of Crosby's training in developing a new quality
culture and implementing the quality improvement process.

In conducting quality education programs on the three
approaches, we had to overcome differences in terminology
used by the experts. Often we had to serve as interpre-
ters, translating Juran's language into Deming's or
Crosby's terminology or vice versa. For example, Crosby,
Juran, and Deming all define quality differently.

To Crosby, quality is conformance to requirements;
whereas Juran defines quality as fitness for use. Although Deming does not give an explicit definition of
quality, he describes quality as a predictable degree of
uniformity and dependability, at low cost and suited to
the market. Dr. Juran relates his definition to Crosby's
by stating that the quality mission of a company is
fitness for use whereas the quality mission of departments or individuals is conformance to specifications.
In their quality definitions, Crosby's emphasis is on
doing *things right* while Juran is stressing the need to
do the *right things*.

Finally, General Motors has developed a definition of
quality that encompasses all three ideas: "Quality is
conformance to specifications and requirements that meet
customer expectations."

Understanding and following the directions from each of
the leading quality experts is necessary, but not sufficient, by itself, for us to reach our destination.
Crosby, Deming, and Juran are interdependent. Companies
using one of their processes need to borrow concepts and
techniques from the others to make their own processes
more successful. A Deming Process, for instance, needs
a Crosby fourteen-step process to assist management in
transforming the organization. It also needs Juran's
breakthrough process as a framework for applying statistics. Juran states that the break-through sequence must
start with a breakthrough in attitude. Crosby helps
achieve this breakthrough with his four absolutes. The
effectiveness of Juran's problem-solving approach is also
enhanced by the application of the statistical tools that
Deming promotes. A company using the Crosby Process
needs these tools and Juran's techniques. It also needs
the teamwork that Deming and Juran emphasize to address
the system problems that keep the individual worker from
reaching zero defects.

In establishing our quality improvement process we wanted to fit Crosby, Deming, and Juran into *our* process and not try to fit our process into one of their programs. In incorporating the best features of all three into our process, we tried to avoid the perception by the organization that we were *jumping* from one "prophet" to the next. To avoid the conflict that comes when an organization tries to choose the proper "champion," we tried to show the benefits of integrating the concepts of Deming, Juran, Crosby, and others into our quality improvement process. We used the metaphor of three preachers, one religion.

Dr. Deming has been called the "fire and brim-stone" preacher. He lays down the fourteen commandments for management. He tells management that they are responsible for 85 percent of the sins and that they must repent or their businesses will go to hell. Dr. Deming also provides the congregation with an SPC "prayer book." Dr. Juran is the theologist who has extensively researched the scriptures of quality management. He provides the quality "Bible." Philip Crosby might be viewed as the evangelist of the three ...exciting, positive, generating enthusiasm. His message is simple: the four absolutes. He preaches that no level of sinning is permissible but he provides management with a way to get to heaven.

Management and the work force make up the congregation at General Motors Truck and Bus. We are learning to sit together and be more than Sunday Christians. As we practice our quality religion, our process is becoming homogeneous. The different concepts and techniques that we have picked up from Deming, Juran, and Crosby are losing their identity with the preacher.

GM's TENETS OF QUALITY IMPROVEMENTS

Therefore, the lessons that we have learned from the masters are best summarized by reviewing the tenets that we have established as the guiding principles of our quality improvement process. The definition of a tenet, as we're using it, is: "a principle, belief, or doctrine generally held to be true; one held in common by members of an organization."

Our first tenet is that quality improvement requires management and union commitment and leadership at all levels. Leadership means comprehending the quality improvement process, developing a shared vision, communicating clear direction, creating an environment for quality and improvement, developing a sense of trust among the people, and establishing a "can do" attitude.

The second tenet is that a quality improvement structure and strategy are necessary for providing a systematic approach to continuous quality improvement. The structure requires the networking, teamwork, and cooperation of all groups within Truck and Bus, as well as throughout General Motors, our suppliers, and dealers. The strategy must be well defined, encompass all the elements in the quality improvement process, and provide a systematic and uniform approach that is clearly understood and followed throughout Truck and Bus.

Our third tenet is that awareness and open and free communications are necessary to create a climate of continuous improvement. All employees must have a shared understanding of our quality issues, challenges, goals, commitment, and accomplishments if we are to establish a new quality culture. This groupwide awareness can only happen in an environment of open, free, and honest communications--in all directions.

The fourth tenet in our quality culture is contingent upon an environment where all employees are learning to apply the quality concepts and techniques; a climate of continuous quality improvement process.

Commitment and leadership, structure and strategy, awareness and communication, and education are all necessary prerequisites for the attainment of our fifth tenet: we (everyone) will continuously improve the quality of all of our products, services, and business processes. Continuous improvement requires the following actions:

- Measurement, analysis, and continuous improvement of our business processes.
- The use of cost of quality as a management tool to help gauge the effectiveness of our quality improvement process.
- The use of statistical methods to identify, understand, and continually improve process capability.
- A corrective action process that includes an error-cause-removal system.
- A focus on preventative actions and on planning and providing capable processes.

The sixth tenet is that employees will be recognized and rewarded on the basis of their contributions to a team approach as well as their contributions as individuals for their continuous quality improvement.

The first six tenets all lead up to and support the seventh tenet: a group quality culture will be achieved when each and every employee at Truck and Bus is constantly trying to improve the quality of his/her processes. A work environment must be established where each and every employee understands and can contribute to the quality improvement process.

29

Dana's Five Steps for Improving People Involvement

Robert A. Cowie

Dana's been around for a long time--since 1904. We've seen a couple of big wars and two or three small ones. We've seen depression, prosperity, and inflation. Over that period of time we've been reasonably successful and profitable. If you looked at our sales chart, you would notice that we've had only three down years since the 1960s. We've had a couple of bad years recently. However, we never went into the red and we're really quite proud of that, because there are many people who can't make that statement.

As do the other chapters in Part III, this chapter focuses on linking human resources with strategic management and how you get the people to move toward the strategic objectives of the company. Those of you who have some way to achieve your strategic objectives other than through people can stop reading right now and start your forty winks. I don't know of any other way to do it. I'm going to tell you some of the things that Dana has done. I'm not prescribing this solution for everybody. All I know is that for Dana it seems to work. If you like the idea, feel free to "steal it."

SHIFT TO PRODUCT ORIENTATION AND REGIONAL ORGANIZATION

Dana has undergone a major shift in strategic emphasis since the early 1980s. We were formerly a product-oriented company. This means that we made a product and then tried to find somebody who could use it. We have moved now to a market orientation, which, in our interpretation at least, means that we look at the market and

then turn around and see what productive facilities we
have and what assets we can marshal to meet the needs of
that market. This is really a fundamental change in the
way people inside the organization must think. We now
try to find out what the customer wants and make it for
him.

One of the ways we did this was to set up product-
market councils, which are made up, generally, of division managers. These product-market councils interface
between the producing divisions and the markets to be
sure that the market needs are met.

We also moved to a regional organization. One of the
slogans we "float" around the company is "Think Global...Act Local." We have four world regions: North
America, Europe, Asia-Pacific, and Latin America.   They
are responsible to execute Dana's world strategic plan
with local tactics; the world strategic plan is adapted
for use in each specific area so as to meet the local
political and economic needs. They are responsible to
use Dana's world assets fully and to cooperate with one
another. That is a very important aspect of this approach, because our markets are now world markets.

Our goal is to be the low-cost, high-quality supplier
in selected markets worldwide. What does that really
mean to us? It means that we must have high productivity, a fast response, and a bottom-up orientation, and we
must be customer driven. The last two items, slightly
paraphrased, are right out of Tom Peters and Bob Waterman's book. We had it before they did, but nevertheless,
that is essentially what they are saying in their book.
We think that this involves a five-step process and that
you must satisfy some requirements in order to accomplish
these objectives.

FIRST STEP: COMMUNICATION

The first step is to communicate. I learned early on
from somebody wiser than I that if you wanted to build a
better mousetrap, the first thing you had to do was learn
how to communicate with the mouse. Business is really no
different. So we work very hard at this, but we probably
don't do enough of it.

Tell All
Let me give you just a few highlights of some of the
things that we do. One motto is "There are no secrets at
Dana." This sets the tone, and our chairman says it all
the time. It's not quite true, because we don't talk
about salaries and other personal information, but after
that, everything else is fair game. I'm talking about
sales, profits, etc. There's an interesting thing about
talking to your people in operating units about sales and
profits. If you don't tell them what the figures are

because you're afraid that they'll ask for more money if
they know how well you're doing, then they will make up
their own number and their number is always more damaging
to your case than the truth.   I'm sure you are familiar
with   the   surveys   showing   that   the   man-on-the-street
thinks that the company is retaining as profit 35% to 50%
of   every   dollar   of   sales.   You   all   know   that   those
numbers are off at least by a factor of ten.

So we tell them everything. We tell them how well the
organization is doing, how much profit is being made, the
return on sales, the return on investment, and so forth.
We try to tell our people before we tell anybody else.
One   of   the   sure   ways   for   a   Dana   manager   to   get   into
trouble   is   to   have   his   people   read   something   that   is
important to them in the newspaper before he's told them.
We do this through a whole variety of schemes that I'll
mention as we go on.   But we do have a serious commitment
to telling our people the important things about their
operation and their company first.

Plant Visits and Meetings

One of the ways we like to tell our people about the
company is through plant visits. Our chairman and president made seventy visits between them to various plant
sites in 1983.   When they visit the plants they try to
meet everybody personally, and we have some plants with
as many as 2,000 people.   That is not a small task.   It
makes a long day. It is a very serious commitment on the
part   of   a   CEO   to   go   into   a   plant,   perhaps   have   a   plant
meeting, meet with the staff, and then walk through the
plant,   shake   hands,   and   maybe   say   a   few   words   to   everybody in that operation.   That's not a trivial commitment
to communication, and a CEO learns a lot by doing it. He
likes to do it, but it's not easy.

During the plant meeting there's an opportunity for the
people at the facility to ask questions. Another interesting thing--many plant managers are a little afraid to
go in front of their people and open it up to questions
and answers. This was particularly the case for some of
our plant managers in the earlier days. To my knowledge,
categorically, we have never had a cheap-shot question
raised with the chairman or any plant manager. The questions that the people ask are usually well thought out,
very serious, and express a concern that they have about
the facility.   The questions are always to the point and
never   intended   to   be   embarrassing.   I   think   industry
sometimes under-estimate our people.   In order to make
sure it's a dialogue, we leave a poster behind with a
tear-off sheet in the corner. We invite our people to
tear off that sheet of paper, write on it, fold it, and
send it to the chairman as a mailer with postage prepaid.
They can question anything or write whatever concern they
may have about their facility or about the company or
whatever.   He answers every single one of them indivi-

dually, provided they sign their names and most do. He
gets about ten to fifteen notes a week.

Newsletter

The *DCN* (Dana Communication Newsletter) is a monthly
bulletin. Everybody has a newsletter, but we think ours
is a little bit different. For one thing, it contain the
monthly operating results for the company. This comes
out about the seventh or eighth working day of every
month. It contains the operating results of the corporation for the previous month. As far as I know, we are
the only major company the publishes its results every
month rather than every quarter. This puts a fair amount
of pressure on the financial staff to make sure that they
don't get any surprises. It also puts a lot of pressure
on the operating managers. They must understand their
operations in great depth and anticipate any situation or
problems that may arise, so they don't get surprised.
Next to not telling his people first, the worst thing a
manager can do is surprise the chairman with news that he
hadn't expected.

We try to publish the hot news. We do not include an-
niversaries, birthdays, service dates, and so forth.
There are no recipes. It is done strictly in what we
call "Kiplinger style." It is very simple and concise
and deals with the issues that are key to the company as
well as the things that the people want to hear about.
We write this at a level so that the readability is high
for everyone.

The chairman sends a letter to all employees every
three months. He discusses very frankly the status of
our markets, what to expect in the company, what world
business conditions are, what the government's doing that
he likes or doesn't like, etc.

Plant meetings are important to us. Our managers are
required to meet with their people and report to them the
results of the operations at least annually. Almost all
of them do it quarterly and some do it monthly. The
question might spring to mind, "Doesn't that cost an
awful lot of money to shut down you operation?" because
that's what we do when we get all these people together
in one place. It's rather interesting if you look at our
numbers. On meeting day, normally, production and productivity increase. The people really appreciate the
opportunity to be there and to be brought up to date on
these events. They show us how much they appreciate it
by making up for the meeting time through increased productivity during the rest of the day. It's not easy for
our managers to become accustomed to making these kinds
of presentations. They're usually a little bit shy about
it. One of the reasons that our president and chairman
make the visits they do is to provide a role model for
our managers. This shows them that it can be done and
that the meetings will be good and constructive.

One of our best communications devices is the "one-on-one." It's out on the shop floor, eyeball-to-eyeball, with the first-line supervisor talking with people. I think you'd all agree that that's probably the key to good communications.

SECOND STEP: PROVIDE UNDERSTANDING OF GOALS

If you do enough communicating and you do it the right way, you gain some understanding. That's the second step. When I say understanding I mean not just an understanding of the words and the material that has been put out, but a sense of common goals. A sense that the success of the Dana Corporation is also the success of the people who work there.

Now, how do we achieve growth through training? One of the things we do is to provide as many growth opportunities as we possibly can. We enroll about 2,800 people year in one-week classes at Dana University. It's a major commitment to training and development and involves conducting thirteen or fourteen different courses with an average class size of twenty. Half of the classes are given at plant sites and half at a very nice building that is adjacent to our headquarter in Toledo.

Dana Style: Keep It Simple

We have made a conscious effort to write down our style in the Dana Style Booklet. In this booklet we try to describe how we do things in the company. This book is widely available. It is a conscious statement of what our corporate culture is and the way we do things. A subtitle from the book is "Working Hard to Keep It Simple!" We're working hard to keep it simple in order to promote the understanding and efficiency that I mentioned earlier.

Here's a good example of simplification. We had a three-volume policies and procedures manual that we used in 1968. Our then-president went to our then-chairman and CEO and said, "Hey, I think we can do better. I want to throw that stuff out and substitute something simpler than all those policies and procedures. I think they're getting in the way." The chairman said, "Oh, you can't do that. There's a lot of good stuff in there. We spent a lot of money to create them. You better leave it alone." So our then-president said, "Well, you tell me what the good stuff is and I'll save that." The chairman turned to him and said, "How would I know, I've never read the books." In any case, we did reduce it to one page. That is all. We do not have corporate procedures at Dana. If a division feels that they need to have procedures, then it's their responsibility to create them. We do not provide them from the corporate office. That one page is really it.

THIRD STEP: INVOLVEMENT

If you can achieve understanding, the next step is involvement. Involvement is really a higher stage of understanding.

Promote from Within

One way to achieve involvement is to promote from within. The nearest thing to an absolute at our company is the dictum "promote from within." We just do not hire people from outside the company at other than entry level jobs. This does two things for us. One is really obvious--that is, it's a motivator. The people know that the job opportunities are there for them. When the time comes and the opportunity arises, someone from the company will be chosen for the job. The other thing is a little more subtle. It forces you to really understand your organization and the people in it because you know that that's all you have. If you've got problems, you've got to fix them. You can't run out and get a new part and plug it in. You have to make do with what's there. That means you choose carefully in the beginning. You develop a keen awareness and understanding of the people and their needs and wants and what will motivate them, and you act on that.

Job Rotation

We do a lot of job rotation in the company. We did a survey and found that, of our plant managers, sales managers, and controllers, 80% were in assignments that were new over the past three years. That doesn't mean that they might not have been controllers or plant managers elsewhere, although in fact, many of them were not. We have chief engineers that became sales managers and controllers that became plant managers and so forth. That happens all the time. So we do a lot of rotation around the company, which helps us to build what we think is a very effective network of people. They know one another personally, so that when they have a problem in Division A, they don't have to go to the vice president for Division A, so he can talk to the vice president of Division B, who in turn talks to the division manager of Division B. They just call up their guy over there directly and say, "I have a problem with you product. Why don't you do something about it?"

Minimum Supervision and Levels of Management

Reduced supervision is another one of our objectives. In order to reduce the number of supervisors and broaden the span of control in an organization, you need better trained and more involved people. In our Hastings, Nebraska, plant we have 150 people and 2 supervisors, one for each end of the plant. It's really run by the people. They have committees that rotate every couple of

months. The folks run the plant themselves with an absolute minimum of supervision, and it seems to be working
out very well. There have been other experiments of this
kind, and most of them were successful.

We strive very hard for five levels of management between the top executive group and the people on the
floor. That's mind boggling for most companies that are
larger than Dana and have eleven or twelve levels. Five
is our number. We try to go from the operating committee
of the corporation down to the shop floor in five jumps.
In most places we are successful.

Autonomy and Entrepreneurship

We provide a high degree of autonomy to all our managers. The regional world organization is evidence of
this. But the same thing is true on the local level.
Our division and plant managers have a great deal of
operating latitude. We call it the "store manager
concept." Each manager is responsible for his own show;
all they have to do is perform.

We have a saying at Dana that, within the twenty-five
square feet where a person works, the person doing the
job knows more about it than anyone else. He or she is
the expert.

We have twenty-four plants that use the Scanlon plan.
Briefly, this is a major way to achieve involvement of
all the people and promote the spirit of entrepreneurship
that we're after.

FOURTH STEP: COMMITMENT

The next-to-last step in the process, and following
involvement, is commitment. This is a word that our
chairman uses a lot. When he visits our plants he talks
about the "five Cs":

1. *Concern.* We all need to worry about the economic
   and market conditions within our industry.
2. *Commitment.* He tells them that if they're committed to the success of the business, then he's
   committed; but they are the ones who have to make
   it go. If they're committed, he'll do everything
   he can to help them be successful.
3. *Communicate.* This is self-evident based on what
   I've said earlier.
4. *Compete.* This sets the tone for the competitive
   position they have to maintain.
5. *Confidence.* This derives from applying oneself to
   the job.

FIFTH STEP: CHANGE

The final result of all this, and the last step in the process, must be change. In order to adapt to a new competitive environment, we must change. In order to achieve productivity increases, we must change. We must have an organization that accepts and promotes change in order to be successful over the long term. The goal of all these efforts is to develop a style that promotes change--that accepts change not as a threat, but as a positive response to the needs of the future.

"FORTY THOUGHTS" ON DANA STYLE

In 1982, in an effort to reduce our style to simple terms and to help us rapidly acquaint new people who come into the company (either through acquisitions or as new hires) with how we do things, we developed the "Forty Thoughts." I'd like to share a few of them with you now. They are all grossly oversimplified, and in many cases they ask more questions than they answer. But that's the intent. It's a great way to start a dialogue on the Dana Style.

- Remember our purpose is to earn money for our shareholders and increase the value of their investment." This is our way of saying that our people programs are not provided just to be nice and humanitarian, but rather they are darn good business. In the final analysis, providing returns to our shareholders is the best and most secure reason for offering people programs.
- "People are our most important asset" is merely our way of highlighting what really is the underlying philosophy of Dana.
- "Promote from within" is an idea I mentioned earlier. We really do it.
- "People respond to recognition" is a shorthand expression of a principle we like to keep in front of us all the time.
- "Decentralize" and "Provide autonomy" really go together and summarize our basic organizational principle.
- "Encourage entrepreneurship" goes along with the decentralization and autonomy ideas. Taken together they are a major means of keeping Dana growing and vital.
- "Control only what is important" is aimed at trying to control only those things that really matter. We try to get people to understand what really matters. This also forces you to understand your organization a little bit better.

- "Promote identity with Dana" is another key ingredient in our program. "This makes all Dana people feel like shareholders."
- "Simplify" has a lot to do with the control aspects and has a great deal to do with getting rid of the policies and procedures manual.
- "Use little paper" means having as little paper around as possible because paper creates problems. "Keep no files." Everybody always asks. "How can you run a business without any files?" Obviously we do have files, but this is one of our favorite questions. It surely generates a lot of comments and conversation. The point is that we keep as few as we possibly can. Every time you put something in a file you have to take it back out again. Sooner or later you're going to have to sort it and throw 90% of it out. Most of it you wouldn't have looked at anyway.
- "Communicate fully" is another article of faith. "Let Dana people know first."
- "Discourage conformity." We try to do things differently. If we have two or three plants that are doing the same thing, then we say to the next plant, why don't you try to do it in some different way.
- "Let people set goals and judge their own performance," since they know when they're doing a good job and when they're not doing a good job. Let them think about their performance for a while and encourage them to do so.
- "Break organizational barriers" is something we're working at all the time. That's one of the things we try to do when we move people around. We get them together in these Dana U. classes and let them talk about their common problems and try to break down those barriers.
- "Develop pride" goes without saying.
- "Insist on ethical standards" is something that we just take for granted. We don't have a corporate policy statement on ethics and corporate behavior. We just assume that our people know what is right and we expect them to do it.

CONCLUSION

We keep these thoughts in the minds of our employees all the time. We try to "keep facilities under 500 people." We think a facility operates better when it's under 500 people. The plant manager ought to know everybody in the facility by his or her first name. He ought to know whether the worker has a son or daughter in college and all about him or her. This is something toward which we are still moving. We still have a couple

of large plants, and they're hard to manage. We like to
have smaller plants.

   We try to "stabilize production" so our work staff
doesn't fluctuate much. We try to stabilize by varying
inventory levels and reducing the impact on our people.
Our customers prefer this. Anticipating market needs is
essential in achieving stability.

   "Do what's best for all of Dana." Whenever we have an
issue or a difference develop between divisions or people
that maybe is not in the best interests of corporation,
we say, "Hey, what hat are you wearing today?" We remind
them that they all wear the Dana hat. That's our key
message.

30

IBM Profits-from-People Programs

H. Don Ridge

Breaking out human resources from the business itself in IBM is a lot like asking a track and field athlete just exactly what it is he does to clear the bar at seven feet. He would probably say, "I don't know how to stand here and tell you how it's done, but perhaps I can give you some pointers." Human resources is such an integral part of the business that we seldom attempt to explain it to others, but I am ready to try and perhaps give you those few pointers.

MANAGERS ESTABLISH AND EXECUTE HUMAN RESOURCE POLICIES

Let me begin by explaining that the corporation is run by two basic committees. One is called the BOC (Business Operations Committee). They are given such tasks as deciding how much to charge for a product, determining when it should be announced, and resolving the honest differences between two divisions vying on a business issue. The second committee is called the Policy Committee, or simply PC. It is composed of the three top executives, and they are involved in all major strategic decisions facing the corporation. Every human resource decision is made by the Policy Committee, not the Business Operations Committee. That alone shows you how important the human resources program is to us.

The second point I want to share with you is that we don't have human resource management programs or personnel programs; instead we have manager programs. The personnel staff does not work with the employees; they work with the managers. The managers are responsible for the program that I'm going to describe, not the personnel people--and that's important.

All managers are held responsible for two things.
First, they're responsible for getting things done--
writing a program, developing a machine, manufacturing a
product. They're held responsible. Second, they're held
responsible for the management of the people reporting to
them. That includes the appraisal process, compensation,
awards, etc. They always get measured in their appraisals on their people management. We insist on that.

COMPANY HISTORY AND PHILOSOPHY

It would be hard to talk about the IBM Corporation
without our familiar THINK sign. I want to take a little
space to review where we are today, the history of the
company and some of the people programs, and the management of people programs. I'll also touch on productivity
and what we see down the road.

We're just a small company trying to make a buck. We're
being somewhat successful, with $40.2 billion gross in-
come in 1983 and $5.5 billion in net earnings. We have
spent much time and effort in getting ready to arrive at
where we think we're going. For example, since 1979
we've added over 25 million square feet of floor space,
of which 1.7 million was completed in 1983; another 3.5
million is under construction. We spent over $10 billion
in land and building development and equipment, and $2.6
billion of that was spent in 1983. Approximately $13.5
billion was spent on research, development, and engineering, of which $3.5 billion was spent in 1983. So we are
trying to ensure the future for the IBM Corporation.

I've been with IBM for over thirty years, and I can
tell you that the business has changed during that time.
Today we're involved in a whole host of products ranging
from all sizes of computers to storage devices, printers,
processors, typewriters, robotics, and so forth. The way
we merchandise and market the equipment has certainly
changed. At one time we sent salesmen directly to all
customers. We now have product centers, retail outlets,
authorized distributors, and other manufacturers selling
IBM equipment.

Who would have ever suspected that someday Charlie
Chaplin would help us sell personal computers?

If you look at the history of IBM, you will see that in
1914 we were the Computing-Tabulating-Recording Company,
basically selling butcher scales, tabulating equipment,
and time clocks. Tom Watson, Sr., left NCR that year,
joined CTR, and soon became president. At that time
there were about 1,300 employees in what was to become
the IBM Corporation.

In 1924, Watson changed the company name to International Business Machines, even though there were no
overseas sites. He foresaw what he was going to do with
the corporation. Tom Watson, Jr., was speaking at

Columbia University's Graduate School of Business and summarized what we believe: "I firmly believe that any organization, in order to achieve success, must have a sound set of beliefs on which it premises all its policies and actions." He also said, "Next, I believe that the most important factor in corporate success is faithful adherence to those beliefs. And finally, I believe that if an organization is to meet the challenges of a changing world, it must be prepared to change everything about itself except those beliefs as it moves through corporate life."

We have done exactly that, if you look at these three beliefs: respect for the individual, providing the best in customer service, and excellence in everything we do. In their book *In Search of Excellence*, Tom Peters and Bob Waterman explain that a company can become excessive or obsessive on a point. I would submit that if IBM is excessive or obsessive on a point, it is one of these three points.

Respect for the individual is a belief that we devote much time to. Tom Watson, Jr., said that this belief was bone-deep in his father. Some of these practices and principles make a lot of sense today, but when they were implemented in the 1920s and 1930s, people must have wondered whether Tom Watson, Sr., had all of his marbles. He talks about the emphasis that he puts on the belief in customer service, and that he wants to give it the best we had. As we become more and more integrated and diversified, such as selling products for home use, we say how do you know that the man who bought the PC and is concerned about its not operating properly or the ability to get it serviced, is not going to make the decision to buy the major computer for his company. If he's unhappy with IBM because his PC doesn't work, he may well decide to be unhappy with IBM when it comes to large-scale equipment. We're spending as much time on the serviceability of the PC as we do on the largest processor.

Mr. Watson, Sr., felt that the thing that makes us effective is our emphasis on excellence. I think that when you start talking about the emphasis on excellence, you can apply it to managing people, to quality products, to your service to customers, or to innovation. We try to apply it to all of those.

We publish a booklet on our business ethics that we give to our employees, including all managers, exempt employees, and some nonexempt employees. They are held responsible to read it and to certify that they have read it. I can tell you that unethical business actions are not tolerated.

PEOPLE PROGRAMS

We also give every manager a book of about forty pages
that enables him to talk to employees about the people
aspects and people programs in the IBM Corporation. In
this book you would find the description of when we took
all the employees off the hourly wage and put them all on
salary in 1958, and it describes taking the time clocks
out of all our facilities in 1970s. It describes our individual work schedules, which allow our people to come
and go as they see fit to a certain extent. It explains
equal opportunity and equal benefits for all employees.
It tells about all kinds of programs. I emphasize that
these are management programs, and that the human resource people and personnel people consult with management in running them.

Performance Planning, Counseling, and Evaluation
Let's look at some of IBM's human resource programs.
The first one--the Appraisal Process--is very simple. We
call it PPCE, which is Performance Planning, Counseling,
and Evaluation. It is done by all managers for all employees.   It involves management by objectives.   The
planning process is individually tailored for each
employee.

Pay
In the salary area we follow a simple philosophy: We
seek to achieve internal consistency. We try to be
competitive with the external environment. We follow a
merit-pay philosophy. We have about 24 salary levels in
which we place our 365,000 people. The salary range is
wide for an individual job, which means that a top per-
former can be making as much as 160% to 170% of the salary paid to a person who's not performing too well in the
same job. That does motivate. Peter Drucker talks about
money not being a motivator, but he deals with different
people than I do.

EEO
With respect to equal opportunity, we feel that this
fits very well into IBM's basic belief in the respect for
the individual. Before the equal opportunity laws were
passed I believe that we were doing many of the things
that are now being done under the Equal Opportunity
Program. I would be first to admit that before the Civil
Rights Act we didn't have an affirmative action program,
but once we had minorities in the business I think that
they were treated with dignity and equal rights.

Employment Security
We spend extensive time and dollars on security in employment. We have not laid off an individual for lack of
work since 1941. I submit that much strategic planning,

education, etc. has been necessary to accomplish such a record, particularly for a company of our size and one that has experienced such a large number of technological changes. We look for employees who have the flexibility and the adaptability to change jobs. When you ask employees through opinion surveys, "What is it that you like about working for IBM?" the number one answer is the security of employment, assuming that you do a good job.

Communication
We devote extensive time to the area of communications. We want the manager to be involved with the employees. We have a very low span of control, averaging about ten employees to one manager. We allow managers time for communications. We have numerous communication programs, such as the speak-up program, in which employees can ask or write almost anything they desire. They can send in a question anonymously. We may publish the answer or we may not. If they send in a question with a return address, they get a written reply. We also have the open-door policy, which allows any employee to go directly to the chairman. I can tell you that some 600 to 800 persons a year do go directly to the chairman. It's not at all uncommon for us to fly an executive from New York to California to deal with a very low-level employee who has a grievance. It may take two or three trips to resolve the problem. *Think Magazine* is another part of our communication program.

Employee Privacy
IBM is very concerned with the subject of privacy because computers are being viewed as invading privacy in many cases. We used national advertising to explain our policies and practices. We made it clear that what we're doing may not fit every company's needs, but what we said was, "We'll gather only the information required to run the business. An employee can check that information for accuracy. We will restrict it to those with a need to know and will release it only with the employee's permission."

Health and Safety
We spend much time on health and safety. Every manager, again, is held responsible and accountable. Du Pont requires a written report of every single accident on the chairman's desk within twenty-four hours. We don't require that, but I can certainly tell you that every critical accident or injury is reported at that level. When the KAL Flight 007 was shot down by the Russians, I learned of a major company that had an employee on that airplane and they weren't aware of it for about four days. That wouldn't happen at IBM. When an employee runs into something like that, everybody in

the corporation who has a need to know, knows it very, very quickly.

Education and Training

Tom Peters and Bob Waterman discuss our educational program in their book and refer to it as the IBM University. If we were to add up all that we have spent on education, it would be a very, very large amount. We started education courses in 1916. Much education is needed in continually retraining people to keep up with the current technology and to avoid lay-offs.

Awards and Recognition

On the subject of awards, we really emphasize money, not gimmicks or products. We have awards for technical achievement, innovation, invention achievement, and so forth. In 1982 we made over 34,000 awards totalling over $24 million. The 1983 awards exceeded the number in 1982. One of our most popular awards is called a "Dinner for Two." This allows any manager, without any further approval, to tell an employee, "You've done a good job on this, take your spouse out to dinner. Here's a check for $100." You can see the reduction of bureaucracy in the process.

Tom Peters and Bob Waterman also discuss Skunk Works. Skunk Works "are those little units that are innovative and create new ideas and products." At IBM we have a program called IBM Fellows. Once we appoint an IBM Fellow--they're appointed because of their technical expertise and ability--they're given about five years to work on almost anything they want to as long as it relates to the mission of IBM. This is an organized Skunk Works.

We also have a suggestion plan, which we started in 1928. We give up to $100,000 maximum on any suggestion, and we've had six $100,000 suggestions in a two-year period. One of our nonexempt San Jose employees was given that award at a recognition meeting in Florida recently. To be given an award of $100,000 was a little breathtaking for him. We've saved about $325 million in ten years on that program, $65 million in '83 alone. We've awarded over $62 million in ten years, $14 million in '83 alone. Just to show that the program is alive and well, we received 36,000 suggestions in 1983.

Community and Education Support

In the area of community responsibility, we established a fund in 1972 for community service. We've had over 30,000 employees, spouses, and retirees submit requests for money for some community project in which they are involved. We've supported over 12,000 projects with $15 million. We also have a faculty loan program in which we allow our employees to work full time at universities. These are primarily minority universities. Over 400 employees have participated in that program. We have over thirty job training projects for the disadvantaged. We opened up nine new ones in 1983. We're also very supportive of the United Way. In San Jose, IBM gave $450,000 to United Way and the employees gave over $925,000 in 1983.

Our financial support program for higher education includes matching employee gifts on a $2-for-$1 basis. Just on three programs alone in 1983 we gave 1,500 personal computers to 85 secondary schools, $10 million in cash to 5 graduate schools to support computer-assisted manufacturing and computer-assisted development, and $40 million to 20 undergraduate schools for the same purpose. Those three programs totalled $58 million and exclude many of the other financial support programs to higher education.

We support IBM employee associations. One is called the IBM Clubs. They basically sponsor Christmas parties and give gifts to dependent children, eight years and under. We also have family days, for example, at San Jose, where we had 24,000 employees attend Family Day extending over a four-day period. We have a Quarter Century Club for employees who have twenty-five years with IBM. There are sixteen-hundred members in the club at that San Jose facility.

Obviously, we believe that employees can devote more attention to the job when their basic needs are satisfied, so all of the benefits are fully paid by IBM. Employees make no contribution. Basically, we lump benefits under three areas: protection, security, opportunity.

Attaining Goals Through People

I've told a little bit about the IBM Corporation today, some of its history, and some of its people programs. Now let me tell about innovation and productivity. In 1956, in San Jose, we announced the RAMAC, or the Random Access Method of Accounting and Control. It was the first disk file in the industry. When we announced that product a new car could be bought for $2,500. Gasoline was selling for 28 cents a gallon. I'm sure you've read that the cost of housing in the Silicon Valley is not cheap, but in 1956 you could buy a ranch-style house for $15,000. Now if you look at what it costs a month to rent a megabyte, which is a million of bits of information, at one time it cost $200 for the ability to store that information for one month. We now have it under $1. If those other things that I mentioned had kept pace with the ability to store product information, you could buy the car for $20, the five gallons of gas for $.01, and the new house for $115.

Every business, in order to succeed, must have its goals. John R. Opel has given us our goals and they're very simple. We're going to grow with the industry.

We're going to maintain product leadership. We're going to be the most effective and low-cost producer. And we're going to continue to be profitable.

Many people thought that when the Thomas Watsons retired from IBM there would be a significant change. We are now three generations past the Watson era and I don't think IBM's changed one bit. For example, here is a quote from Frank T. Cary: "Why have we done so well? Well, I think it's because long before other companies realized it, IBM knew that its most valuable resource was its people. And it did the right thing to get and keep people who could make the company grow. I'm biased, but I believe IBM people are matchless." John Opel reminded us recently, "IBM people are our greatest asset. Increased efficiency cannot be paid for by our defeating our traditional respect for the individual. There can and need be no compromise on that. The management of people remains paramount."

We recognize that we have a challenge. Tom Watson, Jr., said, "We're convinced that any business needs its wild ducks." In IBM we try to have wild ducks, but everyone knows that even wild ducks fly in formation. One of the greatest posters we've ever had showed a duck stuffed with phrases like "Don't fight city hall; easy does it; it doesn't matter; don't overcommit; walk don't run; no way; we tried that."

George Bernard Shaw said, "The reasonable man adapts himself to the world and the unreasonable man persists in trying to adapt the world to himself. Therefore all progress depends on the unreasonable man."

31

Quality: America's Path to Excellence

Joe C. Collier, Jr.

Several years ago, when our company was contemplating whether we dared even think about applying for the Deming Challenge, the chairman of our holding company, Marshall McDonnell, said, "Tell me this. Can you tell me who was the first man to run the four-minute mile?" Immediately everybody said, "Sure. Dr. Roger Banister. We know that." He said, "Tell me who was the second man to run the four-minute mile." How many of you know that? Of course, the point is that if we are going to do something, let's be the first. He challenged us with that, and we have been pursuing that philosophy ever since. We did a little research and discovered that, prior to Roger Banister's feat, no one had ever run a four-minute mile in all the history of mankind. It was a barrier. Conventional wisdom said, "It can't be done." Ever since that landmark day in the 1950s, someone has won a faster mile every year. I believe the record is now down to around 3.47 minutes. In 1910, the first Kentucky Derby was run by a horse in two minutes and ten seconds. Last year the Kentucky Derby was won in two minutes and eleven seconds. Statistically, it looks as though in another forty-seven years a man will be able to win the Kentucky Derby!

We have some great fun with statistical quality control. We have a group in the company whom we call "Applications Experts." We have identified people who want to volunteer to teach graduate-level statistics courses to the rest of our company. They are sort of our gurus of statistical quality control. If a complex question arises, we just turn to them. I challenged them with a study that indicated that a good way to decide what to study in college is to look at the starting salaries of college graduates in various fields. I found

a statistic that said the graduating class in geography
at the University of North Carolina in 1986 made an average starting salary of $280,000. Before everybody rushed
to sign up for geography class, we told them that Michael
Jordan was one of the graduates. Statistics can do some
funny things.

It is wonderful to see you here, and it is good to see
companies talking about quality in America. It is like
when a politician changes his mind. You don't know
whether he has seen the light or whether he has felt the
heat. I think that in America maybe our companies have
felt the heat about quality for the past twenty years.

Twenty years ago, about three out of every four cars in
the world were built in America. Today, that figure is
less than one in four. In 1988, only 60% of the automobiles built in America were manufactured by American companies. Twenty years ago, three-quarters of all of the
television sets and 90% of the radios in the world were
built in America. Today, America accounts for only 6% of
the world production of radios and televisions combined.
It doesn't stop with electronics. Last year the three
leading companies that were awarded patents in the United
States were Canon, Hitachi, and Toshiba. The Japanese
percentage of patents in the U.S. has grown from 4% to
19% in just fifteen short years.

This raises two questions: What happened and what can
we do about it? I think that you all know what happened.
We suddenly found ourselves in a global marketplace with
competitors who had a desperate economic imperative to
succeed.   We discovered something strange--customers
didn't have an emotional attachment to our products. We
are learning that at Florida Power & Light. We are finding that our customers can put in their own generators
and generate their own kilowatt hours. It shocked our
older managers to learn that our customers don't have an
emotional attachment to F. P. L.'s kilowatt hours. They
buy warm water and cold beer. They don't really care
where the power comes from if it does the job more
cheaply.

Well, I think we know what has happened. Now, what are
we going to do about it? I think that the answer is to
adopt an entirely new philosophy toward quality and productivity based on a new understanding and a new economic
imperative for America. Are we going to be a first-class
economy or are we going to be a second-class service
country? The good news, is that business has woken up
and is catching on. You can see it on your television,
in the news and in the commercials. I sort of study
commercials, and I have noticed more and more quality
creeping into the marketing messages of American companies. Some that you are familiar with are very direct--
"Quality is job one" and "Quality goes in before the name
goes on." Some are a little more subtle. MCI "wants you
to hear a pin drop" long-distance. Other companies

proclaim, "The tightest ship in the shipping business,"
"Fly the friendly skies," "Clarity you can see, purity
you can taste." Budweiser has a commercial that says,
"Beechwood aged." I wonder if those steelworkers in
Pittsburgh really care if their beer is "Beechwood aged"
or not.

Everybody has slogans, and that is okay. We had a
slogan when we first started. It was "Do it right the
first time." Dr. Juran came for a visit and said, "Do
what right the first time?" We thought about that and
replied, "Do the right thing right the first time." He
asked, "What is the right thing?" We said, "We don't
know, but we will know it when we see it." Sounds like
the Supreme Court's definition of pornography: the
justices can't define it, but they know it when they see
it. That is the case with quality. We all think we know
what quality is. But without a road map, without a plan,
without a process, you won't know how to get to a state
of excellence in your company. What is more, you won't
know how to maintain it when you get there.

The ten top companies that Tom Peters and Bob Waterman
listed in their book, *In Pursuit of Excellence*, are no
longer the ten top companies today. If, however, you
look at the Deming Prize winners in Japan, the ten top
companies stay on top the next year and the year after
that. Companies who have invested thirty years in becoming excellent stay excellent throughout time.

QUALITY: A MANAGEMENT PROCESS

That is why at F. P. L. we think that quality is first
and foremost a management process, a process that has to
be believed in by everyone from the CEO to the first-line
supervisor. Each member of the team must demonstrate
that sense of commitment by his or her involvement and
constant participation in management. It has been said
that 80% of all business problems lie in the hands of
managers. If they will just get out of the way and let
their people perform, they can solve a lot of those problems. We know that employees want to do the right thing.
It is human nature to want to do a good job. The role of
management then is to provide the environment, training,
tools, and leadership, and then get out of the way. Let
your people do a good job.

Tom Peters has a wonderful story about a gentleman who
had made a very successful career out of turning failing
businesses around. Someone asked him, "What is the
secret of your success?" He answered, "Well, I go to a
business and I take off my coat. I go down on the shop
floor or down to the front line and I ask the people,
'What is wrong with this company?' Then they tell me and
I say, 'Well, can you fix it?' They say, 'Yeah.' I say,
'Then go fix it.' They go fix it, and I make a lot of

money." The people closest to the problem and the people
closest to the customer are the ones with the solutions.
We have to learn to give them the tools, techniques,
motivation, and leadership to do their jobs.

I know that almost all of your companies have objectives. All of you have mission statements, all of you
have quality directions, and all of you want to do the
right thing. We don't take credit for inventing anything. We have discovered a magic formula. Thomas
Edison was credited with inventing the talking machine.
He said, "I didn't invent the talking machine; God did.
I just invented the first one that could be turned off."
We have not invented quality. I give all the credit for
what we have come up with to our friends at Cansi Electric in Osaka, Japan, who have been very generous. They
have shared with us and have allowed us to go over there
year after year after year. They are very gracious and
have shared with us not only their knowledge, but their
people. Their employees come to Florida and spend two
years working with us in our shop. They have been tremendously helpful. There are many different definitions
of quality. If we spoke a common language, maybe we
could share. What I hope to do today is to share some of
our program with you and try to bridge that understanding
gap in explaining what TQC means.

I want to share a personal story with you about filling
in for your boss. About ten years ago, there was a national conference on quality and productivity in Washington. Our current president at the time was Marshall
McDonnell. He was invited to be a speaker, but he
couldn't go and sent me. Dr. Juran, Phil Crosby, Jackson
Grayson, and all of the great names in quality that I had
come to know were there. I was so enthusiastic and excited about quality when I came home that I wrote a long,
thoughtful memorandum to the president of our company
about what we should do. He tracked me down and said,
"Well, what should we do?" I said, "Boss, we need a
quality council." "Well," he said, "who should be in
charge?" I replied, "You should be the spiritual leader,
Boss." He said, "Okay then, we'll start one, and I'm
putting you in charge." Therein lies an important lesson
for junior managers: When you invite a gorilla to dance,
you don't sit down until the gorilla gets tired. We have
had two successive gorillas since then. They have shown
no signs of tiring, and I don't think they ever will.
Our employees have accepted the fact that this program is
not one that is here today and gone tomorrow.

We have tried everything anybody ever published--
management by objectives, managing managers' time,
extended MBO, and so on. Winston Churchill said, "You
can always count on Americans to do the right thing after
they have tried everything else." We think we have tried
everything. Now, we have found the right thing, and

that's this management process we call Quality Improvement or TQC.

DESIGNING IN QUALITY

Most of you are familiar with the continuum of quality.
It was the purview of the manufacturers. People who made
widgets could inspect out the bad ones. Only good quality
widgets would be left. The problem was, 40% of the widgets were being rejected. This was very costly. Eventually the emphasis has shifted to designing in quality.
The trunks of the early Toyotas all leaked, mostly because of weld points. Those early trunks had 57 welding
points. Toyota redesigned them down to seven welds,
thinking that if they could eliminate the trouble points
they could eliminate the problem. The history of Toyota
is, of course, well-known. Designing in quality became
the new continuum. As we moved into a service-sector
economy, managing in quality became a strong part of the
continuum. We think that managing in quality is what we
are doing, what we are attempting with our program.
What is quality? We have more and more philosophical
arguments about that question. Is it Rolls Royce quality, or is it K-Mart quality? It is both. We have
adopted Dr. Deming's statement, "Quality is conformance
to valid requirements." In order to be valid, requirements must meet user needs. They have to be current,
realistic, and somewhat measurable. A man came into a
coffee shop and told the waitress, "I'll have cold
coffee, burned toast, half-cooked eggs, and greasy
bacon." She brought the order just as he requested and
said, "Will there be anything else, sir?" He said, "Yes,
sit down and nag me. I feel homesick." If you satisfy
the customer's needs and wants, then we would argue that
the requirements are valid.
This conformance applies to specifications, procedures,
materials, workmanship, everything that it takes to produce quality. An important part of our program is taking
quality upstream, if you will. We buy 60% of the materials we use in our business from outside vendors. If
their products don't meet our standards and our customers' specifications, we can't produce quality. We
spend $2.6 billion every year with our outside vendors in
an effort to produce quality for our customers. Some of
you are here today. We seek out, recognize, and reward
vendors who work well with us through our vendor quality
program. One of the toughest decisions that businesses
in America must make--we are no different--is to weed out
those vendors who don't want to play according to the
quality rules. We are now at the point where we are
weeding down our suppliers to those few who meet our
standards and help us meet our specifications.

FOCUSING ON THE CUSTOMER

This leads me to the first of four principles upon which our program is based: Focusing on the Customer. We do an enormous amount of research every year to find out who our customers are, what they want, what they need it for, how much they are willing to pay, and how we can better serve them. We were one of the first utilities to spend literally millions of dollars on market research to determine what it is our customers want and how we can supply it better. We measure our performance every quarter on twenty-two quality elements that our customers tell us about. Focus on customers should not be on the external customer only; focusing on your internal customer is also important. Every department must identify its product, service, or output, and then identify the customer for that product, service, or output. It has to negotiate valid requirements between itself and that customer for that service, product, or output. An interesting thing happens when you do that. You find that you have a list of products for which there are no customers. The accounting department found that it didn't need to produce all those monthly reports and stacks of computer printouts. It found that nobody was reading them, nobody wanted them, and once a month would have been better than once a week. We have saved a lot of paper work just through the customer-identification process.

I could give you several examples, but I'll just stick to one. Our customers have told us that accurate bills are one of their high priorities. They want to be confident that their electric bill is accurate and correct. The truth is that 99.99% of our bills are exactly correct. There is a perception, however, that they are not. To get an accurate bill requires that we buy a good meter, test it properly, install it properly, put the paper work in the computer, read the meter accurately every month, and so forth, right down the line to the point where the customer gets his bill in the mail. It is like one big assembly line, with people in varying locations 500 miles apart each playing a role to deliver that customer's accurate bill. We teach our people that everything they do has an impact on that chain reaction, which creates accurate bills for our customers. Each one of them can contribute by keeping his share of the assembly line working properly. By using the quality tools, they can do that and actually calculate their contribution to the chain effect. We can show that in case after case after case. It is a very powerful part of the business.

CONTINUOUS IMPROVEMENT

The second part of our fundamental program is Continuous Improvement. We do it through Dr. Deming's wheel, the Plan-Do-Check-Act Cycle. At the end of the day, all meter readers can check their daily work to see if they have done it correctly. If they didn't get it right, they correct something and get it right the next time. Every supervisor has a process flow chart that helps him keep his process under control. We have moved from measuring things in parts per million to part per billion through PDCA. We have reduced errors through good process control. The beauty of this is that everyone can use it--the first-line employee right on up to management. We are constantly looking for ways to turn the wheel and practice PDCA.

MANAGEMENT BY FACT

The third fundamental aspect of our program is Management by Fact. Believe it or not, this is one of the toughest cultural changes an organization can make, especially one like ours. We have a 60-year history of tough, individualistic people who built a system out of the swamps and the Everglades. We created these supervisors. We put them where they are because they are tough and can make decisions. They operate on what we now know as their calibrated intestines; in other words, gut feel. When these senior managers are confronted by some young engineer with a better set of facts, better data, or better information that calls for a different decision, it is often very difficult for them to swallow and say, "Well, looks like you may be right."

Management by Fact, though, has become a part of our business. Our people no longer say, "Well, it seems to me...." They have been trained to question immediately what the evidence is, what the facts are, what the data show, and why you came to that decision. This has been a cultural revolution in our business. We have a saying that, "Sometimes it is easier to change *people* than it is to *change* people." When you think about that, it *is* tough to *change* people. Last year we had an early retirement program, and 900 people chose to leave. Not all of them did so because of quality programs. It was just a great opportunity for a lot of them. A large number, however, said, "I am too old to learn statistical quality control," and when they found a window they took it. That is what is going to have to happen if we are going to have a new attitude toward total quality control.

RESPECT FOR PEOPLE

The fourth fundamental is Respect for People. We demonstrate respect for people through our quality teams program. As I said, no one knows the customer better than the person who deals with him every day. No one knows the process better than the employee who does the process every day. By allowing these teams an audience, an opportunity to put their ideas forward, we are demonstrating respect for people.

Last year we conducted our very first total employee attitude survey. Believe me, it was not easy to talk our management into letting us do it. We hired an outside behavioral firm and conducted a scientifically-based survey. Ninety percent of our employees said that what would motivate them more than dollars, more than recognition dinners, more than tie tacks and lapel pins, more than anything else, would be having management pay attention to their ideas and put them into practice throughout the company.

Replication of good ideas is a basic part of our program. We do just about the same thing in Daytona that we do in Miami. If we can find a good solution to a problem in Miami, there is no reason that it shouldn't be replicated somewhere else. We even tried to come up with an incentive to get one team to steal another team's idea. We were going to call it the "Buccaneer Award." Respect for people is a strong, strong program.

COMPONENTS OF TOTAL QUALITY CONTROL

I have given you the four basic principles. Now I would like tell you about the three component parts of our program. First of all, there are different types of teams. We have what we call lead teams. I am on a lead team. Every member of management is on several teams. I think I am on five. There is a lead team of all department heads in a cross-functional area.

Functional teams are those people who have similar work assignments. All of the linemen would be a functional team. All the cable splicers get together and talk about cable-splicing techniques.

Then we have cross-functional teams. People from marketing, sales, engineering, regulatory, and accounting would be a cross-functional team. We practice cross-functional management all the way to the very top of the company. We are knocking down all those barriers that it took us sixty years to build between accounting, marketing, engineering, and so on.

Task teams are those teams that we assign to a specific, known problem. When we find a problem, we pick people to work on it. They solve the problem, dissolve the team, and go on.   The other teams are ongoing, continuous team activities.

We initially started with quality improvement teams. We started with two pilot teams back in 1979 or 1980.   In 1981 we developed some formalized teams.   We probably had eight or nine the first year.   We are up to about 2,000 teams now.   Typically, eight or nine people make up a team.   The supervisor is the team leader.   We have someone called a facilitator who helps keep the teams on track.   Facilitators also help with training, teaching about the tools, and recording minutes.

POLICY DEPLOYMENT

The next part of the program is Policy Deployment or Goal Setting.   While teamwork is a bottom-up ap-proach, policy deployment is a top-down approach.   Managment decides what we want to be, when we want to get there, and how we can set the goals, and then asks people to follow. A good example I have used in teaching our people is that each one of us could go up to a freight train and push on it; nothing would happen.   If all of us pushed on the freight train in exactly the same direction at the same time, we could move the train.   You get that kind of synergism from policy deployment.   We can't fix everything all at once, so management chooses four or five high-priority areas on which to concentrate.   Those are typically drawn from what our customers tell us.   Our customers have told us in quarterly surveys that they are interested in (1) reliability, (2) safety, (3) price, (4) courteous, kind treatment, and (5) accurate answers and accurate bills.   We have tried to establish our corporate priorities according to what our customers constantly tell us.   As our Japanese friends say, "The hunter who chases too many rabbits goes hungry."   We try not to chase too many rabbits at the same time.   By focusing the attention of all of our people on those four or five crucial issues at any one point in time, we make some serious breakthroughs.

A good example of setting goals occurred at NASA.   When President Kennedy challenged NASA, we had one goal.   You all know what it was: put a man on the moon and bring him home safely within the decade.   You could walk up to anyone at NASA--from the engineers in Houston to the operations people at Cape Canaveral to the janitor in Huntsville--and say, "What is the mission of NASA?" and they could tell you.   They knew what their mission was.   Unfortunately, when they accomplished it, they didn't have another mission.   NASA fell into some deep problems and took a while to get out of them.   I know there is much more to it than that, but that is a classic example of how having everyone focus helps you meet your goal. Policy deployment then is the process by which we achieve breakthroughs by concentrating and focusing all our efforts on a few selected issues. We publish those issues in a book every January. They all have indicators. Every department makes a contribution to the improvement of those indicators.

QUALITY IN DAILY WORK

The last component of our program is Quality in Daily Work. The Marriott people call it "staying close to your business," because you do it on a daily basis. The supervisor who has process control charts and monitors his daily, weekly, and monthly operations is using this approach. This constant monitoring helps to maintain the gains that we achieve. It promotes consistency and clarifies everyone's contribution. If power plant employee knows that he has to improve his first outage rate by three percentage points and monitors that on a daily basis, he knows how his contribution is going to Affect the overall effort. We operate some thirteen different power plants. Each plant has process control charts for eighty or ninety processes, which it follows every day.

Those are the three parts of our Quality Improvement Program. We should have called it something other than a program, because it is not bounded by any completion date. It is an ongoing, continuous journey. It won't work without committed managers. Our program may be a little different, because we are a service industry with 3 million customers. We deal with an enormous number of things that we have to do on a repeated basis. We believe it is the role of management to bring all of this together by demonstrating commitment, managing throughout the process, staying informed, encouraging employees, and recognizing and rewarding those employees. Without the enthusiasm of management, employees won't know that we are really serious about it.

Zig Zigler, who is a very humorous and warm public speaker, has a wonderful story about enthusiasm. It seems this family of Scots from Tennessee was taking a winter vacation. They were going to Florida for the winter. They passed by a paper mill in southern Georgia. One of the children lifted up his nose, sniffed the air, and said, "My, what is that?" And the father said, "I don't know, but we got to get some of it." We think managers have to get enthusiasm if the quality process is to be successful.

QUALITY AND THE BOTTOM LINE

What about the bottom line? We teach our people that if you achieve quality, productivity will follow. We have about 12,000 people who have gone through basic and advanced quality training and who are on some sort of team. We don't have to sell quality to our customers, we just have to create it. The customers will buy into it. Everybody wants to know about the bottom line. I certainly understand that. As a regulated business, I have to explain to our regulators in Tallahassee how these benefits are flowing to our customers.

One of our worst years was 1977. Our sales started to slide. Total annual energy per customer was sliding, and at the same time our costs were increasing greatly. The conventional wisdom was that electricity was not price-elastic; customers were going to use what they were going to use regardless of the price, and we shouldn't worry about it. We learned the hard way that that is not the case. As our prices went up, our customers began to leave. They went elsewhere, built their own power plants, or just quit using so much. We were in what economists call a death spiral, which occurs when you raise prices to maintain earnings. That depresses sales, so you have to raise prices again to maintain the earnings. You can keep that up only so long before you reach your resistance level. We were dangerously close to that kind of situation. We got hold of our prices and did some drastic things. We started applying TQC at every level; cut our O & M cost growth significantly, and had some good luck with oil prices, because we had stopped using foreign oil. As a result of our efforts, prices are now very stable and sales have rebounded. They still aren't back to where they were in 1977, but they are returning. The situation is much more stable. We have not had a major rate increase since 1985 and don't anticipate one in the near future. We measure service availability because our customers say reliability is their first priority. We are very proud that our service is available 99.9% of the time. But being proud of yourself doesn't help you solve problems. In 1986 we decided to turn the equation around and look at un-availability of service. Now we look at how many hours or minutes per customer our service is not available each year. We started out at 110 minutes, I believe, and it is now down to 60. Since 1986 we have had steady improvement in our customer reliability. We have set a 1992 target of 32 minutes per customer per year for service unavailability. According to the data available to us, if we achieve that goal our service availability rate will be the best in the United States.

We are in a dangerous and sometimes complicated business, so safety is a major concern to us. We have thrity-five hundred construction workers out on lines every day, all day long. Our lost-time injuries have been cut in half, and we propose to cut them even further by 1992. This will be difficult. We cannot always explain the source of the improvements that have been

made. We know that making safety a visible issue has
produced a Hawthorne effect, in that everyone is now
conscious of it, thinking about it, and ultimately
practicing safety procedures. It is very difficult to
measure how much of this improvement came from specific
programs.

Everyone recognizes customer complaints. Ours go to
the Public Service Commission. Ever since we started
measuring the number of complaints per 1,000 customers,
the figures have shown marked improvement. We know that
for every complaint we get, there are another twenty-five
that we don't know about. This is a serious component of
our indicators.

During our formative days, we established a corporate
vision. We have been working to explain what that vision
means to our employees for the past eight years. We do
think that we know how to manage effectively. We have
twenty-five other major utilities in other parts of the
United States. The data that are available to us show us
where we have to be in 1992, assuming that they are going
to continue to improve as well. Recognition is nice, but
it is only good insofar as it motivates us and others to
move forward and do our best.

As our present Chairman, John Hudaburg, testified before Congress, we were instrumental in the establishment
of the Malcolm Baldrige Award. We are very proud of our
role and the fact that Mr. Hudaburg serves as a trustee.
We hope that in time this award will come to symbolize
American excellence in quality, as the Deming Prize has
come to symbolize this excellence in Japan. We would
urge all of you to consider grooming your companies to
challenge for this award, to be aware of it, and to recognize those companies that achieve it. Last year there
were three companies that won it for the first time.
This year I understand the number of applications is up
nine-fold from last year's level.

Coach Vince Lombardi once said, "The quality of a man's
life is in direct proportion to his pursuit of excellence." I would like to paraphrase that and suggest to
you that the quality of life in America in the next
decade or so will be directly proportional to our efforts
in the pursuit of excellence. We encourage you to join
with us in this pursuit.

32

Exploiting Technology to Regain Markets

Bobby Inman

I spent 31 years of my life looking at the outside world. I was an avid user of technology throughout most of those 31 years. I've now had five and a half years to look intensely at my own country. The data base is still shallow, but the opinions are strongly held.

I have listened with growing fascination to what amounts to a public debate on the state of the U.S. economy and how we might deal with it. I watched those who were in public life searching for ways to describe the situation in the kind of simple terms that might capture electoral support. They use pat phrases like "level playing field" and others. You will learn as you go with me that one of our problems in trying to come to grips with the country is that we have a very complex set of issues to face. You have some marvelous speakers on this program to deal with specifics. I will deal in very large generalities. But I will also focus primarily on what I believe we need to do here in this country to regain our competitiveness and not what we need to do to other countries because of the difficulty we're finding in competing with them in the marketplace.

ROLE OF TECHNOLOGY IN U.S. ECONOMIC DEVELOPMENT

Let me dwell first on the role of technology in developing this great economy. Our forefathers imported technology the first 100 years of our existence. They used it with great effectiveness to span a continent and to put in place the infrastructure to permit the growth of what is still the world's largest economy. And you live very near the center of that. I was reminded by the marker driving up yesterday that not all that many miles

away in Ogden is the Golden Spike for the first linkage
of a transcontinental rail system. That was the state-
of-the-art technology in that time frame for moving goods
and services. It was very near that same time frame, in
the heart of the darkest days of the republic (1862) when
the Congress, in its wisdom, enacted the Morrill Act,
creating the land grant colleges, laying the foundation
for creating technology in this country on a broad scale.
That same Congress also passed the enabling legislation,
creating the National Academy of Science, understanding
early that a country that pushed the frontiers of science
and actively used that science has the best prospect of
building and sustaining an economy which would give an
improving standard of living for all its citizens.

In 1984, a major study was done at Massachusetts
Institute of Technology looking at the growth of the U.S.
economy. It was their judgment that from 1865 to 1940,
between 80 and 85 percent of the growth of the U.S.
economy came from creating technology and applying it.
Universities played a critical role in that early on. In
the late 1800s, the state of the art in new technology
frequently was focused on agriculture. And one of the
best processes for technology transfer, the county agent,
was put in place to directly deliver the fruits of that
research to those who could use it in a timely way.

As that great economy was developed, we saw the creation of large corporations. We went through some
interesting times of efforts to create monopolies, efforts to manipulate markets that helped accelerate our
movement into recessions, occasional depressions, and
market crashes. And we set about trying to regulate the
growth of that economy, focusing on the reality that it
was a domestic economy. You could essentially regulate
it almost in its entirety simply by focusing on the
sources of production and the flow of capital inside the
country. You can trace the advent of major additional
investment in research by those large corporations as
they grew, and then, in this century, by the steady
growth of national laboratories sponsored by the federal
government. By 1940, we already had the largest base for
pushing the frontiers of science, for creating new technology, that existed anywhere in the world.

SENSE OF URGENCY TO COMMERCIALIZE NEW TECHNOLOGY

But if you look at it closely, you'll find that also
there was no sense of urgency to move the fruits of that
research into new products. Particularly in the larger
established companies, you can chart pretty easily that
with the great focus on the cost of production, the basic
tenet was: don't rush to introduce new technology that's
going to run up the cost if your competitors aren't
rushing to do that. And it was only in the small busi-

ness sector where you saw some sense of speed to turn new technology into workable products.

World War II began a fundamental change of that. The sense of urgency was instilled by the need to produce weapon systems, but also substitute goods and services to fight the global conflict. And what you saw pretty quickly were collaborative efforts between industry, the academic sector, and government, with government as a catalyst, on a scale that we'd never seen, and that the world had never seen. Out of it did indeed come the weapons for the war. But also out of it came the major impacts on a commercial economy, ranging all the way from synthetic fibers to the first large-scale computers.

From 1946 to 1961 was a period of enormous growth of this economy, untrammeled by the damage that had been done by war to the economies in Western Europe and in Asia. We set out with great generosity to help rebuild those economies. We made major investment in our talent pool. The GI Bill fundamentally changed access to baccalaureate education in this country. Along with it, a very forward-looking program from the government, led initially by the Office of Naval Research and its counterparts in the other services, and subsequently, by other organizations that were created--National Science Foundation, National Institutes of Health--provided major sources of grants for graduate studies, particularly in science and engineering. And by the mid-50s we had opened our already sizable lead to world predominance in talent needed to attack a whole range of problems to create new technology. But you can also chart in that same time frame some slackening of that sense of urgency about turning the fruits of that research into products. You've got occasional surges from the government, the race to the moon through NASA, but they become spasmodic, not a continued focus on timing.

CONCERN FOR GAINING ACCESS TO THE INTERNATIONAL MARKETPLACE

The year 1960 is, for me, the watershed point for a variety of reasons. In 1960, international trade accounted for only 3 percent of our gross national product. No major sector of industry had more than 10 percent of its revenues drawn from international trade. We were still essentially a domestic economy, and that's where growth was to be found. But we were beginning to worry about access to that international marketplace, the European Common Market. Our concern that we were going to be shut out of that market led us to focus on how we could guarantee long-term access to that market, as it grew and created, and perhaps began to close its borders. We pioneered in such things as putting manufacturing facilities in those countries, particularly in Ireland,

looking for the combination of lower-cost labor with the
certainty that we would have production facilities inside
the Common Market. We led in the creation of new organi-
zations--General Agreement on Trade and Tariffs and
others--designed to lower trade barriers, to encourage
the rapid growth of inter-national trade. Of course,
that was an enormous help to countries who looked to exports as the driving feature of their economic growth.
We made very little change in our approach either from
government policy, within industry itself, or in the
academic sector, in beginning to focus on what changes
would be necessary if we were going to make sure we were
competitive at that changing marketplace. In fact, if
you look at the trends from 1961 on, you see a very
different set of activities underway that served to make
us less competitive, not more competitive, in that marketplace.

FORCES THAT REDUCE U.S. COMPETITIVENESS

Beginning in 1963, Defense very sharply curtailed the
availability of grants for graduate studies in science
and engineering, and the flow of equipment to universities. Under the new standard of "Is it cost effective?"
it was not cost effective to make investments unless you
could very specifically tie those investments to a pro-
spective future weapon system. That was a period when
National Science Foundation funding and National Institutes of Health funding were beginning to grow, but the
race to the moon, NASA's effort, helped obscure how
severe the impact was. If you want to document it, the
date you begin is 1968. The cutoff in 1963 shows up in
1968, with the beginning decline in U.S. graduate students in science and engineering. This audience knows
better than most, seats didn't go vacant. Students came
from all over the world to take those vacant seats, often
with full scholarships for the finest technical education
to be had in the world. But it is the point in time at
which, in relative terms, our lead in talent to create
technology and to apply it began to decline relative to
what was happening in the outside world. R & D expenditures began to decline.

From 1946 on to the late 1960s, the federal government
spent about 3 percent of its budget on R & D. Industry
tended to track fairly close to that. As we began to
come to grips with guns and butter, paying the cost of
Vietnam and not raising taxes, one of the areas of cutback was in R & D. You can chart that by the early
1970s--the Office of Management Budget did its calculations on how you got money early--the federal government's investment came down to about 2.2 percent. That
pace continued through most of the 1970s. Industry's
investment, in broad terms, followed exactly that same

profile. So the interest in pushing the investment that would let you take evolving science and turn it into usable technology began to decline in real terms.

Unfortunately, in looking back at this history, one of the real problems was that the changes were gradual. There was no crisis to mobilize us, to wake us up to the fact that the world was changing, and that our involvement in that world was changing, and we weren't working hard at how we adapted to that. We had a process of antitrust regulation and requirements on capital formation and capital flow that continued to look only at a domestic marketplace. We created a business culture that said be very cautious about dealing with your competitors in any environment. Pricing was the clear thing that you were certain to get into difficulty but there was enough ambiguity that even pre-competitive collaboration was worrisome, and there are plenty of cases of corporations that got pulled into court and paid large fines, and even a few whose senior executives went to jail, that helped reinforce that culture to be very cautious about collaboration.

We also built a capital formation process that put the focus on minimizing risk. We required a long standoff distance between the sources of capital and those who were going to undertake production. We required very cautious debt-to-equity ratios. That translated into higher interest rates, higher than those in competing countries. That, in turn, had its impact on business. In the established companies, it led toward a basic approach of being cautious in the pace at which you use new technology. Test market, do some models, test the market again, take the result of that test marketing data to the lending institution, borrow the money to put that production line in process, and then put together a marketing strategy that was aimed at recovering cost as quickly as possible and paying down that expensive debt, rather than how did you go out for broad market share.

JAPAN FOCUSED ON EXPLOITING TECHNOLOGY

What was happening in the outside world? Well, let me turn to the example of Japan. Building an economy aimed at competing and exporting is critical to economic growth. Secondly, they were operating from an environment with a very shallow technology base, with the basic presumption that new technology would be available abroad, in the United States and Western Europe, one year, two years, and maybe three years before it was available to Japanese companies. Therefore, the whole approach was aimed at the speed with which you turned the technology into products once you got it. The banks were actually sitting on the boards of the companies, with no requirement for standoff distance. They were willing to

make rapid decisions on going directly to the market,
cutting back very sharply on that extensive phase of
building test models and going out for test marketing.
But they also added something else. We collectively
laughed at those early Japanese products as they began to
rebuild an economy shattered by war, and they understood
the impact of quality. At the very time we were moving
toward a strategy in the late 1960s of shorter life
cycle, throw away, don't bother to repair products, without much focus on quality, they were beginning to build
quality into every aspect of what they were going to approach.   That led them to a strategy of five times the
number of engineers on the factory floor.   They were
focusing on both the quality and the speed with which the
technology would get used.   And because the interest
rates were so much lower, companies didn't look at how
they would service the debt immediately. The basic strategy was to go for market share.   And once you had the
established market share, then steadily adjust the price
structure that let you service the debt that was nonetheless much less expensive to run.
     I would argue to you that, with those fundamentally
different approaches to capital formation and to the pace
at which you use technology, you aren't going to get a
level playing field simply by barriers to the flow of
products, goods, and services. You may need the threat
of barriers to make sure you get fair access to markets.
It may be the only device you have. You may need to use
some temporary protection to let an industry that's in
deep difficulty transition.   But I will telegraph my
views quickly. I do not believe it is in the public interest to provide protection to permit an industry to
take the investment and use it to move to entirely different sectors, as from steel to oil.

IMPROVED U.S. PRODUCTIVITY NEEDED

     How then do we compete in this changing international
marketplace? And, make no mistake, it is changing dramatically. Now, in the late 1980s, 12 percent of our GNP
is drawn from international trade.   It's not at all
unusual to find 25 percent of the revenues in the industrial sector coming from international trade.   In fact,
some areas like machine tools, small appliances, are
already well past the 50 percent mark. We may even be
re- covering a little from that in machine tools.
     We have no option but to adjust because we already are
experiencing a declining standard of living in our failure to adjust. This marvelous economy has created an
aggregate of about 8.8 million new jobs in the last six
years. That's very remarkable for any economy. But look
more closely at those numbers. The reality is, that over
those six years, we actually created about 10.4 million

new jobs in what we loosely call the service sector. And we lost 1.2 million jobs in manufacturing, and 400,000 in mining. Of the 1.6 million jobs lost, the average weekly wage was $444. Of the 10.4 million new jobs created, the average weekly wage was $272. These figures are obscured sub-stantially by the fact that, increasingly, where there are two adults in the family, both are working. Two incomes have helped sustain a standard of living.

You'll hear the argument that the only way the United States can adapt to this world is to accept a declining standard of living. I don't buy that. I think the real answer is in how we increase our productivity to sustain a favorable level of productivity and the ability to sustain quality with it that lets our goods and services be competitive at that international marketplace.

QUALITY OF U.S. PRODUCTS/UNDERSTANDING FOREIGN CULTURE

I break it into three areas for discussion: creating technology, applying it, and marketing it. I will have very little to say about the marketing side, because I have no direct experience. But I watched it for a long time. I'm persuaded that there are many critical factors, but I can identify two for you, in looking out to that marketplace of the middle 1990s.

One is quality. We've got to get the perception, as well as the reality, that the quality of U.S. products matches that anywhere else in the world. Government has made a lot of effort over the last two and a half years to try to talk down the value of the dollar. They have been very successful with part of our trading partners. But most observers miss the reality that now, as the nature of our trading partners has shifted--the newly emerging countries in the Pacific with about 14 percent of the trade, Latin America or Mexico with 14 percent, Canada with 21 percent, the oil-importing countries taking up another 8 to 9 percent--you're left with those traditional trading partners--Western Europe, 25 percent, and Japan, 17 percent. Those are the ones whose currencies change. For more than half of our trading partners, their currencies are pegged to the dollar and they continue to appreciate to the same two-and-a-half-year time frame. That's why we've not had that much impact on dealing with those markets, not because of the tax policies and discrimination.

The export-import balance still is unsatisfactory, and the only answer I can come up with is that the U.S. customer has proven willing to pay a higher price for imported products that they judge to be of better quality. So we're going to have to tackle that one both domestically and abroad if we are going to grab substantially increased market share.

The second one is the reality that in the growing market, particularly in the Third World, we're going to have to put a lot more effort into understanding the cultures of the countries where we want to market and in being able to market in the language of the country where we want to sell. Painful though it's going to be for us, if we really think we're going to be successful in the year 2000 by telling them all to speak English, we're going to be in for a very rude shock.

MAINTAINING U.S. LEAD IN CREATING NEW TECHNOLOGY

We still have a clear lead in most areas in creating new technology. But there are a few areas where it's either close or we may even have lost the edge. Usually we've lost the edge because of failure to invest here and often for environmental reasons. Nuclear power generation technology is simply one that comes to immediate mind where our own failure to invest, a continuous investment by the French and, to a slightly lesser degree, the Japanese. In some cases they have collaborated with U.S. firms who have exported their activities so that the technology lead, if not already abroad, very soon will be found abroad in that sector. In most areas however we still have the lead. But in a declining pool of talent, we clearly have to insure that we move faster to build on the lead we have. We can't let it slide further. There is a whole variety of activities that need to be undertaken.

We need grants for graduate studies in science and engineering. Five and a half years ago, the conventional wisdom I used to hear was that you couldn't get bright U.S. youngsters to stay on to graduate school. It's all industry's fault. Those starting salaries they paid were simply too attractive. If you get industry to lower the salaries, they might stay on. One of the inducements that got MCC (Micro-electronics & Computer Technology Corp.) to go to Texas was a commitment from the city of Austin of $750,000 a year for ten years in grant aid for graduate students in computer science and electrical engineering.

In May of 1985, I had the pleasure of helping take part in the commencement ceremonies at the University of Texas at Austin awarding advanced degrees to those coming out of the computer science department, ranked number 10 in the country. Half of those getting their doctorates were from East Asia. Almost all of them were going back to East Asia to pursue their careers. In the entering class that fall, every vacant seat was filled by very high quality applicants from the United States, with more than 200 points higher on their GREs than the entering class the year before. What was the difference? $18,000 a year as a grant of study.

The answer is simple. It's the same answer we had in
the 1940s and 1950s and forgot. Bright youngsters will
go to graduate school on grants, but they won't continue
to borrow money. If they borrowed money to go as under-
graduates, most of them want to get out and start paying
it off. And a viable program of grants will fill those
seats and sustain the lead. But they've got to have
equipment in those laboratories as well.

The R & D tax credit, enacted in 1981, clearly brought
a significant increase in industry's investment in that
creative cycle. You get lots of arguments; the congres-
sional budget office did their study saying that all that
industry did really was reclassify things into R & D from
other areas. I'm perfectly prepared to stipulate that
some of that took place. But the reality is still very
clear that in 1982 in one of the deepest recessions of
the postwar period, the overall expenditure by industry
in research went up, not down. That was the first time.
I'm persuaded that the R & D tax credit was the major
ingredient in causing that to occur.

APPLYING TECHNOLOGY

Government investment has gone up in research again
since the early 1980s. That's good news, but there's
also bad news attached to it. That concerns the application of technology. Critical to our long-term success in
that international marketplace is the speed with which
emerging technology becomes available for exploitation.
One of the most vital sectors of the U.S. economy is the
small business sector and the speed with which the right
innovators move to use new technology. The hazard for
innovators is that a year or two later, the industry
leader comes in with a different approach which becomes
the standard. They learn very quickly that it's very
difficult to be in the bed with elephants if the elephant
rolls over and takes a very different approach from the
one you've taken.

BARRIERS TO COMMERCIALIZING GOVERNMENT-FUNDED TECHNOLOGY

Particularly worrisome to me, in looking at this problem from the private sector side, is the time frame that
now applies before much of the technology funded by government becomes available for commercial exploitation.
From the 1940s to the early 1960s, the defense procurement cycle was four to five years. The technology became
available for commercial exploitation in a pretty timely
way. We then set out to reform the defense procurement
cycle. To make no mistakes, we created a cycle of 12 to
13 years, a perfect monstrosity. One of the costs to us
as a country seeking to have no mistakes, all reinforced

with a focus on waste, fraud, and abuse, is that most of
the fruits of the research from that large investment are
no longer available for commercial exploitation in a
timely way.

I would argue that we could afford a lot of mistakes in
the defense procurement cycle and still be ahead, net, as
a country. We could put a ceiling of six years on that
process and cut back on many of the things that have
stretched it out, where what you're looking for is the
earliest availability for broad commercial exploitation
of the research coming out of that funding. What I'm
hearing instead is, "Let's shift that research funding to
a new civilian agency to manage its allocation in the
government." Forgive me, but my 31 years of government
experience leads me to be very skeptical of creating yet
another new agency to parcel out that funding and to make
the wise decisions of where it will do the most for the
long-term growth of the economy.

ACTIONS FOR SPEEDING THE COMMERCIALIZATION OF TECHNOLOGY

We clearly have to have a focused look at how we take
technology to the marketplace faster. Government's side
packs policy to encourage it--some demonstration investment to demonstrate that it can be done--investment in
the education side and in the work force. I give the
government high marks for their decision to invest as a
partner in Sematech, half the money, for a concentrated
effort to focus on process, in this case in the semiconductor industry. Sematech is a consortium created in
1987 by the semiconductor industry to restore U.S. competitiveness in computer chip manufacturing. How can you
move much faster, with some concurrency, into taking that
emerging technology into a high quality product through
the application of automation?

The academic world must focus much more effort on technology transfer. How do we help facilitate the flow of
technology within industry from the university laboratories out to use? How do public universities get in
place patent policy? Another approach is to get rid of
bureaucracy. Again, their focus is the timeliness with
which the technology gets used.

On the private sector side, I'm persuaded that there
must be more collaboration in the pre-competitive phase
in research, pushing the frontiers, making sure that you
get the critical level of effort that's mandatory, and
sustain it for enough time. You have to get a critical
mass. You don't get it with one-year funding, uncertain
about whether it's going to follow in a subsequent year.
We already have several models that prove collaborative
research will work in accelerating the creation of new
technology. But we sure don't have certainty yet that

that's also going to result in use of that technology in a timely way.

FOCUS ON TIME, COST, AND QUALITY IN APPLYING NEW TECHNOLOGY

On the industry side, I believe it's fundamental to bring about a focus on time and quality as well as cost. We've got to build in a process that looks from the beginning, "How do you deal with the cost of change, not just the cost of continuing production with existing technology?" Zero defect has got to be a fundamental rule across the board. None of this will take place without a constant focus on the human element. For indeed, it is preparing a work force that is ready to deal with the changes in environment, automated office, automated service institutions, automated manufacturing, and to servicing those. I don't know what your experience is in getting your automobiles repaired, but I would say that I can give you prima facie evidence that new technology, even in U.S. products, is already substantially outstripping the ability to get service done confidently and quickly to sustain that level, even before we move to the next stage. So the overall competency of the work force must be improved.

The demographics are certain. Given the birthrates, we are going to see a very major difference in the structure of those entering the work force, in some states, as early as the middle 1990s. They are going to impact directly on Utah. In Florida, Texas, Colorado, New Mexico, Arizona, and California, before the turn of the century, more than half those entering the work force will be non-Caucasian. And how we have drawn them into this whole education cycle is going to have a lot to say about how competent that work force is to deal with the world of the year 2000.

Ultimately, there have to be the incentives all across the board to bring everybody to focus on the time, the quality, and the cost if we are going to be competitive at that marketplace in the year 2000. If we don't adapt, we are certain to see a declining standard of living in this country. We are also likely to see very dramatic impact on the world in which we live. Forgive me for one last quick look back at where I spent 31 years of my life.

PEACEFUL WORLD DEPENDS ON ALLIANCE AND ECONOMIC GROWTH

When I was an undergraduate in the late 1940s, one of my learned professors held forth that we've been very fortunate to get 20 years between World War I and World War II. In his judgment, we'd be even luckier if we got

ten years between World War II and World War III. Well,
we're celebrating 40-plus years without a global conflict. We've had some regional ones. We're going to
continue to have a lot of regional ones. We've been
pulled into a couple of those and on the edge of a couple
of others. But we've stayed out of a global conflict.
I'm persuaded that the alliances that we strung together
in the late 1940s and early 1950s have been the key to
keeping us out of that global conflict. If I'm even
close to right, how we manage our own change to be competitive, and then help the whole international economy
grow, is absolutely critical to sustaining those alliances because those alliance partners are our principal
competitors in that international marketplace. We must
adapt or we will not be the leaders but rather those who
suffer from the changes that follow.

33

The Globe Story

Arden C. Sims

Some of you here today are leaders and managers of manufacturing companies. Others of you are leaders, managers,
and owners of small businesses and service organizations,
and some of you are members of the academic community.
You have trained the leaders of today, and you will train
the leaders of tomorrow. My message, and the message of
the Globe story, is that as members and asso- ciates of
the business community, if you understand how quality
relates to profitability, you will be able to build
increasing profitability into your company.

What were some of the problems we faced at Globe over
three years ago before we implemented our quality program? One problem was rising electrical power rates.
The products produced at Globe Metallurgical, silicon
metal and ferroalloys, are some of the most power-inten-
sive products in the world, with electricity accounting
for over 25 percent of our total product cost. At that
time the local utilities were requesting rate increases
in excess of 20 percent. I viewed this as a further es-
calation of power rates that had more than doubled since
1970.

A second problem we faced was an increase in import
competition. There are three major markets for our
products--North America, Europe, and the Far East. Now
at that time the value of the dollar was more than twice
its level of just a few years earlier. So this made the
U.S. the most attractive market for our products. At the
same time, there was an excessive supply of the products
that we produce. Companies mainly in South America had
overexpanded because they had access to cheap labor and
access to power rates less than half of ours. With the
cost advantage and the currency advantage, it was very
easy for them to penetrate the U.S. market.

Third problem was that our market base was shrinking. Historically, ever since Globe was founded in 1873, the company had produced mainly commodity-type products for the aluminum, steel, and foundry industries. We all know what happened to those industries in the mid-1980s. They were closing facilities. They were going through major restructuring because they were experiencing a decline in the demand for their products. They were experiencing increased import competition and cost pressures.

The last major problem we faced at Globe was that the company was for sale. At that time the company was owned by Moore McCormack Resources, a Fortune 500 company that was into a lot of different businesses. They were into oil and gas, Great Lakes shipping, ocean bulk transportation, iron ore and coal mining. They were into concrete, cement, and aggregates, and they were into the metals business with Globe Metallurgical. At that time, over 25 percent of their sales revenue was with LTV. So when LTV filed for Chapter 11 bankruptcy protection, their stock plummeted. It dropped more than 30 percent in a matter of days. So being a large, diversified company, one option they had was to restructure, and that was what they decided to do. They decided to sell their shipping operations, their mining operations, and their metals business--Globe Metallurgical Inc. So you see we had many problems and they were major on every front. We had financial threats. We had competitive threats and ownership threats. But, by implementing quality, we were able to turn the company to a high level of profitability.

How did we accomplish the quality turnaround at Globe? One of the ways was to train all of our employees in quality techniques. Being a small business, we did not have in-house training resources, so we brought in a trainer from The American Supplier Institute. We chose the ASI because of its strong ties to the automobile industry, a major customer of ours. We also decided to use statistical process control as a way to monitor and control our processes. SPC also provided us with a quantitative way to measure the quality of our products. Each one of our employees received six hours of training in basic statistics, in how to use various charts (the meaning of the charts, the meaning of upper and lower control limits), and in how to calculate a point and put it on the chart--even how to use a calculator to calculate the point. Now six hours of training might not sound like a lot, but to a company the size of Globe, that was 1260 hours in the classroom versus being out there on the shop floor producing product.

A second step was to establish QEC committees. QEC stands for quality, efficiency, and cost, and you notice at Globe we put quality first because I believe that with improved quality we will have both better efficiency and lower cost. We have a top management QEC committee of which I am chairman. The other three owners of the company are on this committee, along with the Chief Financial Officer of the company and our two plant managers. We meet once a month.   This committee reviews the activities and establishes guidelines for the plant committees, which meet virtually every day.

The plant QEC committees are chaired by the plant managers and they have people on their committees from departments throughout the plant.   Before every daily meeting, every statistical process control chart (we call them SPC charts) is reviewed and any point that has gone out of control is discussed. Was any action taken, was it the right action, and do any procedures need to be changed?   They also monitor the activities of the quality circle groups, and we have a number of those. We have departmental and interdepartmental committees with people throughout the plant. We have special project groups and interplant groups for which people travel from Beverly, Ohio, to Selma, Alabama, and from Selma to Beverly. These are our hourly people off the shop floor. People from each plant meet in quality circle groups and observe each other working on the shop floor. This is a mixture of union employees from Selma and non-union from Beverly.

We also trained all of our major suppliers in quality techniques--our major suppliers that did not have adequate quality control programs.   First, we brought the top management from those companies into our facilities and gave them the same training as our people received. Then Globe's quality people went out and visited our suppliers.   They took blank charts, training materials, and calculators, and they trained all the hourly and salary people.

We communicated the advantages of quality to every employee in the company. I felt this needed to be on a personal level.   So at Globe we instituted a profit-sharing program for every employee in the company.   During one of my visits to the Selma plant, an employee told me that this was the best thing that Globe had ever done for its employees. He said:

I get this sum of money--a separate check from my regular payroll check every three months. I can take this sum of money and do something with it.   I can buy a television or a VCR or make a down payment on a car or take a trip or put it in savings. If you had given me a pay raise of one, two, or three dollars an hour, I never would have seen it.   It would have gone out every week, the way my regular pay goes out now. Also, this tells me how well I am doing and how well the company is doing. I can now see that when we improve our quality, our sales level increases and profits increase. With improved quality, our costs are lower and our profits are higher. So now I can clearly identify quality with profits.

Another way we accomplished the quality turn-around was to find out just what the quality needs of our customers were. We learned a lot from the audits of Ford, General Motors, Intermet, and John Deere. We also went out and talked to our customers to learn more precisely just what their quality needs were. We found that we were not doing things that were important to some of our customers--and that was waste for them. We found that we were doing things that were not important to them--and that was waste for us. In addition to that, all of our employees, from the shop floor on up, visit our customers periodically. We produce products that go into other products--about 120,000 tons a year, and some of our customers use only one, two, or three pounds at a time. I found that there is nothing like that experience of going to that Ford Motor Company or General Motors foundry and seeing that one, two, or three pounds of product being used; this is less than a coffee cupfull going into molds to produce camshafts, crankshafts, engine manifolds, or differential housings. After seeing this, Globe employees understand the importance of consistency--why the product produced today has to be consistent with what was produced yesterday and every other day. They also get to see the final product going into the automobile in this case. Some of you may drive Ford, Chrysler, or General Motor cars. We have materials in those automobiles. Even if you drive an import like a Jaguar, a BMW, or a Hyundai we have materials in those cars. We have materials in computers, television sets, VCRs, all kinds of electronic equipment, household waxes, automobile polishes, Armorall cleaners, and silicon spray.

We have materials in hair spray, shaving cream, and cosmetics. Earlier this year, I met the president of Mary Kay Cosmetics in Washington, D.C., when I was there to talk about the Globe story, and I learned that we have materials in their cosmetics. We even have materials in surgical implant devices. So you see quality at Globe is not only important to me and to our employees. It is important to you, it is important to everyone.

This is how we accomplished the quality turn-around at Globe. We involved everyone. We involved our company at all levels. We involved our suppliers and our customers. This total involvement gave us the power to achieve tremendous growth and profitability. This total involvement in quality will give you, too, the power to achieve even greater growth and profitability.

What were the major results of our quality efforts? One result of our quality effort was increased business. One place our business increased is in North America. We are now the largest producer of silicon metal and specialty ferroalloys in North America. Our business increased in Europe, to the point that in March of this year, we purchased a company there, a sales marketing and

engineering company, to distribute our products throughout Europe and Africa.

In the Far East, we are now selling products in Korea,
Taiwan, Australia, Malaysia, and India. In that part of
the world, we are competing head to head with the Japanese, and we are winning. Our next target is Japan.

Lower cost was another result of improved quality. We
are now operating the company at full capacity versus
less than 70 percent a few years ago. I am sure that all
of you know how that impacts cost. For every dollar we
have spent on quality, we have gotten a return of forty
dollars. We are now producing more products than in the
1970s when the company was last at this operating level,
with 60 percent less labor.

Because of improved quality, ours is a more predictable
system. When I started with the company, the management
system was to fight the fire with the highest flame that
day. Believe me, there were a lot of fires to fight at
that time, but now with a total quality management system
in place, I know what we are going to do, when we are
going to do it, how we are going to do it, and what the
results are going to be.

The restructuring of our product mix was another result
of improved quality. As I said earlier, the company had
historically, since 1873, produced commodity-type products. But now we are producing high quality silicon
metal for the silicone, chemical, electronic, and solar
cell industries. We are producing high quality silicon
metal for high quality aluminum castings and we are producing high quality ferroalloys for high quality iron
castings. Some people say you cannot change, but I found
at Globe Metallurgical that by implementing quality we
were able to change.

Improved quality has also meant greater recognition:
recognition from the Ford Motor Company Q1 and Total
Quality Excellence Awards; from the General Motors Mark
of Excellence Award; from the Shingo Prize for Manufacturing Excellence; and from the Malcolm Baldrige National
Quality Award--the highest quality honor in this country.

With this recognition, I have had an opportunity to
share the Globe Story--to be on the same program as top
Fortune 500 companies around this country, with people
like Bob Galvin, Chairman of Motorola, and John Morris,
Chairman of Westinghouse. Every time I do that, I feel
like a baseball rookie just called up from the minor
leagues. Here I am with the pros--the people who have
built their companies into giant corporations. I have an
opportunity to listen to how they did it and to learn
from them. And I have an opportunity to share the experiences of Globe Metallurgical.

Sticking with baseball, the issue is not that you have
to hit a home run every time you are at the plate. The
issue with baseball is what you do each time at bat. Do
you bring that home runner who is in scoring position, or

do you move that runner from first base over to scoring
position, or do you get on base? The issue is what you
do each time at the plate, each time at bat. The issue
is the same for quality. With quality, you are at bat,
you are at the plate every day.

You too can achieve results that are measurable in
dollars. You can achieve results that are measurable in
recognition, results that are measurable in positioning
you for a positive, dynamic, and profitable future.

How do we maintain and improve our quality effort? One
way is to understand that quality improvement is a continuous, never-ending, ongoing process every day. The
employees must be motivated to produce a better product
today, every day, than they produced yesterday. When the
employees enter the plant Monday, Tuesday, Wednesday
through Sunday, around the clock for us, they must be
motivated to produce a better product for the company, a
better product for them, a better product for their
neighbors, a better product for you, and a better product
for the world.

We have a very good example at Globe. On the way to
work one evening, one of our employees, at our Beverly
facility had an automobile accident about two miles from
the plant. There is a sharp turn just before a railroad
crossing; he missed the turn, went over an embankment,
hit a telephone pole, and broke it off. Fortunately he
was not injured. Well, he got out of his car and walked
the two miles into the plant to finish his shift of work.
He did not do that because of the money he would lose by
not working that shift, because he could easily have made
that up with one shift of overtime. He did that because
he knew that if he were not there, his co-workers would
have to do his job plus their job, and if they did that,
then quality would suffer. At Beverly, we have a plant
with no supervision, no time cards, and no time clocks.
At Beverly, we have a plant where 135 employees had only
a total of 4 days of absenteeism last year. That is the
kind of motivation that is required.

Another way we maintain and improve quality is to keep
the channels of communication open in all directions,
open with our suppliers, open with our employees, and
open with our customers. With our employees, we have an
open door policy. Anyone at any time can come in and
talk to me, to any of the other owners of the company or
to any of the managers; they do it individually and in
groups. Any time that they come in, whatever we are
doing, we stop and talk and listen.

With our customers, we tell them about any change we
have made in our process, no matter how far upstream it
is. Even if we are confident that it is not going to
hurt the quality of the product, even if we feel it is
going to improve the quality of the product, we tell our
customer, "Hey, we've made a change. We would like for
you to watch our product." Our customers don't check the

quality of our products anymore. They know from their audits that our product is going to be consistent every time. When we make a change, we want another set of eyes looking at it, even after we have done our analysis. Our policy with our customers is "no surprises"!

Another way we maintain and improve quality is to capitalize on this national quality award. We are in the spotlight now. We have been recognized as one of the top quality companies in the U.S., the highest quality recognition that you can get, recognition from the President of the United States, at that time Ronald Reagan. When I was up there accepting this award and shaking President Reagan's hand, on the same stage with Motorola's chairman, with Westinghouse's chairman, and with 250 corporate leaders in the audience from America's Fortune 500 companies, it was a tremendous feeling, a feeling like I was on the top of a mountain peak, the mountain that Globe had been climbing for three years.

But you know what happens when you reach the top of a mountain. You look around and what do you see? One thing you see is your competition trying to climb the same mountain. But you also see another, higher mountain peak, so what do you do? You have to climb the higher mountains, and that is what we are doing at Globe Metallurgical; every day we are climbing the next highest mountain peak.

These are the ways we maintain and improve quality--not on a monthly basis, not on a daily basis. This daily commitment to maintaining and improving quality is our daily commitment to profitability. So you see, if you understand how quality relates to profitability, you will be able to build increasing profitability into your company as well.

34

Linking Merit Pay with Performance at Lincoln Electric

Richard S. Sabo

The Lincoln Electric Company of Cleveland, Ohio, is the world's largest manufacturer of arc welding products and a producer of industrial electric motors.

The Lincoln Electric case is a classic case, as proven by the Harvard Business School. Out of 35,000 cases published worldwide, the Lincoln Electric Company case is the one chosen most often by anyone who purchases a Harvard business case. Today I am going to describe some of the principles that make Lincoln unique, with special emphasis on "linking performance with pay."

TRULY LINKING PERFORMANCE WITH PAY

Every one of our approximately twenty-three hundred workers participates in the company's incentive plan, and all but two have been sharing in the year-end bonus for fifty-three consecutive years. Now, how do you go about fairly and honestly determining how every person in the company should receive over 50 percent of his annual income in one year-end bonus check? Well, it's definitely not easy. It takes a great deal of time and effort, because you must be as fair and as honest as you possibly can in determining each person's share.

The first thing that we do is eliminate the president and chairman from our year-end bonus calculations. We pay those people on the basis of performance by giving them a percentage of sales. In other words, if sales decline, the top executives will take the first pay cut.

Once the top two executives have been removed, we will evaluate each job in the company to determine the fair base rate for that job. This is done by committee, and it is our objective to have the hourly rate for that type of job to be average for the Cleveland area. That keeps us competitive with other industries in our area.

We have another committee that will do the same thing for all salaried positions in the company. All salaried positions in the company are exempt salary positions. In other words, we will pay no overtime to a salaried employee. Now, we take the hourly rate that has been established, and for our roughly 1,200 production workers, we will apply a piecework rate for each individual who is working on production. In essence, we will apply piecework in any area of the company operation where we know how to apply piecework. This definitely links performance with pay, because there is no minimum guaranteed base rate.

After we pay the piecework rate to the employee, we then have roughly 800 jobs in the company that are hourly rate. Those hourly rates have a range, so that an individual needs to perform to his or her highest capability in order to get to the top of the range for that job. So that is a second method of paying for performance.

The salaried people have exactly the same arrangement. Each job in the company has a salary range. An individual may or may not reach the top of the salary range. As you heard earlier, once you have given a person the salary, it is very difficult to take it back. So we are reluctant to give the salary until we are certain that the individual has earned it. Now, all of what we do is well and good, but it still does not guarantee that people will perform at their maximum capability.

EMPLOYEE RECOGNITION

Our next step is to merit rate individuals every six months. You may have heard earlier that merit rating appraisals are rarely used by executives. Nothing could be further from the truth at Lincoln Electric. Our chief executive officer reviews the 2,300 merit ratings every six months, and he looks at every one of them. So, the merit rating is very vital and very important. Essentially, we rate the people on four cards.

To measure output, you simply ask how much work did the individual do, and it doesn't matter whether that individual is a pieceworker, an hourly worker, or a salaried person. You measure their output. Second, we measure the quality of the work. How well did they do the work they were assigned? Third, we measure their dependability, which to us is defined as the ability to work without supervision. We eliminate supervision wherever possible. The average ratio of foremen to workers is 1:100. We do not feel that it is the responsibility of the foreman to make people work. If you hire mature, skilled individuals who have a desire to perform, it is not necessary to make them work; they will do the job. It's management's role to create an environment where they can do their best.

Then we will rate the person's ideas and cooperation. This is the rating card that keeps people from stabbing each other in the back to gain a greater income. The average rating for an employee is 100 points, or 25 points per card. This rating takes place every six months, and we will take the two ratings for a bonus year and develop an average for that person.

The rating may be compared to a grade that you received in school; however, the big difference is that our rating determines what percentage of the year-end bonus each individual will share. So, if you could visualize an individual who earned $10,000 during the year and received a merit rating of 100, he would receive a $10,000 bonus at year-end, if we were, in fact, paying a 100 percent bonus.

Now, for the last fifty-three consecutive years, we have paid an average bonus of 95.5 percent. The merit rating would change the individual's income, depending on what the rating could be. The ratings generally will fall between 90 and 110, but there is no upper limit, nor is there a lower limit, so that people could receive merit ratings of 140, 150, or 200, or more.

But, the bonus payment is paid to everyone in the company except, as I mentioned earlier, the president and chairman.

OTHER BENEFITS TO LINKING PAY TO PERFORMANCE

Now, how successful has our system been? It has allowed Lincoln Electric to maintain its position as the world's largest manufacturer of arc welding products over the entire fifty-three-year period that we have been operating under the principles of incentive management.

Second, our turnover rates are very low. We have a monthly turnover rate of less than .3 of 1 percent. The average age of our work force is just over 40 years of age, and the average number of years of experience in our machine division is 16.75 years.

This experience has resulted in very high quality products. We offer the only five-year warranty in the electric motor field, and in the welder field we offer a three-year warranty. Our rejections rates are minimal. The cost of rejections in our Motor Division has been less than .3 of 1 percent of sales. Add to this the fact that we have never had a strike in our company's history, and you can see why Lincoln's market share continues to increase.

The company has no debt, and we have been able to pay a dividend every year for fifty-three consecutive years.

This is in spite of our industry's experiencing a severe recession over the last four or five years, because the manufacturing base in the United States has certainly declined.

In closing, I do want to call your attention to our Incentive Management Seminars that are periodically scheduled in the Cleveland, Ohio, headquarters. There is no charge. We sponsor these as a service to industry.

35

Boeing's Quality Strategy: A Continuing Evolution

John R. Black

I want to give you an overview of the quality improvement process within the Boeing companies--where it started, how it grew, and where we are today. The process has not always been a smooth one--for we are involved in a major cultural transition. What we are changing to today, however, is not entirely different from the way things were back when Bill Boeing made his first two airplanes in 1916.

He and Navy Commander Conrad Westervelt built a single-engine seaplane, which was called the B & W Number 1, using their initials. Those planes measured only 27 1/2 feet long and had a range of 320 miles. That's tiny compared to today's commercial airliners. In fact, the tail of the 747 is more than twice as high as the B & Ws were long, and the 747 can travel up to 7,000 miles without refueling.

Those first B & Ws were assembled in two locations-- the wings and floats at a shipyard on Puget Sound's Elliot Bay, and the fuselage in a hangar on Seattle's Lake Union. When the first plane was completed in June 1916, Bill Boeing test flew it himself. He didn't delegate the job; he was committed to the belief that his people had done quality work. And he was willing to stake his life on it. By 1928, his company had become one of the nation's largest aircraft builders.

It was the capability and ruggedness of the Boeing B-17 Flying Fortress that helped us win World War II. Some 12,726 B-17s were built--more than any other multi-engine aircraft in history, with Boeing alone producing 6,981 of them. The rest were produced by other manufacturers, following the Boeing plans.

Today, over half of the commercial jet airliners in the free world were built by Boeing. The 707 ushered in the jet age, more 727s have been sold than any other jet airliner, the 737 was 1986's best-selling jet airliner, and the 747 is the flagship of any air-line--with greater passenger capacity and longer range than any other airliner.

CHANGING CORPORATE CULTURE

Our formal efforts to change our culture started in 1980, with the 757 Productivity Program and the birth of quality circles in several of the Boeing companies. Perhaps I should tell you a little about Boeing at this point. There are currently six main Boeing companies, including Boeing Commercial Airplane Company (which I represent, and which also includes Boeing of Canada, formerly DeHavilland). BCAC currently has in excess of 40,000 employees.

The others are Boeing Military Airplane Company, Boeing Aerospace Company, Boeing Computer Services, Boeing Electronics Company, and Boeing Vertol(which makes helicopters). A seventh company, Boeing Services Division, was created in January 1987 to bring together activities that support all of the other companies--such as graphics, medical, security, etc.   Total Boeing employment is 128,000 worldwide, with 82,000 in the greater Seattle area.

Our goal is to deliver products that meet our commitment to excellence--to make Boeing the recognized standard for the quality, after-sales support, and technical and economic performance of those products.

Quality circles began for the most part primarily in manufacturing areas such as the Commercial Airplane Company's giant fabrication division in Auburn, Washington; the Military Aircraft Company's plant in Wichita, Kansas; and the Aerospace Company's manufacturing facilities at the Kent Space Center in Washington State.   And since Boeing Computer Services maintains support personnel at all of the different company locations, they were also early in implementing quality circles at Boeing.

Before I describe how the quality circle process grew at Boeing, I'd like to tell you about a comprehensive attempt we made to change the company culture that began in 1980 and ended in 1984. Established in March 1980, the 757 Productivity Program was far more than just another attempt to encourage our people to work smarter and faster. The program focused on developing a comprehensive and cohesive strategy for implementing employee involvement.

Our first priority on 757 was defined as employee involvement (EI)--an umbrella term that involves the people and the organization in improving productivity and quality of worklife. EI emphasizes changing the management style from "telling" to "listening," and minimizing adversarial relationships. It involves the employee in group decision making, problem solving, and goal setting (team efforts), and vertical communication (primarily upward).

Employee involvement is a process and a discipline for accomplishing an evolutionary change from an existing management structure, system, and style to one that encourages and facilitates less management structure, more participative systems, and maximum openness and communication.

An executive council was established to provide overall guidance and decision making. The management team became the steering committee, responsible for the plan. Department teams became coordinators, and employee teams became active participants in identifying problems and recommending solutions.

We conducted employee surveys at the request of department managers. Over 450 operational factors, both positive and negative, were identified as appearing to influence individual and group productivity. The results were reported confidentially to department managers for appropriate action. Employees were interviewed both individually and through job reaction questionnaires.

A unique aspect of this process was the formation of a Quality of Work Life Committee consisting of employees and managers. The committee addressed survey results, developed recommendations, and presented them to the organization's steering committee for decisions and implementation.

However, when the 757 and 777 projects were merged in 1984, the 757 Productivity Program encountered considerable resistance from managers who were suddenly exposed to the cultural change process. They did not understand what it could do for them. They saw it as unnecessary. Without their support, the 757 Productivity Program was discontinued. And as a result, the momentum to move to a more participative management style within BCAC slowed.

BIRTH OF QUALITY CIRCLES

At the Boeing companies, the quality circle process had been initiated in 1980, with the first three circles. This process has been highly successful and continues to be. By the end of 1986, there were 846 circles active throughout the Boeing companies, and the process is still growing rapidly. Of these circles, 7,901 employees were involved in the process at the end of the year, averaging 9.3 members per circle.

These circle members are not just locating and tackling problems in a haphazard manner; they are all trained, either by their facilitator or by their training group,

in the use of systematic problem-solving tools. The
6,478 circle members and 669 leaders were trained in
1986.

Of the projects worked, half of them provided cost
savings, while the other half resulted in improvements
that are highly significant changes in an organization's
culture. Support at the top isn't enough. Managers
throughout the structure, and especially middle managers,
must be committed to the process for real cultural
changes to be produced. When we created the BCAC Quality
Improvement Center in 1986, we made sure to educate all
managers in the company in the new philosophy as the
first order of business.

Improving quality was also made a special priority at
Boeing Aerospace Company in 1983. However, back then, it
was treated as a motivational program. Just run out the
banners, print brochures, make awards, and suddenly the
front-line troops will do all the improvement for us--so
the theory went. They called it The Pride in Performance
Program and got the graphics guys busy doing a four-color
brochure to tell our people and our customers what
wonderful things we were doing.

There was a lot of truth to that. We were doing a
great job at the time. We were told over and over again
that we were at the top of the aerospace industry for
quality. So we figured we didn't have a lot to do--just
tweak the system a little and get the word out. We put
the Pride in Performance posters up, sent the brochures
out, and waited for the results to come in.

QUALITY IMPROVEMENT CHARACTERISTIC: MANAGEMENT COMMITMENTS

In 1984, Bill Selby, who had been Director of Manufacturing, became Director of Operations--the man in charge
of the Pride in Performance Program. He was convinced
that there had to be more to quality improvement than we
were doing at the time. He said our first priority was
to find out what the experts were saying and what other
companies were doing.

Bill and I went to hear Juran, Deming, Crosby, Conway--
and anyone else who seemed to have a handle on what quality improvement was all about. We visited Tektronix,
ARMCO, Motorola, McDonnell Douglas, Honey-well, Hewlett-
Packard, and IBM--and we were impressed by what we saw.
And so we brought in J. M. Juran, Al Gunderson, and
finally Bill Conway to present seminars to our senior
management on what quality improvement was all about.

The outcome was that the experts and other companies
were saying if we were really going to do quality improvement, it would take a lot more than just launching
into another productivity program or expanding the circle
process. Even the word "program" suggests something

that's only going to be around for awhile. Quality improvement is a process--one that must become a part of the way we do business every day.

All the experts were saying that management commitment to the process is essential if we really wanted it to work. In fact, the estimates were that 85 percent of the benefits to be gained by quality improvement relied on managers working together to change the systems within which their people work. As a result, we decided that our strategy would be to train managers first. We didn't want to get people fired up about the process, only to have them be stopped by their managers or by middle management, who saw the process as a potential threat. We wanted to have them on board first!

At every company we looked at, senior management--usually the CEO or president--was the spark plug behind the quality effort. It wasn't something senior management paid lip service to and then delegated to somebody else. It was something they believed in and led, personally.

QUALITY IMPROVEMENT CHARACTERISTIC: COMMITMENT TO CHANGE

A second common characteristic is a commitment to changing the management style. Managers can no longer sit in their offices and issue edicts. The management role has changed to that of coaching and supporting his or her people to do their very best. It involves a change in the organizational culture.

What is really going on in an organization is not always very obvious. A lot of the time these unwritten rules are only known by people who have been there for some time, and they may be quite different from what is said.

What we must do is to change this culture not only to adopt the new priorities, but also make them clear to all members of the organization and follow through on them.

In order to change the culture, we must change the structure--which means changing our ways. Management must:

- Lead by example.
- Listen--employees are the experts about their own jobs.
- Push responsibility and authority levels down.
- Foster teamwork.
- Provide continuous personal appreciation, recognition, and reward.
- Provide the resources that allow people to excel.

We are accomplishing cultural change through the following five-step process:

1. Identifying the norms that currently guide execu-
    tive behaviors and attitudes.
2. Identifying the behaviors necessary to make the
    organization successful for today and tomorrow--
    not just what worked yesterday.
3. Developing a list of the new norms that will move
    the organization forward.
4. Identifying the culture gaps--the difference
    between desired norms and actual norms.
5. Developing and putting in place an action plan to
    implement the new cultural norms. You have to
    develop agreements that these new norms will indeed
    replace the old ones and that this transition will
    be monitored and enforced.

QUALITY IMPROVEMENT CHARACTERISTIC: TRAINING

A third characteristic we discovered was that everyone
in the company must receive comprehensive training in
both the need for continuous improvement and in the tools
to achieve it. Because only management can change the
systems within the company, it is essential to train
management at the outset of the process. This is the
approach to continuous improvement that was taken at
Boeing Aerospace Center, and it is the approach to
improvement we have taken at BCAC.

When I became Director of the newly formed Quality Improvement Center at BCAC in February 1986, I saw our
first task as training all management to know why it is
vital that we pursue continuous improvement and how to do
it, from the very start. Only in that way are we making
sure we have a true top-down approach. BCAC is a sizable
company, and so this has been no small task. We have
more than 43,00 managers plus about 100 senior executives. And once we train them, we have more than 36,000
other employees to bring into the new system.

We have developed a two-day Managing Quality Seminar
that we will continue teaching to groups of 100 to 250
managers until all BCAC managers are trained. The seminar begins with senior management stating the need for
achieving a cultural change in management. Divisional
directors share what is happening in their areas. And on
the second day of the seminar, speakers are brought in
from other major corporations to tell our people what
they are doing. Already we have heard from IBM, Ford,
McDonnell Douglas, Chrysler, Hewlett-Packard, Harley
Davidson, ALCOA, and many others; and we videotape their
presentations to use with our improvement teams.

We are also bringing in Bill Conway, president of
Conway Quality Inc., to help all our managers understand
the urgency of working to make this cultural transition--
starting today! This year we are hosting ten meetings
with Bill Conway on the University of Washington campus--

for groups of 400 managers plus university students from the business school.

We train team facilitators, team leaders, and trainers. Those trainers work in line organizations to expand the training of quality improvement into all areas of the company. We have designed and taught classes in process control methods, process improvement, and are developing classes in other statistical methods for process improvement.

We believe that the implementation of statistical methods for process control is essential to provide accurate data for decision making and to give us adequate feedback to ensure that we meet our improvement goals. Already some of our divisions are setting up their own courses to expand this training to all their people. We plan to have all of our managers attend the two-day Managing Quality Seminar and the Conway Seminar by the end of 1987.

IMPLEMENTATION STRUCTURE/STRATEGY

To do all this and to make it work requires a structured approach. All of the six major Boeing companies have formed Executive Councils to oversee the process throughout their companies. We have formed steering committees and quality councils, from the president's level on down to make sure that the improvement process is increasingly integrated throughout all of our business systems.

Our companies have also formed Quality Improvement Centers to guide and assist the process. At BCAC, we have a permanent staff of ten people, and a group of twelve functional representatives from major areas of the company. Identified as people who have the potential to become the leaders of tomorrow, these reps come to the center for a one-year rotation, after which they return to their parent organizations, where they continue their efforts to implement the quality improvement process. While at the center, they provide direct contact, consultation, and support for their organizations' improvement efforts.

To make sure that improvement objectives are being met--to find the opportunities for improvement with the biggest payoffs and to accurately track what we are accomplishing--it takes data. A group of top managers in BCAC has formed a team to develop the criteria for measuring the quality of all BCAC products and services. Meanwhile, the new Quality Assurance Division has spearheaded a renewed process of talking to our customers about their quality needs and problems. By fully identifying customer requirements and the highest impact customer quality problems, we can focus our improvement ef-

forts to deal with the most important quality issues our
customers have.

Within BCAC, we have a six-year strategy to achieve the
transition to a total quality improvement process. We saw
1986 as our year of commitment, in which we spent much of
our time educating management on the need to implement
the quality improvement process and to get their commitment to be supportive of the process and personally involved in it. An example of that commitment is the creation of a number of pilot quality improvement teams, who
receive training in QI methods and are given a major
quality problem to resolve--a problem that has a significant effect on a number of organizations.

We call 1987 our year of implementation, as we expand
the number of quality improvement teams, develop measurement systems to locate and quantify waste, identify major
impediments to continuous improvement, and initiate a
supplier improvement process. We see 1988 as the year
for transition and transformation, with inspection becoming more a responsibility of everyone and less relying
solely on traditional methods. We are working to get a
supplier improvement process in place, statistical management implemented, quality planning integrated into the
business planning cycle, and union participation.

We anticipate significant results to be achieved in
1989, with all employees trained in the use of statistical tools, a pilot project on self-regulating work teams
in place, and layers of management reduced. In 1990, we
foresee that we will be using only suppliers that have
their processes under statistical control. And at the
end of the six-year process in 1991, we anticipate that
we will have achieved reduced inspection, restricted
hiring, self-regulating work teams, BCAC business processes restructured to minimize waste, and reduced levels
of management.

This process of continuous improvement, to which we are
committed, is not one that can suddenly be grafted into
a company. Every organization--in our company, in your
company--must make it their own. Top management leadership MUST be provided, and ALL management must be brought
on board. Only when that happens, when all the people
are committed and the process is locked in for the long
term, will it achieve the breakthrough that it is capable
of providing for you and for us--the key to economic
success in the future.

36

Marriott Benefits by Linking Human Resources with Strategy

Clifford J. Ehrlich

The popularity of the topic "Linking Human Resources with Strategic Management" is a relatively recent phenomenon. It's increasingly a subject of meetings and of articles in business publications. I always get a bit wary when that happens. Because a lot is being said on a particular subject doesn't mean that a lot is being done. It's sometimes easier to "say" than to "do" and the challenge of this chapter's subject makes it more inviting to discuss than to act on.

I'll discuss it, but in the process I'll tell you how Marriott is acting too. My remarks will attempt to answer four questions:

1. What factors have catapulted this subject into prominence?
2. Why is it a challenge?
3. How does Marriott attempt to achieve a linkage between strategic planning and human resources activities?
4. What accomplishments have resulted from or have been facilitated by this linkage?

IMPORTANCE OF LINKING HUMAN RESOURCES TO STRATEGY

Let's start with Question 1: What factors have catapulted this subject into prominence? I believe there are two. The first is the ascending importance of strategic planning in the management process. The development of strategic planning techniques is relatively recent, having begun in the early 1970s and becoming commonplace

only since the end of that decade. They were prompted by
a series of economic convulsions that challenged and
strained all businesses: inflation and stagflation, sky-
rocketing labor and energy costs, and declining productivity. Businesses were reeling and realized that they
had to reassess the process by which they managed and
allocated resources. Strategic planning has provided the
response. It asks: What is the mission? Who are your
competitors? What are your opportunities? What resources
do you need? The answer to these and other questions
have shaped the future of most major American businesses
today.

The second factor is demographic change. Except for
periods of war, our nation has traditionally enjoyed an
abundance of labor. In this century, for example, we
saw the movement of people from the rural South to the
urban, industrial North. There has been a sharp increase in the number of women who participate in the work
force. We had a post-World War II baby boom, which star-
ed in 1947 (when there were 40% more births than in 1946)
and continued until 1962, when the birthrate dropped s
sharply. From 1970 to 1975 the work force grew by 25%;
from 1975 to 1980, by 10%. From now to 1992 the work
force will experience essentially zero growth.

Strategic planning and its orientation to factors external to a business smoked out the importance of these
demographics. Sharply rising pay rates during the 1970s
have already shifted labor from a low-cost to a high-cost
resource. Now it also promises to be a scarce resource.
This combination makes it a critically important issue to
any company, particularly a growth company that is also
labor intensive, like Marriott.

WHY IS LINKAGE A CHALLENGE?

My second question is, Why is achieving a linkage between strategic planning and human resource activities a
challenge? What makes it difficult? The long-range plan
projects the future. It describes where the business has
never been, so its managers don't know what it will be
like to be there. It's difficult to appreciate fully the
issues and the problems that will be faced.

By the same token we have yet to experience the jolt of
a scarce labor supply. We don't really know how that
will impact us. Because we're dealing with uncharted
territory, it takes mental gymnastics to figure out how
these two phenomena will interrelate. What processes
will have to change or be discarded? What values will
have to shift? It's just plain tough to do.

Other things also make the linkage a challenge. My
experience is that executives tend to make decisions
almost exclusively on financial considerations, without
adequately considering the human resource implications.

Financial considerations are quantifiable and fairly neat to deal with. Human resource implications are subjective, highly variable, imprecise, and generally messy to deal with: considering them frustrates and distracts most action-oriented executives.

Additionally, many staff people--including, and perhaps most notably, human resource people--are activity oriented. Over the years they have undertaken programs that were "viewed as being good" programs, like training and employee communications. These programs developed an existence unto themselves and met static needs. The activity-oriented people responsible for them have been slow in adjusting to the new economics and have not adequately looked at where the company was headed. I don't intend this remark to be an indictment of the human resource profession, but it does apply to some human resource people I know.

MARRIOTT'S APPROACH

My third question is, How does Marriott attempt to achieve a linkage between strategic planning and human resource activities? It begins with the reporting relationship of human resource executives. I report to the president and chief executive officer, and the human resource executive for each division reports to the general manager of the division. This results in our being present when decisions are discussed and deliberated. It gives us the opportunity to raise issues and assess the human resource implications of what the company plans to do. As a member of the executive staff, I attend and participate in the finance committee meetings at which the corporate strategy is received.

A second linkage occurs in the budget process. The budget I submit for the corporate human resource staff (and the ones submitted by the division of human resource executives) is subjected to close scrutiny. It is challenged and rechallenged. It is imperative that I am able to defend the spending plans for each functional area--compensation, benefits, affirmative action, etc.--and the only successful defense is to show how each area contributes to one of Marriott's vital interests. Unless I can explain how the activities of my staff contribute to the achievement of specific strategic objectives, I know my chances of getting my budget are very low. This process forces my staff and me to go through a rigorous review of the activities before we prepare the budget.

A third linkage is simply the result of the awareness that the division of human resources executives and I have of Marriott's strategic direction. It enables us to steer our activities on the strategic course chosen by the corporation. We know what's important and therefore can ensure that the projects we undertake are making a measurable contribution.

ACCOMPLISHMENTS FROM LINKAGE

My fourth question is, What accomplishments have resulted from or been facilitated by this linkage? The most notable was the development in 1982 of an executive manpower review system. The strategic plan projected our growth for the next five years. When we converted it to a staffing plan it was apparent that we were likely to face a shortage of qualified executives to manage our businesses. A straightforward process was designed that enabled us to identify leading candidates for promotion, establish developed plans for them, and track the results. This process also surfaced a handful of other significant human resource issues on which we had not fully focused and with which we are now dealing.

Another benefit occurred in our compensation program. In the late 1970s our strategic plan revealed an unusual set of economic circumstances that provided an opportunity for unprecedented growth in our segment of the hotel market. Our ability to take advantage of it depended on our ability to vastly increase the number of hotel development projects. We increased the hotel development staff slightly and created an incentive compensation program for a small cadre of hotel developers that was geared to the successful closing of hotel development projects that met return-on-investment goals. It was a program that was well outside the norm for Marriott but that was entirely responsive to a unique situation. The results were far better than anyone expected.

A third example involves one of our restaurant businesses and our recognition of an excellent market opportunity. It involved a business we had acquired and never fully developed because of knotty organizational structure and staffing problems. It was less disruptive to leave these problems alone than to resolve them. But the appearance of a new market opportunity forced us to be creative in producing a solution that seems to have resolved the obstacles. It was a case where the execution of our strategic plan became the mother of a new organizational structure.

CONCLUSION

All in all, we are comfortable with how we are linking human resource activities to strategy, but we're realistic enough to know that there is still much to be learned. I'm sure all of us will be learning together over the coming years.

37

Current Challenges for American Industry

Mark Shepherd, Jr.

The U.S. economy is in the midst of the third longest-running expansion in the postwar period. Inflation is at its lowest level in twenty-five years, and the stock market reaches new highs almost weekly.

Beneath the glitter, however, we still face the threat of large and growing deficits: a budget deficit, whose solution appears out of reach, and a trade deficit, whose impact on our industrial landscape is approaching seismic proportions. In industry after industry, manufacturers are going out of business, curtailing their operations, or giving up on the United States as a suitable place for making their products.

EROSION OF U.S. PRODUCTIVITY

The erosion of American competitiveness in recent years is only a part of the changes now sweeping the global economy, including a massive shift in the focus of world economic activity toward the Pacific Basin. While the United States is struggling to regain its position of leadership, the nations of the Asia/Pacific Region have skillfully exploited their labor-cost and productivity advantages to steadily increase their share of world markets.

Productivity is the key to a country's competitiveness. Since 1960, Japan's productivity gains in manufacturing have increased sixfold relative to the United States, and Europe has outstripped the United States by a factor of two. The United States still enjoys an advantage over our competitors in the *absolute level* of total productivity. Much of this advantage, however, was accumulated over the long period from the Civil War to World War II--

and has been eroded by the low relative rate of U.S. productivity growth in recent years.

This lower U.S. productivity growth has contributed to reduced profit margins, flat production, down-sized capacity in terms of both capital and labor, and an increasing loss of market share to imports.

No single statistic exemplifies the troubles of American industry as much as our manufacturing trade balance. After seventy years of nearly uninterrupted surpluses, the U.S. trade balance for manufactured goods plunged to a $40 billion deficit in 1983, $80 billion in 1984, and to $142 billion in 1986.

The loss of market share has been extensive even in high technology industries--a sector in which we have always taken our leadership for granted. Foreign penetration of the U.S. computer market has increased from 3 percent to 29 percent in less than six years. Communications and instruments have also suffered large losses in market share. These trends are worrisome for a nation accustomed to carrying the banner of world economic leadership.

America's competitive strategy should not rely on forcing our trading partners to give up their legitimate advantages.   Instead, we should be tough with those who take advantage of our good will; and we should develop a strategy that builds on America's strengths to tip the competitive scales in our favor. To this end, we should aim at: 1) balancing the financial scales between the U.S. and its international competitors; 2) improving the skill levels--not only the technical skills, but more importantly, the *basic* skills--of the work force; and 3) accelerating the development of advanced manufacturing processes.

COMPETITIVE STRATEGY: BALANCE FINANCIAL SCALES

The first step in balancing the financial scales is to increase the availability of capital for American companies. The cost of capital for a typical Japanese firm is less than half of that for its U.S. competitors (8.6 percent versus 17.4 percent). High savings rates in Japan, and close ties between banks and industry, have favored highly leveraged financial structures. Despite recent trends toward less reliance on debt, Japanese firms con-continue to exploit the low cost of debt with debt-to-equity ratios that are at least twice as high as comparable ratios in the United States.

Additionally, Japanese companies benefit from a tax system that effectively exempts from taxation much dividend income, interest income, and capital gains on stock. The result is that even if debt/equity ratios were the same in Japan and the United States, the Japanese would still enjoy a cost-of-capital advantage.

This lower cost of capital--combined with different earning standards of the financial community--have allowed Japanese firms to satisfy their investors with only 1 or 2 percent after-tax profit on sales, as opposed to the 5 or 6 percent required in the United States. This difference in acceptable profit margins for a given sales level means more cash available to our Japanese competitors for additional capital investment and research.

Instead of narrowing this cost-of-capital gap, the Tax Reform Act of 1986 increased it still further. According to a recent study by two economists at Stanford University--Douglas Bernhein and John Shoven--the effect of this legislation will be to increase the inflation adjusted cost of capital in the United States by at least 30 percent. This will worsen the cost-of-capital disadvantage of U.S. firms with respect to their Japanese competitors from 2:1 to 2.6:1. If this disparity continues, U.S. companies will not be able to keep up with Japanese investments, and America's technological leadership will continue its erosion.

Future legislation should consider ways of enhancing the incentives for personal saving and for capital formation: 1) by repealing taxes on the interest from savings; 2) by eliminating the double taxation of dividends; 3) by lowering tax rates on capital gains; and above all, 4) by reinstating the investment tax credit. Consideration should be given to a consumption tax as an offset to tax revenues lost through these reforms.

While tax reform could help increase the availability of capital, the federal budget deficit continues to threaten our economy. A return to fiscal discipline on the part of the U.S. government is essential to our continued recovery. The United States *must* reduce the size of the budget deficit by reducing government spending. In the late 1960s, total government spending was about 20 percent of GNP *despite* defense requirements that absorbed more than 9 percent of GNP. In fiscal year 1986, government spending totalled nearly 24 percent of GNP, and only 7 percent of that was in defense.

This is not meant to suggest that defense spending should go back to 9 percent of GNP. But we must go back to the kind of restraint on non-defense spending that has served us so well throughout most of our history.

While fiscal reform is necessary to restore U.S. competitiveness, it is not sufficient. Chronic distortions in exchange rates have played a large role in the deterioration of America's trade balance. Ending these distortions must be an important part of a new competitive strategy.

The extreme undervaluation of the yen in the first half of the 1980s is well documented. Today, Taiwanese and Korean exports to the United States are boosted by currencies that are grossly undervalued--in Korea's case by more than 60 percent--with respect to the dollar. These

relative currency values do not reflect the true positions of Taiwan and Korea in world markets. The use of
more realistic trade weights in computing the value of
their currencies, instead of the current policy of peg-
ging them exclusively to the dollar, would go a long way
toward eliminating this distortion.

But Korea and Taiwan are only part of much larger problems inherent in the present system of flexible exchange
rates--problems that include increased short-term vola-
tility and lack of predictability for planning purposes.
To address these problems, the United States should continue working to establish a system of target zones for
major international currencies. The success of the European Monetary System suggests that the idea of target
zones might be appropriate on a broader scale.

This system would require the identification (and
periodic revision) of a zone, perhaps 20 percent wide,
outside of which rates would be considered in clear dis-
equilibrium. Concerted intervention on the part of major
economic powers, followed by changes in monetary and/or
fiscal policies if necessary, would discourage exchange
rates from straying outside their target zones. This
system would: (1) require governments to consider explicitly the effects of national economic policies on international competitiveness; (2) encourage productive
investment by providing a more stable financial environment; and (3) prevent the "beggar thy neighbor" policies
employed by countries with chronically undervalued
currencies.

Our major trading partners agreed in Paris that exchange rates ought to be stabilized "at about current
levels," but clear target zones--and the specific actions
that would be taken to maintain currencies within these
zones--have not been established.

COMPETITIVE STRATEGY: IMPROVE SKILLS

In addition to balancing the financial scales, restoring America's competitive leadership requires increasing
the skill levels of the work force. The Japanese, with
a national commitment to excellence in education, are
raising an entire population to a standard currently in-
conceivable in the United States. They have succeeded on
the strength of: (1) parents who actively promote learning by cooperating with teachers, supervising extensive
homework, and not accepting mediocre performance; (2)
teachers who are well qualified, and highly motivated
because of the pay and the respect accorded to them; and
(3) a school year that is 30 percent longer than in the
United States (240 days versus 180 days average).

Japanese education is justly criticized for its reliance on rote memorization and its failure to foster the
creativity that is at the heart of American-style innova-

tion. But their system has been very effective in
teaching the "basics."

Meanwhile, we are--for the first time in our history--
producing a generation of high school graduates who are
less educated than their predecessors. SAT verbal and
math scores for U.S. students entering college are twenty
to twenty-five points below the levels achieved in 1967.
And--in contrast to Japan, where more than 90 percent of
students finish high school--a recent study by the Texas
Education Agency showed that one-third of the students
who started ninth grade did not graduate from high
school.

To restore the effectiveness of American schools, we
need to provide the necessary financial incentives to
attract and retain excellent teachers. We also need a
strong national commitment to higher educational standards, especially in math and science. And--most impor-
tant--we need deeper family involvement in all aspects of
education.

An issue of equal concern is the growing shortage of
technically qualified college graduates. Although recent
figures on U.S. engineering graduates show some improvement, these increases in the number of bachelor degrees
are deceptive. Projections of engineering graduates
suggest that we approached a peak level in 1986. Some
engineering schools are actually reducing their enroll-
ments, and a shortage of engineering Ph.D.s is reducing
the supply of qualified teachers.

Universities must work with industry to increase the
capacity of our technical education system and alleviate
this country's technical manpower shortage. To close
this gap, we need to:

1. Encourage more high school students to pursue
    engineering and science by giving them an under-
    standing of the opportunities open to those with
    first-class technical educations;
2. Emphasize co-op programs that allow a student to
    earn the money necessary to pursue a degree and,
    more importantly, provide the student with valuable
    experience with industry and with people;
3. Encourage the growing interest of women in engi-
    neering; and
4. Develop curricula that support lifelong education
    for self-renewal.

COMPETITIVE STRATEGY: DEVELOP MANUFACTURING PROCESSES

A third step in restoring America's leadership is to
develop--and use--more advanced manufacturing processes.
The very recent nature of the deterioration in our trade
balance is a strong indication that neither American
labor nor American management should be accused of being

the *only* cause of our trade deficit. The basic character
of America's industry cannot have changed so radically in
the brief span of five or six years. But we need to recognize the existence of severe structural weaknesses in
our industrial sector. And we must face the challenge of
enhancing our manufacturing skills.

Technological progress has been the driving force behind most of the productivity gains we have made in this
country--and the United States still leads the world in
the absolute commitment of funds to basic research. But
we have been weak in executing the difficult transition
from R & D prototype to full-scale commercial production.
Developing the manufacturing equipment and processes to
make this transition is often more complex than developing the product itself.

The Japanese recognized some time ago the importance of
this critical phase of innovation, and they have committed substantial resources to this area. The National
Science Foundation estimates that Japan spends better
than 60 percent of R & D on manufacturing, compared with
39 percent in the United States. As a result, the Japanese can take ideas into full-scale production in only
half the time we require--and often with lower manufacturing costs.

America's lead in design innovation will do little good
if countries are allowed to acquire our technology at
minimal cost and then, by spending huge sums on manufacturing R & D,consistently beat us to the market-place
with our own designs.

A major weakness in U.S. policy has been the lag between the advances in technology and the use of intellectual property law to protect them. Our competitive
advantage in innovation is seriously threatened by countries that acquire our technology through counterfeiting,
patent infringement, and other forms of piracy, and then
combine that technology with low-cost labor to drive the
original developers out of the market.

The United States has traditionally been the champion
of free trade. But America cannot remain the dumping
ground of other manufacturing nations--nor can we continue to be the victim of government subsidies by our competitors. Prevention of dumping--and the payment of a
fair price for the use of intellectual property--are
essential for assuring the continued development of innovative technologies and products.

At the same time, the government should encourage R &
D--and help provide firms with the cash flow necessary to
develop advanced manufacturing technologies--by:

First, making R & D tax credits permanent. The temporary nature of the current tax credit makes it difficult
to plan long-range projects;

Second, restoring the 25 percent rate that existed
prior to the Tax Reform Act of 1986;

And third, expanding eligibility for R & D tax credits to include the whole range of expenses involved in developing and implementing innovative manufacturing processes, machinery, and facilities.

R & D tax credits are preferable to direct government subsidies because they not only provide the necessary funds but, at the same time, they let the market-place determine where the money goes. Private-sector initiative has been the engine driving our economic growth, and no government bureaucracy can pick the "winners" and "losers" more effectively than the free market system.

But while government can help to provide a healthy environment for manufacturing innovation, industry must focus its attention on manufacturing itself. The infusion of a stronger manufacturing culture in boardrooms and executive offices across the country is an essential element in the revival of the U.S. industrial sector.

Many have suggested that high-technology industry could take up the slack caused by the decline of America's other manufacturing industries. But the absolute levels of output and employment in high-technology industries are not enough to offset the impact of declines in other manufacturing areas.

A much greater economic benefit will be realized if we begin to think of high technology not as an industry, but as a powerful set of tools that can revitalize our traditional industries. Using these tools most effectively will require a fundamental change in the way we think about manufacturing. Most strategic planning focuses on financial numbers, basic research, and designing products to meet market demand--not often enough does it focus on manufacturing. This has produced a mentality that looks on manufacturing as a process separate from design and distribution. For the future, we must broaden this perspective, and consider manufacturing as an integrated process.

By "integrated," I mean two things. First, manufacturing must be an equal partner with R & D and marketing, and become an integral part of a total business strategy.

Second, the manufacturing process itself must be treated in its totality. Traditional strategies for improving manufacturing have concentrated on automating isolated pieces of the process. The most efficient use of resources requires looking at the process as an integrated system and then investing in the resources necessary to optimize that system.

How well we can integrate the manufacturing process, and incorporate it into the overall business strategy, will depend on how well we understand the process itself. This means taking the process apart, piece by piece, and reexamining--and challenging--every task and every procedure. We must be able to quantify, measure, and analyze the process--and to do this, we must have access to complete information. Nothing should move, change, or be

processed in a factory without being captured electron-
ically in a data base.

Traditional approaches to analyzing the manufacturing
process have been of limited usefulness, because the engineers and operations researchers did not have access to
sufficient information and could address only a part of
the problem. Through continuous performance and cost improvements in semiconductor logic and memory, we now have
the potential for accessing more and better information
through distributed computing power, communications networks, and artificial intelligence. These emerging tools,
coupled with the existing tools of modeling and simula-
tion, will enable us to take a true systems approach to
enhancing the overall process, using hard data.

Low-cost computing power--in the form of programmable
industrial controllers and desktop terminals--has taken
computing out of the data processing room and put it on
the factory floor. With local area networks, we can link
together cell controllers, computer-aided design terminals, artificial intelligence work stations, and mini-
computers. And these networks provide a way to integrate
all the different sources of manufacturing process infor-
mation--which means we can now consider any problem in
terms of its impact on the total process.

Distributed computing power brings a problem, the information needed to solve it, and the mechanism for solving it together in the same head. The person with the
problem now has the potential for interacting with the
system from the individual work station, in real time, to
solve the problem.

What local area networks can do for an individual manufacturing plant, worldwide networks can do for an entire
corporation. With telecommunications networks, a semiconductor processing engineer in Dallas can have access
to test data stored in Singapore,to compare initial processing parameters with final test results. This allows
the processing engineer to assume full responsibility for
optimizing total cost and yield for the finished product,
instead of optimizing only one stage of the process.

This combination of computers and communications networks offers the potential of achieving revolutionary
advances in manufacturing efficiency.

Computer-aided design and computer-aided manufactur-
ing--CAD and CAM--are already helping to increase the
efficiency of these individual operations. For example,
in semiconductors, some logic designs that used to take
up to eighteen months are now completed in a few weeks.
But as long as CAD and CAM remain isolated pieces of the
manufacturing process, we will only gain small, evolutionary improvements. The power of Computer-Integrated
Manufacturing lies in its potential for linking together
the entire process.

Human beings will always be the critical part of the
manufacturing process, and part of collecting information

about the process should involve gathering the empirical
data and qualitative knowledge that only humans possess.
But until recently, there has been no effective way of
systematizing and measuring the process knowledge available in the human mind.

"Artificial Intelligence"--the technology that allows
computers to address problems that require human-like
reasoning and intelligence--gives us the key to unlock
this vital source of information. With its potential for
using the information provided by people, Artificial Intelligence opens a new dimension in data processing and
will change the way we think about factory automation.

An early application of Artificial Intelligence is expert systems, which involve capturing the knowledge of
experts in computer programs that can be used by non-
experts to solve a problem. For example, according to
Morgan Whitney, Director of Ford's Robotics Center, Ford
was training thousands of engineers and maintenance
people to service its manufacturing robots, at a cost of
up to $5,000 per person. It still found that "the funda-
mental inability to keep up with repair techniques is a
serious roadblock to the factory of the future."

For a total of $5,000, Ford developed an expert system
that allows a technician to diagnose and repair its ASEA
robots--without a training course and in a fraction of
the time that consulting a manual would have required.

With a thorough understanding, based on both real-time
and empirical information about all elements of the manufacturing process, we should now be able to develop and
implement a comprehensive, long-term plan for integrating
that process and incorporating manufacturing into the
total business strategy. Persistent problems can be
solved, new opportunities found, and maybe even radical
new approaches conceived.

With the widespread availability of these semi-conduc-
tor and computer capabilities, the barriers to increased
efficiency are not technological, but cultural. They
are:

First, a tendency to see manufacturing technologies as
ends in themselves, and not in their proper role as means
to an end. *The goal is not increased automation,* but increased manufacturing efficiency and reduced overhead.

Second, a tendency to substitute automation for understanding. While automation can help, its use must be
based on a total understanding of the manufacturing
process into which it is incorporated.

Third, the misconception that upgrading manufacturing
operations is too expensive. Technologies such as
modular controls and networking make it possible to
achieve step-function improvements without scrapping an
entire factory and rebuilding from a green field.

Fourth, a lack of determination on the part of top
managements. Full implementation might be a five-to
ten-year process, and this means a continuity of project
management that is beyond what is normal for most U.S.
companies.
And fifth, cultural barriers within the workplace.
Changing the culture of the workplace requires significant attitude adjustments. People are threatened by new
and unfamiliar technology and fear the loss of their
jobs. Change creates new pressures on supervisors and
requires operators to be more flexible.

Every individual has a vested interest in his or her
part of the process. Management can create the best
environment for change by involving individual operators
in planning and controlling their part of the process,
along with the responsibility--and the recognition--for
making improvements. Each employee should be seen as a
source of ideas, and not just a pair of hands. The same
technology that allows us to gather data about the manufacturing process also makes it possible for the operator on the factory floor to control the process, experiment with it, and make it better. When people become
involved, they become committed, and commitment produces
results.
In today's global markets, America cannot afford a competitive strategy aimed only at Japan. Even if the Japanese were to implement the structural changes promised
by the Nakasone administration, the competitive battle
would not be over--it would only shift to other countries. Taiwan, Korea, Singapore, and Hong Kong are already powerful forces in world markets; in time, India
and China will be strong competitors. It is time for
American ingenuity to come to bear on the problem of
competing not only against Japan, but against *all* international competitors.
A strong undercurrent of the traditional American
values is still with us. We have plenty of spirit, of
goodness, of patriotism; and the high value placed upon
freedom--at home as well as abroad--remains unaltered.
But in these changing times, our traditional ideals must
be blended with new values: a zeal for winning; a firm
belief in fiscal responsibility; a determined effort to
tilt our nation's resources toward productivity and
investment; a strong commitment to rebuilding an educational system second to none; a revival of the American
work ethic; and a firm determination to manage our destiny. Together, the old and the new will form the strong
foundation American society will need to successfully
meet the challenges that the coming years bring.

PART IV

Strategies for
Competitive Success

38

Managerial Guidelines

Y. K. Shetty and
Vernon M. Buehler

American business is in the midst of stirring action to
improve productivity and quality for gaining greater competitiveness. This concluding section provides general
lessons based on the thinking of experts and companies
that have excellent reputations for productivity and
quality, such as Deming, Juran, Feigenbaum, Crosby,
Grayson, and a wide range of companies representing different industries and technologies. Productivity and
quality leaders suggest that improvements in productivity
and quality can greatly enhance the competitiveness of
American business. The managerial lessons distilled
from the experiences are of increasing interest to companies that are seeking strategies and methods to establish and manage their own productivity and quality improvement efforts.

SOME LESSONS FOR PRACTICE

1. *An unqualified commitment of the top management is
essential for enhancing productivity and quality.* Without
firm top management commitment, these efforts will not
provide optimal results. To say that top man- agement is
committed to productivity and quality is not sufficient,
since employees are looking for a consistent message in
everything top management says and does. To provide such
a guide for employees, productivity and quality improvement efforts must be integrated into the company's total
business philosophy and translated into company goals,
strategies, policies, and culture.
2. *Productivity and quality should receive competitive
focus.* The importance of productivity and quality can
only be understood when viewed within the context of com-

petitive strategy. That means management's concern for productivity and quality must be communicated, integrated, and managed like any other full-scale organization strategy.

3. *The human side of the organization is the key to the ultimate success of productivity and quality improvement efforts.* Employees and managers at all levels should be convinced that productivity and quality are essential for survival, growth, and prosperity in an intensely competitive global market. Research of company experiences shows that when proper attention is paid to employees, productivity and quality naturally follow. Management must clearly explain why productivity and quality are important, and express these concerns in company communications, training, and motivation programs. They must recognize that company employees are the key to productivity and quality, and design a human resource system to promote productivity and quality. Lessons from America's quality leaders, such as Hewlett-Packard, Xerox, Dana, IBM, Marriott, and 3M suggest that excellent performance in production and quality results from giving serious attention to care, training, and motivation of their employees.

Employee involvement is one of the keys to successful productivity and quality improvement efforts. Employees are the natural source of creative input for improvement initiatives. Every person from the CEO to the hourly employee needs to be involved in exploiting the limitless potential of productivity and quality. Employee involvement can be achieved through quality circles, problem solving teams, labor management committees, and other such devices.

4. *Productivity and quality goals and measures are preconditions for success.* Explicit productivity and quality goals and standards should be established on the basis of reliable information. Once customer-driven quality standards are set, the next step is to maintain performance through proper measurement, appraisal, reporting, and corrective action.

5. *A variety of programs and techniques have the potential for enhancing productivity and quality.* America's corporate leaders on productivity and quality credit the teachings of Deming, Juran, Crosby, and Feigenbaum for their success. The American Productivity and Quality Center and The American Society for Quality Control, among others, are dedicated to helping business develop and implement productivity and quality improvement programs. Major techniques for improving productivity and quality include Computer-Aided Design (CAD), robots, Material Requirement Planning (MRP) systems, process controls, automated materials handling, computer controlled machinery (CCM), statistical quality control, Just-in-Time, quality circles, zero defects, and others. All are useful in eliminating waste from transport, stor-

age, inspection, and processing. No single program developed by an expert and no single technique is best for all companies. Programs and techniques must be tailored to a company's business situation and needs.

6. *Optimal benefits are realized through cooperation between functional departments and team efforts.* All functions of a company--product design, engineering, purchasing, manufacturing, sales, and service--can affect productivity and quality. Improvement efforts should encompass all functions of a firm. Each department should provide defect-free products or services to both internal and external customers. The removal of barriers between specialists and the creation of an environment for cooperation and teamwork are essential. Teamwork also shortens the time for product development and commercializing new innovations.

Supplier involvement is crucial. Excellent companies are becoming increasingly selective in developing suppliers who can meet progressively higher standards of quality, delivery, and technical support. These companies work closely with suppliers and develop long-term relationships. They bring suppliers in on the early stages of product design, offer technical and financial help, and propose long-term contracts.

7. *Continuous improvement is the key to productivity and quality leadership.* Initiatives aimed at improving productivity and quality must be institutionalized and managed for optimal results. Improvement must be planned, organized, monitored, controlled, and continuously revitalized. For enduring results, productivity and quality improvements must be fully integrated into the total management of a company.

CONCLUSION

Productivity and quality are two major keys to competitive advantage. Companies that continuously produce high-quality products and are most productive have lower costs, higher profit margins, and capture a larger and larger share of the market. The lessons from America's productivity and quality leaders provide a general framework for making improvement efforts successful. They provide general guidelines, not rigid rules. They have to be creatively adapted to meet the unique situation of each company.

Managers must recognize that productivity and quality improvement efforts require major changes in company philosophy, culture, and operating systems. These changes are difficult and require a major commitment and effort. The ability to improve productivity and quality has little to do with resources, programs, and techniques but depends more on attitudes, corporate philosophy, and operating systems. Companies that are interested in

improving productivity and quality can surely learn from
the success of America's quality leaders. It would be
folly to attempt to imitate the successful companies, but
others might well try to emulate them. Innovation, not
imitation, is the route to successful productivity and
quality efforts.

Selected Bibliography

Abernathy, William J. *The Productivity Dilemma: Road Block to Innovation in the Automotive Industry.* Baltimore: Johns Hopkins University Press, 1978.

Abernathy, William J., B. Clark, and A. M. Kantrow. *Industrial Renaissance: Producing a Competitive Future for America.* New York: Basic Books, 1983.

Baily, Martin N., and Alok K. Chakrabarti. *Innovation and the Productivity Crisis.* Washington, D.C.: Brookings Institute, 1987.

Bain, David. *The Productivity Prescription: The Manager's Guide to Improving Productivity and Profits.* New York: McGraw-Hill, 1986.

Bradford, David, and Allan Cohen. *Managing for Excellence.* New York: John Wiley, 1984.

Buehler, V. M., and Y. K. Shetty, eds. *Productivity Improvement: Case Studies of Proven Practice.* New York: AMACOM, American Management Associations, 1981.

Buffa, Elwood S. *Meeting the Competitive Challenge: Manufacturing Strategy of U.S. Companies.* New York: Dow Jones-Irwin, 1984.

Burgelman, Robert, and Leonard R. Sayles. *Inside Corporate Innovation.* New York: The Free Press, 1985.

Burnham, D. C. *Productivity Improvement.* New York: Columbia University Press, 1973.

Business Roundtable. *American Excellence in a World Economy.* New York: The Business Roundtable, 1987.

Christopher, William F. *Productivity Measurement Handbook.* Cambridge, Mass.: Productivity Inc., 1983.

Committee for Economic Development. *Productivity Policy: Key to the Nation's Economic Future.* New York: Committee for Economic Development, 1983.

Council on Competitiveness. *America's Competitive Crisis: Confronting the New Reality.* Washington DC: Council on Competitiveness, 1987.

Crosby, Philip B. *Quality Is Free: The Art of Making Quality Certain.* New York: New American Library, 1980.

---. *Quality Without Tears: The Art of Hassle-Free Management.* New York: McGraw-Hill, 1984.

Deal, Terrence E., and Allan A. Kennedy. *Corporate Cultures: The Rites and Rituals of Corporate Life.* Reading, Mass.: Addison-Wesley, 1982.

Deming, W. Edwards. *Quality, Productivity, and Competitive Position.* Cambridge: MIT Press, 1982.

---. *Out of the Crisis Cambridge*: Massachusetts Institute of Technology Center for Advanced Engineering Study, 1986.

Dertouzos, Michael L., Richard K. Lester, Robert M. Solow, and the M.I.T. Commission on Industrial Productivity. *Made in America: Regaining the Competitive Edge.* Cambridge MA: M.I.T. Press, 1989.

Dewar, C. *The Quality Circle Handbook.* Red Bluff, Calif.: Quality Circle Institute, 1980.

Drucker, Peter F. *Innovation and Entrepreneurship: Practice and Principles.* New York: Harper and Row, 1985.

Eilon, S., B. Gold, and J. Soesan. *Applied Productivity Analysis for Industry.* New York: Pergamon Press, 1976.

Fabricant, Solomon. *A Primer on Productivity.* New York: Random House, 1971.

Feigenbaum, A. V. *Quality Control.* New York: McGraw-Hill, 1951.

---. *Total Quality Control: Engineering and Management.* New York: McGraw-Hill, 1961.

Fitzgerald, L., and J. Murphy. *Installing Quality Circles: A Strategy Approach.* San Diego: University Associates, 1982.

Fuchs, Victor R., ed. *Production and Productivity in the Service Industries.* New York: Columbia University Press, 1969.

Garvin, David A. *Managing Quality.* New York: The Free Press, 1987.

Gitlow, Howard S., and Shelly J. Gitlow. *The Deming Guide to Quality and Competitive Position.* Englewood Cliffs, N.J.: Prentice-Hall, 1987.

Glaser, Edward M. *Productivity Gains Through Worklife Improvement.* New York: Harcourt Brace Jovanovich, 1976.

Goldberg, Joel A. *A Manager's Guide to Productivity Improvement.* New York: Praeger, 1986.

Grayson, C. Jackson, Jr, and Carla O'Dell. *American Business: A Two Minute Warning.* The Free Press, 1988.

Greenberg, Leon. *A Practical Guide to Productivity Measurement.* Rockville, Md.: BNA Book, 1973.

Griffith, Gary. *Quality Technician's Handbook.* New York: Wiley, 1986.

Gryna, Frank M., Jr. *Quality Circles: A Team Approach to Problem Solving.* New York: AMACOM, American Management Association, 1981.

Harrington, James H. *The Improvement Process: How America's Leading Companies Improve Quality.* New York: McGraw-Hill, 1987.

Hays, Robert H., and Steven C. Wheelwright and Kim B. Clark. *Dynamic Manufacturing: Creating the Learning Organization.* New York: Free Press, 1988.

Hayes, Robert H., and Steven C. Wheelwright. *Restoring Our Competitive Edge: Competing Through Manufacturing.* New York: John Wiley, 1984.

Iacocca, Lee, and William Novak. *Iacocca: An Autobiography.* New York: Bantam Books, 1984.

Ingle, Sud. *Quality Circles Master Guide: Increasing Productivity with People Power.* Englewood Cliffs, N.J.: Prentice-Hall, 1982.

Kanter, Rosabeth Moss. *The Change Master: How People and Companies Succeed Through Innovation in the New Corporate Era.* New York: Simon & Schuster, 1983.

Katzell, M. E. *Productivity: The Measure and the Myth.*
New York: AMACOM, American Management Association, 1975.

Kendrick, John W. *Improving Company Productivity: Handbook with Case Studies.* Baltimore: Johns Hopkins University Press, 1986.

Langevin, Roger G. *Quality Control in the Service Industries.* New York: AMACOM, American Management Association, 1977.

Lawrence, Robert Z. *Can America Compete?* Washington DC: The Brookings Institution, 1984.

Luke, High D. *Automation for Productivity.* Huntington, N.Y.: Krieger, 1972.

Mali, Paul. *Improving Total Productivity.* New York: John Wiley, 1978.

Mooney, M. *Productivity Management.* Research Bulletin No. 127. New York: Conference Board, 1982.

Mudel, M. E., ed. *Productivity: A Series for Industrial Engineers.* Norcross, Ga.: American Institute for Industrial Engineers, 1977.

Murphy, John W., and John T. Pardeck. *Technology and Human Productivity: Challenges for the Future.* Westport, Conn.: Greenwood, 1986.

Naisbitt, John. *Megatrends: Ten New Directions Trans forming Our Lives.* New York: Warner, 1982.

---. *Reinventing the Corporation.* New York: Warner, 1985.

National Center for Productivity and Quality of Working Life. *A Plant-Wide Productivity Plan in Action: Three Years of Experience with the Scalon Plan.* Washington, D.C.: 1975.

---. *Improving Productivity: A Description of Select Company Programs, Series 1.* Washington, D.C.: December 1975.

Peters, Thomas J., and Nancy Austin. *A Passion for Excellence.* New York: Random House, 1985.

Peters, Thomas J., and Robert H. Waterman, Jr. *In Search of Excellence: Lessons from America's Best-Run Companies.* New York: Harper and Row, 1982.

Pinchot, Gifford, III. *Intrapreneuring.* New York: Harper and Row, 1985.

Porter, Michael E., *Competitive Strategy: Techniques for Analyzing Industries and Competitors.* New York: The Free Press, 1980.

President's Commission on Industrial Competitiveness. *Global Competition: The New Reality.* Vol.1 and 2. Washington DC: U.S. Government Printing Office, 1985.

Roberts, Edward B., *Generating Technological Innovation.* New York: Oxford University Press, 1987.

Rogers, F. G. "Buck." *The IBM Way.* New York: Harper and Row, 1986.

Schonberger, Richard J. *Japanese Manufacturing Techniques: Nine Hidden Lessons in Simplicity.* New York: The Free Press, 1982.

---. *World Class Manufacturing.* New York: The Free Press, 1986.

Sepehri, Mehran, ed. *Quest for Quality: Managing the Total System.* Technology Park, Atlanta: Industrial Engineering and Management Press, 1987.

Shaw, John C. *The Quality-Productivity Connection in Service Sector Management.* New York: Van Nostrand Reinhold, 1978.

Shetty, Y. K., and Vernon M. Buehler, eds. *Quality and Productivity Improvements: U.S. and Foreign Companies' Experiences.* Chicago: Manufacturing Productivity Center, 1983.

---.eds. *Productivity and Quality Through People: Practices of Well-Managed Companies.* Westport, Conn.: Quorum Books, 1985.

---. eds. *Quality, Productivity and Innovation.* New York: Elsevier, 1987.

---. eds. *Competing Through Productivity and Quality.* Cambridge, Mass: Productivity Press, 1988.

Sibson, Robert E. *Increasing Employee Productivity.* New York: American Management Association, 1976.

Siegel, Irving H. *Company Productivity: Measurement for Improvement.* Kalamazoo, Mich.: W. E. Upjohn Institute for Employment Research, 1980.

Stebbing, Lionel. *Quality Assurance: The Route to Efficiency and Competitiveness.* New York: Halsted Press, 1986.

Strong, E. P. *Increasing Office Productivity: A Seven-Step Program.* New York: McGraw-Hill, 1962.

Thompson, Phillip C. *Quality Circles: How To Make Them Work in America.* New York: AMACOM, American Management Association, 1982.

Townsend, Patrick L. *Commit to Quality.* New York: John Wiley, 1986.

Twiss, Brian. *Managing Technological Innovation.* White Plains NY: Longman, 1986.

Wadsworth, Harrison M., et al. *Modern Methods for Quality Control and Improvement.* New York: Wiley, 1986.

Werther, William B., Jr., et al. *Productivity Through People.* New York: West Publishing, 1986.

Index

About the Contributors

PAUL A. ALLAIRE is the president and member of the Board of Directors of Xerox Corp. He directs the business products and systems businesses. Mr. Allaire held various financial planning and analysis positions before being named assistant marketing controller. He graduated from Worcester Polytechnic Institute with a B.S. in electrical engineering and earned an M.S. in industrial administration from Carnegie-Mellon University.

DOUGLAS N. ANDERSON is director of Corporate Quality Services at 3M. He is one of the pioneers in establishing and implementing 3M's MANAGING TOTAL QUALITY process. He has over 30 years with 3M in a variety of positions, including new product development, market development, line management in manufacturing, and corporate-based management responsibilities in areas of Staff Manufacturing and Staff Quality. He has B.S. and M.S. degrees in Chemistry from Macalester and the University of Minnesota.

JOHN R. BLACK is the director at the Quality Improvement Center at Boeing Commercial Airplane Company. He is responsible for assisting all levels of management to develop and implement processes leading to a cultural transition throughout the BCAC. He is a graduate of Gonzaga University with a B.A. in sociology, received an M.A. in human relations from the University of Oklahoma, and was granted an M.B.A. from City University in Seattle, Washington.

VERNON M. BUEHLER is a professor of business administration, assistant dean for business relations, and director of Partners Program, College of Business, Utah State University, Logan, Utah. He holds the M.B.A. from the Harvard Graduate School of Business Administration and a Ph.D. in economics from George Washington University, Washington, D.C.   He has been active in the field of government and business relationships, and his articles have been published in the *Academy of Management Journal* and other journals.   He has taught public policy and business environment courses since 1972.   He co-edited, with Y. K. Shetty, six books during the 80's on productivity, quality and competitiveness.

JOE C. COLLIER, JR. became president and CEI of Central Maines Power Company on July 1, 1989., At the time of the presentation included in this book, he was a senior vice president at Florida Poawer and Light, where he was resonsible for corporate planning and regulation.   While at FPL, he was part of the management team that developed the corporate quality program that resulted in Florida Power & Light winning the prestigious Deming Award.

ROBERT A. COWIE is vice president for public affairs in the Dana Corporation, Toledo, Ohio.   He is a former director of the Marine National Bank of Janesville, Wisconsin, and a trustee of Cornell University, where he serves as vice chairman of the Executive Committee and as a member of the Advisory Council of the engineering college.

PHILIP B. CROSBY is a quality management consultant and the author of books on quality management, zero defects, and human behavior.   He is chairman and chief executive officer of Philip Crosby Associates, Inc., the firm he founded in 1979 to work on quality improvement.   PCA has four divisions: The Quality College; Professional Services; Creative Services; and International.   His book, *Quality Is Free*, is well known as a best seller, along with *The Art of Getting Your Own Sweet Way* and *Quality Without Tears: The Art of Hassle-Free Management*.

W. EDWARDS DEMING, consultant for improvement of quality and productivity, Washington, D.C., is an internationally renowned productivity expert whose career spans six decades.   In addition to the Japanese statistical quality control that he instituted in the 1950s, he has advised clients in diverse organizations.   He was an engineering instructor at the University of Wyoming, where he received a B.S. degree.   He earned his M.A. at the University of Colorado and his Ph.D. at Yale University.   In 1946 he began private consulting work and became a professor of statistics at New York University, where he still teaches.   In addition to having written several books and articles on statistics, he has been a consultant worldwide.   Dr. Deming gained recognition for his contribution to the economy of Japan from the Japanese Union of Science and Engineers.   They instituted the annual Deming Prize, which is awarded for the advancement of precision and dependability of products. Dr. Deming received the Shewart Medal from the American Society for Quality Control and was awarded the Second Order Medal of the Sacred Treasure by the Emperor of Japan in 1960.

CLIFFORD J. EHRLICH is senior vice president of human resources, Marriott Corporation, Washington, D.C., and has held this position since April of 1978. He works with the American Red Cross and is a member of the Labor Law Committee of the Conference Board. Mr. Ehrlich is past president of the Personnel Council for the Food Service and Lodging Industry.

DALE P. ESSE is Manager of Production Quality Assurance for the Copy Products Division of Eastman Kodak Assurance Programs for production of all Kodak Ektaprint Copier Equipment. In the course of his 18 years as an engineer and manager, he has traveled extensively in the development and implementation of quality programs. He received his B.S. in Mechanical Engineering from the University of Wisconsin. He has completed several courses in both quality and management, including the Juran course on Management of Quality and Management of Managers Seminar at the University of Michigan Graduate School of Business Administration.

RODNEY J. FALGOUT is the manager of Personnel Operations in Monsanto Company. He received his B.S. degree from the University of Southwestern Louisiana with a major in personnel management and a minor in psychology. He is involved in the American Society for Personnel Administration and the Human Resources Management Association of Greater St. Louis, Inc.

ARMAND V. FEIGENBAUM is president of General Systems and the originator of Total Quality Control (TQC). General Systems designs and installs integrated operational systems for corporations worldwide. He is the author of *Total Quality Control*, now in its 3rd edition and in several languages. His honors include the Edwards Medal of the American Society of Quality Control, the National Security Industrial Associations Award of Merit, and the Union College Founders Medal. He holds M.S. and Ph.D. degrees from the Massachusetts Institute of Technology.

ED FINEIN is chief engineer and manager of Competitive Practices and the Product Delivery Process for Xerox Corporation. He is a member of the Strategic Business office in the Business Products and Systems Group at Webster, New York. He manages all group competitive evaluation and analysis activities including benchmarking. He is a graduate of the University of Rochester with degrees in math and physics.

C. JACKSON GRAYSON is chairman of the American Productivity Center in Houston. He has an M.B.A. from the
Wharton School and a Ph.D. from Harvard Business School.
He served as chairman of the U.S. Price Commission, where
he received national recognition. He is a CPA and member
of the Board of Directors of Lever Brothers, Sun Company,
IC Industry, and Potlack, Tyler, Harris, and Browning
corporations. He has also been a newspaper reporter, a
special agent of the FBI, and a manager of a cotton farm.

ANDREW S. GROVE graduated from the City College of New
York with a bachelor of chemical engineering degree and
received his Ph.D. from the University of California,
Berkeley. Upon graduation, he joined the Research and
Development Laboratory of Fairchild Semiconductor and
became assistant director of research and development in
1967. In July 1968, he participated in the founding of
Intel Corporation, where, after serving as vice president and director of operations and executive vice
president, he became president in 1979. He has written
over forty technical papers and holds several patents on
semiconductor devices and technology. His latest book is
High Output Management.

JULIE HOLTRY is corporate quality marketing and com-
munications manager for Hewlett-Packard Company, in Palo
Alto, California. She is responsible for promoting
company-wide quality control (CWQC or known as Total
Quality Control) to HP employees and customers worldwide.
She was national merchandising manager for Atari Corpora-
tion and senior director of customer service for a major
U.S. airline. She received her B.S. in Business Adminis-
tration from the University of Arizona in 1969 and an
M.B.A. in 1983 from Pepperdine University.

BOBBY INMAN is chairman, president, and CEO of Westmark
Systems, Inc., a Texas-based defense industry holding
company. He graduated from the University of Texas in
1950 and entered the Naval Reserve as an Ensign. Be-
tween 1974 and 1982 he served as director of Naval
Intelligence, director of NSA, and department director of
the CIA. From 1983 to 1986, he served as chairman and
CEO of the Microelectronics and Computer Technology
Corporation (MCC) in Austin, Texas. He is Chairman of
the Federal Reserve Bank of Dallas and a member of the
Boards of Directors of Flour, Oracle, Science Applica-
tions International, Xerox, Southwestern Bell, Texas
Eastern, and Tracor. He is a member of the National
Academy of Public Administrators and the Trilateral
Commission, and a trustee of the Brookings Institution,
Southwestern University, and Saint James School.

F. KENNETH IVERSON has been chairman and CEO of Nucor
Corporation since 1984. He received a B.A. in aero-

nautical engineering from Cornell University and a M.A. from Purdue University.   He is a director of Rexham Corporation, Wikoff Color Corporation, Cato Corporation, Southeastern Savings and Loan, S.H. Heist Corporation, the Council for a Competitive Economy, and the Greater Charlotte Foundation. In 1981 and 1982, the *Wall Street Journal* named him the "Best Chief Executive in the Steel Industry."

JOSEPH M. JURAN is chairman of Juran Institute, Inc. He has authored hundreds of published papers. Juran recently published *Juran on Quality Improvement*. It includes a series of 16 color video cassettes plus related training manuals designed to help companies get started on annual quality improvements and cost reduction.   Dr. Juran received the Order of the Sacred Treasure awarded by the Emperor of Japan for   "development of Quality Control in Japan and the facilitation of U.S. and Japanese friendship." He holds degrees in both engineering and law.

ROSABETH MOSS KANTER is an entrepreneur, business leader, best-selling author, and respected scholar. A magna cum laude graduate of Bryn Mawr, she earned both her M.A. and Ph.D. from the University of Michigan. She taught at Brandeis and Yale before joining the faculty at the Harvard Business School in 1986. She is the recipient of many national honors, including the Guggenheim Fellowship, four honorary doctoral degrees, and four "Woman of the Year" awards.   She has written several books, the latest of which is *The Change Masters: Innovation and Entrepreneurship in the American Corporation*.

JOHN W. KENDRICK is a professor of Economics at George Washington University and a member of the Board of Directors of the American Productivity Center in Houston, Texas. He has been the chief economist for the U.S. Department of Commerce and, in 1972-1973, was vice president for Economic Research at The Conference Board. He is currently on the research staffs of The Conference Board and the National Bureau of Economic Research. He has written several books, including *Productivity in the United States*.

THEODORE A. LOWE is a graduate of the University of Michigan, receiving both a B.S. in mechanical engineering and an M.A. in business administration. He is also an ASQC-certified quality engineer. He is currently manager of quality improvement for General Motors Truck and Bus. In this position, he is responsible for leading the development and implementation of the GM Truck and Bus Quality Improvement Process.

WAYNE R. PERO is a manager of Quality Assurance and Quality Performance at the Dow Chemical Company. He oversees development and execution of the quality performance effort at Dow divisions in the United States and is responsible for maintaining a strong Quality Assurance function. He is a graduate of Bucknell University, where he received a B.S. in chemical engineering.

THOMAS J. PETERS is the founder of the Palo Alto Consulting Center and the Pal0 Alto Management Institute, Palo Alto, California. Since 1978 he has worked almost full time conceiving, conducting, writing about, and acting on the findings of the "McKinsey Excellent Company Survey." The findings were published in the best-seller he co-authored with Robert Waterman, *In Search of Excellence: Lessons from America's Best-Run Companies*. He was in the Navy Civil Engineer Corps in Vietnam and in Washington.

H. DON RIDGE is director of personnel for IBM's General Products Division in San Jose, California. He joined IBM in 1954 and in 1957 was appointed instructor in the Atlanta Education Center and made manager of the Education Center in 1960.

RICHARD S. SABO is the manager of Publicity and Educational Services at the Lincoln Electric Company. He is responsible for educational programs, publicity, public relations, and technical publishing. He also heads the book division and handles the editing, publishing, and sales of all books. He graduated from California University and was awarded a master's degree in education from Edinboro University. He has majors in industrial arts, safety education, and counseling.

WILLIAM W. SCHERKENBACH is director of Statistical Methods at Ford Motor Company, Dearborn, Michigan. He is responsible for guiding the implementation of Deming's philosophies, including statistical management methods, throughout the company worldwide. Prior to joining Ford, he was a private management and statistical consultant and a member of a major management consulting firm specializing in reliability and maintainability.

MARK SHEPHERD, JR. is chairman of the Board of Texas Instruments Incorporated. He received his B.S. in electrical engineering from Southern Methodist University, graduating with honors in the class of 1942. Before joining Texas Instruments Incorporated, he had several work experiences, one of which was being a lieutenant in the U.S. Navy on the cruiser USS Tucson, specializing in radar and electronics maintenance.

Y. K. SHETTY is professor of management at the College of Business, Utah State University, Logan, Utah. He holds an M.B.A. and Ph.D. from the Graduate School of Management, University of California, Los Angeles. He is currently engaged in research on the problems of productivity, quality, and innovation at the firm level. His articles have been published in *Academy of Management Journal, California Management Review, Business Horizons, Advanced Management Journal, Management Review, Journal of Management Studies, Management International Review,* and other journals. He coedited, with V. M. Buehler, six books during the 80's on productivity, quality and competitiveness.

ARDEN C. SIMS graduated with a B.S. in electrical engineering from the West Virginia Institute of Technology in 1970. Mr. Sims became president of Globe Metallurgical Inc., then a division of Interlake, Inc, in 1984. Globe was sold to Moore McCormack Resources in 1984 and in 1987, Mr. Sims was a member of the group that purchased Globe from Moore McCormack. He now serves as President and CEO, as well as an owner and director. Mr. Sims, on behalf of Globe Metallurgical Inc., was presented witht he Malcolm Baldrige National Quality Award in 1988. Globe has won the Ford Motor Co. Quality Q1 and Total Quality Excellence, The General Motor's Mark of Excellence, and the Shiego Shingo Prize for Manufacturing Excellence. Mr. Sims is a member of numerous professional and civic organizations.

WICKHAM SKINNER is the James E. Robinson professor of Business Administration Emeritus, Harvard Business School. He graduated from Yale University with a B.S. in engineering, and earned his M.B.A and D.B.A from Harvard. Skinner joined Harvard after ten years with Honeywell Corp and has lectured worldwide on production management, manufacturing, and operations. He was also associate dean in the M.B.A program. He is the recipient of the McKinsey Prize for best article in *Harvard Business Review.*

MARTIN STARR is professor and director of the Center for Operations at Columbia University. He earned his B.S. at the Massachusetts Institute of Technology and his M.S. and Ph.D. from Columbia University. He is the past president of the Institute of Management Sciences and is on the faculty of Columbia's School of Engineering and Applied Sciences.

LESTER C. THUROW is the Gordon Y. Billard Professor of Management and Economics at MIT where he has taught since 1968. Previously, he served as staff economist on the President's Council of Economic Advisors from 1964 to 65, and visiting professor at the University of Arizona. Other positions include: economics columnist for the *LA Times, NY Times, and Boston Globe.* He has authored numerous books including *Zero Sum Solutions: Building a World Class American Economy* (1985) and *The Management Challenge: Japanese Views* (1985).

LEWIS C. VERALDI is vice president of Car Programs Management, Car Product Development of Ford North American Automotive Operations. He holds a B.A. in mechanical engineering from the Lawrence Institute of Technology in Michigan and now serves as a trustee on the board of that institution. He is a member of the Society of Automotive Engineers and holds a patent on a vehicle chassis front-suspension mechanism.

STEVEN C. WHEELWRIGHT is the Kleiner, Perkins, Caulfield, and Byers Professor of Management, Graduate School of Business, Stanford. He received a B.S. in mathematics from the University of Utah, an M.B.A and a Ph.D. from Stanford, and taught at INSEAD in France and the Harvard Business School before joining Stanford. He teaches in the areas of business policy and strategy, manufacturing policy, and production/operations management. His most recent book is *Restoring Our Competitive Edge: Competing Through Manufacturing*, coauthored with Robert Hayes.

JOHN YOUNG is president and CEO of Hewlett-Packard Company. In 1983 he was appointed by Ronald Reagan to be chairman of the President's Commission on Industrial Competitiveness, which was chartered to explore means of improving the competitive posture of U.S. industry at home and abroad. In 1986, the Council on Competitiveness, a private-sector group led by Young, was founded to continue the goals of improving U.S. industry's competitive posture. In 1985, he was named Manufacturer of the Year by the California Manufacturers Association, Business Communicator of the Year by the Business/Professional Advertising Association, and was the recipient of a leadership award by the U.S. Council for International Business.